A critical introduction to twentieth-century
American drama

For Gareth, Kirsten, Bella and Ewan
with love

A critical introduction to twentieth-century American drama

1

1900–1940

C. W. E. BIGSBY

CAMBRIDGE UNIVERSITY PRESS

Cambridge

London   New York   New Rochelle

Melbourne   Sydney

Published by the Press Syndicate of the University of Cambridge
The Pitt Building, Trumpington Street, Cambridge CB2 IRP
32 East 57th Street, New York, NY 10022, USA
296 Beaconsfield Parade, Middle Park, Melbourne 3206, Australia

© Cambridge University Press 1982

First published 1982
Reprinted 1983

Printed in Great Britain at the University Press, Cambridge

Library of congress catalogue card number: 81-18000

British Library Cataloguing in Publication Data

Bigsby, C. W. E.
  A critical introduction to twentieth-century
  American drama.
  Vol. 1: 1900–1940
  1. American drama – 20th century – History
  and criticism
  I. Title
  812'.5   PS351

ISBN 0 521 24227 4 hard covers
ISBN 0 521 27116 9 paperback

CONTENTS

ILLUSTRATIONS

PREFACE

American drama, as a serious form, is a product of the twentieth century. But, as Walter Meserve has established in his multi-volume study (the first instalment of which appeared in 1977), it has a long and fascinating pre-history. A public form, it has self-consciously engaged the public issues and private tensions of a nation and a culture in search of itself. Few countries have lived their history so self-consciously, dramatising, with political rhetoric and fast-congealing myths, the opening of a continent and the creation of a national identity. The theatre played its part in this process. Particularly in the nineteenth century it attempted to devise a spectacle commensurate with national expansionism, the revealed splendours of the American topography and a new technological mastery. And from time to time it also expressed a concern for the erosion of American idealism and the pressures on national and personal values which were a product of rapid social process.

But it was in the twentieth century that American drama began to attend to its own processes, to test its own boundaries and possibilities. For all their amateurism the Provincetown Players were concerned with fostering American writers who wished to test the potential of the stage. The explosion of experimental theatre, which had marked European theatre at the turn of the century, was long in reaching America but when it did so it found a group of people who combined a studied aesthetic eclecticism with a conviction that drama could have a central role in cultural and social life, as paradigm no less than as subtle instrument of analysis or as sculptor of language and movement.

Where once the actor and, to some extent, the ingenious machinery of stage effects, had dominated, now it was the writer and even the director who did so. And the central theme of this new drama became alienation. Reborn in its modern guise in a largely urban and industrial environment which seemed, in many ways, to be a denial of animating myths that drew their strength and credibility from a predominantly rural world in which the individual's responsibility for his own fate and identity was an article of national no less than individual faith, it tended to take as its primary subject the loss of an organic relationship with the natural world, with one's fellow man and with oneself.

The dominant image was of the loss of space: physical, emotional and moral. In so far as American idealism had been consciously rooted in the fact of American space, romantic notions of the moralising impact of nature, political convictions about the democratising effect of the frontier and the availability of land, in the simple absence of economic and social determinants, the loss of those convictions threatened the very basis of that idealism. And twentieth-century American drama has engaged that conviction directly, presenting dramatic correlatives of that process, on the whole taking the expansive and confident stage of the nineteenth century and compressing it until the sensibility of the individual is made to bear the weight of this social process.

For some writers this diminution of personal space, this collapse of a liberal dream, becomes an image of metaphysical process. For if the connections between the individual and a redeeming idealism, a liberating imagination, have been threatened by simple fact and by an implacable materialism, so the connection between the self and its own sense of available transcendence is seen as having been threatened. And so social alienation deepens into metaphysical *Angst*.

This book attempts to describe this process by concentrating on the major figures and theatre groups of the period. It does not attempt to be exhaustive. It is offered as a *critical introduction*. Many playwrights are mentioned but not discussed, others are not even mentioned: this does involve an act of critical judgement. The American theatre at this time could boast a large number of competent playwrights, but little, I think, in the context of this book, would be gained by offering an extensive critical reading of writers such as Sidney Kingsley, Sidney Howard, Marc Connelly, Paul Green or many others. Admittedly, one or two of those I do choose to discuss are not markedly superior to these but are offered as being in a sense representative.

For the most part this is a book about the central figures and principal groups of the period – those, that is, who shaped the nature of the American dramatic imagination. It is offered as an account of a theatre excitedly discovering its own power and potential. The American theatre moved with incredible rapidity from adolescence to maturity. It bears the stress marks of that fact. This is part of its fascination. It was a drama in the making as, in a sense, was America. This is the source of its energy as, perhaps, of its imperfections. On occasion those imperfections proved disabling but more often they were indicative of sensibilities struggling to make sense of a swiftly changing environment in a language and with a form that were themselves aspects of those changes.

ACKNOWLEDGEMENTS

I would like to express my gratitude to the British Academy and the United States Information Agency for financial assistance. I would also wish to acknowledge the generous help of the librarians and staff of the Beinecke Library at Yale, Harvard University Library, the Humanities Research Center at the University of Texas at Austin, the New York Public Library at Lincoln Center and the Federal Theatre Archive at George Mason University.

Permission to reproduce illustrations is gratefully acknowledged: for numbers 1, 7, 9, 10, 11, 12, 13, 14, 15, 16, and 26 from the Billy Rose Theatre Collection, New York Public Library at Lincoln Center; for number 2 from the Louis Sheaffer Collection; for numbers 3, 4, 5, 6, 8 and 21 from the Hoblitzelle Theatre Arts Library, Humanities Research Center, the University of Texas at Austin; and for numbers 17, 18, 19, 20, 22, 23, 24, and 25 from Fenwick Library, George Mason University, Fairfax, Virginia.

Letters from Thornton Wilder to Alexander Woollcott reprinted by permission of the Houghton Library, Harvard University. Eugene O'Neill and Elmer Rice letters and manuscripts reprinted by permission of the Librarian, Collection of American Literature, Beinecke Rare Book and Manuscript Library, Yale University.

1 Provincetown: the birth of twentieth-century American drama

The decline of the theatre in the nineteenth century was not an especially American phenomenon. It was a century of mass art. It was, above all, a century in which the novel predominated. This was the social art of the new bourgeoisie celebrating its own literacy and leisure. For Shelley, the decline of drama was especially alarming because he assumed a direct correspondence between that and a kind of social entropy, suggesting that 'the corruption or extinction of drama in a nation where it had once flourished, is a mark of a corruption of manners, and an extinction of the energies which sustain the soul of social life'. As George Steiner has suggested, there was a kind of historical justification for such an assumption in that the corollary notion, which Shelley equally urged, that the 'highest perfection of human society has ever corresponded with the highest dramatic excellence',[1] could be plausibly argued with respect to England, France and Spain. It was not that theatre was unpopular but rather that it lacked subtlety, that it offered a literal platform for a posturing which was not unconnected with the celebration of bourgeois individualism and the display of a new technological sophistication. Romanticism, with its emphasis on the individual, with its admiration for the dominating, self-dramatising figure, had exacerbated the situation by placing the self as actor at the centre of attention; the revolutionary as actor striding the world stage. And in nineteenth-century America, with its public myths of upward mobility, of the self as a plastic form easily mouldable into the contours of successful businessman, rising politician and hero, the actor was in a sense a model of the age. He was everything the public could aspire to be: a Protean figure. No longer locked into a European fixity, for the American, acting out a self-created destiny, all things were possible. And so the theatre provided both distraction and a displaced sense of potential. And it was perhaps a certain logical hubris as well as a twist of insanity which sent John Wilkes Booth leaping onto the stage of Ford's Theatre after killing a president of the United States. The theatre had established itself not merely as a mirror of events but as a correlative to the national spectacle.

The American theatre was not quite the total wasteland it was taken to be, though serious drama was almost invariably touched with melodrama. Indeed, even James O'Neill's version of *The Count of Monte Cristo* was not without a certain wit and verve. But its real claim to seriousness lay in its concern with locating the individual in a social context, with examining moral and social problems against a background which in part explained those

1

problems and in part lent authenticity to their treatment. In 1873, Emile Zola had announced that 'there should no longer be any school, no more formulas, no standards of any sort; there is only life itself, an immense field where each may study and create as he likes'. The need, he insisted, was to 'look to the future'. And the future would 'have to do with human problems studied in the framework of reality'.[2]

A consideration of social problems was not new to the American stage. Dion Boucicault's *The Octoroon* had tackled the question of miscegenation in 1859, receiving its première just four days after the execution of John Brown. But, despite some intelligent dialogue, it was essentially a melodrama with a host of stock characters and contrived events. Much the same might be said of the work of Bronson Howard, who was more concerned with morals than morality. His observation that America needed plays which lauded virtue and attacked vice, his belief that 'the wife who has once taken the step from purity to impurity can never reinstate herself in the world of art on this side of the grave',[3] suggests the limitations that he willingly embraced.

James A. Hearne was rather more willing to challenge such presumptions. Indeed, in *Margaret Fleming* (1890) he created an Ibsenesque heroine who was not merely capable of challenging convention but who deftly asserted her autonomy within marriage. The play is concerned with the infidelity of a successful businessman. A young woman dies bearing his illegitimate son and when his wife discovers the truth she insists on taking the child into her own home, though the shock exacerbates an eye condition and makes her blind. Her husband is suitably cowed and the play ends on a note of somewhat smug contentment all round.

The distinction of the play clearly did not lie in its freedom from melodramatic elements; the usual farrago of revealing letters, concealed identities, sudden affliction, abound. It resided rather in the frankness with which the intimate details were confronted and in the figure of Margaret Fleming herself who, if capable of a sickening piety, was also capable of confronting her husband with the double standard of social morality that gave him a freedom it denied her. As William Coyle and Harvey Damaser have pointed out, the play was regarded as sufficiently shocking for the *New York Times* reviewer to comment that

> *Margaret Fleming* is, indeed, the quintessence of the commonplace. Its language is the colloquial English of the shops and the streets and the kitchen fire place. Its personages are the everyday nonentities that some folks like to forget when they go to the theatre. The life it portrays is sordid and mean, and its effect on the sensitive mind is depressing...the stage would be a stupid and useless thing if such plays as *Margaret Fleming* were to prevail.[4]

James A. Hearne was, however, finally upholding the bourgeois system. He assaulted immorality not because it was a consequence of social convention but because it inhibited the felicitous functioning of a fundamental institution of bourgeois life – the family. Ibsen may have been a source but he was perceived only at the most superficial level. Far from breathing life into the family, Ibsen dissected it, exposing the hypocrises, the moral evasions, the self-betrayals and the casual inhumanity which were the price paid for a stability that only seemed to imply private and public control over the flux of experience, instinct and emotion. To compare Ibsen with any product of the nineteenth-century American theatre is to compare two different levels of perception, two wholly disproportionate worlds. The self-doubt of *The Master Builder* simply has no parallel in the American theatre until after the middle of the twentieth century; the subtle enquiry into the ambiguous nature of the ideal contained in *The Wild Duck* no like until O'Neill's *The Iceman Cometh.*

But the impulse was clear. It was to define a notion of reality, which consisted of locating human action in a social context which partly explained and partly justified that action. And that required a particular style of production – a style placing the individual in a more direct relationship to a material world which was increasingly seen as a generator of action and character. The naturalistic convictions of the novelist applied equally to the stage, where the *mise-en-scène* becomes the equivalent of the detailed description offered by the novel. As André Antoine had explained of his own innovations at the Théâtre Libre, 'it is the environment that determines the movement of the characters, not the movements of the characters that determine the environment. This simple sentence,' he suggested, 'does not seem to express anything new; yet that is the whole secret of the impression of newness which came from the initial efforts of the Théâtre Libre.'[5]

In America the chief exponent of naturalistic stage setting was David Belasco, who arrived in New York City in 1882 and quickly made himself the dominant influence. Stanislavsky actually made him an honorary member of the Moscow Art Theatre many years later, following that theatre's visit to America in 1923. He declared his faith in realism, took advantage of the new system of electric stage lighting to produce naturalistic effects and insisted on realistic stage sets. 'I will allow nothing to be built out of canvas stretched on frames. Everything must be real. I have seen plays in which thrones creaked on which monarchs sat, and palace walls flapped when persons touched them. Nothing so destructive to illusion or so ludicrous can happen on my stage,'[6] he wrote in *The Theatre Through Its Stage Door*, which appeared in 1919. Indeed when he produced *The Easiest Way*, which contained a scene set in the hall bedroom of a cheap theatrical boarding-house in New York, he 'went to the meanest theatrical lodging-house I could find in the Tenderloin district and bought the entire interior of one of its dilapidated rooms – patched furniture, threadbare carpet, tarnished and broken gas fixtures, tumble-down

3

1. Belasco's production of *The Governor's Lady*, 1912. A stage replica of the well-known Broadway restaurant, Child's.

cupboards, dingy doors and window-casings, and even the faded paper on the walls'.[7]

Like all innovations, however, stage naturalism had a constricting as well as a liberating effect. Where stage sets had originally been either simple backdrops for bravura acting or spectacular enterprises offered as marvels of technical accomplishments and substitutes for subtlety of dramatic construction and character, they now assumed a defining power, a conventionalised significance, which became a shorthand for character and moral enquiry. Yet it did result in serious attention being given to the need to create a homogeneous effect with lighting, setting and acting which made possible the naturalistic acting of the twentieth-century theatre. It introduced an artistic unity which had not formerly been required. In common with those directors who transformed the European theatre Belasco announced his concern for truth.

But if the stage was acquiring techniques to serve a more forthright realism, the playwrights lagged somewhat behind. And as Adolphe Appia rightly pointed out:

> the theatre has always been bound strictly by the special conditions imposed by the age, and consequently, the dramatist has always been the least independent

of artists, because he employs so many distinct elements, all of which must be properly united in his work. If one of these elements remains subject to the conventions of the age, while the others free themselves to obey the will of the creative artist, the result will be a lack of balance which alters the essential nature of the dramatic work.[8]

The effect is a disabling dislocation. But things were changing.

In his autobiography, Floyd Dell, editor of *The Masses* and *The Liberator*, describes the sense which he and his generation had that they were part of a fundamental revolution in values, aesthetics and lifestyles:

> The year 1912 was really an extraordinary year, in America as well as in Europe. It was the year of the election of Wilson, a symptom of immense political discontent. It was a year of intense woman-suffragist activity. In the arts it marked a new era. Color was everywhere – even in neckties. The Lyric Year, published in New York, contained Edna St. Vincent Millay's 'Renascence.' In Chicago, Harriet Monroe founded Poetry. Vachel Lindsay suddenly came into his own with 'General William Booth Enters Into Heaven,' and commenced to give back to his land in magnificent chant poetry its own barbaric music. 'Hindle Wakes' startled New York, as it was later to startle Chicago. The Irish Players came to America. It was then that plans were made for the Post-Impressionist Show, which revolutionized American ideas of art. In Chicago, Maurice Brown started the Little Theatre. One could go on with the evidence of a New Spirit come suddenly to birth in America.[9]

There was, indeed, a sense, even before the First World War opened a gap of experience and perception between the generations, that the world was on the move. Partly it was the natural hubris of a new century, the feeling that forms and conventions adequate to the nineteenth century could hardly be adequate to the twentieth, but partly it was a genuine reflection of signs of change. Nor was Dell the only one to detect it. Indeed the air was thick with manifestos and prophecies. The previous year the London *Athenaeum* had remarked that 'few observant people will deny that there are signs of an awakening in Europe. The times are great with the birth of some new thing. A spiritual renaissance.' The prophecy was approvingly quoted in the *Chicago Review* which Dell edited, while his friend and fellow Iowan, George Cram Cook, expressed the hope that America would be 'moved by the same perception of the beauty and wonder of the world, and not be voiceless'.[10] Dell, Cook and a third citizen of Davenport, Iowa, Susan Glaspell, felt themselves to be a part of this movement.

George Cram Cook, born in Iowa in 1873, was repelled by the bourgeois values which he saw as suffocating the individual. He eagerly embraced the modern but wished to employ it to breathe life into American idealism. The problem, as he saw it, was to re-establish lost values and in particular to generate a literature with the power not only to embody but to promote these values. Moving to Chicago he found himself on the fringe of the Chicago renaissance, reviewing the work of his contemporaries for the *Evening Post*. The writer did indeed seem a key to unlocking the imagination which would regain the past while embracing the language and the forms of the present. 'Suppose,' he wrote, that the renaissance 'depends not on blind evolutionary forces, involving the whole nation, but on whether or not the hundred artists who have in them potential power arrange or do not arrange to place themselves in vital stimulating relationship with each other, in order to bring out, co-ordinate and direct their power'.[11]

In 1911 he published *The Chasm*, a socialist novel, but his real model of an organic society in which culture and life were fused was Ancient Greece, not a notably socialist society. But Cook was never a man to subordinate vision to tiresome realities.

In 1913 he married Susan Glaspell, leaving his wife and three children to do so, itself something of a challenge to mid-western moralism. Glaspell had published a first novel, a sentimental book with pretensions to artistic accomplishment. But in 1907 she had met Cook and was pulled into the world of socialism, a concern with women's suffrage, and a more realistic apprehension of the world around her – a new vision – which was expressed in her second novel, *The Visioning* (1911).

As Dell describes it, Davenport was an 1848 European revolutionary foundation which had a liberal and socialist superstructure. There was also, he suggests, a certain native mysticism, deriving from romantic libertarian ideas. And certainly the renaissance which he, Cook and Glaspell jointly urged, created and celebrated, was a curious blend of anarchism (by which they seem to have meant individuals living intensely and acknowledging no authority), visionary socialism, and a mystical assertion of life against death. The significance of sex, the role of women, the liberating nature of art were discussed in small groups of enthusiasts and in the journals and newspapers to which they contributed, and which on occasion they edited. For all the naive political thrust there was an equally powerful lyrical pull. Certainly this was as true of Glaspell's novels as it was of George Cook's writing which subsumed his anarchist interests in a fascination with Greek theatre.

And for the first time in America it seemed possible that the theatre might actually play a role in a literary renaissance. Maurice Brown established the Chicago Little Theatre, which opened with Yeats's *On Baile's Strand*. Admittedly, it turned to a European rather than an American writer for its inauguration but the choice of play was not without significance to those wishing to see the emergence of a renewed national theatre. The arrival of the Irish Players the following year compounded this. When they reached Chicago, Cook and Glaspell were enthusiastic supporters, while a young man in New York, suffering from the effects of alcohol and tuberculosis and depressed to the point of attempted suicide, paid repeated visits to the theatre when the Players arrived there. He, of course, was Eugene O'Neill.

The main thrust of the renaissance was clearly poetic, with the appearance of Carl Sandburg, Edgar Lee Masters, Vachel Lindsay and Edna St Vincent Millay, but the theatre began to exert a fascination which it had hardly commanded before – a concern reflected by the publication, also in 1912, of Gordon Craig's book on the theatre. Cook's enthusiasm for the Greek theatre was strengthened by Maurice Brown's production of Euripides' *The Trojan Women* and it was by no means an eccentric concern. Craig was also fascinated by the achievement of classical tragedy, while Isadora Duncan's idiosyncratic version of Greek dance had a surprisingly direct influence on Russian ballet, helping to liberate it from its heavy classical formality.

But for all the strength of the Chicago art scene, New York still exerted a powerful lure; and Dell, Cook and Glaspell all moved there, joining the new colony of artists and writers then establishing themselves in Greenwich Village. Although their experiments took different forms, there was a sense of community in their endeavours, a sense which chimed with Cooke's desire for an organic society led by its artists. The world of the arts became a paradigm for social action. As Susan Glaspell herself explained:

> We were supposed to be a sort of 'special' group – radical, wild. Bohemians, we have even been called. But it seems to me we were particularly simple people, who sought to arrange life for the things we wanted to do, needing each other as protection against complexities, yet living as we did because of an instinct for the old, old things, to have a garden, and neighbors, to keep up the fire and let the cat in at night...Most of us were from families who had other ideas – who wanted to make money, played bridge, voted the republican ticket, went to church, thinking one should be like everyone else. And so, drawn together by the things we really were, we were as a new family.[12]

Perhaps, as Nick Carraway says at the end of *The Great Gatsby*, theirs had been a story of the West after all. For the revolt against contemporary American values was waged in the name of older American values, and when Cook and Glaspell formed the Provincetown Players in 1915 it was with a determination that they would stage American plays. And, as Arthur Waterman has pointed out, though they regarded themselves as socialists they never espoused pacifism or a fashionable anarchism during the First World War – though they did stage Edna St Vincent Millay's anti-war play, *Aria da Capo*.

Relations were not as cosy as Susan Glaspell's account would suggest; indeed Greenwich Village was composed of a number of overlapping groups who believed rather different things. Arnold Goldman has identified the elements which went to make up what he calls the culture of the Provincetown Players in a fascinating article in the *Journal of American Studies*. As he reminds us, there were those like Hutchins Hapgood who shared Cook and Glaspell's impatience with current convention and combined this with a visionary outlook. From the year 1911 Hapgood began to spend the summer at Provincetown, and was soon the nucleus for a group of summer expatriates in retreat from the heat of New York. But in the summer of 1914 they were joined by what Hapgood called 'the extreme left wing of the Socialists, the females militantly revolutionary about sex-freedom'.[13] And to these – people like John Reed and Louise Bryant to whom Reed was pointedly not married – were added the aesthetes of Mabel Dodge's salon. But one thing did unite them – a more or less profound sense that a particular model of aesthetic and moral development had been disrupted, that just as classic liberal principles were inadequate to describe their sense of a world no longer susceptible to Jeffersonian idealism, and of a human sensibility more anarchically various than such a paradigm suggested, so a simple art of surfaces could not hope to describe a human or environmental reality which operated behind conscious and unconscious concealments. The outbreak of war in Europe certainly strengthened these convictions but it did not create them.

The experimental theatre movement, which had produced the Théâtre Libre in Paris in 1887, the Freie Bühne in Berlin in 1889, the Moscow Art Theatre in 1898 and the Abbey Theatre in 1904, was a considerable time in reaching America. The cultural lag in theatre was greater than in the novel, perhaps because the theatre is a collaborative exercise that requires a concerted decision as to the acceptability of the new. But Maurice Brown had founded his theatre in Chicago, and in 1912 the New York Stage Company was founded. A little later the Liberal Club on Macdougal Street, run by Henrietta Rudman, a meeting-place for writers, socialists and university people, formed its own drama group which specialised in skits satirising the beliefs and commitments of its own members. Floyd Dell himself wrote a number of them (including *The Perfect Husband*, *What Eight Million Women Want* and *The Idealist*) acting as his own stage designer and scene painter. In 1914 what were to become the Washington Square Players performed their first play. Lawrence Langner and Max Eastman's wife, Ida Rauh, were dissuaded from renting a theatre by Albert and Charles Boni who offered their own bookshop, which adjoined the Liberal Club, for their first performance. With the aid of Robert Edmond Jones, who had studied in Europe under Max Reinhardt, a makeshift acting space was devised and Lord Dunsany's *The Glittering Gate* became the somewhat curious inaugural production. In February 1915 they acquired the Bandbox Theatre and staged their first season, consisting of plays by Langner, Edward Goodman, Maurice Maeterlinck, John Reed and Philip Moeller, and Leonid Andreyev. The ideological stance was not consistent but they were clear as to the identity of the enemy which was the commercially oriented, artificial and vapid world of Broadway, and beyond that, rather less clearly, the social system that created it.

One other experiment in theatre should perhaps be mentioned. The Neighborhood Playhouse, established in 1912, grew out of the activities of the Henry Street Settlement. This had been established in 1890 to deal with the influx of immigrants and the social problems of the area. Urged to form a drama group, Alice Lewisohn Crowley decided to launch it with a production of *The Shepherd*, a play by Olive Tilform Dorgon, about the revolutionary movement in Russia. Assisted by Agnes Morgan, a former member of George Pierce Baker's Workshop 47, she immediately began planning a purpose-built theatre. But for all their interest in recent developments in European production theory and stage design, they were not interested in a revivified American theatre. Indeed, their second production was Galsworthy's *The Silver Box*. They were concerned with serving a community. The audience they sought was not that which attracted Floyd Dell or Lawrence Langner. But it was an eclectic theatre, drawing on Noh drama and Hindu plays as well as work by Leonid Andreyev, Arnold Bennett, Harley Granville-Barker, George Bernard Shaw and Scholem Asch. Indeed it also produced Susan Glaspell's *The People* and Eugene O'Neill's *The First Man*. But its real significance lay in the presumption that theatre could play a role in uniting the heterogeneous elements of an immigrant community, that the theatre spoke a language which was relevant to people trying to read the code of American society and looking for a reflection of their own uncertain apprehension of the real.

Though George 'Jig' Cook was himself involved in the first performance of what were to become the Washington Square Players, they were not experimental enough for him nor were they sufficiently interested in fostering native talent. And as evidence of that they turned down *Suppressed Desires*, a satire on the current vogue for Freud among the sophisticated, which Cook and Glaspell had written together. For Cook that was provocation enough. Accordingly, in the summer of 1915, in the Hapgoods's house, they staged the play themselves, along with *Constancy*, a brief play by Neith Boyce (Hapgood's wife) which was based on the love affair between John Reed and Mabel Dodge. Once again Robert Edmond Jones designed the simple set. This was the beginning of the Provincetown Players and, in effect, the beginning of modern American drama. Pleased with their success, they repeated the plays together with two more, *Change Your Style* by Cook and *Contemporaries* by Wilbur Steele, in an old wharf at Provincetown owned by Mary Vorse.

For George Cook naturalism was no answer to the deficiencies of theatre

2. The Wharf Theatre, Provincetown, Massachusetts, in 1915. By courtesy of Louis Sheaffer.

and no adequate response to a contemporary constriction of the spirit. 'The reinterpretation which is to be the great spiritual event of the coming years will not be a reinterpretation of the facts of science by the intellect to the intellect, but their interpretation – for the first time – by the poetic imagination to the collective heart of man.'[14] By this he meant the writer's sense of a direct relationship to his society, not simply through locating his characters in a concrete environment of fact and social relationships but through acknowledging art as itself a unifying force – an expression of community. 'I glow,' he said on reading Halévy's *Life of Nietzsche*, 'with a white sense of the relation of a modern writer's social feeling to his art', seeing this as a 'vital intimate thing'.[15] And this could not be expressed simply by asserting the naturalist's nexus between the individual and his physical environment. He wished to provoke a renaissance in American writing, a resurgence, socialist in spirit and poetic in its ability to generate dramatic images of human unity. The model and inspiration was always the Greek theatre, which dominated his imagination and which led him to stress the correspondence of the arts. 'The arts fertilize each other,' he insisted, 'the dancer creates in space attitudes of sculpture and in time makes them flow rhythmically into each other like the successive notes of melody. Our minds are now full of the madness of painting that wants to be like music.'[16] In this respect, of course, not only was he embracing Wagnerian theories, and reflecting the *symbolistes'* convictions, but he was also anticipating the experiments, first of the dadaists and then of the surrealists. But the real force was always the Greek. Life was to be confronted not with the prosaic directness of the naturalist but with the sensibility of the poet: 'One thing we're in need of is the freedom to deal with life in literature as frankly as Aristophanes had.'[17] And this required not merely new writers but a new spirit in drama and, indeed, a new audience, for the special quality of theatre lay in its ability to re-create the community which was also its subject.

> One man cannot produce drama. True drama is born only of one feeling animating all the members of a clan – a spirit shared by all and expressed by the few for the all. If there is nothing to take the place of the common religious purpose and passion of the primitive group, out of which the Dionysian dance was born, no new vital drama can arise in any people.[18]

Beneath the visionary jargon, what Cook was calling for was a symbolic language, a realisation that theatre is not simply a verbal act nor a spectacle external to the observer, a crust of experience. The film was, anyway, already in the process of taking over that limited function. In the very year that Cook was reading Nietzsche, James O'Neill was making a film version of *The Count of Monte Cristo* (while his son was also reading Nietzsche). Cook was not an original thinker but he did combine a personal vision with a practical energy and an inspirational power which makes him a crucial figure in the history of American drama. He was the man for the moment, a man for whom popular success meant failure, a failure which eventually drove him out of America, still pursuing his dream of a revivified Greek drama.

Suppressed Desires marked a somewhat curious beginning to this brave new theatre. This first play of the Provincetown Players was an inconsequential comic satire in two scenes, with George Cook playing the role of Stephen Brewster, an architect whose patience is tried by a wife, played by Susan Glaspell, whose obsession with a modish psychiatry is aptly symbolised by her subscription to the *Journal for Morbid Psychology*. The play would have worked very well at the Liberal Club. Seen in the context of the Players' later work, it is a very slight piece, distinguished only by its humour. A minor irony is that a theatre which began by satirising Freudian theory should subsequently have produced the work of the man who, perhaps more than any other American writer, bore the mark of Freud; while its portrait of disintegrating marriage was far from irrelevant to a group so concerned with marriage as the focus of feminist ideas and an image of social institutions. Indeed, there is some evidence that Cook did look on the group and on drama as having some therapeutic dimension.

If the Provincetown was in a sense created by accident – the original performance at the Hapgoods's house had been impromptu – once the idea of creating a theatre had established itself in Cook's mind he hunted assiduously for the new playwrights which his own convictions told him should be simply waiting for the opportunity. The amazing thing is that he was right.

When they reassembled in 1916, Cook had already sold tickets for a season which was not only not yet planned but for which they had insufficient scripts. The arrival on the scene of Eugene O'Neill was thus doubly fortuitous. He met their immediate need for an additional script, and he was the embodiment of the American writer for whom they had been looking. And the difference between their mid-western and, in effect, very sheltered lives and the experience-packed life of a man who at the age of twenty-eight had been married and separated (like Cook) but had also prospected in South America, been a sailor, attempted suicide and suffered from tuberculosis can have done nothing to diminish his appeal.

O'Neill had been living in Greenwich Village and went to Provincetown with Terry Carlin, an anarchist who was much later to become the basis for the character of Larry in *The Iceman Cometh*. Asked if he had any scripts available, Carlin referred the group to O'Neill who by now had a trunk full. He offered them *Bound East for Cardiff*, rejected by George Pierce Baker when he had sent it to him at Harvard as 'not a play' at all. He read the script aloud at the Cook home and then, as Susan Glaspell observed, they knew what they were for.

The play, with its evocation of stumbling articulacy, its claustrophobic setting, its concern with a poetic vision of death and its powerful sense of a group hero, could hardly have suited their purpose better. Its tragic implications were also likely to appeal to George Cook, as was the use of seamen as a kind of choric context. The play was a great success and served to consolidate the Provincetown.

At the end of the summer season they met to consider their future. It was decided that they would retain their title and that they would form themselves as a club, active membership of which was restricted to those who wrote, acted, produced or in some way offered their labour to production. In order to underscore its commitment to new writing O'Neill proposed that the theatre which Cook was anxious they should acquire in New York should be called the Playwrights' Theatre.

Cook found a building to his liking – actually an ordinary brownstone terrace whose dividing wall could be removed – and plans went ahead for its conversion. Thanks to a deal arranged by John Reed, four hundred season tickets were sold in advance to the Stage Society, thus guaranteeing the venture. Accordingly, on 3 November 1916, *Bound East for Cardiff* opened not only the first New York season of the Provincetown Players but also the history of twentieth-century American drama.

The Provincetown Players were never reticent about their objectives. In the folder announcing the first New York season they explained that:

The present organisation is the outcome of a group of people interested in the theatre, who gathered spontaneously during two summers at Provincetown, Mass., for the purpose of writing, producing and acting their own plays. The impelling desire of the group was to establish a stage where playwrights of sincere, poetic, literary and dramatic purpose could see their plays in action, and superintend their production without submitting to the commercial manager's interpretation of public taste. Equally, it was to afford an opportunity for actors, producers, scenic and costume-designers to experiment with a stage of extremely simple resources – it being the idea of the Players that elaborate settings are unnecessary to bring out the essential qualities of a good play.[19]

Clearly the statement contains a good deal of rationalising after the event, since their aesthetic was at least in part born out of the circumstances in which they found themselves; and when it seemed to Cook that a more sophisticated staging was necessary – for O'Neill's *The Emperor Jones* – he did not hesitate to blow virtually the whole reserves of the organisation in order to facilitate it.

Their faith in the group as a unit, however, was more deeply rooted. For Cook it was primarily an attempt to recapture an organic unity which he saw as quintessentially Greek. But the attempt to relate a central icon of American mythology (the individual) to the new icon of emergent socialism and a restructured liberalism (the group) posed a problem which was actively engaging other social thinkers of the day. And the Players in due course, when they moved into 133 Macdougal Street, attempted an explanation of their broader objectives:

That a closely knit group of creative and critical minds is capable of calling forth from the individuals who compose it richer work than they can produce in isolation is the basic faith of the founder of our playhouse. He knows that the art of the theatre cannot be pure, in fact can not be an art at all, unless its various elements – playwriting, acting, setting, costuming, lighting – are by some means fused into unity. There are two possible ways of attaining it: the way of the director and the way of the group. Unity in the theatre has been attained, especially in the case of Reinhardt, by imposing upon all the necessary collaborators the autocratic will of one mind – the director's – who uses the other minds involved as unquestioningly obedient instruments. This method of attaining unity leaves room for one and only one free spirit in a theatre.

It was not so when drama first came into the world. Primitive drama, the expression of the communal or religious life of the organic human group, the tribe, had spontaneously the unity of pure art. There may be two hundred actors dramatically dancing the conflict of Winter and Spring, but all that all of them do in the drama springs from one shared fund of feelings, ideas, impulses. Unity is not imposed on them by the will of one of their number but comes from that deep level in the spirit of each where all their spirits are one. The aim of the founder of the Provincetown Players, as yet imperfectly fulfilled, is to make all hands work from that level and to do it by recreating in a group of modern individuals, individuals far more highly differentiated than primitive

13

people, a kindredness of minds, a spiritual unity underlying their differences, a unity resembling the primitive unity of the tribe, a unity which may spontaneously create the unity necessary to the art of the theatre.[20]

The language is clearly Cook's, so much so that it casts an ironic light on his disavowal of the director's central role. Indeed, as was the case with the building of the plaster dome, required for certain sophisticated lighting effects in *The Emperor Jones*, he showed himself quite willing to ignore group decisions when they failed to coincide with his own predilections. Floyd Dell was particularly scathing in his response to Cook, more especially since he did not share Cook's enthusiasm for O'Neill. Dell regarded Cook as a romantic, and the evidence for that of course is fairly secure, but he also regarded the group as essentially egotistic, saying that 'I saw new talent rebuffed – though less by George than by the others – its fingers brutally stepped on by the members of the original group who were anxious to do the acting whether they could or not – and usually they could not.' It seemed to him simply Broadway in miniature. 'And what did astonish and alienate me,' he insisted, 'was the meanness, cruelty and selfishness which this little theatrical enterprise brought out in people.' He saw its style of production as wilfully experimental. George Cook, in particular, 'fell madly in love with one toy after another – when a wind-machine was acquired, hardly a word of dialogue could be heard for months, all being drowned out by the wind-machine'. Even the dome 'became a nuisance, it was so over-used...Nothing,' indeed, 'was too mad or silly to do in the Provincetown Theatre, and I suffered some of the most excruciating hours of painful and exasperated boredom there as a member of the audience that I have ever experienced in my life.'[21]

Cook's own plays, *The Athenian Women* and *The Spring*, the latter of which he tried to run on Broadway with the assistance of an inheritance, Dell regarded as undramatic though worthy. The only two plays to justify the existence of the theatre, in his eyes, were Susan Glaspell's *Inheritors*, which he described as 'a beautiful, true, brave play of war-time',[22] and Edna St Vincent Millay's *Aria da Capo*. Dell's bitterness seems to have derived a least in part from the treatment of one of his own plays which an over-enthusiastic producer at the Provincetown staged by placing the actors on stilts, thereby rendering the dialogue inaudible as they clumped around the stage. As a consequence, and alarmed by what he called 'the incredible fussiness into which the Provincetown Players had descended', he chose to design the sets and paint the scenery himself for a subsequent play.

But the hostility said as much about Dell as it did about the Provincetown Players. Cook could clearly be exasperating as well as engaging, and he had all the crankiness which is liable to accompany obsessional enthusiasm. But he was artistically successful. He had actually given birth to the renaissance of which they had all spoken in Chicago. And if there is one unforgivable crime among friends, it is success. Certainly the notion that Cook was seduced by the idea of success on Broadway is hard to reconcile not only with his own private and public statements but also with the man who eventually abandoned the Players to travel to Greece, not because of their failure but because of their success. Hutchins Hapgood in his autobiography, *A Victorian in the Modern World*, offers another explanation. He attacks Dell for his assault on Cook, suggesting that Dell thought Cook a failure because he had failed to write any successful books, because, in effect, he had failed to conform to the conventionalities which Dell continued to respect despite his socialist pretensions. It is also true that Dell's enthusiasm for Edna St Vincent Millay's play may not have been entirely unconnected with his own romantic attachment to her, which led him on one occasion to chase her through Greenwich Village.

But it is worth bearing his criticisms in mind when reading Susan Glaspell's celebratory *The Road to the Temple*, which is rather less a biography than a respectful homage. And certainly Cook's poetic vision meant that the group sailed perilously close to pretentiousness. Consider the programme note to *The Game* by Louise Bryant, which followed *Bound East for Cardiff* on the bill and which is quoted by Arnold Goldman: '*The Game* is an attempt to synthesize decoration, costume, speech and action in one mood. . .[T]he play is symbolic of rather than representative of life. . .the decorations [have been designed] to suggest rather than to portray; the speech and action of the players used as the plastic element in the whole unified convention.'[23]

The Provincetown Players did not invent the one-act form. It was well established both in England and America, and continued to be so into the 1930s. But it did lend itself to the circumstances of a small theatre. Certainly a play like Susan Glaspell's beautifully economical *Trifles* could scarcely have survived elaboration, while O'Neill's fascination with claustrophobic settings, his central image of the human body crushed into ever smaller spaces, made the Provincetown an ideal environment for his work.

Under the influence of Adolphe Appia, theatre became alert to the significance of space, the three-dimensional force of the stage. Space, created by lighting and its effects on a newly perceived *mise-en-scène*, not merely located stage characters in a tangible world in which object and person interacted but also created a void which was available as a powerful image of the individual's spiritual location. Because of this sense of space the human body moved once again to the centre. As Appia wrote:

> Today, the resurgence of the body as an expressive medium essential to our aesthetic culture is a concept which possesses many minds, animates the imagination, and gives rise to diverse experiment, doubtless not all of equal value, but all directed toward the same reform. We now feel that the performer tends,

almost implicitly, to come closer to the spectator; we also feel (some more deeply and sensitively than others) a mysterious involvement on the part of the spectator with the performer. Our modern productions used to force us into such miserable passivity that we veiled our humiliation in the shadowy recesses of the auditorium. But now, as we behold the body's effort finally to rediscover itself, our emotion is almost a fraternal collaboration: we wish to be that body on stage; our role of spectator is now a responsibility; the social instrument awakens in us, an instinct which has been heartlessly stifled until now, and the result of our own egoism.[24]

In the 1960s this moved to the very centre of interest but there is a sense in which the circumstances of production in the Provincetown Theatre facilitated an erosion of that barrier between performer and audience which was equally a basic of Cook's philosophy. Also it is clear that one of O'Neill's gifts to the theatre lay in his concern with the body, with placing the physical and psychological reality of the individual at the centre of attention. It was his luck, of course, that in George Cook he had someone who recognised this fact, spending $500 of the Provincetown's meagre reserve of $540 on building the plaster dome which, when lighted, created precisely that sense of depth and space which Appia had called for and which, in *The Emperor Jones*, was so crucial to the isolation of the human figure: ' *The Emperor* has *got* to have a dome to play against...it begins...thick forest at first...steadily thinning out...scene after scene...to pure space.'[25]

When Robert Edmond Jones remarked that 'Great plays have nothing to do with space'[26] he was rejecting not this kind of metaphysic of space but the idea that the setting for a play is governed by realistic laws of space composition, for 'the artist should omit the details, the prose of nature and give us only the spirit'.[27] A basic theme of O'Neill's, and indeed of Arthur Miller's, is the loss of space, physical and moral, in which the individual can move with freedom and confidence. Indeed, he repeatedly dramatises the human figure crushed by a mechanised world, compressed by social and psychological forces and abandoned by the collapse of reassuring myths of consonance and metaphysical purpose. And the proximity of audience and performers at the Provincetown can have done nothing to undermine that social instinct which O'Neill, no less than Appia, wished to awaken. Appia had announced as a principle what the Provincetown arrived at by chance. 'Let us proclaim it strongly,' Appia had insisted, 'the dramatist will never be able to liberate his *vision* if he insists upon projecting it in a place rigidly separated from the audience.' And Cook clearly shared Appia's awareness that the social community for which he called had its roots in the past of drama. For as Appia suggested, 'There is no art form in which social solidarity can be better expressed than in drama, particularly if it returns to its noble origins in the collective realisation of great religious or patriotic feeling, or simply of human feeling, transforming them into our modern age.'[28]

O'Neill's early plays, in particular his sea plays, are plays of feeling in just this sense, plays concerned with a desperate groping for meaning, a meaning to be constructed out of memory rather than experience, out of a sense of loss countered by surface solidarity. The human figure, pressed back atavistically to pagan self (*Emperor Jones*), or brute existence (*The Hairy Ape*) or seen as forming part of the harmonics of community, especially in the sea plays, lay at the centre of his concern. The lyric potential of the self was projected either against the blank pre-social world of natural space or the largely unreal solidarity offered by isolated selves grouped together in the configuration of community. O'Neill was less willing than most dramatists to permit a *mise-en-scène* unfiltered through the writer's mind. From his earliest work he offered detailed instruction as to the nature of the setting. Inanimate setting is made to relate directly to the real form of the actor, and, as Appia suggests, this gives the writer's text more control over the actor's role. The setting becomes an active part of the text rather than an arena for the actor. Theatre language, in other words, is recognised as a more complex concept. Belasco had already wrought important changes through his use of lighting and through a sophisticated three-dimensional conception of the *mise-en-scène*. But his tendency was to allow stage to dominate text. O'Neill's tone poems sought an integrative approach. And often it is music which provides the integrative force – the sea shanties and Negro songs of the sea plays, the contrastive songs of *All God's Chillun Got Wings* and the organic pulsations of the drums in *The Emperor Jones*. Appia was aware that the average audience 'will always ask to be deceived, and to be given what the ordinary man enjoys most, that is the most exact replica of what he is *capable of seeing* in the outer world' and that 'the drama, of all the arts, is best suited to satisfy such a desire'.[29] But O'Neill offered an inner world, distorting the stage to express the temporal and spiritual dislocation of the self.

In their first New York season the Playwrights' Theatre produced four plays by O'Neill (*Bound East for Cardiff, Before Breakfast, Fog* and *The Sniper*). And though *The Sniper* and *Fog* had little to recommend them, *Before Breakfast* gave notice of his continued commitment to experimentation. Heavily influenced by Strindberg whose inspiration he acknowledged, it is a dramatic monologue in which a woman drives her failed husband to suicide. He makes a single appearance when his shaking hand is seen through a doorway clutching a razor. It is a deceptively simple but powerful play. Once again the set becomes a claustrophic cell, an active image of the drastically reduced possibilities of those it contains. And this in turn becomes an image of the marriage whose expansive hopes have collapsed. The relationship which should have provided some sense of relief from the relentless rigour of their situation becomes the source of pain. It is a familiar Strindbergian theme but it becomes so endemic to O'Neill's work that it can hardly be explained simply as a borrowing. In some ways it is superior to *The Stronger*, the Strindberg play from which it clearly derives. O'Neill has a sharper eye for the realistic detail that creates the sense of menace in which the play operates. In keeping his other character off stage he also focusses the drama more completely on the woman whose tortured monologue destroys both herself and her husband. But his insistence on pursuing the action to the point of the husband's suicide discharges the tension which he has been at pains to establish; it is a melodramatic gesture which Strindberg more wisely denied himself. And this is a weakness which dogged O'Neill's career. In a sense it seems to suggest a failure of nerve. For although, in this case, the man's death clearly leaves the woman to live out a solitary existence, ties her indeed more irrevocably to her fate, these subtleties are lost in the impact of an action too thoroughly signalled throughout the play.

However, with plays additionally coming from John Reed, Louise Bryant, Floyd Dell, Neith Boyce and Hutchins Hapgood, Susan Glaspell and ten others there was no doubting the success of the Playwrights' Theatre. In the end there were eight bills and a review bill, each offering three plays. Each bill ran for a week, with members of the Stage Society having Sunday and Tuesday evening privileges in return for their lump sum payment of $1600. There were additionally 450 regular subscribers. Attendance was strictly limited to members in order to circumvent the various city ordinances. Even so, the planned tenth bill had to be cancelled when the Building Department invoked a technicality to close them down – a fate which was to haunt off-Broadway groups well into the 1960s.

The following season, 1917–18, the number of bills was cut to seven but the subscription kept at four dollars. The building inspector was appeased and they opened with O'Neill's *The Long Voyage Home*, Susan Glaspell's *Close the Book*, and James Oppenheim's *Night*. But the original list of active members began to shrink. By April 1917, only fifteen remained out of twenty-nine and when the next season opened at least seven of them were in the army. The First World War, indeed, brought about the collapse of the Washington Square Players but the Provincetowners, who still most importantly included O'Neill, Cook and Glaspell, decided to continue. They raised the subscription to five dollars, remodelled and moved into 133 Macdougal Street (their original base having been at 139). But the war raised another question. Just what was the responsibility of the theatre during wartime? Should they take the war as their subject or, on the contrary, should they offer escapist material for a country which was getting enough brutal reality? The result of this debate was a document which they issued at the beginning of their third season in New York:

It is now often said that theatrical entertainment in general is socially justified in this dark time as a means of relaxing the strain of reality, and thus helping us to keep sane. This may be true, but if more were not true – if we felt no deeper value in dramatic art than entertainment – we would hardly have the heart for it now. One faculty, we know, is going to be of vast importance to the half-destroyed world – indispensable for its rebuilding – the faculty of creative imagination. That spark of it which has given this group of ours such life and meaning as we have is not so insignificant that we should now let it die. The social justification which we feel to be valid now for makers and players of plays is that they shall help keep alive in the world the light of imagination. Without it the wreck of the world that was, can not be cleared away, and the new world shaped.[30]

The season certainly made no attempt to deal with the war directly. O'Neill's *In the Zone*, which is set on a British tramp steamer as it sails through submarine-infested waters, was actually performed by the Washington Square Players and not Provincetown, leading to suggestions that that group had been the real discoverers of O'Neill. Edna St Vincent Millay's *Aria da Capo*, a specifically anti-war play, was not produced until the 1919–20 season.

Slowly the nature of the organisation began to change. A greater degree of professionalism became apparent. For a time, as Arnold Goldman has pointed out, Nina Moise, who like Edna St Vincent Millay had recently left Vassar, directed O'Neill's plays until she had to leave to undertake war work. At the same time the personnel was changing. Only four of the original list of active members were still with the group and in the 1919–20 season Cook withdrew to Cape Cod and left things in the hands of James Light.

Then in 1920 came their greatest success. *The Emperor Jones*, with which Cook was so impressed that he committed virtually all their funds to its production, was an immediate success. It became impossible to maintain their original plans for the season and the play ran for weeks, disrupting their schedules but swelling their subscription lists. It was finally moved to Broadway together with its cast. It was a brilliantly innovative play. Like *Before Breakfast* it was, in effect, a monologue since for most of the play there is only one character on stage. But now O'Neill liberated the *mise-en-scène*, giving it a dynamic force which no other American play had attempted. At the same time his use of the regular beat of the native drums, besides sustaining a constant tension, could be seen as representing the pulse of a man whose psyche was carefully dissected layer by layer. The play was a brilliant exposition of physical and psychological collapse. It was also the greatest achievement of the new theatre for which they had all been working. Sound, light, theatre design, and writing all combined to create a stunning effect.

But if *The Emperor Jones* represented the summit of their achievement it also in effect marked the end. Cook became increasingly discontented, perhaps only partly because the increasing professionalism of the group seemed to him to be a step in the wrong direction. It is true that what had started out at least in his mind as an experiment in living as much as an experiment in theatre had become a show-case for Broadway. For him theatre was important, but it was important as a means to an end. The transfer of *The Emperor Jones* was thus in part a betrayal. Anyway, he had a new dream, or rather a new way of realising an old one. He decided to go to Greece and attempt to re-establish there the classic Greek theatre which to his mind was not simply a product of a particular set of cultural presumptions but an agent of those presumptions. He did undertake the direction of O'Neill's next Provincetown play, *The Hairy Ape* but was replaced. When he and Susan Glaspell sailed for Greece it was decided that rather than disband the Players they would call for an 'interim'. Officially the reason was that they all needed some leisure from the demands of the schedule they had imposed on themselves. There was also a suggestion that they had exhausted the available plays. In fact it was more a crisis of spirit.

It has been suggested that the Provincetown failed because it only turned up one major talent and it is true that its policy of producing only American drama meant that it sometimes staged plays whose only virtue lay in the nationality of the author. But in Susan Glaspell it produced a writer much more accomplished than her present dwindled reputation would suggest, while Edna St Vincent Millay's *Aria da Capo*, if not the work of genius that Dell's besotted imagination suggested, was an interesting and subtle experiment in form, a reflexive work which made the process of play-making as much its subject as the generalised anti-war sentiments on which reviewers fastened. The accomplishment of the Provincetown was considerable. In eight seasons, consisting of two summer and six winter programmes, it produced ninety-three plays by forty-seven American playwrights. O'Neill was responsible for sixteen of these and Susan Glaspell for eleven. But its achievement did not simply lie in its discovery and encouragement of playwrights, nor yet in the innovations which it thereby fostered. It established the theatre for the first time in America as a serious focus of artistic activity. Its ensemble acting and its emphasis on the central importance of a group working together and integrating all elements of performance, established a model later embraced by other groups. Together with the Washington Square Players it laid the foundations for the modern American theatre.

In 1923 George Cook, looking back on his experience with the Provincetown, offered the following analysis:

> Three years ago, writing for the Provincetown Players, anticipating the forlornness of our hope to bring to birth in our commercially-minded country a theater whose motive was spiritual, I made this promise: 'We promise to let this theater die rather than let it become another voice of mediocrity.'

I am now forced to confess that our attempt to build up, by our own life and death, in this alien sea, a coral island of our own, has failed. The failure seems to be more our own than America's. Lacking the instinct of the coral-builders, in which we could have found the happiness of continuing ourselves toward perfection, we have developed little willingness to die for the thing we are building.

Our individual gifts and talents have sought their private perfection. We have not, as we hoped, created the beloved community of life-givers. Our richest, like our poorest, have desired most not to give life, but to have it given to them. We have valued creative energy less than its rewards – our sin against the Holy Ghost.

As a group we are not more but less than the great chaotic, unhappy community in whose dry heart I have vainly tried to create an oasis of living beauty.

Since we have failed spiritually in the elemental things – failed to pull together – failed to do what any good football or baseball team or crew do as a matter of course with no word said – and since the result of this is mediocrity, we keep our promise. We give this theater we love good death; the Provincetown Players end their story here.

Some happier gateway must let in the spirit which seems to be seeking to create a soul under the ribs of death in the American theater.[31]

It is clear from this that Cook's sense of failure was not really rooted in theatre. He pursued that same quest for organic unity which Eliot and Pound were equally locating in a classical past. He, in common with many others, recognised that *Gemeinschaft* had given way to *Gesellschaft*, that alienation was a primary fact of his age. In common with Paul Goodman in the 1940s, he felt that the recreation of community through art offered a possible means to restore a lost sense of belonging. Perhaps that was why he responded so immediately to O'Neill's work, for the word 'belong' echoes through his plays, most of which focus on a sense of lost purpose. People are grouped together in O'Neill plays rather as they are in the aggregations of the un-communal city which had increasingly become the dominant reality for the majority of Americans. They have the appearance but not the reality of community. Cook hoped to fill this space in people's lives with a sense of shared purpose. It is here that his sense of failure really focussed, for he found that his fellow players did not all share his therapeutic sense of theatre, nor his communitarian ethic. And although O'Neill was a fellow enthusiast for Nietzsche he lacked Cook's missionary zeal for life enhancement. At the heart of his disillusionment was perhaps his own breach of faith in pressing for a Broadway production of his own play and perhaps his own act of desertion. But he was right in one thing: the Provincetown Players were dead. Though O'Neill did restructure the group and launch it again, its primary work had been done.

The next stage of the Provincetown tended to emphasise theatrical experimentation. Kenneth Macgowan, associate editor of *Theatre Arts* magazine (founded in 1916), was to be in charge. Macgowan had collaborated with Robert Edmond Jones on *The Theatre of Tomorrow* (1921) (an implied reference to Hiram Moderwell's book of 1915, *The Theatre of Today*), which not only described the achievement of the new European theatre but advocated the need to move beyond realism and 'attempt to transfer to dramatic art the illumination of those deep and vigorous and eternal processes of the human soul which the psychology of Freud and Jung has given us through study of the unconscious, striking to the heart of emotion and linking our commonest life today with the emanations of the primitive racial mind'.[32] Since this book appeared the year after O'Neill's *The Emperor Jones* it was perhaps inevitable that the two men would respond to one another. They had also collaborated on *Continental Stagecraft* (1922) which again urged the writer to move beyond the surface, and, with the assistance of more imaginative designers and directors, to tap psychological and archetypal truths. The paradigm for this new 'expressionist' theatre was, indeed, O'Neill's *The Hairy Ape*.

O'Neill began working with Macgowan in 1921 and when the re-launching of the Provincetown was discussed he saw himself at first not primarily as contributing new works but as offering ideas as to production possibilities. But inevitably his real effort went into his plays, plays more manifestly experimental in form and intent, and, although the restructured Provincetown had some success, even acquiring a second theatre, he broke with it in 1926. He had virtually from the beginning been uneasy with the use of the old name, seeing it as 'a dead issue', an albatross. In the end, like George Cook, he preferred to lay it to rest. It had done its job. The American theatre was now firmly launched on a new path.

The Washington Square Players are accorded less attention here for a number of reasons. They lacked an individual with the drive and personal vision of George Cook. They lacked also a resident playwright of the power and stature of O'Neill, though O'Neill, Cook and Glaspell all had plays produced by the Players. They were also less concerned with creating a specifically American repertoire. Their first programme announced: 'We have only one policy in regard to the plays which we will produce – they must have artistic merit. Preference will be given to American plays, but we shall also include in our repertory the works of well-known European authors which have been ignored by the commercial managers.'[33] Following the first impromptu performance of Lord Dunsany's *The Glittering Gate*, the group, which included, among others, Robert Edmond Jones, Ida Rauh, Albert Boni and Lawrence Langner, acquired The Bandbox theatre at 57th and Third Avenue. The first public performance was of Maeterlinck's *Interior* on 19 February 1915. At first they offered only two performances a week but this was gradually extended. In the first season seventeen plays were produced, of which five were European in origin. In the second season performances at the 299-seat theatre were given nightly, and admission raised from fifty cents to a dollar so that the actors could earn twenty-five dollars a week. In the third season the Washington Square Players moved from The Bandbox to the Comedy – in the words of Oliver Sayler, 'from the byways to Broadway, from spiritual freedom hampered by material bondage to material freedom hampered by spiritual bondage'.[34] The move signalled an increased emphasis on foreign plays, so much so that Waldo Frank was led to protest at their irrelevance to American audiences, at the degree to which transposed realism can become a form of exoticism. Nevertheless they were clearly correct in their claim to produce plays which commercial managements would not touch, and in addition to fostering new drama they could also boast a young stage designer, Robert Edmond Jones, who was to dominate the next decades. And though, faced with financial difficulties and the absence in Europe of a number of their personnel, they closed their doors in 1918, from the ashes emerged the Theatre Guild, which was a direct successor, formed by the same group with a capital of $500 and a lease to the Garrick Theatre. Its declared objective was:

(1) To improve the Guild standards of play production;
(2) To improve the Guild standards of acting;
(3) To experiment to a greater extent than heretofore, especially with the works of American dramatists;
(4) To develop a permanent ensemble acting company;
(5) To maintain a repertory of fine plays which shall be presented from year to year;
(6) To establish a Studio for all branches of the Art of the Theatre, in which young people of talent may study as an inherent part of the life of the theatre.[35]

Though Oliver Sayler could regret four years later that 'whatever it may hope to accomplish with more elaborate equipment, the Guild on its record is not an experimental theatre. It has taken no more chances than the average earnest Broadway producer, not so many as Arthur Hopkins, the Neighborhood Playhouse, the Provincetown Players or its own earlier self, the Washington Square Players...Nor is the Guild non-commercial.' He added that 'It has paid its way from the start without gift or charity.'[36] It was a somewhat harsh judgement. It is true that most of the productions in these years were of foreign plays but it survived at a difficult time and it did commit itself to professional standards of a kind that the old Provincetown had frowned on.

3. Susan Glaspell.

SUSAN GLASPELL

Besides Eugene O'Neill, the Provincetown Players produced one major talent in Susan Glaspell. Her work is in many ways more controlled than O'Neill's. Her style is more reticent. Where possible she works by indirection. Yet she shared her husband's visionary drive, his sense of a Nietzschean life force operating as a counterweight to a tragic potential. And this breaks through on occasion in lyrical arias, apostrophes to the human spirit, at times unbalancing and sentimental, at times affecting in the simplicity of their expression.

Her first play for the Provincetown, apart from the sketch which she wrote with her husband, was *Trifles*, which was first produced at the Wharf Theatre in Provincetown on 8 August 1916. *Trifles* was a well-observed study of male arrogance and insensitivity. Following the murder of a man, apparently by his wife, the County Attorney, the Sheriff and his wife, and a neighbouring farmer and his wife arrive at the empty house to collect clothes for the imprisoned woman and to look for clues. But while the men wander around the house baffled as to motive, the women slowly piece together the reason for the crime from the trifles which they find – a poorly stitched quilt, a song bird with a broken neck in a fancy box. And as they assemble the evidence of her guilt so, without a word between them, they conceal that evidence, recognising their own failure to help a woman whose desperation they had done nothing to soothe. Childless, with her spirit broken as her husband had broken the neck of the song bird to which she had looked for consolation, she had struck back against the man who had stifled her own lyricism. The women recognise the pain out of which the crime had come, a crime in which they feel themselves to have shared. 'Oh, I *wish* I'd come over here once in a while! That was a crime! That was a crime! Who's going to punish that?' It is the women and not the men who acknowledge the shared experience which both gives them their insight and breeds the compassion which they offer, for 'we live close together and we live far apart. We all go through the same things – it's all just a different kind of the same thing.'[37]

The brief play is economically constructed. And just as the women create their instinctive theories out of trifles, so the playwright builds her play out of small gestures (a broken hinge on a birdcage which reflects the broken neck of the bird, the broken neck of the man, but also the broken spirit of the woman who had bought the cage). The man imprisons the woman, the woman imprisons the bird. And yet they are all imprisoned in a system equally implacable. So too, the disordered state of the stitchwork on her quilt reflects the tensions which finally turn her from a creative to a destructive force. The principal character, as in her later plays, *Bernice* and *Alison's House*,

25

never appears. It is a play which works by understatement. The melodrama inherent in the scene is rigorously excluded. It is an ensemble piece, lyrical but spare.

At the same time several of Susan Glaspell's one-act plays for Provincetown were genuine trifles, comedies which revealed a playful sense of the egocentrism of those in the anarchist movement (*The People*, first performed 9 March 1917), the inverted social snobbery of the non-conformist (*Close the Book*, 2 November 1917), the conflicting roles of women (*Women's Honor*, 26 April 1918), and, in a play written in collaboration with George Cook, *Tickless Time* (20 December 1918), the ironic pull of reality undercutting grand gestures of moral and metaphysical independence. In other words, they were to some degree in-jokes, gentle deflations of their own pretensions, a mockery of their own over-seriousness. But as plays they offered nothing of real interest beyond an unusual stance of self-consciousness.

Susan Glaspell's primary weakness lay in a tendency to a somewhat mawkish sentimentality, at its worst in *Bernice* (21 March 1919) and *The Comic Artist* (24 June 1928), both ringing affirmations of life, portraits of individuals whose vital commitment to others and to the spirit of a transcendent life force survives even their own death, which becomes a kind of joyous sacrifice. The sentiment is perhaps that of O'Neill's *The Iceman Cometh* – 'we die so soon ! We live so in the dark. We never become what we might be. I should think we could help each other more'[38] – but it is expressed in a disturbing pseudo-poetic prose and projects a view of the principal character as a kind of secular saint for this vague religion. Bernice had, we are told, 'the gift of being herself',[39] but somehow that self never becomes anything more than a simple piety. Similarly, in the later *The Comic Artist*, written in collaboration with her second husband Norman Matson, the spirit of a cartoonist, committed by virtue of his profession to sustaining laughter, survives even his destruction at the hands of a wife whose materialism is simply an image of a society which has abandoned the old ways. The principal characters have retreated to Provincetown to rebuild their lives, a restoration of values which is symbolised by their attempts to restore an old house. The setting is a clue to the sense of mission, of mystical purpose, which Susan Glaspell and her first husband had. Evil is presented as the desire to remove to New York and cash in on one's talents. Since this is of course what, from one point of view, they both did, the play in a sense also stands as a kind of critique of, and elegy for, the experiment which had brought such energy to the American theatre but which had led to her husband's own sense of disillusionment, a disillusionment which, by some curious act of loyalty, she seems to embrace in this play.

The early plays were flawed. They pressed effects too far. The symbol becomes at times too overt. In many ways Susan Glaspell's early work, however, was more impressive than some of O'Neill's. There is more control, a natural reticence which charges language and gesture with a significance the more powerful because of their subtlety. *The Outside* (28 December 1917), for example, compares more than favourably with O'Neill's early sea plays, though with some of the same faults. It begins with realism but quickly blurs the hard edge of that realism towards abstraction. The tactile precision of the setting dissolves into an insistent but vague significance; the prose dissolves into poetry. The spaces in the text at the beginning of the play are more forceful than the later loquacity.

The Outside is set on Cape Cod, near to Provincetown itself, in an old life-saving station now turned into a house. And the notion of life-saving becomes central to the play's meaning. Outside, the sand dunes can be seen threatening to overwhelm the woods beyond. There is, in other words, a struggle for existence in the setting itself. On the outer edge of Cape Cod is the open sea, with the wind driving a destructive sea before it. On the inner edge is the calm of the harbour. The action takes place between the two and the play begins with a fruitless attempt to revive a drowned man. Although he appears dead, his rescuers struggle on trying to breathe life back into him. The owner of the house, Mrs Patrick, is indignant at their intrusion but the men persist, ignoring her objections and the silent presence of her woman companion, Allie Mayo.

As the play develops it becomes clear that Mrs Patrick's resistance to the life-savers is an expression of her own deeper misanthropy, a conviction that death dominates life, as the sand overwhelms the woods. Her transformation of the life-saving station into a silent house is an image of this. For some reason she has decided to bury herself in a house itself half buried in sand and Allie Mayo, who has 'a prejudice against words',[40] is a natural companion, having herself lost a man to the sea some twenty years before. But the appearance of the life-savers acts as a catalyst. Allie utters her first words and then, through a faltering language, feels her way back towards life. Clearly the life-savers have lost one life only to save another. Slowly her staccato sentences give way to a lyrical invocation to life – a conceit which Glaspell handles with considerable tact. As Allie realises the significance of what she has seen, so she regains control over her surroundings by re-enacting the process of language acquisition. She sees the event which she has witnessed as showing the strength of the life principle; Mrs Patrick as revealing the ironic and overwhelming power of death. And so both women argue for their own interpretation in terms of the natural struggle for life symbolised by the battle between the woodland and the smothering sand, the open sea and the harbour. The testing point is the edge, the interface between order and anarchy, safety and danger. It is at the margin that meaning coheres, that real identity is forged. It was a territory which in many ways O'Neill was to make his own but for Glaspell too it was the crucial area. Mrs Patrick resists the spring, which she (like Eliot and Hemingway) feels to be simply ironic. The only guarantee against suffering is an absurdist stasis. She seeks the invulnerability of the inanimate. For her companion, newly awakened, spring is an image of the eternal renewal which ultimately defeats death. The outside edge contains and defines life. It is where the battle is and, despite herself, at the end of the play Mrs Patrick is won over to this Nietzschean image of recurrence.

In a sense the play suffers from its own basic strategy. It works best when it is least articulate. The woman, stunned into silence, watching the wordless efforts to bring life back to a dead body, communicates more powerfully than the over-explicit arias with which the play ends. Her struggle for language is an apt correlative of her effort to find her way back to a social world from which she has wilfully excluded herself. But language, once acquired, discharges the tension, makes literal what derives its strength from its reticence, uncoils the images which gain their power from their refusal to render up immediate meaning. The religious fervour with which each argues her position presses language towards a poetic self-consciousness which is paradoxically bathetic.

By contrast *Inheritors* (21 March 1921) engages a public world pitching American historical idealism against a politically reactionary and morally pragmatic present. The first act, set in 1879, establishes the vision. Silas Morton, who had acquired his land directly from the government, which had itself appropriated it from the Indians, wishes to assuage his sense of guilt by returning it to the people. Together with his friend Fajevary, who had fought for democracy in his native Hungary in 1848, he plans to leave the hillside which dominates the town as the site for a university. They are motivated by the conviction that we '*made* ourselves – made ourselves out of the wanting to be more – created ourselves you might say, by our own courage – our – what is it? – aspiration'.[41]

Forty-one years later the dream is both realised and betrayed. Another war has just passed but it has left a residue not of hope and idealism but of materialism, political reaction and self-interest. Fajevary is now the banker president of the college board of trustees, anxious to extend the university and willing to take such steps as are necessary. In particular this means persuading a radical member of faculty to adopt a discreet silence and, more painfully, controlling Madeline Morton, granddaughter of the college's founder, who now adopts the cause both of a conscientious objector and a group of Hindus who wish publicly to press their case for Indian independence. By a rather too adroit irony, therefore, she finds herself in a position to exorcise the guilt felt by her grandfather towards the Indians of her own country while, through her relationship to the Indians and to Emil Johnson, a 'crudely Americanized

Swede', she re-enacts the friendship between her grandfather and his Hungarian friend. She is also able to reassert an idealism which has surrendered to simple chauvinism. She thus assaults the police and the play ends as she prepares to accept the consequences of her action, convinced that, 'What you are – that doesn't stay with you.' The crucial thing is 'to be the most you can be, so life will be more because you were'.[42]

Well-constructed, articulately argued, *Inheritors* is essentially a non-tragic version of the conviction which animates much of O'Neill's work. But it presents the struggle as essentially a social battle. Susan Glaspell is less concerned with elemental battles between the self and its environment than with differing versions of the social ideal. Since the individual and the race create themselves, they possess a moral responsibility which is in part mystical, in part a consequence of a kind of ethical Darwinism and in part a necessary product of social living. Fate may intervene – Madeline's mother dies of diphtheria having unselfishly rushed to the assistance of the Johnson family – but such is the manifest goodness of the act that it redeems the contingency. And this is the weakness of the play. Good and evil are self-evident. And despite her efforts to blur the clear outlines of the moral argument by saddling her radical academic with the sick wife whose treatment depends on his continuing employment, the world which she creates renders itself in simple terms. Indeed the weakest character of the play, Madeline's brother, is a rabid patriot who regrets Abraham Lincoln's remarks on social justice. For Ludwig Lewisohn, writing in *The Nation*, it was

> the first play of the American theatre in which a strong intellect and a ripe artistic nature have grasped and set forth in human terms the central tradition and most burning problem of our national life, quite justly and scrupulously, equally without acrimony and compromise. No competent critic, whatever his attitude to the play's tendency, will be able to deny the power and brilliancy of Miss Glaspell's characterization... She has recorded the tragic disintegration of American idealism. The memorable dramatic occasion of the year is on Macdougal Street where Susan Glaspell has added to the wealth of both her country and her art.[43]

It was a reaction which did more than justice to a play whose epic pretensions founder finally on characters and a plot which are too manifestly manipulated to command conviction. Yet this concern with the fate of American idealism placed her squarely at the centre of literary enquiry while her conviction that materialism and a resultant political conservatism were destroying American idealism was felt sharply by those socialists and liberals intent on constructing a credible response to the reactionary politics of the 1920s.

The Verge (1921) is a remarkable play which takes as its structural principle its subject – the refusal to be contained by form or by language. It begins as a social comedy but the Wildean wit is quickly exposed as a mask concealing a metaphysical yearning that collapses by degrees into hysteria and ultimately madness. It is a play in which the failure to penetrate through the word to the meaning, and through the personal to the universal, is mirrored by the disintegration of character and the loss of social form. Here, as elsewhere in American writing, the twin fears are a suffocating and constricting sense of stasis on the one hand, and a total formlessness, anarchic, amoral, non-definitional on the other.

The ironically named Claire Archer is obsessed with breaking through to a new order of being. She pursues transcendence and consequently rebels equally against her role as wife and mother and against the banality of the forms with which she feels herself to be surrounded. At the beginning of the play this desire is sublimated in the breeding of exotic plants. She tries to create a hybrid which will in some sense break through the boundary of being, will transcend its own physicality. One such, accurately named the Edge Vine, fails her, reverting to its biological type. As a consequence she tears it up by the roots. 'The leaves of this vine,' we are told in the stage direction, 'are not the form that leaves have been. They are at once repellent and significant.' But not, it seems, significant enough, although Glaspell coyly indicates that 'you might see the form of a cross in it, if you happened to think of it that way.'[44] And this is a clue to the ambiguity at the heart of the play, for in tearing up the vine because of its failure to enter a new sphere of being, she is also violating a principle which is competing for her attention – a humanity, a compassion, a human responsibility which ties the individual to his or her fate and which traps that individual in a world of familiar forms. But Claire places her faith elsewhere – in a plant called Breath of Life, delicate, strange, too fragile to exist outside a hothouse environment but visibly pulsing with life. In other words the flower is a patent image for Claire herself.

At the beginning of the play Claire's insistence that 'we need not be held in forms moulded for us. There is outness – and otherness'[45] seems to have a social dimension. She is the new woman who dominates her world and refuses to be defined by social roles that derive from sexual roles. She wishes to smash the system, however, not in the name of anything so simple as sexual justice but because 'there would be strange new comings together – mad new comings together, and we would know what it is to be born, and then we might know – that we are'.[46] It follows, however, that her rebellion against forms is also a revolt against socially derived notions of sanity. She wishes to breed insanity to see what it may spawn. She had, indeed, married an artist and then an aviator, hoping thereby to break through into another realm of experience through them. But the painter turned out to be a conventional realist and the flyer returned to earth the same man who had left it. She sees no option but to make the leap which she believes to characterise the natural world, for she places her faith in the fact that 'plants do it. The big leap – it's called. Explode their species – because something in them knows they've gone as far as they can go. Something in them knows they're shut in to just that. So – go mad – that life may not be prisoned. Break themselves into crazy things – into lesser things, and from the pieces – may come one sliver of life with vitality to find the future.'[47]

She hopes by destroying to create. Accordingly she tries to smash her marriage through a largely spiritual affair with the painfully symbolically named Tom Edgeworthy. She refuses to be defined by her maternal responsibility towards a daughter who has become the embodiment of bourgeois American values. She breaks with her sister who is called in to reassert the values of familial life and who reminds her that 'you must see yourself that you haven't the poise of people who are held – well, within the circle... There's something about being in the main body, having one's roots in the big common experiences, gives a calm which you have missed.'[48] For she wishes precisely to violate such presumptions, indeed to press beyond a world in which language itself has been conventionalised. 'Life – experience – values – calm – sensitive words which raise their heads as indications. And you *pull them up* – to decorate your stagnant little minds... And because you have pulled that word from the life that grew it you won't let one who's honest and aware, and troubled, try to reach through to – to what she doesn't know is there.'[49] She seeks a world, an experience, a level of being, which is not 'shut up in saying'. But the problem is clear. The act of expression is definitional. It freezes energy into form. 'Why does the fabric of life have to – freeze into its pattern?' she asks. 'It should flow.'[50] Here is the paradox (one that Tony Tanner has shown to be endemic to American writing). She attempts to resolve it by resorting to poetry but this, more than anything, is pattern and structure.

> Thoughts take pattern – then the pattern is the thing
> But let me tell you how it is with me.
>   [*It flows again.*]
> All that I do or say – it is to what it comes from,
> A drop lifted from the sea.
> I want to lie upon the earth and know.
> But – scratch a little dirt and make a flower;
> Scratch a bit of brain – something like a poem.
> Stop *doing* that. Help me stop doing that![51]

Experience demands communication and communication denies experience. It is an observation more subtle than O'Neill's crude metaphysics and a concern which Glaspell allowed to enter her own aesthetic. It is a problem which the symbol can resolve and the metaphor cannot. But just as Claire is unable to hold her personal world together, having forsaken the tension which keeps its component parts in place, so the play de-creates itself. Claire disengages from the rational world, plunging into a self-destruction which she trusts will prove regenerative. The play correspondingly shifts from social realism into wild impressionism, a symbolism which has cut free of its roots in the social and linguistic world. Claire toys with the idea of killing herself and actually does kill Tom because his love threatens a form of stasis. She throttles him, destroying by possession. It is a form of metaphysical baroque, not entirely unlike plays Edward Albee was to write forty years later.

Clearly Glaspell is critical of Claire who retreats into a tower, who is able to envisage a world entirely bereft of moral values, who cuts the links between herself and her fellow men, who advances the cause of ultimate beauty above that of ethical consciousness, who searches for selflessness with a romantic egotism so fierce that it destroys herself and those who surround her. She is Ahab defying the world through challenging it. But there is a kind of authority and glory in that. She is a dangerously ambiguous figure in the same sense as Gatsby; an equally odd combination of the ideal and the corrupt, and in that sense, perhaps, a natural enough product of her time, which was not only fascinated with literary notions of innocence and evil but which even invested its political language with like presumptions. And her distrust of a language drained of meaning by a world unreasonably satisfied with its own sense of self-evident values (the mid-western world of her own upbringing) was not remote from that which Hemingway (another mid westerner) would voice a few years later. Which is to say that Susan Glaspell was also acutely aware of that sense of the collapse of structure and meaning mirrored in so much writing of the 1920s. But she was also alive to the danger of a personal morality of action and imagination which took the crude form of romantic hedonism, of the substitution of quantity for quality in experience, and the more sophisticated form of a desire to see social, moral and linguistic worlds disassembled in order to give birth to values powerful only by virtue of their abandonment of a teleological world. Art is, finally, not an ultimate value in her lexicon. And if others found it a comfortable and even logical strategy to counterpose the imagination to a disintegrating social world, she did not. For the imagination has its own coercive power and the price of locating meaning in aesthetics was finally a surrender of humanity. She had read Nietzsche but she had not swallowed him whole.

The Verge is an imperfect work. There is a precious quality about the dialogue, whish is not entirely a function of character. The collapse of comedy (and the early scenes are extremely witty), is part of the play's basic strategy (just as Claire's growing seriousness is a function of her failure of moral vision) but it also serves to underline a certain pretentiousness in her writing. Nonetheless, it is a play of real invention and intellectual energy, a play which compared favourably with O'Neill's early work, with the single exception of the achievement of *The Emperor Jones*. The stage set was itself an expression both of the play's subject matter and the state of mind of the heroine. The tower into which the heroine retreats is described in expressionistic terms. It is 'thought to be round but does not complete the circle. The back is curved, then jagged lines break from that, and the front is a queer bulging window – in a curve that leans. The whole structure is as if given a twist by some terrific force – like something wrung...The delicately distorted rail of a spiral staircase winds up from below.'[52] Glaspell, no less than O'Neill, had found her way to expressionism without the help of the Germans, though in her anthropomorphic flowers there is more than a hint of Strindberg's final plays, as there is in the visionary quality of her work.

The reviews were mixed. There was general agreement that it was a failure, but a failure which distinguished itself from the banalities of the American theatre. As Percy Hammond wrote, 'The play is good, but not great. Yet, it must be added, most of our American dramatists would be proud of such a default of greatness; indeed, only two or three could so fail.'[53] But to Stark Young, writing in *The New Republic*, the fault largely lay with the Provincetown's uncertain acting. He conceded Glaspell's tendency, already noted, towards an over-explicitness. There were, he admitted, 'too many words and phrases that run toward cant, too much about otherness, farness and so on'. But he also recognised 'a mixture of matter that is fresh on our stage' and is 'at the same time scientific, vivid, intimate and searching; and through all these is exciting. And what's more,' he added, 'this immediacy and truth and freshness make an excitement that is the same as that which good poetry has always achieved with its method and imagery.'[54] For Thomas Dickinson 'the language in which Miss Glaspell has written this play is more richly allusive than of any other play written in America.'[55]

If this was something of an overstatement it remains true that few American dramatists approached Susan Glaspell's originality of mind or her ability to create symbols of human desperation. And though Young is right in detecting her tendency to replace the poetry *of* the theatre with a poetry *in* the theatre – a wish, that is, to make language express too directly abstract ideas or spiritual aspirations – she was aware of this weakness and builds into her work a scepticism which does not resolve but does identify this paradox. And here her sense of an identity under such pressure that it begins to fragment in front of us is handled with such skill that it never lurches into melodrama.

Her last play, *Alison's House*, was first performed on 1 December 1930. It is, perhaps, a rather slight affair, a piece of self-justification by a woman who had, in effect, run off with a married man and who in this play offers a justification of her violation of social taboo. But nothing by Susan Glaspell is less than an articulate attempt to render experience in a form that neutralises her own acknowledged tendency to sentimentality.

Alison's House is a lyrical celebration of the human spirit, set on the final day of the nineteenth century. Alison Stanhope (whose name is clearly not without significance), dead some fifteen years, had been an Emily Dickinson figure, a spinster whose work had only been published after her death. Now, with her sister Agatha becoming ill and mentally unstable, the family have gathered to assist her removal prior to the sale of the house. As the day progresses so we learn more about the mid-western poet and her family. Alison, it transpires, had fallen in love with a married man but had bowed to her family's wishes and refused to go with him. Her poetry was a product of that act of self-denial. But the same temptation has come the way of her brother and his daughter. He, like his sister, resisted; but his daughter, the product of another age, had followed her instincts.

The buried side of Alison Stanhope is now exposed. Agatha dies, poised between destroying and passing on the previously unknown poems with which Alison had described her affair. These poems become the focus for an argument between the generations, with her brother intent on suppressing them to preserve appearances, as he has done in his own unhappy marriage, and the younger generation arguing for the survival of a truth-telling art. The logic of the passing century endorses the final decision which is to allow to language and to instinctive response an authenticity denied by a century which believed that passion should defer to duty and art offer its due respect to convention. Admittedly, the thumb is securely on one side of the scales. The only happy marriage is that of the daughter who had ignored convention while the romance that unfolds during the play is the result of a spontaneous meeting of minds and spirits which occurs between a young secretary and a reporter, who, as himself a putative poet and a newspaperman, is wedded to a pursuit of truth. Yet the play also expresses a revulsion from the prosaic materialism which is equally a product of the new century. For Alison's house is to be sold to a couple who plan to make it into a garishly decorated boarding-house. Their harsh practicality has no place for the poetic values which were enshrined in the poetry of the mid-western spinster. The ambiguity is revealing. Glaspell regarded herself as a radical but there was a strong conservative streak in that radicalism. And so she produces a play in 1930 which in effect celebrates those values which economic crisis had suggested to be ineffectual in tackling problems which were proving resistant to liberal notions of moral identity. At a time when art was required to engage the brutal social and economic realities of American life, she was in effect proposing an intensely personal art. And despite the fact that the play was awarded the Pulitzer prize for 1931 she never published another play. Her idealism was displaced by a rather more hard-nosed political pragmatism; her visionary celebration of the life force and the individual sensibility deferred to the simple biological persistence and group ethic of a John

Steinbeck. She did become the director of the Mid-West Play Bureau for the Federal Theatre for a year and fostered local talent but she produced no more of her own plays and eventually died in 1948.

Hers was an original voice. She was contemptuous of social and artistic evasion and hence was suspicious of the moralistic pieties of her upbringing. But she shared with her first husband a belief in an uncorruptible human nature and the persistence of a desire to transcend a materialism which was the primary enemy of the spirit. Her imagination worked primarily in terms of symbols, potent images which she transposed to the stage with economy and grace. Her doubts about language were an expression of her modernity and were shared by the O'Neill who, in *The Emperor Jones*, showed the collapse of verbal structure as a correlative of a reversion to archetype. If she had a contrary tendency to prolixity, in her best work this was kept under control and even inspected for its falsity. Certainly the success of the Provincetown Players owed almost as much to her as it did to O'Neill. The eclipse of her later work and the very real accomplishment of O'Neill have tended to conceal the extent of her achievement.

2 Eugene O'Neill

Of all writing I love only that which is written with blood. Write with blood:
and you will discover that blood is spirit.

Nietzsche, *Thus Spake Zarathustra*

O'Neill was born into the theatre. His father, James O'Neill, was a famous
actor who early in his career had been hailed as a potentially great tragedian
but who had settled for the financial security that came with his acquisition
of the rights to *The Count of Monte Cristo*, a play whose continuing success
trapped him in the same role for two decades. This surrender of a poetic self
to a prosaic materialism was one which haunted O'Neill's imagination in
later years and became the basis for much of his work.

Eugene's home life was painful. His father was domineering, his mother a
morphine addict, his brother an alcoholic. He spent a year at Princeton but
never finished his course. Then, having made a young woman pregnant he
secretly married her – an act which seems to have been an odd compound of
duty and spite since he immediately allowed his father to ship him off to
South America, where, out of funds, he camped out on the docks and learned
about the underside of life at close hand. On his return to America he made
no attempt to see his wife and child, abandoning them and living in a bar-
hotel in New York. Following a suicide attempt he was rescued by his father
but a tubercular infection necessitated a stay in a sanatorium,* where he began
his first attempts at playwriting. The result was a series of brief plays, sketches
in which he tried out his talent.

O'Neill's was a double inheritance. From his father's theatre, the theatre of
nineteenth-century melodrama, he derived the central significance of event,
and from the naturalistic tradition of Crane, Zola and London the determining significance of environment, the tendency to see setting as a concrete
image and central mechanism of fate. He had no respect for the theatre as he
found it, regarding most of its products as ludicrously gimcrack, and from
the first he attempted to write dialogue which was authentic in language and
tone, itself something of an innovation. But his interest in examining human
nature under pressure, his concern with placing his characters in extreme
situations left him open to the charge of creating melodramas. Certainly his
early works, later collected under the title *The Lost Plays of Eugene O'Neill*,

---

* Many years later the novelist Walker Percy occupied the same bed in the same sanatorium.
For him, too, it meant a transformation in his life.

36

4. James O'Neill as Edmond Dantes in *The Count of Monte Cristo*, a part which he played more than 6000 times in twenty-five years, and which earned him in excess of $800 000.

are a catalogue of suicides, shipwrecks, abortions and moral ironies almost wholly lacking in subtlety.

Like Nietzsche, whose work he read avidly, he saw little evidence of ethical progress and his early plays in particular tend to be accounts of the collapse of social and moral worlds. Class disintegrates under pressure (*Thirst*, 1916; *Fog*, 1917; *Recklessness*, *Abortion*, 1914), but so too does character, though a good deal faster for the rich. But he was equally capable of offering a Shavian satire of Nietzschean thought, as he did in *Servitude*, which is the most polished and accomplished, though not the most original, of his early plays. *Servitude* also stands as O'Neill's considered response to Max Stirner's egoistic philosophy as exemplified in *Ego and His Own*.

The self in these early plays is very much a product of arbitrary forces. It inhabits a contingent world. Ships are constantly running into submerged wrecks, lives being destroyed by stray pregnancies and by tuberculosis, by sudden affliction or ill-considered marriages. His seas were scattered with icebergs, his society with the flotsam of social injustice. Confident material success existed only to be betrayed by event, youth to be destroyed by dissipation, illness, poverty and even death. His romantic attachment to blighted lives, consumptive young women and a pervasive smell of death, allied to a fascination with the wealthy, is in some ways reminiscent of F. Scott Fitzgerald, who followed him at Princeton some years later.

In part, however, this process of stripping his characters of the apparent solidities of the social world was a strategy for exposing the falsities of that world. It was evidence of a generalised political commitment which he soon abandoned. So, later he chose to contrast the sailors whom he had met on shipboard, and whose relations were kept honest by the exigencies of shipboard life and the constant danger of death, with those who submitted to the conventions and traditions of society. He admired the sailors precisely because 'they have not been steeped in the evasions and superficialities which come with social life and intercourse...Their real selves are exposed. They are crude but honest. They are not handicapped by inhibitions.'[1]

His plays became precisely concerned with exposing what Pirandello was to call 'naked figures'. And for O'Neill, concern with prostitutes, down and outs, and sailors was not wholly a romantic pose. These were people he knew well. And if they too had dreams and illusions, the deceits were at least their own. They spun life-lies out of necessity, as a compensation for real deprivations, and not as part of an elaborate charade of moral decency and social status. The spiritual dimension of life was rendered in his work through a lyric perception of the natural world and a nostalgic regret for the loss of harmony between man and nature – a harmony disrupted by the modern. Or, more especially in his early dramatic experiments, the gaps left by the collapse of faith were filled by sentimentalities – mother love (*The Web*), selfless acts of heroism (*Fog*), moral self-sacrifice (*A Wife for a Life*). Crudely handled in these early sketches, such sentimentalities became a kind of moral and artistic bathos. Towards the end of his career, however, they are seen as part of a strategy of self-delusion, consciously employed by his characters and available for criticism.

For a time he regarded himself as a socialist, and then an anarchist. In other words experience could still be regarded as offering a meaning, as expressing forces which could be analysed. But for the most part this survives in his drama only as a conviction of the irremediable triviality of the wealthy and their conviction that wealth buys immunity not only from outmoded conventions but from natural moral demands, demands which O'Neill still acknowledged without being able to offer any justification for invoking them beyond an adolescent notion of honour and personal dignity. Characters in his early sketches have a tendency to commit honourable suicide when confronted with the evidence of their own caddish behaviour. He may have boldly announced his freedom from convention and lived a life which seemed to epitomise his contempt for respectability, but his moral values were at first clearly as conventional as could be desired. God may be dead but he is replaced by a conscience every bit as rigorous in its demands. If in *The Sniper* (1917) he comments on the 'crushing irony' of futile prayer, it is clear enough that irony is both his central moral agent and the concept which serves as a substitute for divine justice; it is, in fact, an expression of the constricting power of internal and external fate – that is the power of heredity and environment.

The early one-act plays are obsessed with death and madness. Human relationships are destructive by definition. Character collapses under pressure. Dissolution is a natural law. Experience is less a process of acquiring knowledge than of suffering psychological and literal wounds. In *Where the Cross is Made* (1918) a sea captain is driven mad by the privations of shipwreck and his son physically maimed and eventually driven mad. In *Before Breakfast* (1916), an experiment in monologue, a young woman and her off-stage husband are physically debilitated and morally crushed by their incapacity to sustain themselves. The play ends with his death and his wife's hysteria. *The Dreamy Kid* (1919) ends with two imminent deaths and *The Rope* (1918) centres on a deranged old man and a retarded girl. And cementing these gothic elements together is money. Buried treasure, concealed money, hard-earned dollars are the source of the bitterness that characterises human relationships.

The model of personal character and individual behaviour was crudely naturalistic. A mad parent spawns a mad child; a physically constrained environment produces a warped personality. He created, in other words, a psychopathology of the self which was, in a sense, clearly the product of his

5. Eugene O'Neill

own traumatic recent past. The drug addiction of his mother, the alcoholism of his brother, his own wilful self-degradation and his tuberculosis contributed to a vision which was brutally deterministic.

The Eugene O'Neill who presided over four decades of American drama was a playwright of genuine force and originality. But his was an eclectic imagination and an undisciplined intelligence which created powerful but imperfect works. Virtually nothing he wrote was without flaw. He stumbled on ideas and techniques with an enthusiasm seldom less than total. When he conceived of the mask as a major symbol and practical tool, he immediately regretted his failure to use it in a whole range of plays. Once he had discovered the dramatic aside as a practical expression of the subconscious he looked for reasons to employ it in works for which it was demonstrably unsuited. There can be few writers whose best-known works are so deeply marred by failures of imaginative and intellectual control. *Desire Under the Elms* (1924), *Strange Interlude* (1928) and *Mourning Becomes Electra* (1932), milestones in the history of the American theatre, are deeply imperfect. Even *The Iceman Cometh* (1948), a play of haunting grace, presses character and image too far, surrendering to its own logic, pulling O'Neill into the vortex of his echoic method.

When he strained for poetic effect the result could often be bathetic. But when he engaged the painful experiences of his own family life, or when he recalled lyrical moments from his own life at sea, he created sustained moments of poetry in the theatre which have not been equalled since.

O'Neill spent the first fifteen years of his life as a Catholic. And though he abandoned that faith with melodramatic suddenness, he spent the rest of his life seeking some other faith to neutralise a persistent pull toward nihilism. At the end of his life he found the solution in something more immediate and less abstract than anarchism, socialism or Nietzschean ideas of eternal recurrence – he found it in those very human relationships which had been at the root of his early sense of alienation.

To him theatre was trivial if it did not tackle what he regarded as the 'big issues'. He was always concerned with penetrating the social, with tracing experience to its root in metaphysics. The consequence at times was a humourless engagement of abstraction through characters whose sensibility and even form is bent to serve thematic purposes dependent on a conception of character denied by his own art. By the same token, after his early efforts, he never wrote an inconsequential play, merely, occasionally, ill-conceived and crude thesis dramas. Although the Provincetown Players were originally struck by the differences between their own mid–western aestheticism and O'Neill's manifest engagement with experience (as gold prospector, sailor and habitué of dock-front saloons), in fact O'Neill shared their enthusiasm for Nietzsche and Schopenhauer, for Freud and Jung – the influence of these four runs throughout his work, as does that of Strindberg. For all that, and for all the variety of his subjects, his work remains distinctive. The clotted prose, the moments of pure poetry, the self-conscious experimentalism, the anguished engagement with the dilemma of free will and determinism, the creation of characters pressed to the very extremes of the social world and of experience itself are the mark of a writer whose imagination was always drawn to excess but who was always concerned with discovering a way in which the human spirit could survive the rigours of a painful and disillusioning life.

In an interview with Oliver Sayler, published in *Century Magazine* in 1922, O'Neill outlined his artistic credo. Though this was a mere six years after his first play had been produced by the Provincetown Players it can stand as an accurate description of his basic theme.

> The theatre to me *is* life – the substance and interpretation of life...[*And*] life is struggle, often, if not usually, unsuccessful struggle; for most of us have something within us which prevents us from accomplishing what we dream and desire. And then, as we progress, we are always seeing further than we can reach. I suppose that is one reason why I have come to feel so indifferent toward political and social movements of all kinds.[2]

Early in his career this was the basis of what he presented as a tragic perception; but it could equally well be seen as the basis of an absurdist stance. And despite his public statements, the distinction between the two was never as clear as he implied. Accused of pessimism he insisted that, 'There is a skin deep optimism and another higher optimism, not skin deep, which is usually confounded with pessimism. To me, the tragic alone has that significant beauty which is truth. It is the meaning of life – and the hope.'[3] The statement was unequivocal: the plays were not. His fundamental belief in human ambivalence – a conviction which he derived partly from Nietzsche, partly from Schopenhauer and partly from Freud – was productive of an irony which he wished to see as tragic but which he was inclined to dramatise as absurd.

It is no wonder that O'Neill should have been drawn to Schopenhauer, who regarded the drama as 'the most perfect reflection of human existence' and shared O'Neill's belief that tragedy was the highest form of drama, for in that form, he insisted:

> we are brought face to face with great suffering and the storm and stress of existence: and the outcome of it is to show the vanity of all human effort. Deeply moved, we are either directly prompted to disengage our will from the struggle of life, or else a chord is struck in us which echoes a similar feeling.[4]

But O'Neill could equally have found in Schopenhauer a perfect expression of his own sense of human dualism, of the irony which attaches itself even to those consolations which life appears to offer, more especially through a sexuality which proves both release and imprisonment, for the individual and the race.

> We now contemplate [said Schopenhauer] the bustle and turmoil of life, we see everyone concerned with its cares and troubles, exerting all his strength to satisfy infinite needs and to ward off suffering in many forms, yet without daring to hope for anything else in place of it except just the preservation of this tormented existence for a short span of time. In between, however, we see in the midst of the tumult the glances of two lovers meet longingly: yet why so secretly, nervously, and furtively? Because these lovers are the traitors who

secretly strive to perpetuate the whole trouble and toil that would otherwise rapidly come to an end.[5]

This sense of a conflict, a tension, between the desire for death, for a final resolution of an unconsummatable desire, and the will to life implicit in man's sexual being can be found equally in Freud. In *Beyond the Pleasure Principle*, which O'Neill read and which had been published in translation in 1924, Freud identifies a tension between the ego, or death instinct, and the sexual or life instinct, for he too acknowledges the drive for the organic to resolve itself into the inorganic and announces that '*the aim of all life is death*',[6] but sees this aim as being constantly frustrated by contrary instincts. And this, of course, is potentially the source of that ironic comedy identified by Schopenhauer and which, in truth, identifies the real force of many of O'Neill's plays. Indeed, Freud himself was aware of the consonance between his own approach and that of the philosopher, conceding that 'we have unwittingly steered our course into the harbour of Schopenhauer's philosophy'.[7] But whether its origins lay in philosophy or psychology it is in this tension that O'Neill found his subject, finding in it sometimes a sense of irony and sometimes a sense of the tragic.

Indeed his public statements about the tragic ennoblement in his plays were always at odds with an absurdist reality. It is this absurdist observation which is mirrored in *Before Breakfast* and then again in *Strange Interlude* in which sexuality is presented as a 'trap' (also Hemingway's phrase in *A Farewell to Arms* published in 1927) and an indifferent God is described as looking down on 'our trifling misery of death-born-of-birth'.[8]

In 1922 he outlined his own sense of the tragic, objecting that:

> people talk of the tragedy [in his plays] and call it 'sordid,' 'depressing,' 'pessimistic' – the words usually applied to anything of a tragic nature. But tragedy, I think, has the meaning the Greeks gave it. To them it brought exaltation, an urge toward life and ever more life. It raised them to deeper spiritual understandings and released them from the petty greeds of everyday existence. When they saw a tragedy on the stage they felt their own hopeless hopes ennobled in art...Any victory we *may* win [he insisted] is never the one we dreamed of winning.
>
> The point is that life in itself is nothing. It is the *dream* that keeps us fighting, willing – living! Achievement, in the narrow sense of possession, is a stale finale. The dreams that can be completely realized are not worth dreaming. The higher the dream, the more impossible it is to realize it fully. But you would not say, since this is true, that we should dream only of easily attained ideals. A man wills his own defeat when he pursues the unattainable. But his *struggle* is his success! He is an example of the spiritual significance which life attains when it aims high enough, when the individual fights all the hostile forces within and without himself to achieve a future of nobler values. Such a figure is necessarily

tragic. But to me he is not depressing; he is exhilarating! He may be a failure in our materialistic sense. His treasures are in other kingdoms. Yet isn't he the most inspiring of all successes.[9]

As a description of the tragic mode this is perhaps unexceptionable but as an account of his own drama it was somewhat misleading. For the trans-figuring Apollonian vision, the dream designed to aestheticise life and give it the shape which in reality it lacked, devolved all too often into simple self-deception. More often than not his plays are not about a glorious struggle against fate, an heroic pursuit of the unattainable. They are concerned with the desperate illusions which are the acknowledgement of defeat. It is difficult, indeed, to think of any of his plays, prior to this statement, which actually expressed this heroic potential. In *Beyond the Horizon* (1920) the visions are wilfully abandoned, as fate intervenes to deflect the aspiring mind into simple irony. *The Emperor Jones* (1920) is an account of the collapse of illusion and character, the dissolution of a personal universe. *Anna Christie* (1921) pitches sentimentalities against a determinism partly a product of hostile environment and partly a consequence of wilful self-destruction. Its cosy conclusion specifically deflects the work from tragedy into pathos. *The First Man* (1922) contains no vision beyond a biological urge for procreation on the part of a woman and the self-pitying cowardice of a man who has substituted science for humanity. Yank, in *The Hairy Ape* (1922), is ironically transfigured but his vision is hopelessly naive and self-destructive in a way which has very little to do with the tragic.

O'Neill proposes no sense of historicity. Tragedy is to be dramatised in terms of the individual who represents the ever-present potential of the race. But the year before Susan Glaspell had proposed a non-tragic version of the same perception about human aspirations, locating it in a Darwinian or, perhaps, more strictly, a Lamarckian context of evolution and historical progress underlining her socialist convictions. One of her characters remarks:

> when you think we have hands because ages back - before life had taken form as man, there was an impulse to do what had never been done – those of best brain and courage who wanted to be more than life had been, and that from aspiration has come doing, and doing has shaped the thing with which to do – it gives our hand a history which should make us want to use it well.[10]

For O'Neill, such a notion of human advance falsified history. He saw Darwin less as identifying a progressive mechanism than as depriving the individual of a conscious role in his own making. For him Darwin represented that environmental and hereditary determinism which could only be resisted by the transcending imagination, a spiritual yearning to transgress the barriers of the possible. But it was not always a concern which he succeeded in trans-lating into tragic perception. He proposed a gap between aspiration and what

Susan Glaspell called 'doing', but it was a gap which was more likely to generate absurdity than tragedy. And yet, in 1925, in a letter to Arthur Hobson Quinn, he still announced that his objective as a writer was

> to see the transfiguring nobility of tragedy, in as near the Greek sense as one can grasp it, in seemingly the most ignoble, debased lives. And just here is where I am a most confirmed mystic, too, for I'm always acutely conscious of the Force behind – Fate, God, our biological past creating our present, whatever one calls it – Mystery certainly – and of the one eternal tragedy of Man in his glorious, self-destructive struggle to make the Force express him instead of being, as an animal is, an infinitesimal incident in its expression. And my profound conviction is that this is the only subject worth writing about and that it is possible – or can be – to develop a tragic expression in terms of transfigured modern values and symbols in the theatre which may to some degree bring home to members of a modern audience their ennobling identity with the tragic figures on the stage.

As he himself recognised, his own aspiration was of a piece with that which he insisted to be the distinguishing characteristic of man. 'Of course,' he confessed, 'this is very much of a dream, but where the theatre is concerned, one must have a dream, and a Greek dream in tragedy is the noblest ever!'[11]

He was, of course, confident that in *Desire Under the Elms* (1924), produced only the previous year, he had created such a tragedy. But it is hard to agree. The fated couple in that play are driven equally by sexual and financial lust and if Eban is conscious of a transfiguring beauty in the natural world, that vision is subordinated to a drive for possession which leaves him possessed. The true passion with which their lives seem finally ennobled is in fact simply a product of desire and guilt which provides a false link with the natural world. The play begins with sunset in a world of distorted emotions and frustrated dreams and ends with a sunrise and the momentarily united young couple. But there is little ennobling in the scene, except in so far as they exult in the results of their own manipulation and embrace their role as cosmic victims. There is no real sense in which they have won a victory over themselves. Their selflessness is simply a mirror image of their earlier selfishness. It is a total reversal unaccompanied by any sense of moral or spiritual value. One obsession is exchanged for another.

The real force of the plays lies elsewhere. It lies in a rather less grandiose but equally harrowing conception of character as a moral constant forced to an acknowledgement of fate. And this too O'Neill could have derived from Schopenhauer whose work he knew well. For in his essay on character Schopenhauer observes that:

> since *a man does not alter*, and his *moral character* remains absolutely the same all through his life...since he must play out the part which he has received, without the least deviation from the character; since neither experience, nor philo-

sophy, nor religion can effect any improvement in him, the question arises, what is the meaning of life at all? To what purpose is it played, this farce in which everything that is essential is irrevocably fixed and determined? It is played that a man may come to understand himself, that he may see what it is that he seeks and has sought to be; what he wants, and what, therefore, he is. *This is a knowledge which must be imported to him from without*...it is only by life that a man reveals what he is, and it is only in so far as he reveals himself that he exists at all.[12]

And though O'Neill resists the implacable nature of such a complete determinism, this is a clue to his sense of character and to the nature of the transcendence for which he searches.

His objective was essentially that identified by another major influence on his work, Nietzsche. Speaking as Zarathustra, Nietzsche had identified his art and his aim as 'to compose into one and bring together what is fragment and riddle and dreadful chance in man'. Indeed, it was 'as poet, reader of riddles, and redeemer of chance' that he identified the need 'to create the future, and to redeem by creating all that *was past*'.[13] And it was in Nietzsche that O'Neill eventually found the basis on which the conflicting powers of life and death could be resolved, expressing his new conviction in the unwieldy *Lazarus Laughed* (1928).

It is clear that O'Neill like Nietzsche saw tragedy as life-affirming: as, in a sense, closing the gap between man and his experience. The fact of suffering becomes a unifying principle and 'having looked boldly right into the terrible destructiveness of so-called world history as well as the cruelty of nature' the individual is offered metaphysical comfort – the conviction that 'life is at the bottom of things, despite all the changes of appearance, indestructibly powerful and pleasurable' – through art. In Nietzsche's words, 'Art saves him, and through art – life.'[14] As O'Neill wrote to his nurse from the tuberculosis clinic in 1923:

> I know you're impervious to what they are pleased to call my 'pessimism'. I mean that you can see behind that superficial aspect of my work to the truth. I'm far from being a pessimist. I see life as a gorgeously-ironical, beautifully-indifferent, splendidly suffering bit of chaos, the tragedy of which gives Man a tremendous significance, while without his losing fight with fate he would be a tepid, silly animal. I say 'losing fight' only symbolically, for the brave individual always wins. Fate can never conquer his – or her – spirit. So you see I'm not a pessimist. On the contrary, in spite of my scars, I'm tickled to death with life![15]

Despite the cavalier posturing, this does indeed convey a fundamental conviction, if one which he does not sustain in all his works. It is the unequal nature of the battle which gives significance to characters who have no social status and who are morally distinguishable from the bland bourgeois society which exists, frequently, in the background, or from those for whom simple endurance and unquestioning acceptance are primary virtues, by virtue of the weight placed on them by environment, hereditary burdens or the ironic indifference of the natural world. O'Neill shares Nietzsche's contempt for the cheerfulness of the slave who has nothing of consequence to be responsible for, and who does not value anything in the past or future higher than the present.

Like Tennessee Williams's protagonists, O'Neill's are dreamers forced to operate in a real world, poets who inhabit prose. Life is a series of adjustments and constraints, retreats from a purity of heart and imagination which make the individual simply vulnerable. The greatest enemy is time, eroding the grace of human features as it carries the individual further from the source of his innocence. In O'Neill's world the brow becomes lined abnormally fast, the body bends, the spirit breaks. Personal and public histories are thus ironic. This is no Hegelian world. The spring uncoils, the energy dissipates. The union of selves, and of self-hood and nature, is disrupted. Consolations become the source of further pain. And faced with this fact the self constructs a mask, a carapace, to protect a vulnerability and a surviving imaginative yearning whose vestigial existence becomes the source of a continuing irony. And yet its existence, together with a stoical acceptance and a compassionate spirit, somehow neutralises this irony, which is perhaps to say, as did Nietzsche, that life is a means to knowledge, that its justification lies in the fact of process. It is in this sense that suffering is a path to truth. Nietzsche put it thus:

> Could it be possible that, in spite of all 'modern ideas' and the prejudices of a democratic taste, the triumph of *optimism*, the gradual prevalence of *rationality*, practical and theoretical *utilitarianism*, no less than democracy itself which developed at the same time, might have been symptoms of a decline of strength, of impending old age, and of physiological weariness? These, and not pessimism? Was Epicurus an optimist – precisely because he was afflicted?[16]

The O'Neill hero is caught between two fates: the stasis, the surface satisfaction of bourgeois existence, and the pain and self-knowledge of spiritual daring. The one creates pathos, the other tragedy. For Nietzsche, 'the tragic myth...has to convince us that even the ugly and disharmonic are part of an artistic game that the will in the eternal amplitude of its pleasure plays with itself...The joy aroused by the tragic myth has the same origin as the joyous sensation of dissonance in music.'[17] It is this dissonance which seizes O'Neill's imagination. This is the 'joy' which he affects to identify. It is not only a dissonance between the individual and his setting. It is, in Nietzsche's words, 'dissonance become man'. It is a dissonance which 'to be able to live, would need a splendid illusion that would cover dissonance with a veil of beauty',[18] an Apollonian life-lie of a kind to be found at the heart of O'Neill's work.

His work, his plays, are not only metaphors in themselves. They constitute the history, or a metaphor for the history, of his life. From the brutal, despairing images of the early one-act plays – apocalyptic in tone, dominated by a concern with decay and debilitation, obsessed with the constricting nature of the personal and social world – through to the compassionate, bleak work of his later years, he sifted through the painful misunderstandings and private agonies of his life, looking for a key to that experience. And he offered that experience in turn as itself an apt key to human experience which he felt equally balanced between despair and stoical aesthetic energy.

For Heywood Brown, writing in the *New York Tribune*, O'Neill's first produced play, *Bound East for Cardiff* (1916) owed 'more to the creation of mood and atmosphere than to any fundamentally interesting idea or sudden twist of plot' while its appeal lay in the 'successful approximation of true talk'.[19] But to O'Neill, writing some time later, 'in it can be seen, or felt, the germ of the spirit, life-attitude etc., of all my more important future work'.[20] Both were clearly right. The difference between them lay primarily in the fact that for Brown plot was sacrificed to mood, while for O'Neill the lack of plot was a metaphysical as well as a theatrical fact.

At the heart of the play is Yank, badly injured in a fall. He lies dying as life goes on around him. The play fluctuates between silence and sound, as his shipmates retreat from the fact of his impending death through a neurotic chatter and a desperate reliance on routine. Language becomes a retreat. The presence of death transforms their conversations and their actions, creating an ironic undertow, an absurd commentary on life. But Yank himself faces death with a certain dignity, a grace under pressure which O'Neill and Hemingway alike chose to characterise as tragic. If there is no 'plot' it is because there is no conception of private or public history in the play, no sense of progression or direction, no development. Yank may regret the domestic life which he likes to feel that he sacrificed by going to sea, but there is no suggestion that his character could have been other than it is, no suggestion that his fate could have been deflected. The fog which obscures Yank's sight and which on a literal level pervades the naturalistic setting of the play, is symbolic not only of death but of the imperfect perception which these characters permit themselves.

The sea plays (*Bound East for Cardiff*, 1916; *The Long Voyage Home*, 1917; *Ile*, 1917; *The Moon of the Caribbees*, 1918; *In the Zone*, 1917) bring together an aggregation of national types, clearly designed to give them authority as images of the human experience. The 'SS *Glencairn*' series (the above plays, less *Ile*), conceived as separate works, nonetheless adds up to a symbol of life as a directionless journey which was to recur in his work. In a sense this is to say that these plays rest on a cliché and certainly they are imperfect works. But against a naturalistic setting he creates a series of plays without a single protagonist – an ensemble of lost souls whose only connection lies in a shared situation.

Their accents differ, their characters, crudely drawn, are sharply contrastive, but the effect is a harmonic threnody of lost opportunities, failed dreams, and relationships attenuated by time and experience. The plays' weakness lies in their sentimentality, in the melodramatic clichés which are a substitute for observation. The dying Yank, in *Bound East for Cardiff*, for example, sees a woman in black beckoning him – a piece of romanticism which is derived less from Yank's character than from the clutter of theatrical job lots picked up by O'Neill through association with his father's theatre. Likewise, the bar-tender and his crony in *Long Voyage Home* are casual stereotypes, off-the-peg comic villains. The real power of these plays lies in the force of the image of abandonment which they elaborate. Marginal figures, his characters struggle to make sense of their marginality, creating a provisional society, elaborating a system of values, generating a sentimental account of their own situation.

Smitty, like Larry in *The Iceman Cometh*, is cursed with a full awareness of himself and the depth of his failure. For the most part the others have blunted their sensibilities to all but the most sentimental pathos. But Smitty's life consists of 'thinking and – drinking to stop thinking'.[21] The melancholy Negro chant in *The Moon of the Caribbees* must be blotted out for the crew by the raucous note of popular music. Indeed, this musical dialectic is a reflection of a society which O'Neill sees as in transition. The natural world is already in process of being transformed. The SS *Glencairn* is a steamship, and its sailors are already products of a mechanical world. One of the crew begins to play 'You Great Big Beautiful Doll' with 'a note left out every now and then'. The seamen and their black companions (whose prostitution is at odds with the lyricism of the distant black music and further evidence of the collapse of moral value) perform a 'jerk-shouldered version of the old Turkey Trot as it was done in the sailor-town dives, made more grotesque by the fact that all the couples are drunk and keep lurching into each other every moment'.[22] Indeed the grotesque nature of the occasion is highlighted by the fact that two of the men start dancing with one another. The violence that follows is in a sense a logical consequence of the anarchy which lies just below the surface in this world of lost souls. The drink-maddened men fight indiscriminately. They fill the void of their lives with sound and fury. Smitty alone is fully aware of the vacuum which exists at the heart of this. He goes to his cabin as, in the silence that follows, he hears in the distance 'the haunted, saddened voice of that brooding music, faint and far-off like the mood of the moonlight made audible', a music which contains the unrealised potential of his life, the feeling transformed into sentimentality, the consonance destroyed by a force which is only partly external. The real death instinct is within. The mechanical world in which he lives is merely the concrete expression of that instinct.

O'Neill regarded this play as his favourite because it seemed to him to break new theatrical ground. It was indeed conceived as a kind of tone poem, a play of shifting moods in which silence becomes unbearable because it forces the individual back upon himself. Action is less a function of plot than of character – a desperate need to evade a silence which becomes a spiritual void. Sex, alcohol, music, reminiscences are the desperate armoury against truth. And Smitty, the principal focus of the play, stands to one side of this action, too shocked by a sudden glimpse of his situation to drink himself into oblivion.

Their voyage is an odyssey which they can only accept and transform through imagination. And since there is no authenticating principle, no source for moral authority, and no ultimate purpose or direction to their lives, meaning lies simply in process. It was a familiar Nietzschean idea. And it is perhaps not without significance that R. J. Hollingdale, editor of the Penguin edition of *Thus Spake Zarathustra*, in looking for an image to explain Nietzsche's convictions, should have turned to the sea journey:

> The concept of purpose becomes meaningless. But the opposite concept is invested with infinite meaning: not what I *do*...my purpose – but what I *am* – my state of being – is what counts for me. It is as if one were on an unending sea journey. The destination is immaterial, since it is never reached; but whether one is sea-sick for much of the time is material: it is really all that matters.[23]

O'Neill is the poet of stasis. The world which he describes is static in the sense in which a ball, thrown into the air, is static at its apogee. The past was promise; the future can only be entropic. In a sense all of America's major playwrights have been concerned with society caught in a moment of transition (the same, of course, is equally true of Ibsen and of Chekhov). But for O'Neill, in the sea plays, there has been a fundamental change in the rhythm of life. There is a painting ('The Fighting Téméraire') by the British artist Turner in which an iron steam tug is shown towing an old wooden sailing ship (one of the victors at Trafalgar) to the breaker's yard. This is the essence of the change which fascinates O'Neill, both here and in *The Hairy Ape*. But he sees no sense of dynamic energy in this image; only a sense of abandonment, of a gulf between the self and the natural world which is the basis for the sense of loss that dominates the lives of his characters. It is a space which they try to fill by evading the present in which they are trapped. And so they dwell on what might have been: Smitty travelling with the letters from the girl he might have married, and Yank recalling the domestic life ashore which would have given his life the meaning that it lacks. Or, alternatively, they make an ideology out of tomorrow. So, the sailor who has spent his life on board ship regards himself as a natural farmer; as, later in O'Neill's work, the social derelict sees himself as a putative mayor, the addict as a selfless mother, the miser a compassionate man. These dreams are the potential other selves which convince the individual that he is something other than pure surface. They are a response to the fear of being reduced to simple role. But in fact O'Neill's characters tend to be trapped in an unending present. Their Sisyphean task is to accept that and by accepting it to transform it. 'You tell me: "Life is hard to bear",' says Zarathustra. 'But if it were otherwise why should you have your pride in the morning and your resignation in the evening'.[24] For O'Neill, their dreams, the moments of lyricism which Yank and Smitty and Olson experience, are evidence of a resistant self. For, he was still insisting, the fact of absurdity does not necessitate capitulation. Had not Nietzsche, in a phrase which would have struck O'Neill as particularly telling, described as 'consumptives of the soul' those who 'are hardly born before they begin to die and to long for doctrines of weariness and renunciation... They encounter an invalid or an old man or a corpse; and straightaway they say "Life is refuted!" But only they are refuted, they and their eye that sees only one aspect of existence.'[25] It was not, however, a convincing assertion when applied to O'Neill's work and certainly not felt as such by those reviewing his first success, *Beyond the Horizon*.

Beyond the Horizon (1920) marked his Broadway début. It was his first play performed by a professional cast and presented by a major commercial producer and when it received the Pulitzer prize in 1921 he had clearly staked his claim as America's leading young playwright.

The play is the story of two brothers: one, Robert, a dreamer who wishes to go to sea, to encounter the world beyond the horizon, the other, Andrew, a practical farmer for whom the daily routine of farm life provides meaning enough. But both men love the same girl. And when, to everyone's surprise, she chooses the dreamer, he relinquishes his place on his uncle's boat and decides to stay on the farm, while his brother, bitter at having lost her, goes to sea. The marriage proves disastrous. Robert is no farmer and the decline of the marriage and of the farm are conterminous. Eventually he dies of tuberculosis, his body as emaciated as his spirit. With his dying breath he asks his brother, physically fit but morally damaged, to take his place. With his remaining strength he drags himself out onto the road and dies looking at the horizon that he had never managed to transcend.

Beyond the Horizon is, in effect, a portrait of O'Neill's own warring instincts. One brother is drawn to the practical world. He is unimaginative, creative only to the extent that he has the will to dominate his circumstances and imprint his identity on a world with which he is at harmony. The other is a delicately featured dreamer, prone to consumption, cowed by the environment which he allows to dominate him. The one constructs the world out of fact, the other out of pure imagination. But both betray themselves, wilfully going against their natural instincts – a fact unnecessarily underscored by O'Neill. For when Andrew destroys his harmonious relationship with the land by becoming a property speculator O'Neill has his brother spell out the moral: 'You used to be a creator when you loved the farm. You and life were in harmonious partnership. And now... You – a farmer – to gamble in a wheat pit with scraps of paper. There's a spiritual significance in that picture.'[26] Indeed! But the significance lies in an action which has no need of explication.

The other brother, Robert, has equally betrayed his creative gifts, marrying on impulse (reminiscent of O'Neill's own marriage) and abandoning his dreams, subordinating his talents to the simple determinants of daily existence. Like so many of O'Neill's characters he is obsessed with the constrictions which fate – expressed through character and environment – has placed around him. The hills surrounding the farm become 'like the walls of a narrow prison yard shutting' him 'in from all the freedom and wonder of life';[27] the house, a place where he had been 'cooped' up. His daughter dies from inherited consumption. Life is a process of disillusion, of disintegration, manifested in a loss of control over physical being (the ravages of time on the various characters are stressed by O'Neill in his stage directions and constitute evidence of dissolution) and the decay evidenced by the setting itself, which expresses a sense of exhaustion. And though this suffering is offered as a form of grace by the dying Robert, the final stage direction suggests a sense of stasis from which recovery is impossible. For Ruth is too debilitated, physically and spiritually, to be redeemed by a suffering which has simply brutalised and not ennobled. She remains silent 'with the sad humility of exhaustion, her mind already sinking back into that spent calm beyond the further troubling of any hope'.[28]

O'Neill was, as he said in a letter to the critic Arthur Hobson Quinn, 'always acutely aware of the reality and power of determinism' but he wished to view this in the context of a tragic vision which could transform that determinism. As he said shortly after the premiere of *Beyond the Horizon*, which had been hailed as an American tragedy (and even by one critic as the first modern native tragedy), 'It is the meaning of life – and the hope. The noblest is eternally the most tragic. The people who succeed and do not push on to greater failure are the spiritual middle classes. Their stopping at success is proof of their compromising insignificance. How petty their dreams must have been.'[29] But it is hard to see how this statement can be said to apply to *Beyond the Horizon*. The failure of the characters derives not from the greatness of their dreams, or even the courage with which they tackle a task imposed by fate. It is a consequence of their capitulation to biological impulse, of their capacity for self-destruction, of their wilful abandonment of dreams for immediate satisfactions of one kind or another. The potential spiritual unity which both brothers, in their different ways, glimpse is abruptly and arbitrarily aborted by a fate in which the heavy hand of the playwright becomes a simple extension of a romantic sense of inevitable doom. The setting is, in effect, Hardy's dark star. The game is so thoroughly rigged and so precipitately enacted that the concept of moral authority, of a resistant self, of a courageous challenging of the determined, makes no sense. The self is too thoroughly infected, literally and symbolically, for it to sustain a tragic mode. The one brother fails in large part because his strength is taken away by disease, the other because, removed from our attention, character is arbitrarily changed to permit him to betray a nature laboriously established earlier in the play. Suffering implies a grace but it is a grace which remains unexamined and which is unconvincing.

For Nietzsche, the problem of the meaning of suffering resolved itself into a Christian or Dionysian one. As he explained in *The Will to Power* 'In the former case it is to be the way toward holy being, in the latter, being itself is holy enough to justify an enormity of suffering... The god on the cross is a curse on life, pointing to a redemption from life. Dionysus, torn to pieces, is a promise of life – it will be eternally reborn and return again from destruction.'[30] In *Beyond the Horizon* the ideas are confused. Robert simultaneously invokes a Christian version of redemption through pain, and a Dionysian encomium on life. He looks forward to the next world, while recalling the purity of his original vision. But he capitulates, finally, to a Christian and hence non-tragic perception and by doing so ensnares his brother in the same anti-life vortex from which death alone has rescued him. He bequeaths his wife to a brother who is now tied to his fate by a moral imperative which leaves no room for an expansive soul. Prosaic himself, he must now mortgage his future to a woman drained of all energy, vision and hope. The play ends not on a tragic but an ironic note: hence the division among the reviewers who called it, on the one hand, tragic, and on the other, gloomy. The world of *Beyond the Horizon* is essentially that of Nietzsche's madman alter ego in *The Gay Science* who identified a world in which a sponge had wiped 'away the whole horizon', a world through which the individual strayed, 'an infinite nothing' feeling 'the breath of empty space'.[31]

If *Beyond the Horizon* established O'Neill's popular reputation, there is little doubt that his finest and most original play in these early years was *The Emperor Jones* (1920). It opened to almost universally approving notices and,

6. Charles Gilpin in the Provincetown Players' production of *The Emperor Jones* which opened in December 1920. In later productions he was replaced by Paul Robeson.

despite occasional baffled allusion to tragedy, O'Neill having successfully planted the idea of his tragic intent in reviewers' minds, it was in fact a brilliantly original account of a disintegrating private and public world.

His dramatic strategy in the play lay in the deconstruction of character, in the dismantling of social forms and the unhinging of language. Assurance about the substantiality of the self, the sequentiality of history and the subordinate nature of event and environment crumbles under pressure. The collapse is not simply atavism of a kind which might make the play racially suspect. His concern is with dramatising an unconscious whose irrationalisms are ultimately the generators of meaning and the expressions of an anarchy within, which the conscious mind is designed to suppress. Here, the desire for order and the awareness of the world's refusal to render any coherence beyond the ultimate stasis of death are dramatised within the individual. The irony is self-contained.

Brutus Jones, an American Negro who has escaped from America where he had committed two murders, finds himself on an island in the West Indies 'as yet not self-determined by White Mariners'. (The capitalisation implies a level of social criticism which the play never really takes up.) By dint of judiciously pandering to local superstitions, he quickly establishes himself as Emperor and begins salting away money. He protects himself from assassination by asserting that he can only be killed by a silver bullet. When the play begins, however, a rebellion is already under way and Jones begins a prepared retreat through the tropical forest, with the sound of drums in his ears. Once in the forest his social assurance collapses. He abandons his clothes, fires his revolver at his own formless fears and memories as they materialise in the darkness, and is ultimately killed by a silver bullet specially prepared by the natives, whose spells may or may not have liberated the anarchic spirits which in fact destroy him. The final remark of the play, delivered by Henry Smithers, a cockney trader who has profited from Jones's seizure of power, is singularly inappropriate. His observation that the natives are 'stupid as 'ogs, the lot of 'em! Blasted niggers!'[32] is a sign of his failure to understand what he has seen.

On one level the play is clearly a comment on imperialism, as it is an assault on the more obvious presumptions of racism. Its observations on the mercenary motives and coercive methods of government, its identification of that government's method of enforcing its power through the manipulation of opinion and through capitalising on prejudice, its suggestion that government is in effect a criminal enterprise, are clear enough. But the play is not primarily a satire. Its basic concern is with exposing the unconscious, dramatising the imagination, tapping the anarchic truths, the discontinuities of the mind. Below the level of narrative is a contra-flow of images destabilising the surface. Past and present mix. Sequence defers to simultaneity as the nodal points of personal and race history coalesce. Character fragments into pulses of experience, alternating fears and certainties. It is a play of considerable originality – a genuine achievement which showed the real resources of a playwright whose territory was the mind and its conflicts rather than the social world. The *mise-en-scène* itself becomes a character – the forest trees closing around Jones, expressions of the terror that suffocates and immobilises him.

And yet there is a version of history unfolded here. For the memories that well up into Jones's consciousness are not only of events which he had experienced. They are race memories derived from a history of oppression. He sees a vision of a slave auction in the 1850s, a fiction into which he is drawn, becoming himself the object of the sale. He re-enacts the experience of the voyage to America on board a slave ship, joining his voice with that of the other slaves in a wail of agony as they experience the roll of the ship (some fifty years later Amiri Baraka also tried to forge a theatrical ritual out of the same material). Ultimately Jones finds himself the victim of a pagan ritual sacrifice – a Jungian dramatisation of race consciousness and of an archetypal experience.

Indeed, the play seems to bring together and develop in parallel a personal unconscious and a collective unconscious. As Jung was later to explain in an essay entitled, 'The concept of the collective unconscious':

> the collective unconscious is part of the psyche which can be negatively dis-tinguished from a personal unconscious by the fact that it does not owe its existence to personal experience and consequently is not a personal acquisition. While the personal unconscious is made up essentially of contents which have at one time been conscious but which have disappeared from consciousness through having been forgotten or repressed, the contents of the collective unconscious have never been in consciousness, and therefore have never been individually acquired, but owe their existence exclusively to heredity. Whereas the personal unconscious consists for the most part of *complexes*, the content of the collective unconscious is made up essentially of archetypes.[33]

The archetype, as Jung indicates, is what Adolf Bastian, perhaps more tellingly in this context, had called 'primordial thoughts'.

In the final vision/experience which Jones undergoes in O'Neill's play a witch-doctor enacts a ritual, a play within a play, which comments on the experience which Jones is himself going through:

> The WITCH-DOCTOR sways, stamping with his foot, his bone rattle clicking the time. His voice rises and falls in a weird, monotonous croon, without artic-ulate word divisions. Gradually his dance becomes clearly one of a narrative in pantomime demanding sacrifice. He flees, he is pursued by devils, he flees again. Ever weaker and wilder becomes his flight, nearer and nearer draws the pursu-ing evil, more and more the spirit of terror gains possession of him.[34]

The collapse of language creates rather than destroys meaning. All the images from the past are presented in mime. The process of pressing back into the past towards pre-history is a process of dispensing with language. It is also presented as a move towards truth – simultaneously a Freudian and a theatrical assertion of the primacy of non-verbal communication. At the level of language lies are possible; at the level of instinctual behaviour, of gesture, and of unconscious impulse there is an available truth. By the same token the accretions of 'civilisation' have served merely to obscure this truth. Language has become the agent of exploitation, identity a disguise to facilitate theft. The conscious world is a world of deceit, of deliberate obfuscation.

O'Neill sets himself the task of penetrating an equal mystery – the unconscious roots of action – precisely the world which Macgowan and Jones were urging as the real subject of the modern dramatist in their books on theatre. As Freud said, in an essay called 'The unconscious and consciousness' (1901–2), 'The unconscious is the true psychological reality; *in its innermost nature it is as much unknown to us as the reality of the external world, and it is as incompletely presented by the data of consciousness as is the external world by the communications of our sense organs.*'[35] But for Emperor Jones there is no distinction. The membrane dividing real from unreal, conscious from unconscious dissolves. The superstitions of the natives seem successfully to have invaded his mind. Hence their sense of triumph at the end of the play, as they believe themselves to have defeated him. But Freud himself had described superstition as '*nothing but psychology projected into the external world*'.[36] Indeed, he sought a parallel in paranoia for the process whereby psychical factors are mirrored in 'the construction of a supernatural reality'.[37] And, of course, *The Emperor Jones* is a study of a paranoid individual as it is an observation about the psychopathology of a group. Jones's reactions are readily explicable in Freudian terms. His superstition is not only a race memory, a trace element of history. It is explicable in clinical terms. For Freud, superstition 'is in large part the expiation of trouble; and a person who has harboured frequent evil wishes against others, but has been brought up to be good and has therefore suppressed such wishes into the unconscious, will be especially ready to expect punishment for his unconscious wickedness in the form of trouble threatening him from without'.[38]

The Emperor Jones (1920) was a startlingly innovative play. O'Neill later objected to those who saw it primarily as a Freudian work, and certainly its force lies elsewhere than simply in its account of repressed guilts. Like Strindberg in his last plays, O'Neill discovered with *The Emperor Jones* the plasticity of the stage, deconstructing its new-found solidities alongside his dislocation of character, language and plot. He discovered, what Robert Edmond Jones was to assert in his book on *The Dramatic Imagination*, that the setting was potentially 'a presence, a mood, a warm wind fanning the drama to flame. It echoes, it enhances, it animates. It is an expectancy, a foreboding, a tension.'[39] Likewise his use of sound. In the sea plays he had experimented with contrapuntal rhythms which were expressive on the one hand of the natural world of the natives and on the other of the degraded and disjointed world of the sailors. Now he uses sound, throughout the play, in the form of a drumbeat which is offered as a resonant correlative of Jones's pulse, a blood rhythm not to be denied by time or by evasive role-playing. The continual throb of the tom-tom – a projection of Jones's heartbeat which ceases abruptly with his life – emphasises another of the play's themes, the slow process of deconstruction which is the process of life itself. For Jones's physical and mental collapse provides a foreshortened, temporally collapsed, version of the entropic process of mortality.

Three years later O'Neill returned to the question of race and the regressive pressures of the social world. *All God's Chillun Got Wings* (1924) describes the relationship between a black man and a white woman. As children they had been largely free of prejudice, using the language of racism but drained of real meaning. Like most of O'Neill's early work, the setting is claustrophobic, with tenements closing around the figures who in some senses become mere extrusions of their environment – in this case an environment rigidly divided along racial lines. The mechanical rhythms of the street are an image of the mechanical lives of those who exist in the constricting boundaries of the city. To cross boundaries of any kind is to invite suspicion. When Jim Harris wishes to become a lawyer this is seen as an act of defection by his fellow blacks. 'What's all dis dressin' up and graduatin' an' sayin' you gwine study to be a lawyer? What's all dis fakin' an' pretendin an' swellin' out grand an' talkin' soft and perlite? What all dis denyin' you's a nigger... Tell me befo' I wrecks yo' face in! Is you a nigger or isn't you? Is you a nigger, nigger?'[40] So powerful are the myths of colour that Jim is unable to deal with the effortless superiority of whites, internalising their values and unconsciously accepting their assertions of his inadequacy. Even the desire to succeed as a lawyer is a sign that he has accepted the values of the society he struggles to join. The passing of the examinations will enable him to 'pass' as white, not because he has a white skin but because his language, his appearance and his values will be those of white society. The effort is simultaneously legitimate aspiration and a fundamental betrayal of himself – a perception which in some ways makes O'Neill close kin to those black dramatists of the 1960s who made a similar point. Jim believes that he must pass the examinations before he can claim Ella, the white girl, as his wife – indeed he is doubtful whether he can ever aspire to that status, being content to live in her shadow. But she is equally trapped in her own myths. Though used and abused by a callous white man she is ambivalent about Jim. She both loves and despises him and the pressures drive her to psychosis as equally they lead Jim to physical and mental breakdown. As in *The Emperor Jones*, O'Neill is concerned with the disintegration of personality, the subordination of the individual to history and to myth. And once again the *mise-en-scène* becomes an actor in the drama – not merely with respect to the racially divided streets but more especially with regard to the primitive

Negro mask which hangs on the wall of Jim's apartment and which becomes the embodiment of the social prejudices which Ella has absorbed.

The fact of race taunts her as it does Jim. They try to escape the dilemma by running to Europe but are pursued by it. And, as in *The Emperor Jones*, the physical world seems to shrink, compressing them to the point at which character is reduced to type and the space for social action is destroyed. The stage directions indicate that 'The walls of the room appear shrunken in, the ceiling lowered, so that the furniture, the portrait, the mask, look unnaturally large and domineering.'[41] Jim wants to break out of his constraints, not to see his life in terms of history and myth. 'You with your fool talk of the black race and the white race!' he objects to his sister, 'Where does the human race get a chance to come in? I suppose that's simple for you. You lock it up in asylums and throw away the key.'[42] But this, of course, is exactly what does happen as both the principal characters are driven to the point of breakdown. And so they re-enact the only period in which the schizophrenia of race had been inoperative – childhood. The adult world must be rejected. Sexuality must be denied. Career must be abandoned in favour of a pre-lapsarian world. Ella, who has been almost literally consumed by hatred, by self-contempt and by remorse, is reduced to a frail figure, her womanhood withered and denied. She is saved, paradoxically, only by Jim's failure to establish his adult status by graduating as a lawyer. His failure is ambiguous. In one sense it re-establishes the ordered world in which racial roles are paradigms of metaphysical purpose; it reasserts the constancy which she desperately wishes to cling to. But on the other hand it isolates them in a childlike innocence. As O'Neill indicates in a stage direction, she can at last freely kiss him but 'she kisses his hand as a child might, tenderly and gratefully'.[43] And Jim joins her in this new innocence by falling on his knees and embracing the religion which is equally a product of an innocent world.

It is an apparently sentimental ending with a fierce undertow of irony. It is also, once again, an ending consonant with Freudian theory, for Freud observed, in his essay 'The horror of incest', that 'a neurotic…exhibits some degree of psychical infantilism'.[44] Indeed Jim and Ella are actually described as having lived 'like friends – like a brother and sister'.[45] O'Neill clearly sees the pressures of race as having created this neurosis. For as Freud says of the neurotic, 'He has either failed to get free from the psychosexual conditions that prevailed in his childhood or he has returned to them – two possibilities which may be summed up as developmental inhibition and regression.'[46] Intimidated by myths of racism Jim never considers himself an apt sexual partner for Ella. He offers himself as a friend, indeed as a worshipper. He is, in other words, from the beginning an example of 'developmental inhibition', socially created.

59

But O'Neill was conscious that race was not the only prejudice with the power to warp the sensibility. As he insisted, 'the Negro question, which, it must be remembered, is not an issue in the play, isn't the only one which can arouse prejudice. We are divided by prejudices. Prejudices racial, social, religious. Tracing it, it all goes back, of course, to economic causes.'[47] The 'of course' is expressed in the play only through the oppressive nature of the tenement buildings but it is indicative of O'Neill's cast of thought, his early plays generating poetic images of a human unity disrupted by the forces of capitalism. The play's title is ironic. It is only in heaven that freedom can be a reality – hence Jim's reversion to a simplistic faith at the end of the play. In the words of the spiritual from which the title is derived:

> When I get to Heav'n
> Gonna put on my wings
> Gonna fly all over God's Heav'n.

In this world such freedom is not so readily available. Metaphysical absurdities are compounded by social absurdities. It is a mark of O'Neill's social iconoclasm that he should tackle the question of race, forging from it a powerful metaphor of alienation in a play which takes a naturalistic setting and exerts an expressionistic pressure on it of a kind which parallels the social pressure exerted on his protagonists. The walls of the tenement close in on the fatal couple as do the walls of prejudice and myth. The light changes from the brilliant glow of the setting sun on a hot spring day to that of an arc lamp which 'discovers faces with a favourless cruelty'. The growth from childhood to maturity becomes a moral regression. The bright faces and laughter of the children disappears. 'There is no laughter from the two streets',[48] O'Neill tells us. The faces have begun to distort. The collapse of style is a correlative of the collapse of individual and human purpose.

For Kenneth Macgowan and Robert Edmond Jones, O'Neill was *the* American expressionist, and the play which best exemplified his expressionist impulse was *The Hairy Ape*. Indeed, in a review in *Theatre Arts*, Macgowan hailed it as the first American expressionist play, ignoring the expressionist achievement of *The Emperor Jones*. Not surprisingly, but also not at all accurately, the reviewer of *Industrial Solidarity* saw it as one of the most helpful and legitimate defenses of the IWW (International Workers of the World) position. Even Mike Gold attacked Heywood Broun for failing to recognise the social reality in the play. But in truth the alienation that lies at the heart of the play is more fundamental than most reviewers were prepared to grant, while the clash between rich and poor which seemed to lie at the heart of a profoundly social drama was in fact simply further evidence of a sense of incompletion, of displacement which lies at the heart of most of his work.

7. *The Hairy Ape*, production at the Provincetown Playhouse, New York, 1922. Design by Cleon Throckmorton and Robert Edmond Jones. Scene 5, with Louis Wollheim and Harold West.

The Hairy Ape (1922) is a play about alienation. The ship, which stands as a central image of society, sails aimlessly, its only function to give pleasure to the wealthy who in fact find very little pleasure in it. It is on one level clearly a bitter social indictment – a satire on the vacuous world of the rich, and the soulless existence of the poor. But the prime value is not the need to revolt but to 'belong'. Indeed this is the only value which Yank, leader of the stokers in the boiler room, can identify. There is no ideology, no real communal sense which can claim their allegiance. Sexuality has been displaced. Masculinity now goes into the service of the machine which becomes a substitute for a life-giving feminine principle. And so Yank urges on his fellow stokers, as they feed the furnaces, in a language which is deliberately sexually suggestive: 'Dat's de stuff! Let her have it! All togedder now! Sling it into her! Let her ride! Shoot de piece now! Call de toin on her. Drive her into it! Feel her move!' But no sooner does he cry out 'Dere she go-o-es' than the voracious appetite of the machine demands their attention again. 'We had a rest. Come on, she needs it! Give her pep!'[49]

The image of misplaced sexuality becomes a dominant image of the 1920s in the work of Pound, Eliot, Lewis, Fitzgerald and Hemingway. And for O'Neill it operates as a symbol of the reductive power of a modern

61

world in which the individual is always alienated from himself, from his fellow man and from his environment. Like Elmer Rice, he dramatises man as a machine. The stokers' voices have 'a brazen, metallic quality as if their throats were phonograph horns'.[50] But the rich are equally mechanical. When Yank confronts them they appear nothing more than 'a procession of gaudy marionettes, yet with something of the relentless horror of Franken-steins in their detached, mechanical unawareness'.[51] The real force which opposes this is not so much the 'Wobblies' (International Workers of the World), who are seen as setting their faces against injustice, as the lyric reminders of a past world in which man was in tune with the natural world – a world celebrated by the old Irishman, Paddy, who recalls the 'fine beautiful ships' and the 'fine strong men in them...for we was free men... 'Twas them days men belonged to ships, not now. 'Twas them days a ship was part of the sea, and a man was part of a ship, and the sea joined all together and made it one.'[52] The unity has been destroyed by a selfishness which Yank and the débutante alike epitomise.

Mildred Douglas and her aunt are described as being conspicuously out of time with the natural world which is the setting but not home for figures who are described as being 'two incongruous, artificial figures, inert and disharmonious' in contrast to the 'beautiful, vivid life of the sea all about'.[53] If Yank's vitality is misdirected, sapped by the mechanical demands of the modern, Mildred betrays the fact that the vitality of her stock had been sapped before she was conceived, so that she is the expression not of its life energy but merely of the 'artificialities that energy has won for itself in the spending'.[54] The weakness of the play lies in the fact that O'Neill feels it necessary to make Mildred state explicitly what is apparent in the play's action, and in the images which he deploys. The reiterated references to Yank's ape-like appearance, the insistence on the aridity and inhumanity of the rich press the allegorical dimension too hard.

Yet the play transcends the social terms that it erects. Confronted by the Wobblies who find him as impossible to incorporate in their schema as does Mildred in hers, Yank characterises their stance as a conviction that if they can 'cut an hour offen de job a day' they would 'make me happy! Gimme a dollar more a day and make me happy! Tree square a day, and cauliflowers in de front yard – an ekal rights – a woman and kids – a lousey vote – and I'm all fixed for Jesus, huh?' Yank's alienation goes much deeper. 'It's way down – at de bottom. Yuh can't grab it, and yuh can't stop it. It moves, an everyting moves. It stops and de whole woild stops.'[55] Yank is in effect an absurdist figure, suddenly dimly aware of the unbridgeable gulf between his simply conceived aspirations for harmony and order and the refusal of the world to manifest it. He is stranded in a world to which he cannot relate. He finds himself in a present which lacks any causal relation to the past.

As he senses, 'I ain't got no past to tink in, nor nothin' dat's comin', on'y what's now – and dat don't belong.' For O'Neill, as later for Beckett, the only moment of consonance is the moment of death. As he slips to the floor, the author's stage direction indicates that now, 'perhaps, the Hairy Ape at least belongs'.[56]

The current always sweeps O'Neill's characters backwards, back to a pre-social, pre-literate, pre-conscious past, in which primal emotions dominate, the complex arabesques of self defer to simple type, and language is dismantled into phatic gestures. Brute existence exerts a gravitational pull and his characters have little or no purchase on an alternative world.

For O'Neill, the space available for character to form, for language to coalesce, and for social visions to expand, is minimal. The dominant image is one of constriction. In *The Emperor Jones* the forest closes around the protagonist, driving him back to meet the terrors of his own mind. In *The Hairy Ape* character is reduced to type and compacted into a political, moral and physical space which allows no scope for manoeuvre. 'The ceiling crushes down upon the men's heads. They can't stand upright.'[57] In *Desire Under the Elms* the action takes place under two huge elms which embrace the house and stand as a symbol of the natural world subduing and crushing the spirit of those within. When they go to their bedrooms the steeply sloping roof makes them bend their bodies in a grotesque image of the extent to which they are forced to bend their actions to a sexuality they cannot control.

At the heart of O'Neill's work is a moral anarchy. In *Desire Under the Elms* this is expressed through the quasi-incestuous relationship between a son and his stepmother. Eben's father, an old and bitter man, remarries, thus potentially disinheriting his son. But the new wife is young and is powerfully attracted to Eben – an attraction which does battle with the acquisitiveness which had driven her to marry a man so much older than herself, and which becomes the basis for a series of overlapping ironies. For not only is Abbie Eben's stepmother but she insists that their first sexual experience together should take place in his own mother's parlour, untouched since her death.

For Freud, incest was an image of anarchy and for O'Neill likewise it represents the pressure towards disorder that typifies so much of his work. His sexual pairings have all the fated character of Hardy's but the disproportion that he chooses to stress has metaphysical overtones. Old man is mated with young woman, stoker attracted to débutante, black to white, son to quasi-mother. And the consequence is either sterility or a life which must be destroyed, a synthesis which must be denied. The only freedom is to embrace one's fate – a Sisyphean triumph whose irony represents the only victory. Crushed by circumstance or a willed collision with a destructive facticity, they celebrate their imprisonment which is itself the only generator of meaning which they can find.

O'Neill's characters seem to live at emotional extremes, switching from one mood to its opposite with a mechanical suddenness. Hate changes to love, reproach to apology, self-contempt to pride. Emotional intensity becomes a substitute for personal and social meaning, an expression of the disjunction between self and environment. To some degree, of course, it is also a reflection of O'Neill's melodramatic imagination which tends to need the kinetic energy which derives from emotional disproportion. But beyond this it becomes a strategy of emotional dialectics. The chief fear is of an habituated norm, a plateau of intellectual and imaginative blandness, a stasis which is the equivalent of death. And so his characters lacerate themselves and others, pressing experience to its extremes, living intensely as a substitute for living meaningfully. And yet the alternating moods are equally an expression of baffled incomprehension, an uncertainty about the value of truth and illusion, of compassion and strength, of acceptance and rebellion. Though each emotional moment is intense it contains and implies its opposite. The Yank who expresses his hatred for the young débutante cannot help but imply his attraction for her. Much the same could be said of Eben's response to Abbie, of Ella's reaction to Jim, or Jones's assertion of his courage in the face of his actual cowardice. The absolute implies the relative. It is not merely that O'Neill's is a Manichaean imagination but that, as in Beckett's world, contradiction is the essence of the absurdity which he identifies.

In *Desire Under the Elms* (1924) he presents a melodrama of multiple ironies. The sons are ironically dispossessed by the young wife whom their father introduces into the house. But he is defeated by the love that springs up between that woman and one of his own sons. Then, when a child is born of that alliance, a child who will inherit the farm, it in turn threatens the son with dispossession and is killed as the result of an ironic misunderstanding. The young couple, having found in one another some purpose in life, are now to be separated for life. Irony thus develops to the point of mannerism. It becomes the mechanism of the social and metaphysical world. It becomes, indeed, the primary expression of an absurd world. Thus, when Cabot, the father, is persuaded to go West, he does indeed find the land of plenty. 'We come t' broad medders, plains, whar the soil was black an' rich as gold. Nary a stone. Easy. Ye'd on'y to plough an' sow an' then set an' smoke yer pipe an' watch them grow'[58] but 'somethin' in me fit me an' fit me – the voice o' God.'[59] And so he rejects the easy life. The irony is generated from within, as it is for his son. And part of the weakness of the play lies not only in the lurid incidents and reified characters but in a fatalism which is pressed to the point of collapse.

His sense of religion as a contricting irrationalism is powerfully expressed.

8. *Desire Under the Elms* at Greenwich Village Theatre, 11 November 1924, with Mary Morris and Walter Huston. Setting by Robert Edmond Jones.

But the sense of emotion as an almost supernatural force (Eben and Abbie seem able to detect one another's feelings through a solid wall), his truncation of emotional subtlety, his insistence on simplistic modes of plot development, all betoken a man still feeling his way toward a form and a language which can adequately expose the savage constraints of myth, superstition and custom on the one hand, and ethical anarchy, an antinomian universe, on the other. Either way disaster seems to wait.

It is true, as Edgar F. Racey Jr, for example, argues, that the play can be seen as a version of the Hippolytus–Phaedra–Theseus plot but it is misleading to see it primarily in these terms. It is certainly unhelpful to suggest that 'as a classical tragedy – *Desire* is both successful and complete'.[60] Though a considerable advance over the early sketches, it remains crude in its characterisation and contrived in its plotting.

In a letter to George Jean Nathan in 1921, O'Neill offered a defence of the melodramatic element in his work, what Nathan himself had attacked as his tendency to 'intensify and even hyperbolize a theme as to evoke the dramatic effect from its overtones rather than...from its undertones'. Speaking of *Anna Christie* he said that

> with dumb people of her sort, unable to voice strong, strange feelings, the emotions can find outlet only through the language and gestures of the heroics in the novels and movies they are familiar with – that is, that in moments of great stress life copies melodrama...In real life I felt she would unconsciously be compelled, through sheer inarticulateness, to the usual 'big scene', and wait hopefully for her happy ending...the happy ending is merely the comma at the end of a gaudy introductory clause, with the body of the sentence still unwritten.[61]

In fact, he had once considered calling the play *Comma*.

The problem, then, was to articulate the suppressed aspirations of those who could not voice those aspirations simply through language. And here perhaps is a clue to O'Neill's concern with socially marginal characters. For this is less a product of the naturalist's concern with pure environmental mechanism than of his conviction that 'it's where the poetic is buried beneath the dull and crude that one's deep-seeing vision is tested'.[62] Thus in *Desire Under the Elms* he is not only concerned with the pressure of a crudely determining world but also with making the inexpressiveness of New England's inhibited life expressive.

There was, as I suggest above, a crudity about O'Neill's imagination which sometimes comes through as brute power and sometimes as simplistic analysis. Emotions are perceived in primary colours. Psychology resolves itself too often into a Manichaean battle between conscious and sub-conscious, mind and body. His morbidness, like Poe's, was an attempt to break through to a different level of experience, to place the sensibility under stress in the faith that some kind of authenticity was to be found at the extremes of experience. Abortion, insanity, disease and death placed the self under a pressure which rooted identity in something more substantial than social role. In part he is like Marsden, the novelist in *Strange Interlude*. He turns aside from creating 'fairy tales for grown-ups' to shout 'this is life and this is sex, and here are passion and hatred and regret and joy and pain and ecstacy, and these are men and women and sons and daughters whose hearts are weak and strong'.[63] In part his was a gothic imagination which sought to dramatise the underside of the mind, to tackle the permanent and fundamental issues of life and death rather than the ephemeral problems of manners and the simple drama of social relationship.

O'Neill was a self-conscious experimenter. He was eclectic to a fault. He read widely and was struck by the achievements of the European theatre. In 1907 he made ten visits to see Alla Nazimova's group perform *Hedda Gabler*. He was entranced by the visit of the Irish Players and in 1913 discovered Strindberg. 'It was,' he confessed, 'reading his plays when I first started to write back in the winter of 1913-14 that, above all else, first gave me the vision of what modern drama could be, and inspired me with the urge to write for the theatre myself. If there is anything of lasting worth in my work,' he asserted, 'it is due to that original impulse from him.'[64]

With *The Great God Brown* (1926) he experimented with masks and with *Strange Interlude* (1928) he tried to breathe life back into the dramatic aside, refurbishing it to do duty as an expression of a highly conscious subconscious. Meanwhile both *The Great God Brown* and *Lazarus Laughed* revealed his debt to Nietzsche and Schopenhauer.

O'Neill's experiments with masks, ancient in origin but modern in concept, were both an expression of his dissatisfaction with the theatre which he inherited and an assertion about the direction in which he believed the theatre should go. 'For I hold,' he insisted,

> more and more surely to the conviction that the use of masks will be discovered eventually to be the freest solution of the modern dramatist's problem as to how, with the greatest possible dramatic clarity and economy of means, he can express those profound hidden conflicts of the conscious and unconscious mind which the probing of psychology continue to disclose to us. He must find some method to present this inner drama in his work, or confess himself incapable of portraying one of the most characteristic preoccupations and uniquely significant, spiritual impulses of his time. With his old – and more than a bit senile! – standby of realistic technique, he can do no more, at best, than obscurely hint at it through a realistically disguised surface symbolism, superficial and misleading. But that, while sufficiently beguiling to the sentimentally mystical, is hardly enough. A comprehensive expression is demanded here, a chance for eloquent presentation, a new form of drama projected from a fresh insight into the inner forces motivating the outer actions and reactions of men and women, a new truer characterization, in other words – a drama of souls, and the adventures of 'free wills' with the masks that govern them and constitute their fate.[65]

In many ways his statement constitutes the manifesto of the new American theatre – a theatre which wished to dispense with an art of surface appropriately symbolised by the painted backdrop, the falsification of character implicit in grandiloquent acting, and the moral equivocation dramatised through the banalities of stage convention. 'For what, at bottom, is the new psychological insight into human cause and effect,' asked O'Neill, 'but a study in masks, an exercise in unmasking?' The dogma for the new masked drama, he announced, was that 'One's outer life passes in a solitude haunted by the masks of others; one's inner life passes in a solitude hounded by the masks of oneself.' His weakness lay in his failure to press these propositions further.

In the same essay, 'On Masks', he dismissed as 'of no importance here' the question of whether 'the attempted unmasking...has only created for itself further masks'. But that, of course, is a crucial question. For once you have struck through the pasteboard mask are you in touch with reality? Have you reached rock or exposed sheer flux? It was a worry which nagged at his mind but which only rarely surfaced in his work as disturbing symbols: incest, the sea. He did, it is true, regret the fact that in *The Great God Brown* he had allowed the masks to stress 'the more superficial meaning that people wear masks before other people and are mistaken by them for their masks', and wished that he had made the masks 'symbolize more definitely the abstract theme of the play'. But there, of course, was the problem – to convey the abstract 'definitely'. Indeed, in *Strange Interlude*, which he described as 'an attempt at the new masked psychological drama without masks' (a crucial indication that the mask's most powerful meaning for O'Neill was meta-phoric), he felt that he had succeeded only 'in so far as it concerns...surfaces and their immediate sub-surfaces, but not where, occasionally, it tries to probe deeper'.

For O'Neill it was always depth that attracted him – depth meaning sophistication of perception but also depth meaning the abyss, the loss of that surface tension which offers a reassuring form and structure to experience but which can only do so by concealing the hollow beneath. He wished to appeal to what he felt to be the spiritual need of a new audience who wished to 'participate imaginatively in imaginative interpretations of life rather than merely identify itself, mentally and emotionally, with faithful surface resemblances of living'. In other words, from the same essay, he wished to create 'a legitimate spiritual descendant of the first theatre that sprang, by virtue of man's imaginative interpretation of life, out of his worship of Dionysus...theatre...as a Temple where their religion of a [practical] interpretation and symbolic spiritual celebration of life is communicated to human beings, starved in spirit by the soul-stifling repetition of their daily struggles to exist as masks among the masks of the living'. The messianic tone is unavoidable, as are the images of constriction and release that run throughout his work. The theatre was to be spiritually and emotionally liberating and its weapons were in some ways those of poetry, the striking image, a condensed language. And it was this which he saw as distinguishing it from modern novels which were 'padded with the unimportant and insignificant...obsessed with the trivial meaning of trivialities'. Novelists appeared to him to be 'mere timid recorders of life, dodging the responsibility of that ruthless selection and deletion and concentration on the essential which is the test of the artist – the forcing of significant form upon experience'.

· For O'Neill the theatre offered depth; not simply three-dimensionality, but the ability to present appearance and reality simultaneously, person and persona, internal and external reality. Past and present could be brought into immediate dialectical relationship, the body's response to its environment literally dramatised and language undercut by action.

In many ways *The Great God Brown* (1926) is about the parallel between the process of self-creation and the invented world of the theatre. The masks of the one become the masks of the other. The theatricality of the stage is deliberately foregrounded as a means of implying the aesthetic nature of life. So, the backdrops to the various scenes are painted cloths, deliberate parodies of the two-dimensional realism of late nineteenth century theatre. But these backdrops are themselves contrasted. The Dionysian world is pictured as bright, natural, exultant and disordered: 'The background backdrop is brilliant, stunning wall-paper, on which crimson and purple flowers and fruits tumble over one another in a riotously profane lack of any apparent design.'[66] The Apollonian world is apparently static, dull, heavy and ordered: 'A backdrop of carefully painted, prosperous, bourgeois culture, bookcases filled with sets.'[67] And yet both remain backdrops, two-dimensional fictions. The use of masks implies a more problematic reality, its combination of Dionysian vitality and Apollonian structure offering a synthesis for the dialectical elements of the drama. In the play, Brown, the architect, produces cold, symmetrical, ordered structures without imagination or a spark of inspiration. Dion, his literal alter ego, adds the magic, the embellishments that give life to these structures. Together they are the complete artist.

The Great God Brown is a very conscious Nietzschean drama. Dion, the protagonist, in a moment of manic lucidity, recognises the ironic death-drive of society invoking Silenus, Dionysus' companion, himself presented as exemplary by Nietzsche in *The Birth of Tragedy*. For it is his assertion that 'what is best of all is...not to have been born, not to *be*, to be *nothing*. But the second best for you is...to die soon,'[68] which exposes the horror of existence which has to be neutralised by art.

For the most part O'Neill's bleak vision of human affairs was, in his mind, primarily transcended through a tragic perception, but in his next play, *Lazarus Laughed*, he proposed a more completely Nietzschean solution.

O'Neill rightly remarked of *Lazarus Laughed* (1928) that he knew no play like it and was not even sure that it was actable, in that its central character was required 'to laugh as one would laugh who had completely lost, even from the depths of the unconscious, all traces of the Fear of Death',[69] inspiring a similar laughter in what amounted to an operatic cast of 166 actors. Lazarus, brought back from the dead by Christ, brings with him an affirmative and infectious laughter, 'Are you a speck of dust danced in the wind? Then laugh, dancing! Laugh yes to your insignificance. Thereby will be born your new greatness! As Man, Petty Tyrant of Earth you are a bubble pricked by death into a void and a mocking silence! But as dust, you are eternal change, and everlasting growth, and a high note of laughter soaring through chaos from the deep heart of God!'[70]

It was a philosophy derived in large part from Nietzsche who, in the person of Zarathustra, asked 'What had been the greatest sin here on earth? Was it not the saying of him who said; "Woe to those who laugh!" Did he himself find on earth no reason for laughter? If so, he sought badly. Even a child could find reasons. He – did not love sufficiently: otherwise he would also have loved us the laughers! But he hated and jeered at us, he promised us wailing and gnashing of teeth.'[71] Exultance lies in what Nietzsche called 'eternal recurrence', 'for in laughter all evil is present, but sanctified and absolved through its own happiness'.[72] So, O'Neill's Lazarus says, 'there is hope for Man! Love is Man's hope – love for his life on earth.'[73] The same point was made in Schopenhauer's essay on 'The indestructibility of being', for though 'death announces itself frankly as the end of the individual...in this individual there lies the germ of a new being. Thus nothing that dies dies for ever'. Indeed Schopenhauer draws on an image which would have appealed to the O'Neill who made full use of masks in *Lazarus Laughed*: 'However much the plays and the masks on the world's stage may change it is always the same actors who appear... The contrivance which prevents us from perceiving this is *time.*'

Lazarus, then, is plainly an apt image of the human spirit reborn to the world but O'Neill seeks to establish the significance of the event by resonating it through a chorus of citizens. These are masked according to age and type, collapsing time and individuality and expressing only the archetypal forms of youth and age, pride and sorrow. The strategy of the play is again that outlined by Schopenhauer's 'Indestructibility of being', for, as he suggests there:

> one can regard every human being from two opposed viewpoints. From the one he is the fleeting individual, burdened with error and sorrow and with a beginning and end in time; from the other he is the indestructible primal being which is objectified in everything that exists...We sit together and talk...just so did *others* sit and talk a thousand years ago; it was the same thing; and it was the *same people*: and it will be just so a thousand years hence.

O'Neill's play collapses this time and locates the individual against this primal being. Only Lazarus has no mask. Only he has glimpsed the truth and understood. Only he realises, with Schopenhauer, what Caligula cannot understand, the distinction between individual death and racial survival.

> Death announces itself frankly as the end of the individual, but in this individual there lies the germ of a new being. Thus nothing that dies *dies* for ever; but nothing that is born receives a fundamentally new existence. That which dies is destroyed, but a germ remains out of which there proceeds a new being, which then enters into existence without knowing whence it had come nor why it is as it is.[74]

This was finally also the most that O'Neill could then say, the closest he could come to affirmation until the compassion of his final plays.

Strange Interlude was an attempt, by means of a systematic use of the dramatic aside, to express the continuing dialectic between conscious and unconscious. The mask now becomes assimilated to a realistic mode, becoming simply the public face of an inner consciousness which was now to be allowed direct access to the audience. It is also manifestly a play in which the influence of Schopenhauer becomes a dominant fact.

It was four and a quarter hours long and consisted in large part of dramatic asides, commenting on speeches remarkable for their lack of humour. There was little in the way of incident. Yet not only was it extremely popular, receiving the Pulitzer Prize, O'Neill's third, but it was also very successful as a published text and was made into a film.

It was clearly his attempt to make the theatre enact the tension between inner and outer life which he felt to be the essence of Freudian thought. But while several of his characters display textbook symptoms of Freudian complexes – Charles Marsden being oedipal to the point of absurdity – O'Neill himself claimed in a letter to Joseph Wood Krutch (July 1927) that:

> as for the complexes of the characters in 'Strange Interlude', I must confess that before or in the writing I never thought of them as such in any Freudian sense and that's probably why no exposition of them obtruded. I'm no great student of psycho-analysis although, of course, I do know quite a bit about it, without ever having gone in for a complete analysis myself, and I'm enormously interested to see what will eventually emerge as sciences out of these theories and the Behaviouristic ones.[75]

The final remark is especially interesting, for all the characters in the play are, in effect, 'typed' on their first appearance. Their future is apparent in their present. They are 'weak' or they are 'strong'; they dominate or they are dominated, as though that were imprinted on their genes as securely as the madness is, apparently, on the family of Sam Evans, whose own success is a function of his weakness. Beneath the modern appearance, the experimental mode of O'Neill's play, is a sense of character which would not have been out of place in his father's theatre. He claims to be 'sort of half in one camp and half in the other' but no one in this play crosses the boundary of a character exposed in the first few words which he speaks. But O'Neill claimed that although *Strange Interlude* 'is undoubtedly full of psycho-analytic ideas, still those same ideas are age-old to the artist and...any artist who was a good psychologist and had had a varied and sensitive experience with life and all sorts of people could have written "the play" without ever having heard of Freud, Jung, Adler and Co. This doesn't apply in my own case,'[76] he confessed. But in fact this notion of an immutable character derived not from Freud but from Schopenhauer whose work O'Neill had been reading and who believed precisely that the individual was born with his character already fully formed.

The asides were in part his attempt to breathe life into a theatrical cliché; in part an appropriation of the novel's ability to present an inner world. But he was himself aware of a deeper failure. As was suggested in his notes, the play was a successful attempt 'at the new masked psychological drama... without masks' only in so far as it concerned 'surfaces and their immediate sub-surfaces, but not where, occasionally, it tries to probe deeper'.[77] The failure was partly one of psychological complexity. The spoken word is consistently deceptive; unspoken motivation, as exposed by asides presumed to be 'voiced' by the mind, is fully formed and coherent, expressing emotional truths. The irrational explains itself rationally – a paradox which seems not to disturb O'Neill. His society is effectively described as being an extension of the setting with which the play begins, 'a cosy cultured retreat, sedulously built as a sanctuary where, secure with the culture of the past at his back, a fugitive from reality can view the present safely from a distance'.[78] His characters are, indeed, fugitives from reality but he never probes the question of the substance of that reality outside of a sexual drive and a mystical urge for completion. Social behaviour is seen as an elaborate fiction; culture, not a means of access to truth but an evasion of it. But that truth is too reductive, too consistently demeaning, to make its demands carry any moral compulsion, while the obsessive neuroses of Nina, the central character, make the social and even metaphysical extension of her plight suspect. As her father remarks, 'in the present state of her mind the real and the unreal become confused'. Marsden's reply, 'As always in all minds... or how could men live',[79] though described by O'Neill's stage directions as 'cynical', is obviously a key observation but not one which the play engages with any sophistication. For the most part real and unreal are simply consigned to different levels of perception and experience. The moral and metaphysical complexities generated by a confusion of the two remain largely unexplored. On the contrary the 'thinking' self, expressed through the asides, is all too clear and expressive. It is pitiless in its exposure of motivation, determinedly clear in its recognition of reality. It is the written and spoken word that lies. Marsden's life as a novelist, indeed, has been dedicated to the propagation of such falsehoods. Clearly O'Neill's play is an attempt to expose this but it simply sidesteps the paradox in which O'Neill as writer and speaker might be thought to be ineluctably trapped. Nonetheless, this is clearly one of his central themes. *Strange Interlude* is in many ways about writing. Nina's father is a specialist in dead languages, lecturing and writing about 'the past of living'.[80] As a writer Marsden misrepresents the truth or produces novels which consist of 'just well-written surface...no depth'. Nina's husband writes copy as an advertiser. Language is deceit.

'How we poor monkeys hide from ourselves behind the sounds called words,'[81] laments Nina. 'You know – grief, sorrow, love, father – those sounds our lips make and our hands write.'[82] The only relief from this knowledge comes for her in the exultance of pregnancy when she feels that the world is 'whole and perfect...all things are each others...life is...and the is is beyond reason'.[83] She becomes the life principle, the real creator of life and hence an image of the only available God, the only possible source of transcendence. Yet in the play this is a source of further irony. Birth stands for the passing on of hereditary defects. She aborts her first child, and the second is the result of a calculated act of adultery who grows up to mock her and the meaning she had felt herself to be imprinting on life. The play ends with a triple irony: the sexless mating of Nina and Marsden, the commitment to biological research by Darrell – research which can render neither life nor truth – and the sexual pairing of the spiritually vapid Gordon and his girl-friend, which amounts to nothing more than the instinctual propagation of the species, a blind serving of biological law which the individual conceals behind the sentimental and deceptive banalities of love, and which the race justifies through the production of art and literature.

An unwieldy work, the play is nonetheless designed to be a confession of O'Neill's own culpability, his collaboration in a process which continues even in the face of knowledge as to its mechanisms. Neither as artist nor as scientific observer can he finally render truth because he is part of the thing which he observes. As an artist he is trapped with words; as a scientific observer he is left with the accusatory definition which Nina offers of the scientist as one who 'believes if you pick a lie to pieces, the pieces are the truth'.[84] But this pre-thematic self-doubt is never allowed to obtrude, to surface as a genuine reflective concern. Though Darrell objects to Nina that 'You've got to give up owning people, meddling in their lives as if you were God and had created them,'[85] he never considers his role as artist-controller and manipulator.

Doris Alexander, in an article in *American Literature*, has indicated O'Neill's debt to Schopenhauer, and it seems clear that much of this play can be seen as a dramatic version of his theories of love and sex. Nina's sense of life-enhancing oneness with creation is an echo of Schopenhauer's assertion that sexuality is an expression of the race's will to live – what Nietzsche preferred to call a 'will to power'. The play also, like so much of O'Neill's work, deals with the irony of a sexuality which in full flood is evidence of a fierce determinism, neutralising reason and tying the individual to his biological fate, but which is also the source and evidence of vitality. In *Strange Interlude*, with the passing of sexual potency *all* meaning drains away. Indeed, O'Neill seems to share Schopenhauer's conviction, expressed in 'The ages of life', that 'when...passion is extinguished, the true kernel of life is gone, and nothing remains but the hollow shell; or, from another point of view, life then becomes like a comedy, which, begun by real actors, is continued and brought to an end by automata dressed in their clothes'.[86] Indeed this is exactly how O'Neill presents it in a play which is essentially about the ironic comedy of human life.

The very setting owes something to Schopenhauer. The play opens in Professor Leeds's study, whose walls are lined with classic texts in Greek, Latin, French, German and English. Here he feels 'secure with the culture of the past at his back',[87] as Schopenhauer, in 'On books and reading', speaks of the array of books on the shelves of a library as being like fossils, storing up the errors of the past. So, too, some of the more arbitrary aspects of the play, such as Nina's physical deterioration after her two pregnancies, seem to owe something to Schopenhauer's conviction that 'after giving birth to one or two children, a woman generally loses her beauty' because she has served her biological function. O'Neill's curious belief that the meno-pause marks the end of female attractiveness owes more to Schopenhauer's biological theories than it does to reality. Schopenhauer regarded the years from eighteen to twenty-eight as the period during which women are attractive (perversely adding that 'outside those years no woman can attract us'.[88]) Likewise O'Neill's emphasis on the menopause as marking the effective end of a woman's power and personal meaning is derived directly from Schopenhauer where it is a natural consequence of his theory of the central and defining significance of the sexual impulse. But, since the indi-vidual consciousness resents this determining power it creates a fiction, a mask, by talking of love and individualising a general impulse. In other words he establishes two levels of reality which O'Neill simply transposes into two modes of discourse. Indeed both men use the metaphor of the mask to explain the process. As Schopenhauer explains:

> what appears in consciousness as sexual impulse, directed to a definite individual, is in itself the will-to-live as a precisely determined individual. Now in this case the sexual impulse, though in itself a subjective need, knows how to assume very

skilfully the mask of an objective admiration, and this to deceive consciousness; for nature requires this strategem in order to attain her ends.[89]

The essential thing thus becomes 'not...mutual affection, but possession', a fact which we evade because of its demeaning connotations. As Marsden says in O'Neill's play, 'forgive us our possessing as we forgive those who possessed before us'.[90] So, the play is a conscious attempt to dramatise Schopenhauer's conviction that, 'as in the case of all instinct, truth assumes the form of delusion, in order to act on the will', and as a consequence it has all the hallmarks of a thesis play in which idea dominates character and action and the mechanical exposition of that idea becomes more important than its dramatic realisation. And this was even more true of his 1928 play, *Dynamo*.

Dynamo begins with something of the barely contained frustrations of *Desire Under the Elms*. Once again the set suggests a sparse, reduced world charged with sexuality but his interest now is less with charting the distorting power of physical passion than with pressing beyond the fact of desire to a concern with the nature of God. Indeed O'Neill announced that it would be the first part of a trilogy on religious problems. Scepticism and blind belief are set side by side on a stage which is literally divided between those two positions. The play becomes an examination of the individual's attempt to get in touch with the source of energy which lies behind the reductive mask of daily existence. For the ironically named Reverend Light, it is vengeful God; for his neighbour, Ramsey Fife, a militant atheism, a Darwinian drive. Yet both ignore the real vitality in their own lives, a sexuality which they suppress in the lives of their offspring, Reuben and Ada. The first act is a powerful dramatisation of suppressed emotion. But the play effectively collapses with the second act. Reuben Light is now transformed into a mentally unstable visionary and pursues his image of a female god in the form of a giant dynamo at a local power station. At this point the symbolism dominates both character and action, and presses the play perilously close to farce. The dynamo becomes associated with Reuben's mother and O'Neill welds together an oedipal theme with a metaphysical enquiry – the latter predominating.

In June 1929, after its first production but before its publication, he wrote to Joseph Wood Krutch confessing that the play had failed to measure up to his own hopes. His expectation was that the published version would throw 'a new light on my intent, which was psychological primarily in spite of the published quotes from my letters on the trilogy' (the other two plays, which were never written, were to have been called *Without Ending of Days* and *It Cannot Be Mad*). Indeed he came to regret the use of the term 'trilogy', choosing instead to regard them as plays united only by a concern with 'the general spiritual futility of the substitute God search'. He came to feel that his

9. *Dynamo* at the Martin Beck Theatre, 11 February 1929, with (left to right) Catherine Calhoun-Doucet, Claudette Colbert and Glenn Anders. A Theatre Guild production, set designed by Lee Simonson.

own comments had put 'all the emphasis on the abstract scheme for the trilogy at the expense of the human drama in the foreground'. He was plainly right. And though the published version did perhaps make clear 'the emphasis on the identity of Reuben's dead mother with his Dynamo-Mother God... with all its connotations in the electrocuting of his Father God and his final blood sacrifice of the girl who had made him unfaithful',[91] the psychological drama merely served the symbolism. The value of human relationship, implicitly contrasted to the sterile business of locating meaning in an external force, is never established because the characters never break out of the constraints of their metaphoric roles. The mother is betrayer, the father God the father, the girl the human sacrifice which he feels constrained to make to a maternal deity and to the principle of motherhood which must be appeased for the betrayal implicit in a son's dawning sexuality. Religion is revealed as a product of deep psychological need, as well as a sense of spiritual inadequacy. Indeed, in this play it is difficult to say whether psychological tensions create religious needs or vice versa. But either way the play is hopelessly flawed by his inability to sustain the credibility of character or the adequacy of his symbolic structure.

As has frequently been noted, O'Neill derived the symbol of the dynamo from Henry Adams, where it stood as an image of energy, a female principle of life lacking only the power to reproduce. But it would be a mistake to see the play's ending, in which Reuben dies, electrically crucified on the terminals of the dynamo, as 'a triumphant return to the source of life' as does Travis Bogard.[92] Far from being a 'plunge toward identity with the God force' by which Reuben finally 'belongs', it is surely a sign of the ultimate futility of a search for transcendent meaning outside human experience. The dynamo, finally, is not that remote from those other mechanistic images which appeared in the drama of the period, plays like *Frankenstein*, *RUR*, *Processional*, *The Adding Machine*. If it was not presented as an image of the destruction of individuality by the new machine age (though the play was originally to have included an explicit attack on materialism), it was offered as a symbol of the sterility of looking for spiritual meaning in the fact of modernity.

O'Neill was inclined to dismiss the play as a product of a difficult period in his life (his first marriage had collapsed and the details of his divorce were being completed), one which he had not given the kind of attention that was his norm. But his real problem lay in his determination to tackle what he regarded as 'big work'. For, as he remarked in his description of the trilogy, 'it seems to me that anyone trying to do big work nowadays must have this big subject behind all the little subjects of his plays or novels, or he is simply scribbling around on the surface of things and has no more real status than a parlor entertainer'.[93] The problem was that he failed to embody these ideas in characters who carried any conviction or in action which sustained belief. Idea won out over a sustained engagement with a fallible human nature.

The growing maturity of O'Neill's imagination is apparent in *Mourning Becomes Electra* (1932). His notes for this reveal, above all, an implicit reexamination of his own theatrical methods. His theme remained essentially the same, as did the dominant image of the world as mask, but he had come to feel that it was possible to expose that inner world without resort to the simple and potentially simplifying device of the 'aside' ('Warning!' he wrote to himself, 'always hereafter regard with suspicion hang-over inclination to use "Interlude" technique regardless – that was what principally hurt "Dynamo", being forced into thought asides method quite alien to essential psychological form of its characters – did not ring true – only clogged up play arbitrarily with obvious author's mannerisms'). It had been appropriate to a play in which the dissociated sensibility, the disintegrated ego, had been the focus for his concern; outside of that he came to feel it was 'superfluous show-shop business'. In similar vein he abandoned an early version which contained stylised soliloquies because these 'reveal nothing of character's motives, secret desires or dreams that can't be shown directly or clearly suggested in their pantomime or talk'. Out, too, went the use of masks as such because they 'obtrude themselves too much into the foreground' and because they 'introduce an obvious duality-of-character symbolism' outside his interest. He relied now on make-up, on dialogue and the skill of his actors to communicate what formerly he had conveyed through simple theatrical device. In other words, he was moving towards a psychological drama in which character would have to carry a weight which had previously been borne by a theatricality which had, he now admitted, been on occasion distorting and distracting.

But his themes remained unchanged. He was still concerned with locating a sense of determinism in human affairs, still concerned with exposing the deadly effect of a presumption that 'life was a dying. Being born was starting to die. Death was being born.'[94] His attraction to a Greek drama which had tackled such issues and which had so successfully tapped the insecurities and spiritual needs of that society now found direct expression in a trilogy deliberately based on that drama.

The idea first occurred to him in the spring of 1926 and by the October of 1928 he had settled on the story of Electra and her family. By the following spring he had decided that his own play could be most appropriately set at the time of the American Civil War, an event suitably remote from the present, and possessing, thereby, 'sufficient mask of time and space, so that audiences will unconscously grasp at once it is primarily [a] drama of hidden life forces – fate – behind lives of characters'.[95] It had the added advantage of providing a perfect rationale for setting the play in a house built in imitation Greek style thereby creating a functional irony around which the play turns, for the New England setting, with its puritanical view of sexuality and the life force, stood in sharp contrast to the iconography of its Greek setting.

The play is concerned with the fated family life of the Mannons. In the previous generation, before the action of the first part of the trilogy, David Mannon (Thyestes) is dispossessed by his brother Abe (Atreus) because he falls in love with a Canuck (part Canadian, part Indian) nurse whom his brother had himself desired. Indeed, not content with this, Abe actually razes the family home to the ground and builds a new one. These events are the coiling of the spring which now unwinds. For in O'Neill's play David

10. *Mourning Becomes Electra* at the Guild Theatre, 26 October 1931, with Alice Brady (seated) and Alla Nazimova. Settings and costumes by Robert Edmond Jones.

Mannon's son, Adam Brant (Aegisthus) seeks vengeance on the Mannon family for his father's death (he had subsequently committed suicide). He does this by seducing Christine Mannon (Clytemnestra) away from her husband, the present head of the Mannon family, Ezra (Agamemnon). However, in doing so he actually falls in love with her. But Christine's daughter, Lavinia (Laodicea), herself in love with Brant, discovers the truth of their relationship.

Christine and Brant conspire together to poison her husband and duly succeed but Lavinia convinces her brother, Orin (Orestes), both of the real nature of his father's death and of the nature of the relationship between Brant and Christine. Ostensibly to revenge his father but in effect to revenge himself, since his relationship with his mother is charged with sexual overtones, he kills Brant. On hearing the news of her lover's death Christine commits suicide, leaving Orin distraught, having, in effect, killed the woman he loves. He can no longer stand the idea that his sister and he should marry the suitors who have waited patiently in the wings for them – Paul and Hazel (Pylades and Hermione). He feels that they have been taken outside the normal world by their abnormal act – a state symbolised by the incestuous proposal which he makes to his sister. She finally buys his silence by agreeing to renounce her marriage and Orin concludes by killing himself, leaving his sister to live with her Furies.

For O'Neill, the New England setting, redolent with notions of sin, guilt and punishment, and with Calvinist belief in determinism, was an entirely appropriate setting for such a trilogy. The self-destructive fatalism of Greek theatre, symbolised by the Furies, is transmuted into a Calvinist conscience which makes the self its own enemy. Love is corrupted by puritan values into lust, thus losing its redemptive and creative aspects. When Christine turns to Brant she is trying to restore a sense of romance and vitality to a world drained of life. For in the Mannon family values are so distorted that there is a psychic inbreeding, an anarchic inward-turned sexuality which is the mark and explanation of their self-destructiveness. The physical resemblance of the Mannons underlines this closed world which feeds off itself and breeds only death. The external world remains just that – external to their real concerns, barely intruding in the form of the local townspeople, who constitute a simple chorus, or the would-be lovers, Paul and Hazel, whose bland normality lacks the imaginative power to penetrate the psychological reflexiveness of the Mannons.

The mask-like faces, constantly referred to in the stage directions, are, as earlier in his work, an expression of his sense of the 'unreal behind what we call reality which is the real reality! – the unrealistic truth wearing the mask of lying reality'.[96] The psychology which is required to be the embodiment of this vision remains somewhat simplistic – the oedipal complex is here balanced by an electra complex (love of daughter for father) – setting up a dualism of false surface and true depth, a false mask and true face which rests rather too heavily on Freudian archetypes. But the mask is at least now generated by character. It is not only an image of a shared fate which links the Mannon family; it is also shaped by their own denial of change, of the living flux of experience, by an obsession with the past which allows the mask a dominance which denies the individual his individuality. In other words the notion of the mask becomes internal to the character, it becomes expressive of an interpretation of experience which concedes authority to time, which allows no resistant self to violate the given. And this pattern of exterior and interior is reflected both in the stage set – the house itself being described as a mask – and in the formal structure of the play, which alternates exterior and interior scenes, scenes in which the external world impinges on, if it does not penetrate, the world of the Mannons, and those in which that world is absent.

The townsfolk who represent that external world are themselves seen only in their externals. Not merely are they a backdrop to the drama of the central characters – a chorus – but they are in some essential way character-less. They lack depth. If they suffer none of the extremes of the Mannon family, neither do they look into their own lives. At their most admirable they crystallise into the form of Peter and Hazel, the Starbucks of O'Neill's Melvillian drama; what he, in his notes, calls the 'untroubled, contented "good"', the sweet 'constant, unselfconscious, untempted virtue'.[97] It is a telling description. We see no depth in their lives because there is none. They are not the material of tragedy.

And Melville is not an inappropriate name to invoke in a play in which *Typee* is quoted as an image of escape and release. The South Sea Island motif recurs as a symbol of a pre-lapsarian world, the world to which the principal characters are drawn. Here the rigid puritanism of New England would no longer apply. It is a place in which causality has no power, a pre-moral world. And yet, as in *Typee* itself, there is a judgement to be made on a world so totally deprived of tension. For the price which the inhabitants of Melville's island pay for their paradise is the surrender of that intellectual perception which is the essence of individuation and the generating force of history. For a world deprived of pain, a world with no sense of sin, a world in which the pleasure principle dominates the reality principle may also be a world without profundity, without energy, a world of surfaces, bland, homogeneous and ultimately static. Which is to say that the South Sea Island motif is also a part of the concern with masks, with levels of experience and perception which in some ways is the subject of the plays.

The sea is thus an escape which these characters cannot permit themselves or, rather, it is a world which they ultimately invest with their own fears and neuroses so that even this retreat is denied them. They are characters who, like Arthur Miller's, meet after the fall and that fall is the source of their meaning. And although both male and female Mannons respond to the romantic spirit – Brant living for a time in the South Seas and Christine marrying Ezra for his romantic quality – that aspect of their character is always held in check by the gravitational pull of their Calvinist consciences, or their inability to break free of their heritage, to challenge the happiness which seems too insubstantial to their spirits. Vengeance, for them, is a way of challenging the world as it is. They wish to recreate it, to mould it in such a way that it will meet the demands of their insistent consciences. They are creator-destroyers whose dignity lies in their acceptance of total responsibility for their actions. David, Christine and Orin Mannon even assume the godlike attribute in taking their own lives, as the latter two and Brant had taken those of others. If social propriety, morality and religion stand between them and their objectives then they will ignore them as Ahab was willing to challenge the sun itself. This is their folly and their greatness. And if both Lavinia and Orin are tempted to lay aside their severe view of the world, to settle for the romantic mask, this is a temptation which their own inherited nature will not finally allow. The world of innocence is, after all, not recoverable.

What O'Neill calls the 'simple sad rhythm of hopeless sea longing', represented by the reiterated singing of the sea shanty, 'Shenandoah', is rejected in favour of a relentless engagement with the self. Indeed, this is a world in which the only authority is self. The many crimes of the play go unpunished. In fact, for all the blandness of the immediate vicinity, the world which they inhabit is itself in a state of collapse. Orin returns from a war in which words like 'dignity' and 'glory' and 'honour' have been as effectively eroded as Frederic Henry had felt them to be in *A Farewell to Arms*. America, too, is a house which has been at war with itself, like the Mannons. And Lincoln's death denies even the apparent restoration of order. It is not simply a case of the Mannons inhabiting their own antinomian world; the whole world envisaged by the play is deprived of order, form and meaning.

And yet O'Neill still wishes to set them apart. Hence his dramatic isolation of the house from the town and his notion of the characters as locked up behind their own deterministic masks. They are the forces of death and their faces are like death masks. The impetus is towards destruction and death. The only force which holds them back is love and O'Neill sets up a Freudian battle between the ego, or death instinct, and the id, or life instinct, with his thumb securely on one side of the scale. The death-mask make-up becomes an expression of that inanimate state which can only be vivified by passion – a passion which at times disrupts the mask but which eventually becomes the agent of the death instinct in a world as completely inverted as that which the Mannons inhabit. Indeed Ezra Mannon, a death dealer both as a judge and a soldier, is given the speech, quoted above, which is a simple paraphrase of Freud's observation in *Beyond the Pleasure Principle*: 'Life was a dying. Being born was starting to die. Death was being born.'[98]

And so O'Neill establishes a *mise-en-scène* which reflects his dramatic strategy in the play. We move from an external to an internal view of the world which he creates and the characters who inhabit it. The audience is confronted with a special curtain which shows the house as it is seen from the street. From this, as he explained in a descriptive note, 'in each play one comes to the exterior of the house in the opening act and enters it in the following act'.[99]

But, despite O'Neill's suggestion of a gap separating the Mannons from their society, it is clear that in this regard at least they are scarcely aberrant. The iconographic significance of the town's white church is as usurped by irony as that of the similarly white Mannon house. If the Mannons splatter that whiteness with blood then so too does the world beyond their estate. As Ezra himself replies, when charged by his wife with being obsessed with death (an ironic charge of course since she is at that moment plotting his murder):

> How in hell people ever got such notions! That white meeting-house. It stuck in my mind – clean-scrubbed and white-washed – a temple of death. But in this war I've seen too many white walls splattered with blood that counted no more than dirty water. I've seen dead men scattered about, no more important than rubbish to be got rid of. That made the white meeting-house seem meaningless – making so much solemn fuss over death![100]

It is not only the Mannons who are death-centred; it is the world which they inhabit.

If the mask stood as a barrier between the Mannons and life, it also stood as a barrier between themselves and other people. In particular Ezra belatedly realises that there has been a barrier between himself and his wife, a gulf which he tries first to bridge with words and then with passion. But they are shut up inside themselves, so in love with their own conception of themselves that only a mirror image of that self can make a suitable mate. And so Orin loves his mother, and his sister when she takes on the appearance of that mother. By the same token Lavinia loves her father, and the image of that father which she detects in Brant. And so the circle closes, a series of repetitive actions reflected in the reiterative structure of the play, the echoic nature of some of the lines, and the fundamental strategy of creating characters who are themselves the mirror images of their own parents. The principal force of the play lies in O'Neill's dramatisation of this desire to embrace one's own image – an egotism which can only be death-oriented. The play ends as Lavinia's bid to escape her fate founders when, with a literally Freudian slip, she addresses Peter, the man who could release her, by the name of her mother's lover. This reflexive truth traps her and she retreats into the house, earlier described as a tomb, the last Mannon. Ibsen signifies the freedom of Nora with the sound of the door slamming as she leaves the house which has become the image of her mental and moral subservience. O'Neill ends his trilogy with the sound of the shutters slamming shut as Lavinia enters the house, closing the door behind her. With this action she wilfully retreats into the inner world which the house has symbolised.

Mourning Becomes Electra is an advance in that he has learned to subordinate theatrical devices to psychological needs. As he wrote in a letter to Kenneth Macgowan in 1929, 'No more sets or theatrical devices as anything but unimportant background – except in the most imperatively exceptional case where organically they belong.'[101] His imagination was now more firmly under control and the energy was not dissipated by diverting it into a self-conscious concern with mechanism. Here, everything was to be seen through, or to serve, character.

The weakness of the play lies in the studied Freudianism which frequently surfaces in naively expressed statements of incestuous attraction, and in repeated self-analysis. Also, in so far as he ascribes the relentless sufferings of the Mannon family in part to a distorting Calvinism, he fails to account for the play's other characters who seem to have derived theirs not from sin but innocence, or perhaps, more accurately, banality. Two different modes seem to clash. On the one hand he seems to project a dualistic vision, whereby the corrupting inward-turned Mannons are contrasted with figures like Peter and Hazel; on the other hand he wishes to describe a world which is itself in a state of moral collapse, the Mannons in some senses being the epitome of a self-directed violence.

There are still elements of melodrama – poison bottles, guns, overheard conversations, revealing documents – and these serve to heighten the gothic notion of the curse, the predisposition of the Mannon family which is supposed to do service for the Greek sense of determinism. The striking similarity between the Mannons (a lost member of the family is recognisable by his strong family resemblance), while functional, is also reminiscent of nineteenth-century melodrama, indeed specifically of *The Count of Monte Cristo*. The process whereby Lavinia and Orin are in effect possessed by the spirit of their parents, transforming before our eyes into versions of those parents, is a Poe-like contrivance whose psychological truth is in danger of being neutralised by its literary origins. Indeed the fall of the house of Mannon is not remote in spirit from the fall of the house of Usher.

O'Neill has a disturbing tendency to an over-explicitness which implies a lack of faith in his own dramatic powers. So, in the first play of the trilogy, Amos Ames, one of the townspeople, seems to exist simply to provide the audience with information in the most literal-minded way. So, too, Seth, another townsman, informs us, as he would surely not need to inform his fellow citizens, to whom he is ostensibly speaking, that Ezra Mannon had

> been a soldier afore this war. His paw made him go to West P'int. He went to the Mexican war and come out a major. Abe died that same year and Ezra give up the army and took hold of the shippin' business here. But he didn't stop

there. He learned law in addition and got made a judge. Went in fur politics and got 'lected mayor. He was mayor when this war broke out but he resigned at once and jined the army again. And now he's riz to be General.

To which his companion can only say:

Ayeh? This town's real proud of Ezra.[102]

Despite the length which O'Neill permitted himself, a length which strengthens the epic pretensions, we are once again required to accept sudden transformations not merely of mood but of appearance as an adequate account of reality. Hence, Lavinia, who, on her first appearance, is described as being flat-breasted and angular, unattractive, wearing a black dress, after her mother's death undergoes what O'Neill has the grace to describe as 'an extraordinary change'. 'Her body, formerly so thin and underdeveloped, has filled out. Her movements have lost their square-shouldered stiffness.'[103] And, lest we should miss the significance of this, she is required to wear her mother's green dress while Orin remarks, 'you don't know how like Mother you've become'.[104] By the same token, Orin, who on his first appearance had carried himself 'by turns with a marked slouchiness or with a self-conscious square-shouldered stiffness that indicates a soldierly bearing unnatural to him', ends the trilogy bearing himself like a soldier, wearing a beard like his father and, in the process of a single month, ageing to the point at which he looks as old as his father had in his portrait. O'Neill's comment is that the 'resemblance between the two is uncanny'.[105] And once again the point is needlessly underscored: 'Can't you see,' he asks, 'I'm now in Father's place and you're Mother?'[106] Lightness of touch was never O'Neill's strong point. And so, in a play in which fate was to be securely rooted in psychological reality, Christine decides to murder her husband with poison because 'some fate' had forced her to read a book on poison a few weeks before. So, too, her husband's heart condition which, we are told, Christine had deliberately exaggerated, obligingly becomes real and serious at a convenient moment.

O'Neill recognised this tendency in his own work and, reading through an early draft, he was conscious of its melodramatic qualities. He hoped to mitigate this by establishing a psychological veracity and by tightening his control over tone, mood, structure and rhythm. But his psychology was equally schematic. He may have avoided a simple dualism of character by dispensing with literal masks, but he substituted an equally simplified version of human dynamics. Fate is hardly domesticated by asserting that what once was external and supernatural is now internal and psychological. He still plays with dualisms. External falsehood and internal truth remain operative modes, while the O'Neill who had been informed in 1926 that he was suffering from an oedipus complex presents a drastically simplistic and explicit version of oedipal and electra complexes.

Viewed in one way the fallibility of the Mannons derives from their tendency to see the world in simple terms: passion must be pursued, slights must be avenged, problems must be resolved by violent action. And yet this process is compounded by a dramatist who applies a similar Manichaean model to the world which he creates. The psychology is imposed on the character rather than derived from it as it would be in *Long Day's Journey Into Night* (1956). Both myth and psychological model are too close to the surface. What we see is character as exemplification and action as re-enactment of archetype. George Steiner rightly objects, in *The Death of Tragedy*, to 'the lesser men' (O'Neill, Giraudoux, Hofmannsthal, Cocteau) who 'often proceed with wanton artifice' trying to 'have it both ways, combining the resonance of the classic theme with the savour of the new'.[107] He complains that such writers set ambushes for the imagination, setting off majestic echoes through reliance on familiar stories. O'Neill, in particular, attracts his opprobrium because he 'commits inner vandalism by sheer inadequacy of style. In the morass of his language,' Steiner asserts, 'the high griefs of the house of Atreus dwindle to a case of adultery and murder in some provincial rathole.'[108] The objection may be unnecessarily patrician, and his notion that 'half the work is done for the poet before the curtain rises' a failure to recognise the special problems of transforming classical models, but he is right in identifying O'Neill's failure to produce an adequate modern equivalent for a classic resonance, and right, too, in identifying his stylistic and linguistic inadequacies. The speech of the Mannons is deliberately contrasted with that of the townspeople. The latter speak in banalities, a flatness of perception underlined by the use of dialect. The Mannons converse at a high emotional intensity, with neurotic directness. All tensions, pains and fears are allowed to bubble to the surface in language, discharging themselves in words. The effect is an hysterical intensity which permits little variation beyond the simple contrast between the Mannons and the others. The emotional and linguistic range of the Mannons is severely restricted and this underscores the melodramatic nature of the action. The inner life tends to rush into an outer existence in a way which is neither psychologically nor poetically convincing. The tension between inner and outer world is lost. Everything must be stated just as every whim must be pursued to the point of action. And the result is a kind of banality which is not restricted to a linguistic sphere. And if, in a sense, it is the fate of the Mannons to be fully known, that explicitness is the undoing of the plays as well as of the characters. Language loses the tension which comes from the unspoken, from that which is concealed from the speaker as well as from the listener. And that tension, that energy, is replaced, in the text, by the exclamation mark, a sign which signifies a truth flourished openly and therefore a truth which has lost much of its kinetic energy. Indeed, the very supposed rationality of the psychological analysis on which the play rests neutralises the tragic impulse. The inscrutable forces behind life which he had set himself to expose at the beginning of his career have become all too scrutable. Psychopathology is finally no substitute for the tragic imagination.

Mourning Becomes Electra did, however, indicate a direction in O'Neill's work which was to lead eventually to the achievement of his final plays. The landscape which he describes here is a landscape of the mind. And in moving through the gauze curtain, which his stage directions indicated should be painted with the social location of the Mannon estate, through the external walls of the house to the interior, we are moving from the social to the psychological, from the public to the private – a path which took O'Neill to his central subject, a Strindbergian drama of sexual tension and moral implosion. As he had said earlier in his career, '[man's] struggle used to be with the gods, but is now with himself, his own past'.[109]

The Iceman Cometh, though written late in his career, was psychologically a product of the same traumatic year which was to produce Long Day's Journey Into Night. It was an attempt to track his personal demons to their lair by returning to the year of his attempted suicide, the year, also, which had turned him into a writer. It clearly has its literary echoes – of Gorky's The Lower Depths and Ibsen's The Wild Duck – but its inspiration was psychological rather than literary, intensely personal rather than public.

The play has a single set, Harry Hope's bar. And this functions symbolically as both womb and tomb for the desperate souls who inhabit it. It is a protection from the world outside, from the need to accept a personal history and a social role; but it is equally a static, enclosed world, which denies any development. It is a reified world which has a deconstructing effect on character. On the face of it, indeed, the play would seem to be flawed in precisely the way that Strindberg had suggested nineteenth-century theatre to be. He had, in particular, warned against the creation of character through simple linguistic or physical mannerism of a kind which typifies The Iceman Cometh. But, for O'Neill this was not simple shorthand for the establishment of character, it was a self-imposed reductivism, the consequence of a willed surrender of complexity and depth. His group of isolated figures face a classic dilemma. On the one hand they are threatened by the viscosity of time, a flow of events which ties them to a past they wish to evade and a future which implies dissolution and death; on the other hand they are menaced by a stasis which abstracts them from time at the price of a denial of substantive identity and any sense of vital development. They opt for narcosis but, despite their semblance of community, the spaces between them seem unbridgeable. They wake from their drunken sleep in order to mumble a drunken phrase and then slump back into unconsciousness, having sounded the note which contributes to an elegiac whose totality they are unable to grasp.

In many ways we are offered an absurdist vision. A group of individuals are suspended in a timeless void, cut off from past and present, killing time as time will in due course kill them. Their vulnerability, the irony of their situation, seem simply exacerbated by action. Love serves to emphasize the gap between ideal and actuality. The only possible reaction, it seems, is a kind of vaudeville in which they parody their own social roles. As in Beckett's world, safety apparently lies in moving as close to the inanimate as possible. Thus they pass the time sitting motionless, using drink to deny the consciousness which is the source of their pain, the origin of those aspirations which, invoked to sustain life, become the embodiment of that discrepancy between aspiration and fulfilment which makes them such ironic figures. Their only consolation lies in the fact of their shared situation, a consolation seemingly out of all proportion to their sense of loss. But it is all they can offer to shore up a collapsing world. Read thus, Hickey becomes a Godot figure who offers himself as a source of coherence, as possessing a key to the riddle of their existence. But his failure to proffer this meaning merely exacerbates their situation for he offers to resolve the paradox of life by ending it. He is the iceman, death. And so the original text ended with a description of Larry, staring out of a window, oblivious to the frenetic attempt of his companions to blot out the knowledge of their situation, 'his face beginning to set in an expression of indifferent expectancy',[110] a paradoxical description entirely appropriate to that Sisyphean self-knowledge which, to Camus early in his career, had constituted the essence of the only victory available to the absurd hero.

Like Hickey, virtually all the inhabitants of Harry Hope's bar are betrayers. They have failed the causes which they had served, the people they had loved, the world which they had perceived in their youth as opportunity but see now as a lost cause. Their drunkenness, their retreat into self, into unreality, is a protection against knowledge of that imperfection. They are all committed to sustaining their own innocence. And yet, as with Hawthorne, there is a crucial and inelectable connection between their imperfection and the compassion which is equally generated by despair. Imperfection is definitional, but so, it seems, is the instinct to console.

Larry's conviction that the pipe-dream 'gives life to the whole misbegotten mad lot of us'[111] is plainly self-deceiving, as is Hickey's hawking of 'truth'. For clearly the brief flurries of activity, the spasms of energy, evidenced by Harry Hope's roomers is, like Strindberg's lethal gavottes, a parody of life. Indeed Larry himself recognises it as a 'death dance'. But so, too, Hickey's notion of grace through truth is designed to win the roomers not to some sense of life but to a destructive egotism. In a speech deleted from the first draft, O'Neill has Hickey tell Hope after the failure of his excursion into the street, 'You can stay in here drunk for the rest of your life now without feeling any guilt about it. You needn't make up lying excuses. You don't have to cheat yourself with false hopes about tomorrow. You're really rid of the past and Bessie now. *You needn't give a damn about anyone or anything.* You're free to be what you really want to be [my italics].'[112]

The real choice seems to be less one between a public and a private world, or between truth and illusion, than between narcissism and a concern for others. This, indeed, is the spirit in which O'Neill assured Lawrence Langner he had written the play, for 'there are moments in it that suddenly strip the secret soul of a man stark naked, not in cruelty or moral superiority, but with an understanding compassion which sees him as a victim of the ironies of life and of himself. Those moments are for me the depth of tragedy, with nothing more that can possibly be said.'[113] Larry's moral criticism might shade off into misanthropy, a Calvinist insistence on man's innate moral depravity and fundamental inconsequence, but his own irrepressible compassion denies this. Indeed in the first draft that compassion is emphasised even more, as he reaches out to console those who surround him. His apparent nihilism is a literary pose. He repeats absurdist aphorisms, O'Neill pointedly tells us in a stage direction, 'as if he were trying to hammer something into his own brain'.[114] But this does battle with his instinctive nature. O'Neill can no longer offer the kind of confident assurance which he had expressed in *Lazarus Laughed* and *Ah Wilderness!* but he does find room for consolation in the gap between nihilistic language and compassionate action. In *Waiting for Godot* a naive announcement of purposive action is undercut by the failure of reality to conform. Hence, the injunction, 'Let's go', is deflated by the stage direction, 'They do not move.' In *The Iceman Cometh*, on the other hand, the pronouncement that man is a mixture of mud and manure is negated by a human sympathy expressed through action. In the form of Hickey's wife this religion of man even has a kind of secular saint. For her pipe-dream was that human nature, though fallible, was constantly renewable – that love could prevail.

The question of illusion, so often seen as the central concern of the play, is subject rather than theme. Indeed, in a passage in the first draft not included in the final version, O'Neill has Larry pose a question which takes the issue beyond a mere choice between truth and illusion. Having identified the desire of his fellow roomers to rest content with their present situation, he observes, 'That's the truth, but what is truth?'[115] For truth is problematic. Is Hugo to be defined by the ten years in prison which he served for the cause or by the contempt for the masses which he equally betrays? The play is less an embodiment of Eliot's observation that humankind cannot bear very much reality than it is an assertion of the paramount need for compassion. Pressed into the world of reality·by Hickey, the roomers betray 'an atmosphere of oppressive stagnation and a quality of insensibility'. They are 'like wax figures', behaving 'mechanically', sprawling in 'sodden slumber'.[116] But, drugged with alcohol their state is much the same. However, enlivened by the demands of mutual support, they sustain a level of imaginative sympathy which itself becomes a value.

Much the same could be said of the characters in *The Wild Duck*, which is not concerned with endorsing illusion but with identifying a necessary and redeeming humanistic commitment. Thus, in that play, the 'life lies' offered by the drunken doctor Relling, express a human sympathy which distinguishes them from the self-deceptions of Gregers Werle and the fiercely egotistical illusions of Hjalmar Ekdal to whom others are required to sacrifice their lives. The Ibsen who was capable of such virulent assaults on social and moral mendacity was not likely to elaborate a philosophy of necessary falsehoods. The O'Neill who had seen his mother and brother destroyed by addiction and who had devoted much of his art to exposing the false masks of private and public life, was unlikely to advocate an existence sustained by alcohol or a life based on lies. The truth, which he had searched for first in religion, then in anarchism and socialism and subsequently in a Nietzschean sense of eternal recurrence, he found, finally, in the simple fact of human relationship. And if these relationships were equally capable of exacerbating a fundamental absurdity, it is their redemptive quality which provides the only ground for hope which he can identify. The movement is essentially that identified by Camus. For, having sought for hope first in a sense of absurdist exultance, a Sisyphean transcendence through sheer acceptance, and then in a sense of identity deriving from the fact of rebellion, he came, finally, to identify a progression which went beyond the simple acknowledgement of paradox, asserting that: 'The end of the movement of absurdity, of rebellion, etc....is compassion...that is to say, in the last analysis, love.'[117]

The Iceman Cometh was, O'Neill suggested, a denial of any other experience of faith in his plays and it was so primarily through his acceptance of this new logic. Certainly his dedication to *Long Day's Journey Into Night* speaks of a 'faith in love' inspired by his marriage to Carlotta, which enables him at last to face his dead in a play written 'with deep pity and understanding and forgiveness'. *The Iceman Cometh*, in which he faces his own crucial experiences of 1912, and, perhaps most directly, the sense of despair which had led him to the brink of the grave, was a necessary prelude to writing about his own family and his own former self who could, finally, only be approached through love, and only portrayed in their complexity if they could be approached with compassion.

O'Neill's real ancestor was Melville. His art was born out of the same spirit of rebellion. He had the same conviction, expressed most centrally in *Moby Dick*, that truth had little to do with fact, that the true man was the man of sorrows, that the world was indeed a pasteboard mask and that to find the truth it was necessary to strike through that mask. It is not simply that for both men the sea was a central symbol. They saw the same world. A world of innocence, without pain, was conceivable but it was also a world without direction, drained of the energy which is life. Both men brought a tragic perspective to bear. Both men created work which constantly flirted with melodrama, which dealt in extremes and pressed language beyond its prosaic function. Both were capable of bathos, of misplaced effects. Both had a Manichaean vision but doubted the extremes which they identified. If both were romantics their work also implied a critique of that romanticism. Neither could settle for the domestic values of a Starbuck. The most they could envisage, outside the doomed figures who challenged their fate, was the individual who, knowing all, continued to exist with that knowledge while offering a necessary gesture of compassion, of human solidarity – Melville's Ishmael, O'Neill's Larry Slade. It was a limited victory but finally, of course, an accurate reflection of their own roles as novelist and playwright, truth-tellers, survivors, who see and tell the story as the price and method of their survival, and as a gesture of community with their audience.

Earlier in his life O'Neill had tested a series of animating faiths – the faiths enumerated in that curious testament to rediscovered religious faith, *Days Without End* (1934): 'First it was Atheism unadorned. Then it was Atheism wedded to socialism...and the next I heard Atheism was living in free love with Anarchism, with a curse by Nietzsche to bless the union.'[118] The same play identifies a fear that the protagonist, fascinated with death, is cursed with 'the inability to reach a lasting belief in any faith, damned by a fear of the lie hiding behind the mask of truth'.[119] It was an apt self-criticism. It was equally offered as a criticism of his own society which had lost its ideals and surrendered notions of individual responsibility. And though the play ends with an uncharacteristic and unconvincing affirmation of religious faith, the strategy which lies at the heart of his work is that identified by his protagonist when he asserts the individual's responsibility as 'daring to face his eternal loss and hopelessness, to accept it as his fate and go on with life.'[120]

After *Days Without End*, indeed, he had turned more completely inwards.

Ill health drove him to an increasing privacy. His very handwriting became illegible to others. He wrote now, he explained, primarily to be read, though he assumed that what worked on the page would work in the theatre. The man who had complained that the stage had suffered from 'the banality of surfaces' was now increasingly driven into the depths of his own self. The mask he now chose to penetrate was his own.

For O'Neill, human nature is dual. As he said in an intriguing aside in his article on masks, Faust and Mephistophiles are one. For him, character is action and reaction. The individual is equally drawn to the material and the spiritual, symbolised sometimes, though not invariably, as the land and the sea. He inhabits a Baudelairian universe of poverty, deprivation and pain from which he retreats into dream or narcosis. Love is the spur and the reward but, though born of a spiritual yearning, a selfless vision, it has to struggle for survival in a real world. For O'Neill, as for Baudelaire, the purity of the blue sky and sea is tainted by the fog, which is partly a product of the abyss and partly a welcoming concealment of truth.

O'Neill creates an aesthetic out of the tentative. No statement can be allowed absolute authority. Despair is no sooner expressed than it is balanced by a persistent hope. A hand raised to strike ends by consoling; a gesture of compassion is immediately aborted. There is a fear of completion, of resting in a singularity of experience which will prove definitional. Since the principle fear is of determinism, the restless, neurotic self becomes a central strategy for survival as well as evidencing a human pathology. Character is placed under such pressure that it breaks up into its component parts as though it had been through a centrifuge. The qualities of hope, despair, misanthropy, compassion, are thrown off in pure form but not allowed dominance beyond the moment. Thus character, and, indeed, the play itself, becomes a kind of kaleidoscope of intense emotions. If there is a dominant characteristic it is the self-destructive impulse, a gravitational pull towards death as a final synthesis which will bring ultimate peace, escape from the irony which comes from a persistent desire to deny the potency of that pull. But, denied that death which achieves synthesis only through annihilation, character is dualistic rather than dialectical. In some cases that dualism is pressed to the point of creating double characters, as in *The Great God Brown* and *Strange Interlude*, thereby precipitating out opposing characteristics. More often the conflicting selves are held together, forced to co-exist in a continuing tension which becomes a trope for that conflict which O'Neill seems to accept as a defining image of existence. It is a tension which is the source of irony, but it is also a tension which is the sign of continued life. The real enemy is the stasis of death towards which his characters are drawn but to which they seldom capitulate.

O'Neill began his career with a revolt against his father – rejecting the very kind of theatre that James O'Neill epitomised. But he ended it with a series of portraits of that father, honest, living and self-revealing: exorcism and grace. The process had less to do with bringing him to terms with his family than with reconciling himself to himself. The tracery of guilt that scarred that family was, he came to feel, largely what kept it together. It was, indeed, a love-hate relationship, a meeting of opposites which established the rhythm of his plays. He saw man as an amalgam of warring impulses, of spiritual longings and physical failings, of outer falsities and inner truths. His art was a quest for some way of reconciling these elements – through politics or a visionary unity. But it was only in his final plays that he succeeded in locating that principle of harmony in the nature of human relationships. Only here that his quest came to an end.

The underlying rhythm of O'Neill's plays, the regular pulse of action and reaction, is seen by John Dewey, speaking not of O'Neill but of the relationship between art and life, as a natural product of the relationship between man and his setting, since

> all interactions that affect stability and order in the whirling flux of change are rhythms. There is ebb and flow, systole and diastole...Contrast of lack and fullness, of struggle and achievement, of adjustment after consummated irregularity, form the drama in which action, feeling, and meaning are one. The outcome is balance and counter-balance. These are not static nor mechanical. They express power that is intense because measured through overcoming resistance. Environing subjects avail and counteravail.[121]

It is an apt description of O'Neill's method and of his apprehension of the process of a life operating between the twin threats of pure flux and stasis. As Dewey observed:

> There are two sorts of possible worlds in which esthetic experience would not occur. In a world of mere flux, change would not be cumulative; it would not move towards a close. Stability and rest would have no being. Equally it is true, however, that a world that is finished, ended, would have no traits of suspense and crisis, and would offer no opportunity for resolution. Where everything is already complete, there is no fulfilment. We envisage with pleasure Nirvana and a uniform heavenly bliss only because they are projected upon the background of our present world of stress and conflict. Because the actual world, that in which we live, is a combination of movement and culmination, of breaks and re-unions, the experience of a living creature is capable of esthetic quality... In a finished world, sleep and waking could not be distinguished. In one wholly perturbed, conditions could not be struggled with.

For Dewey as for O'Neill 'inner harmony is attained only when, by some means, terms are made with the environment'.[122] But in O'Neill's world such moments are rare – Eben's sudden sense of the beauty of the farm in

93

Desire Under the Elms, Edmund's lyrical memory of a moment of harmony with the sea, the wind and the sky, in *Long Day's Journey*. But that harmony is inhibited by an oppressive sense of time. And once again Dewey identifies the source of that disruption, for 'most mortals are conscious that a split often occurs between their present living and their past and future. Then the past hangs upon them as a burden... It rests upon the present as an oppression' and 'only when the past ceases to trouble and anticipations of the future are not perturbing is a being wholly united with his environment and therefore fully alive'.[123] And there lies the dilemma of the O'Neill protagonist – isolated in time, oppressed by the past, terrified of the future. But if the emotional systole and diastole of O'Neill's characters can be seen as reflecting a natural rhythm it is also a product of a neurotic uncertainty, an internal conflict, while, as Dewey recognised, too total a harmony with the natural world can 'in extreme cases' lead 'to the point of insanity'.[124] And that is as apparent in Edmund's encomium to the natural world, as it had been in Ishmael's dangerous mental plunge into the heart of nature in *Moby Dick*.

Early in his career he decided that his subject was to be Man and not man, and the consequence was a reduction of character to agent rather than principal. In search of underlying human principles he was too disposed to see abstractions rather than people. And so he regarded the human face as a mask concealing abstract qualities rather than itself being the evidence of a complex identity. The characters of his early plays tend to be types, defined by profession, class, nationality, social role. And though he was determined not to be distracted by surfaces, somehow the depth which he projected had less to do with people than with ideas. Losing his Catholic faith early, he still retained a belief in the necessity for some kind of transcendent principle which could charge the apparent futility of life with meaning. And he looked for that in the ideas of Schopenhauer and Nietzsche and the poetry of Baudelaire. The significance, in this regard, of *Long Day's Journey* is that it is an admission that this was the wrong place to look. The father and the son are always ready with an apt quotation. Indeed, in a sense they live fictional roles, play out the literary conceits which they derive from art rather than life. But the truth lies elsewhere. It lies, his final plays seem to assert, in the power of the individual to create or destroy the lives of others; in the absolute necessity to renew even the love which is itself the source of irony. For where else can opposites be reconciled but in the human heart; how else can meaning be generated but in the relationships, bitter and loving, between individuals who meet not as embodiments of abstractions, but as expressions of conflicting but real emotions, and as evidence of the losing struggle to imprint order, and at least a provisional purpose, on a life defined by the absoluteness of its ultimate end? He comes much closer to tragedy in these final plays than he ever did when he tried to recreate the structure, but not the spirit, of the Greek theatre. And he did so because he came at last to realise that the essence of the tragic lies in the individual's struggle with his own conflicting self as much as in his foolhardy but ennobling challenge to the world. O'Neill's characters are doomed and know it all too acutely. What they fail to recognise is the nature of the rebellion which they sustain, which has nothing to do with their retreat into alcohol, drugs, or a wilful capitulation to guilt and death, but everything to do with the love which makes it impossible for them finally to desert their fellow sufferers. Mary Tyrone's end is pathetic; that of her husband potentially tragic.

Relationships are as much battles for dominance as they are in Strindberg or Pinter. And language is only one of the weapons employed. But it is a subtle one. In *A Touch of the Poet* (1958) a simple shift of linguistic register can constitute a challenge, an ironical comment, a deflating gesture. The discrepancy between what Con Melody is and what he pretends to be is underlined by a subversive language, a thick, clotted brogue, viscous, entrapping him in his past. And yet that discrepancy, to some greater or lesser extent, is a mark of most of O'Neill's characters and shifts in verbal patterns frequently betray that crucial gulf. This is at its most obvious in *Strange Interlude* and *Days Without End*, but it applies equally to a work like *Long Day's Journey* in which the lyrical language of ideal form and spiritual potential is counterposed to a deflationary prose, a parodic tone, and an assertive present tense. What once was can be no more because of a tense which is constantly reasserting the present moment. They are trapped, in a sense, in language which simultaneously betrays the past and asserts the present.

In *A Touch of the Poet*, Nora Melody's subservience is underlined by her accent, as her daughter's rebelliousness is by hers. It is clear, also, that Con's seduction of his wife had been a linguistic as well as a sexual act, that the two processes were intimately connected. There is, indeed, a melody to his speech, a mellifluousness, when he is intent on seduction, which is the lubricant to an assault whose directness could not otherwise be borne by the religious Nora. So, too, with James Tyrone and, of course, James O'Neill. It is not for nothing that 'intercourse' has a crucial linguistic ambiguity. Their control of language is not merely evidence of their physical power, it is the essence of it. So much so that silence acquires a special poignancy. It becomes an admission of impotence. And both James Tyrone and Con Melody are stunned into silence, forced to acknowledge the loss of control and, more crucially, the loss of hope which ultimately undermines their egos and the language through which they exert themselves.

Nora's linguistic reticence marks both her social impotence and her proximity to reality. In O'Neill's work, the greater the flood of language the greater the distance from the real. The stripping of Brutus Jones is a process of linguistic as well as social deconstruction. His language and his pretence are in the end intimately connected.

O'Neill's characters suffer from a moral autism, a narcissism which constitutes a deliberate withdrawal from the social. Con Melody, admiring himself in a mirror in his dilapidated inn, a self celebrating itself free for a moment from the mocking ironies generated by relationship, is a paradigm. They react favourably only to those aspects of others which are a reflection of themselves. The only safe world is a world in which the self is comfortably replicated, a cloning which leaves no room for an otherness which is the source of social, moral and spiritual complexity. And yet the mirror also reflects time. And thus, the former self becomes the other, and the strategy finally fails.

Meaning, happiness, lies in the past. The future is defined by images of disintegration and death. The present is simply a void – a purgatory, an anteroom to death. His subject is the individual's effort to sustain himself after the momentum of life has slowed, after the events which seemed to generate meaning have passed. The roomers of Harry Hope's bar can remember the genuine achievement of their youth; James Tyrone his real promise as a tragic actor; Con Melody the acts of bravery which once distinguished him. O'Neill's late plays are concerned with the process of coming to terms with the fact of time – with unmaking as a fundamental fact of existence. His characters live a life in which the active has given way to the passive voice.

O'Neill maintains an ambiguous response to the mode in which he writes. His characters are forever quoting – usually from poets, on occasion from playwrights. In doing so they are attempting an ironic distancing from themselves. Apt or not, the words they speak are not their own. They are retreating behind language, a language which has already been shaped by other consciousnesses. Art itself thus becomes a kind of mask, another protective device. And this was the paradox of his art. The touch of the poet, which is the mark of so many of his characters, betrays a desire to reshape the world which is equally the origin of that evasion of the real which is at times the essence of their self-betrayal. The writer, as in *The Arabian Nights*, is in effect staving off death. The story becomes life giving or at least death defeating. O'Neill's characters are poets manqués. Language is the essence of their resistance.

Greek and Shakespearian tragedy assumed the existence of a moral universe in which justice would eventually exert its supremacy. It took for granted that man was a part of an homogeneous world and that to place oneself in opposition to that world was to invite destruction. O'Neill's characters inhabit a very different world. For him there was a fundamental gulf between the individual and the world, a gulf which he and his characters sought to close through holistic schemata, through religion, politics or a Nietzschean assertion of pagan continuities.

In the synopsis which he wrote at Le Plessis and which is dated June 1939, O'Neill tried out various titles for his new play. Two of these were *The Long Day's Retirement* and *The Long Day's Retreat*. Both titles identify a basic theme of the play and, indeed, of O'Neill's work. For the play is patterned around the various strategies of retreat adopted by the tortured Tyrone family, while, again like so much of his work, the rhetorical method of the play is patterned on statements made and then retracted, sentences which are withdrawn before they are completed, cruelties interdicted by compassion, kindnesses unmade by bitterness. Theirs is a world of incompleted gestures, needs never satisfied, longings never realised.

The whole Tyrone family is in retreat. They live in a house set back from the harbour road on the fringe of the town (O'Neill's sketch for the house is an almost exact reproduction of his family's New London home). They seem to have no real friends. Their isolation is underlined by the fog that swirls in from the sea, separating them more completely and acting as an image of that progressive withdrawal from the world which is in some ways the subject of the play and which is embodied most directly in the figure of Mary Tyrone, originally to have been called Stella. Her gradual eclipse lies at the centre of *Long Day's Journey Into Night*.

Her retreat had begun long before. On the death of her first child, a death for which she blamed herself and her husband since she had left the baby to join him on tour, she had conceived James Jr as a way of blotting out the fact of that death and denying that guilt. Thus, ironically, James's birth had been the first stage in a progressive retirement from self-knowledge, from personal responsibility and from the meaning of death. And when a quack doctor gives her morphine to relieve the pain of that birth he opens another avenue of escape.

When the play begins, having successfully withdrawn from her addiction for several months, she has just returned to her dependency, frightened by by Edmund's illness. But the drug only provides the most tangible evidence of her retreat. Her most obvious resource is a retreat into language. Her family's bitterness and suspicion make them unavailable for consolation, so that she staves off self-awareness with a nervous loquacity as her hands flutter with an equally aimless movement. 'I know it's useless to talk,' she admits, 'but sometimes I feel so lonely.'[125] Her solipsism, however, is merely an intense form of an isolation which is more generally applicable. As O'Neill indicates in his scenario for the play, she and her husband 'stare helplessly at each other, the helpless stare of a man and woman who have known each other and never known each other'.[126] O'Neill's, like Tennessee Williams's characters, are sentenced to solitary confinement inside their own skins for life.

The intensification of isolation is given concrete form in Mary's retreat into the spare room, always a sign of the detachment, and will for detachment, which comes from her resort to morphine. And this movement is intensified by the fog which stands as an image of her withdrawal. Indeed in his notes O'Neill outlines what he called the 'weather progression' of the play. The action begins on a fine morning. The fog is clearing. In the second act, as his notes indicate, the sunshine dims and with it Tyrone's optimism. In the third act the first distant sound of a fog horn acts as an ominous sign which Tyrone still resists, hoping that the fog will stay out at sea. But in the fourth act it finally arrives and encloses them. For Mary and for Edmund it is welcome, for the former because it makes concealment possible, for the latter because it destroys the distinction between the real and the illusory.

But if her retreat is described in terms of present reality, a kind of horizontal schema, it also has a vertical dimension. Unable to face a future consisting of her own addiction and guilt and her son's illness, she retreats into the past. The dead son becomes the only son she had loved because he represents the unambiguous. Beyond that she recalls the days of her courtship and trails her wedding-dress behind her, finding a lyricism in her description of its simple beauty which has disappeared from her own life. And behind that she turns to a religious faith which is the last possible retreat, to the Virgin Mary who conceived without sin and who thus was free of a guilt which in some ways is inseparable from sexual knowledge. What she yearns for, in other words, is innocence, as do all the Tyrones. And in order to assert that innocence they are ready to accuse one another.

The shifting alliances which they form were very much a part of the original plan for the play. Relationships resolve themselves into 'battles' (O'Neill's word in the notes for what he called his 'New London Play'), and O'Neill reminded himself, in his notes, to ensure that the movement of the play would correspond to these shifting alliances. But this hostility does continuous battle with an ambiguous love, ambiguous because it is both the source of consolation and of pain and as such is an expression of a basic paradox of existence. Hence it is James Tyrone's love for his wife which leads him to want her with him on tour. Yet it is that presence which leads to the death of her child. It is a paradox which baffles and bewilders her and which O'Neill planned that she should only perceive clearly in the final act. His notes for what was to have been a fifth act (he eventually divided the second act into two scenes) read: 'Just before end, she *snaps* [*partly illegible*] into awareness again – the trouble is all love each other – so easy to leave if indifferent, or could just hate – but no, we have to love each other – even you, Jamie – when you say wish father would die – oh, I know you mean that at times – I have meant it, too – but you know very well you love and respect, too.'[127] It is a realisation which she is not permitted in the final version, a journey towards self-perception and clarity of thought which would have been inconsistent with her clouded mind, her retreat into the past and the pervasive imagery of fog. But it is a perception which still lies at the heart of the play. As it is, the irony is caught more delicately in the final reverie about her youth and her observation that 'in the spring something happened to me. Yes, I remember. I fell in love with James Tyrone and was so happy for a time.' The ironic implications of a blighted spring, of life turned against itself, were familiar enough. There seems a clear echo of the concluding sentence of *The Sun Also Rises*. But the final image of the play is reminiscent of the stasis of a Beckett play and, indeed, the final moments of *The Iceman Cometh*. For after the emotional turmoil and the unnerving articulateness of the play we are left with silence and immobility. Mary 'stares before her in a sad dream. Tyrone stirs in his chair; Edmund and Jamie remain motionless.'[128] And there is a sense in which they are involved in an endlessly repeated ritual. Though the play is specifically located in 1912, the characters are in a sense merely re-enacting an archetypal experience. Edmund's attempted suicide had its parallel in the suicide of Tyrone's father while Edmund's tuberculosis reflects that of Mary's mother.

His notion of character remains much as it had been in the earlier plays. It is reactive. It bears the imprint of heredity and environment, though his concern is less naturalistic than metaphysical. And clearly in the context of this family, in which the baby Eugene had died, Edmund has been arbitrarily struck down by illness, and his mother saddled with an addiction which controlled her before she was aware of it, there is a validity granted to Mary's lament that 'None of us can help the things life has done to us. They're done before you realize it, and once they're done they make you do other things until at last everything comes between you and what you'd like to be, and you've lost your true self forever.'[129] Except, of course, that the true self has no existence outside the ironies generated by the collision between platonic form and reality. Jamie's cynicism, parodied by Edmund – 'Everything's in the bag! It's all a frame-up! We're all fall guys and suckers and we can't beat the game'[130] – is inadequate because it presumes no resistant impulse, because it fails to take account of the imperfect but constantly asserted compassion which is in part generated by that sense of shared victimisation. The Catholic faith is seen as purely a retreat from truth, but love, though implicated in the deterministic drive, is not simply anodyne. It operates even in the face of a full knowledge of the real. Nor does it ever

11. *Long Day's Journey Into Night*, New York, 1956. Act IV with Florence Eldrich, Bradford Dillman (standing left), Jason Robards (standing right) and Frederic March.

become a simple piety, as it does, for example, in the work of James Baldwin, or Tennessee Williams at their weakest. It may be invoked, as it is by Mary, as an excuse for not facing the truth about herself but she is right in refusing to grant her addiction as constituting an adequate definition of her life. As she says to her husband, 'We've loved each other! We always will!

Let's remember only that, and not try to understand what we cannot understand, or help things that cannot be helped – the things life has done to us we cannot excuse or explain.'[131] And it is true that, though love and happiness have not proved synonymous, love does still operate.

And though Mary is the principal focus for the theme of blunted aspirations (the girl who wanted to be a concert pianist and now has crippled hands; who wanted to be a nun and married an actor), the other characters stand as variations on that theme. Tyrone is sensible of having thrown away his chance to be a great actor by settling for material rewards; James is jealous of his brother's talents and has become a pathetic drunk; Edmund's poetic sensibility has been deflected into a self-pitying admiration for other writers, literature itself becoming a retreat. And so the Tyrones cling together, afraid of the future and unable to face the past because that is to remind themselves of a promise which was in part blighted by their own wilfulness as well as by the operation of something they wish to dignify with the name of fate. For the truth is that they all allow absolute authority to the past. As Mary says, 'The past is the present, isn't it. It's the future, too. We all try to lie out of that but life won't let us.'[132] They, like her, accept the present as itself only as illusion. O'Neill's description of Mary's state could apply equally well to the rest of the family. For they, like her, have 'found refuge and release in a dream where present reality is but an appearance to be accepted and dismissed unfeelingly – even with a hard cynicism – or entirely ignored'.[133] The only refuge is the past, the world of childhood innocence. Indeed Mary even suggests that it would have been better had Edmund died, for then he would have been spared suffering. Thus life is suffering which can only be avoided by death.

And Edmund himself is attracted by this oblivion – seeing the fog as blotting out the real, removing him from the social context which is the source of his pain. 'I didn't meet a soul. Everything looked and sounded unreal. Nothing was what it is. That's what I wanted – to be alone with myself in another world where truth is untrue and life can hide from itself.' In other words only by destroying the other can he destroy pain, but by destroying the other he denies himself not only consolation but identity itself. And the logical extension of this is death, literal or figurative. 'I even lost the feeling of being on land. The fog and the sea seemed part of each other. It was like walking on the bottom of the sea. As if I had drowned long ago.'[134] Alcohol and morphine are simply ways to approximate this death, attempts to annihilate time which is the source of all ironies, for it is that which turns spring into autumn, childhood into adulthood, hope into the frustrated dream.

Man's fate, as O'Neill sees it, is to glimpse order and unity and live with disorder and chaos. As Edmund remarks, 'For a second there is meaning!

101

Then the hand lets the veil fall and you are alone, lost in the fog again, and you stumble on towards nowhere for no good reason.'[135] This is the absurdist vision against which the individual can only pitch compassion and a poetic sense, a creative reshaping of the world which creates a provisional beauty. They all possess a touch of the poet. For them, as for O'Neill, this is the source of meaning, and Edmund's comment on his own talent is essentially O'Neill's description of his own position as a playwright. 'The *makings* of a poet. No, I'm afraid I'm like the guy who is always panhandling for a smoke. He hasn't even got the makings. He's got only the habit. I couldn't touch what I tried to tell you just now. I just stammered. That's the best I'll ever do. I mean, if I live. Well, it will be a faithful realism at least. Stammering is the native eloquence for us fog people.'[136] The gap between language and experience is akin to the gap between aspiration and fulfilment.

This stands, paradoxically, as O'Neill's most eloquent statement of his own achievement. Having looked for an adequate response to existence he found it in the end in the love with which he was able to approach his wife and his family and in the art with which he faithfully rendered the imperfections and ironies of the life which had given him such pain (a pain now literally undermining his ability to write), but which had also given him a glimpse of meaning, a sense, finally, of belonging to the world from which he had felt so alienated. For through his art he achieved a loss of self which was transcendence rather than death, a denial of time which was not evasion but recognition of higher values.

> I became drunk with the beauty and singing rhythm of it, and for a moment I lost myself – actually lost my life. I was set free! I dissolved in the sea, became white sails and flying spray, became beauty and rhythm, became moonlight and the ship and the dim-starred sky! I belonged, without past or future, within peace and unity and a wild joy, within something greater than my own life, or the life of Man, to Life itself. [And this is] the end of the quest, the last harbour, the joy of belonging to a fulfilment beyond men's lousy, pitiful, greedy fears and hopes and dreams.[137]

And yet they do move closer to truth, admitting to their own failings, to the jealousies, the unrealised dreams which had made them turn against others in preference to facing the guilt which can be located nowhere but in their own hearts.

It is not just that in Saint Augustine's sense the past, in these last plays, is ever-present. The past is actually made into an icon. It overwhelms the present. It is not the literal past to which they turn but an embalmed past, remodelled to serve present purposes. It consists of images, tableaux. It becomes an object of which time has deprived the individual and which derives its power from that felt absence. Hence, Mary Tyrone handles the past as though it were tangible, passing her fluttering hands over its perfect form as in reality she clutches at the platonic shadow of her beautiful wedding-dress which represents that past. It is not simply that the past had set the mechanism in motion, that it contained a key to an enciphered present, as it did for Ibsen. Rather it presents itself to the mind as a self-contained world, a pre-lapsarian model, in which no gap existed between wish and fulfilment, the individual and his setting. It is less the past which creates the present than the present which recreates the past, turning it from verb into noun. Looking back creates a kind of inverted and retrospective vertigo, a terror at the height from which the character has already fallen. The past tense is constantly intruding, usurping the present, undermining those relationships which depend upon a shared apprehension of present reality. There are moments in which Mary Tyrone and Con Melody simply no longer inhabit that present, when they turn themselves into objects, become, in effect, dead to the present and hence lost to those around them. The past is too strong a lure. It is the Gorgon. And though O'Neill rejects Simon Harford's observation in *More Stately Mansions* that 'all we are is the past', and his mother's equally assertive remark that 'the past is the present', it assumes a primary significance.

The past is reassuring because it deals in completed actions. The present is concerned with incompletions and that is the nature of its menace. Hickey invokes a future tense only in order to demonstrate the impossibility of a dynamic way of viewing that future; to sever the lines to that future, to deprive others of hope and create a community of despair in which he can hide.

To acknowledge the future is to acknowledge entropy. George Steiner reminds us that Lévi-Strauss proposed that the science of man should be described as an *entropologie*. And certainly O'Neill was profoundly aware of the fact that whatever future the individual may plot for himself – a future which implies a process of becoming – is accompanied by an inevitable physical decline, a process of unbecoming. The reality of entropy is the one unambiguous fact about the future of any individual. It follows that the future tense is inherently suspect and that all projected futures are undercut by that irony. And so, in his final plays, O'Neill deals in petrified moments. The past has become fossilised but the present is equally static. Earlier in his career he had peddled Nietzschean notions of eternal recurrence; now that recurrence is simply a constant re-enactment of the fact of individual morbidity and an account of the self's attempt to resist the fact of its own decline. Time leads to an increase of perception but the reality perceived is by definition one of increasing decay. Renewal, then, is not a mystical concept of seasonal recurrence but a compassion born of increasing knowledge of mortality. In O'Neill's work the grammar of futurity is shunned. It is

Lavinia's door slammed shut or Larry Slade's dead stare, or the silence with which the Tyrones await the next moment.

In his early work he was inclined, with Schopenhauer and Nietzsche, to say that the individual may die but the species survives; in his later work, closer himself to the fact of personal decline, he was more inclined to invert the sentiment and find in that a disturbing irony. Hence the futurities of *Lazarus Laughed* are not those of *The Iceman Cometh*. But in *A Touch of the Poet* a final benediction is contrived. As in Hawthorne's *The House of the Seven Gables*, a young, resilient, tough-minded member of the lower classes is to marry a representative of the naively idealistic but enfeebled aristocracy – thereby projecting a future which lies beyond the pages of novel or play and which implies a thoroughly bourgeois and non-mystical sense of continuance. And hence there is, perhaps, a faint echo of Nietzsche's description of man as an animal not yet fully defined. It is an odd ending to the play, a lurch back to a kind of benign stance akin in some respects to Shakespeare's gentling of his own harsh vision in *The Tempest*. But last plays are perhaps the moment for gestures of reconciliation, for weddings pregnant with the possibility of new orders which cannot be described or even fully imagined but which are simply committed to the wind. Indeed to trap them too thoroughly in language is to deny them the freedom which the future tense also implies. But they can, of course, only be dramatised through language.

In a sense, in O'Neill's plays, the language which should be secondary has become primary. His characters live through the words which they utter. Language is detached from reality and becomes the only house they can inhabit, infinitely preferable to action, to fact, to a genuine engagement. To be called a tart rather than a whore is to transform the meaning of action. They settle for the banal prose of apparent dialogue, suppressing that part of themselves which once responded to the ideal, that part which could not so easily be contained by language. Speech becomes a pose, a front, a mask. It is a mockery because it cannot finally penetrate to the root of real fears or express a genuine transcendence. How can life move towards transcendence if it is pulled back into the physical world of language? Hence O'Neill's sense of himself as a stutterer. The lyricism which occasionally breaks through the prosaic crust constantly threatens to crystallise into a merely literary apprehension of beauty and harmony. It stands out as a performance, an aria, which is recognised as such, as it is by James Tyrone in *Long Day's Journey*, who sees in his son a touch of the poet. But his son is not at that moment reaching for poetry. He is trying to find a language which can genuinely express his ephemeral but vivid sense of transcendent meaning. But the conventions of art have used up the available language and all that he can communicate is the aesthetic rather than the moral and spiritual content of his vision.

Yet when O'Neill indicates that a pause should be a 'dead silence' he indicates, consciously or not, the implications of abandoning language altogether. They may inhabit intense privacies but they are constantly hounded out of them by the fear of a silence which is death. The language into which they retreat, however, overlaps rather than conjoins. Take, for example, the various expostulations of Harry Hope's roomers. Suddenly shaken into consciousness they speak, but they are not really involved in dialogue with anyone but themselves. Their speeches become like those in Albee's *Quotations from Chairman Mao*, parts of a collage. Or, more realistically, consider the conversation between Nora Melody and her daughter in which neither hears the other in any real sense:

> NORA (*aroused at the mention of police*): Call the police is it? The coward!
>
> SARAH (*goes on unheedingly*): Simon was terribly angry at his father for that. And at father too when I told him how he threatened he'd kill me. But we didn't talk of it much. We had better things to discuss.
>
> NORA (*belligerently*): A lot Con Melody cares for police, and him in a rage! Not the whole dirty force av thim will dare interfere with him!
>
> SARAH (*goes on as if she hadn't heard*): And then Simon told me how scared he'd been I didn't love him... [138]

And so on. The monologues fail to engage because they come out of different experiences, express different hopes and fears. Where communication should be at its most lucid, within the family, it fails. Or, rather, the gulf is such that it takes a special effort to bridge it.

George Steiner has said that 'Language is the main instrument of man's refusal to accept the world as it is.' [139] Indeed he has gone so far as to insist that it is facile to regard falsity as primarily negative in that without the facility to deny evidential material, simple facticity, 'we would turn forever on the treadmill of the present'. And it is worth bearing this in mind when approaching O'Neill's *The Iceman Cometh*. No moral distinction is made between truth and illusion. Indeed the two have interpenetrated themselves so thoroughly that it is by no means easy to see what motivates each individual – a confusion which exists equally in their own minds.

Nor should it be too surprising to find this shading of the line between truth and illusion, for it was Nietzsche, his chief philosophical mentor, who observed that man's genius lay in his lying ability and that since experience is mediated through the mind it is fictionalised in the process of perception. Is Con Melody any less true when he is playing the role of country gentleman than when he is playing the role of peasant? Man is an actor first and foremost. Some falsehoods destroy, others sustain. And yet O'Neill still seems to present us with brief moments when that self is seen at rest as roles change; in which the self passes through a zone of authenticity. But even that moment is suspect.

O'Neill began his playwriting life with the stark, organic fact of death. In his earliest one-act plays people die, more or less well, with varying degrees of awareness of their situation. It is a central reality brought directly before us. He deliberately foreshortens the lives of his characters, putting them on a lifeboat or presenting them *in extremis*. As his career continued he tried to invoke various antidotes to the entropic nature of existence. He remained obsessed with the collapse of form (in *The Emperor Jones* brilliantly paralleling the disintegration of a social and moral being with a disintegrative theatrical style). The faces which he created for his characters bore the marks of premature aging. Breasts drooped, bodies were quickly contorted by the warping power of their social or metaphysical plight. They were sustained against this insistent irony by their pursuit of hollow material objectives, by grand passions which swamp their minds, or by quasi-religious invocations of continuity. But finally he comes close to accepting Nietzsche's analysis in *The Will to Power*, 'There is only *one* world...and that world is false, cruel, contradictory, misleading, senseless... We need lies to vanquish this reality, this 'truth', we need lies *in order to live*... That lying is a necessity of life is itself a part of the terrifying and problematic character of existence.'[140] It is not that lying is preferable to truth but that it is a mechanism for survival. Sarah Melody deceives her lover in order to ensure her future just as Con Melody deceives himself in order to protect his vision of the past. Lying is a human activity. It is definitional. Accordingly O'Neill abandons the simple opposites of his early work. And that question deleted from the early text of *The Iceman Cometh* – 'but what is reality?' – becomes central. Death is real. But almost everything else is constantly being invented as it passes through the senses, the mind, the memory. And this is pre-eminently true of human relations in which nothing is assuredly shared, but moments of apparent consonance become the basis for what amounts to an ideology of relationship. The gulf between the various Tyrones and the Melodys is not a product simply of time. It is primal, basic, not just in a Strindbergian sense that the sexes derive their perceptions and needs out of fundamentally different contexts, but in the sense that all individuals inhabit discrete and unique worlds. The only thing they share is death – hence sharing, establishing a relationship, is a reminder of mortality. But, of course, it is also a consolation, a way of blunting an awareness of death – hence its fundamental ambiguity in O'Neill's work, its constant oscillation; the desperate need for and fear of the other.

'Metaphysics, religion, ethics, knowledge – all derive from man's will to art, to lies, from his first flight before truth, from his negation of truth,'[141] said Nietzsche. He might well have added 'art' to his list. So that if O'Neill's career was in effect given over to an investigation of these strategies for survival, it itself constituted such a strategy. He is part of the conspiracy which he sets out to expose. No wonder he takes such an understanding stance with respect to his fellow fictionalisers who choose to make their own world rather than simply to suffer the ignominies of the minimal world presented to them.

O'Neill is a long way from validating narcosis. But his work is a celebration of the resistant spirit, whose acts of transformation, like his own art, are offered as means of survival in a world which offers nothing but the bare bones of birth, dissolution and death.

Just as it is the imprecision of language, its failure to communicate totally, which gives birth to literature, so it is the imperfection of human intercourse which leaves room free for invention, which prevents the banality of total knowledge. That gap is the source of energy as well as pain. O'Neill's characters do not know one another fully. They remain mysteries to one another, responding sometimes with baffled rage, sometimes with genuine affection. But that is precisely what keeps them together. They are incomplete and look to one another for crucial completions. The real terror is when those invented worlds break entirely free of one another and dependency is lost. The real fear is of completion which has no need of the other: zero energy. And so, at the end of *Long Day's Journey Into Night* Mary Tyrone no longer requires collaborators or an audience. Her fiction has become a form of autism.

For Heidegger 'being consists in the understanding of other being'.[142] Relationship is not simply a method; it is the essence of identity and the justification and source of meaning. But understanding is also an act of aggression. It is an intrusion into private meaning. To know another person is to gain power; to surrender private truths is to volunteer vulnerability. And this is precisely the ambiguity which one finds in O'Neill. Individuals are driven to relate, indeed in a sense derive their meaning from that relationship. But they are also harrowed by a process which is akin to assault. The female protagonists of his plays are often virginal figures assaulted by male arrogance, an intrusive force which invades not only their bodies, but the simple placidity of their minds.

Relationships are not equal. Mary Tyrone and Sarah Melody are swamped by the sensibility of men whose aggressive knowledge is not limited by an implicit contract of secrecy. To be known is in some sense to be used up. Subtleties of feeling are coarsened. An inner energy has been tapped and earthed. But, like Hölderlin, O'Neill felt that it was in this curious collision of opposites, this dialectical exchange, that meaning resided.

107

The familial conflicts of the late plays are not simply the destructive residue of psychological variance, as perhaps are those between Jim and Ella in *All God's Chillun Got Wings*, though they clearly have a destructive dimension. They are also the source of dialectical energy. And this doubleness – the fact that vitality and enervation, tragedy and irony, coexist, that they inhabit the same psychic and metaphysical space – is at the heart of O'Neill's apprehension of the social, moral and psychological universe. By contraries we exist; by contraries we die. The fact of death informs the lives of O'Neill's characters, frequently taking the form of a literal illness, a touch of death to balance the touch of the poet which is invoked to transcend the finalities of the former. This is, of course, a romantic pose but that after all was a central truth of O'Neill. He was at heart a romantic.

O'Neill lived at a time of remarkable change. The pace of life was literally accelerating and in *The Hairy Ape* and *Dynamo* he caught the staccato tempo of the new age. But his work also expressed a different rhythm. In the sea plays, and then again in his last plays, the world slows to a halt. Time suddenly stretches out like a flat plain leaving the individual or, more usually, the group, stranded, with no temporal landmarks. But this is not that bourgeois contentment of nineteenth-century life nor is it Schopenhauer's great ennui. It is life lived with a dreadful sameness in which only the moral topography is shifting. It is an inertia, a deceleration of time, which leaves the individual nowhere to look but at those similarly stranded, or, more destructively, at a self which cannot bear such inspection.

Though a number of his plays are set in the city, that city penetrates those plays only through the maimed figures which it disgorges. For the most part the fact of the city is not confronted directly. The vortex is moral rather than social. The naturalist dwelt on the tactile surface of the city, finding in the blank face of its tenements an explanation for behaviour assumed to be a product of the simple pressure of facticity. For O'Neill the city did not occupy that central position. The flotsam of urban life – the prostitutes, the drunks, the has-beens – are not adduced as evidence of the collapse of identity and will but as examples of people treading on the edge of existence. Stripped of the lineaments of a public life, cut off from history, they have to elaborate their own response without the protective banalities generated by social form. His settings themselves tend to be remote from where the flux of life is at its strongest. And so he chooses the remote farm, the distant sea, the back room of a bar, a country inn, a tropical island, the hold of a ship, a life-raft, a seedy hotel, a house set back from the road. His characters share a sense of isolation, a temporal and spatial isolation. They seem indeed to be treading a narrow line between life and death, frequently carrying the marks of death on their faces. And though the *mise-en-scène* does not disappear it reflects rather than determines the psychology of the characters. The buildings threaten at times to turn into tombs, as does Eben's farm, in *Desire Under the Elms*, the Mannon house, in *Mourning Becomes Electra*, and the Tyrone house in *Long Day's Journey*. They do so literally in *Dynamo* and *The Iceman Cometh*, while the ship in *Bound East for Cardiff* and the forest in *Emperor Jones* play a similar role. The *mise-en-scène*, in other words, plays a metaphysical rather than a naturalistic role. It becomes an image of the metaphysical rather than social constraints within which the individual lives. On the edge there is an intensity, a crucial pitching of the self not against social forms or public versions of self and history but against the simple fact of existence. The social world tends to be a Baudelairian whirl of detritus, a miasma, an occlusion of human vitality. And this provokes a sense of crisis as the individual seeks to survive the constrictions which may take a social form but are metaphysical in origin.

Indeed the same suffocations are to be found in the country. The extreme becomes part of a romantic strategy for dealing with this sense of moral trauma. The emphasis on incest, on a refusal to recognise sexual taboos, is Byronic – a sexual extremism which is an attempt to press back against constraints. The consequent damnation is equally romantic. So, too, with drugs and alcohol. They are not merely escapes; they are self-dramatising acts which involve a public and willed surrender of self which is intended to contrast with a self destroyed by its environment. It is a death chosen rather than imposed. Alienation becomes a grand gesture. To flirt with doom is to tread the ultimate margin, to assume a tragic aura. But O'Neill did not only celebrate the romantic spirit; he also criticised it. The line between quixotic flirtation with annihilation and simple torpor is not easy to define. It becomes painfully easy to overbalance into extinction. And nowhere is that better expressed than in *Long Day's Journey*. Early in his career he would have been tempted to see the bland crust of existence as concealing a building pressure of social revolt. That was very much the spirit of *The Hairy Ape*. Later, that pressure has been dissipated or seen simply as a baffled and misdirected passion. The incubus lies deeper than the social. A world of honest men, such as those pictured in the 'Wobbly' scene in *The Hairy Ape*, would be a world still fraught with fundamental ironies of a kind they would have been ill-equipped to perceive. Believing that disjunctions are social in origin they believe them to be rectifiable. But as O'Neill implies the homogeneous world which they work towards holds terrors of another kind.

O'Neill certainly never lost a simple social conscience. As late as the *Moon for the Misbegotten* (1957) the battle between rich and poor is still being waged but it is now simply the focus for broad humour. The disproportions with which he now deals are not social in origin. Indeed, in retrospect neither were those of his early plays. They may at times have taken a more clearly social form, but the sense of unease, of a dislocation of personality and a disruption of continuity between the self and its social and natural surroundings, disturbs less because of economic imbalances than because the individual has been dislodged from his own sense of himself. He can no longer read the symbols which surround him in such a way as to reassure himself that he belongs, that he is anything but marginal and extraneous.

O'Neill's was a world deprived of exigencies. There are no necessary commitments – to culture, to history, to values. The figure of a night porter in a seedy hotel idling away his time, with his mind turning from media-influenced dreams to a dull neutrality, becomes an apt image of one pole of human experience. *Hughie* (1958), indeed, is in some senses akin to *Krapp's Last Tape*. The roomer's monologue slowly disinters the corpse of his life as the night clerk lapses into a protective silence. He remains painfully blind to the signs of his own other self – to the genuine affection for the now-dead Hughie, trying to absorb this worrying evidence of his vulnerable humanity into the cynical self-image which he projects. The baffled sense of loss which both men feel, the sense of something in life which evades them, is expressed in the silences which are built into the text.

Hughie is a delicately orchestrated piece with the understatement of a Hemingway short story. The sense of life as a night terror, a dream of implacable dissolution, is strong in O'Neill's work. Nor is it always completely balanced by a conviction that the very shared nature of that fate offers some degree of redress. There is a crucial ambiguity in the night clerk's observation that, 'It is a goddam racket when you stop to think, isn't it... But we might as well make the best of it, because – Well, you can't burn it all down, can you? There's too much steel and stone. There'll always be something left to start it again.'[143] But the dominant mood is one of emptiness. There is a vacancy about his characters. They are radically incomplete in ways which they themselves often detect. Jamie, in *Moon for the Misbegotten*, recognises it, as does Yank in *The Hairy Ape*. And the primary thing which is missing is any sense of how the individual can relate to his own yearnings or his own situation. It is not only the pressure from without but the vacuum within which threatens the implosion of identity. Required to create their own meaning, they lack resources. The failure is partly one of imagination and partly one of will. The weight proves too great. But if O'Neill was obsessed with this primal wound he was also capable of peopling it, with indicating a possible relief.

O'Neill's nostalgia was kept tightly reined but it was central. Though creating pictures of a harsh rural environment he allowed his characters moments in which they saw beyond that starkness. The lyrical moments in his plays tend to be about the land, the sea and the sky, because they are not bounded by time. Absurdity is plainly a product of man, it is a consequence of the gulf between aspiration and fulfilment, it is the product of being trapped in time, saddled with a shrinking temporal horizon. Indeed, it is the discrepancy between an eternal natural world and an ephemeral personal one that creates the anxiety from which O'Neill's plays emerge.

Of course there is a patent sentimentality about O'Neill's vision. He was not always as remote from the wilful plunge into annihilation which his characters take as one might wish. His pictures of an existence whose meaning has been voided into space with the withdrawal of God has a theatrical grandiloquence. He did, indeed, have an enthusiasm for the disintegrative and the pathological which, while wholly explicable in terms of his personal psychology, pressed towards melodrama. But for the most part his work was concerned with the necessity to embrace one's fate and to generate such meaning as the world could be made to contain.

Those who run away (Smitty in the sea plays, the two brothers in *Desire Under the Elms*, Parritt in *The Iceman Cometh*, Mike in *Moon for the Misbegotten*) are pathetic or bland. O'Neill is interested in those who do not run, who are tied to their fate and through acknowledging it gain a certain dignity. As the young James Tyrone says to Josie in *Moon for the Misbegotten*, 'We can kid the world but we can't fool ourselves, like most people, no matter what we do – nor escape ourselves, no matter where we run away. Whether it's the bottom of a bottle, or a South Sea Island, we'd find our own ghosts there waiting to greet us.'[144] It was, of course, precisely when he chose to confront these personal ghosts that O'Neill created his greatest drama.

For all his disavowals O'Neill was clearly influenced by both Freud and Jung, either directly or through his colleagues. Indeed the vogue for Freudian theories in the Greenwich Village of the post-war period is hard to imagine today. Not only did O'Neill himself undergo analysis, in 1927, but he was part of a group for whom Freudian theories were the main subject of discussion. John Reed and Hutchins Hapgood were members of Mabel Dodge Sterne's group and she herself made a profession of being analysed, actually leaving her husband on the advice of her analyst. Floyd Dell, a fellow contributor to the Provincetown theatre, was a primary advocate of psychoanalysis and himself underwent analysis.

O'Neill certainly shared with Freud a conviction that the instinctual drive contributes to the destruction of the organism. And it is, perhaps, from both Freud and Jung that he derived his basic model of human nature as fundamentally divided, as composed of warring instincts: ego and id; unconscious wish and conscious repression; false surface and true depth. As Simon Harford observes in *More Stately Mansions* (1962), man has 'a continual conflict in his mind, so that he lives split into opposites and divided against himself!'[145] The notion of the mask, fundamental to his work, can itself be found in Jung, as David Sievers has pointed out. For as Jung observed,

> Through his more or less complete identification with the attitude of the moment, he at least deceives others, and also often himself, as to his real character. He puts on a mask, which he knows corresponds with his conscious intentions, while it also meets with the requirements and opinions of his environment, so that first one motive and then the other is in the ascendant. The mask, viz. the ad hoc adopted attitude, I have called the *persona*, which was the designation given to the mask worn by the actors of antiquity.[146]

O'Neill's obsession with the oedipal theme, which runs throughout his work, and breeches like a whale in *Desire Under the Elms* and *Moon for the Misbegotten*, is evidence of a profound ambivalence discharged through an art of equal ambivalence. There can be no doubting his drive toward death – it is manifest not only in his attempted suicide but in the single-minded plunge into the depths of the waterfront in South America and again in New York City. There is equally no doubting his energetic commitment to life and to his art, painfully writing his plays in cramped longhand long after control of his hands had been destroyed by disease. It was a contradiction which dramatised his own sense of the perverse mechanism of the biological and social world. The boy who one day returned from school to find his mother shooting drugs into her veins was likely to be left with a bewildering series of confusions, guilts and paradoxes which art could only express but never really resolve.

O'Neill's work was often crude. His characters' desire for self-revelation is more often an expression of the author's desire to force his way through to hidden meanings than a product of a willed expressiveness on the part of characters whose privacies are often the heart of their painful dilemmas. The dynamics of social action are frequently dramatised in a form whose simplicities belie the force which he clearly wishes to grant them. For O'Neill the theatre was a form of cultural and self-analysis and he tended to feel that his plays, like psychoanalysis, did not benefit from brevity. After his one-act dramas his plays tended to get longer as though he could not let them go until each contrariety had been allowed to progress to its extremes, for truth lay somehow in the tensions between those extremes. Truth could never be singular and hence the debates which he appears to establish between reality and illusion do not bear directly on the centre of his concern, which was, rather, always with locating those human strengths and weaknesses that defined and transcended an overpowering sense of absurdity.

And since he believed that individual psychology was at the root of experience, by dramatising those tensions locked in the unconscious he felt he was also offering a description of the history of culture itself. Freud proposed a similar account of that nexus in *Totem and Taboo*, a book which O'Neill had read. There he suggests that 'the animistic phase corresponds in time as well as in content with narcissism, the religious phase corresponds to that stage of object finding which is characterized by dependence on the parents, while the scientific stage has its full counterpart in the individual's state of maturity where, having renounced the pleasure principle and having adapted himself to reality, he seeks his object in the outer world.'[147] O'Neill collapses the time scale and destroys the sequentiality in his characters who often become trapped in a single phase, unable to break out of a hermetic but protective self, or desperate to sustain a literal or figurative childhood. O'Neill's is a drama of personal and cultural neurosis, for his analysis of American society suggested that it, too, had failed to break free of a hieratic onanism, that narcissism had, in the form of a culturally sanctioned materialism, simply enshrined the animistic phase in a national ideology, a myth of self-interest as moral value. And the family becomes an obvious focus for this concern, partly because it played a central role in Freudian mythology, partly because it played a similar role in American mythology, and partly, perhaps mostly, because of his awareness that his own family life held the key to his own compulsions, guilts and phobias.

It is arguable that, lacking any real ideological base, America is best understood in psychological terms. Certainly O'Neill was part of a recognisable tradition in approaching his culture through the dislocated psyche. And in seeing his culture as profoundly neurotic he was essentially doing no more than Poe or Melville had done, and than Sherwood Anderson and Scott Fitzgerald were doing in his own age. Indeed, Hemingway's psychologically maimed figures, haunting an America or Europe drained of meaning, an America whose language no longer adequately expressed reality and whose code no longer concealed a living truth, were not remote from O'Neill's own protagonists. There is the same sense of nostalgia for an irrecoverable lost unity between man and the natural world, the same recognition of love as at one go both a sign of maturity and an agent of fate, the same sense of an unnaturally prolonged adolescence, the same rejection of the father and the religion and social authority which that father represents, the same desperate sense of cultural collapse which makes personal trauma an adequate key to history. And this perhaps explains O'Neill's epic pretensions, his desire to create cycles of plays, a grand panorama, in which the individual sensibility is placed in a wider context and the relationship between private and public elaborated.

Ironically, perhaps the clearest expression of O'Neill's belief is to be found in one of the last works which he wrote, a work whose early drafts were studiously burned and which only survived by chance – *More Stately*

113

Mansions. A weak play in which the symbolism is overt, the social criticism simplistic, the plot contrived, and characters arbitrarily manipulated, it nonetheless reveals his sense of the dynamics of self. The very directness of the statements make them dramatically weak but fascinating for the light which they shed on O'Neill's ideas.

Deborah Harford, unable to adjust to the loss of her son, who has left her to marry Sarah, daughter of Con Melody, a drunken Irish innkeeper, retreats into a self whose hermeticism promises only death. For Freud a fundamental axiom is that the ego cannot escape itself. To O'Neill this was the basis for a determinism which at times he saw as tragic and at times as absurd. Here Deborah flirts with insanity, symbolised by the dark room in a small summer-house which is located in a garden whose artificiality is an image of her own constrained nature. She develops a misanthropy which is the reverse of her son's utopian view of human nature, exposing her own suppressed sexual aggression through a waking dream whereby she becomes a courtesan at Versailles. But this sexual aggression is posited as the opposite of a redemptive love which is presented as the key to escape from the prison-house of the self. Thus pure imagination is offered as an evasion, a symptom of neurosis. But equally her definition of the real as constituted by time, age and death is presented as an inadequate triangulation. When she says she has disciplined her will 'to be possessed by facts – like a whore in a brothel'[148] she offers, it is apparent, an inadequate description of reality. O'Neill's hesitancy about defining the real in *The Iceman Cometh* becomes here the subject of his play. And Deborah's comment that 'I have deliberately gone out of my way to solicit even the meanest, most sordid fact, to prove how thoroughly I was resigned to reality',[149] stands not only as an indication of this but as an indictment of naturalism. Deborah lives only in the mind. She is incomplete, as is her definition of the real, because she is able to engage the world only as absurd fact or irrational dream. What she prays for, however, is a 'resurrection from the death in myself'.[150]

So, too, with Simon, who is wooed away from his Rousseauesque view of human nature by the accumulating evidence of fallibility. And the book which he now wishes to write sounds very like a description of O'Neill's own artistic credo:

> There's the book that ought to be written – a frank study of the true nature of man as he really is and not as he pretends to himself to be – a courageous facing of the truth about him – and in the end, a daring assertion that what he is, no matter how it shocks our sentimental moral and religious delusions about him, is good because it is true and should, in a world of fact, become the foundation of a new morality which would destroy all our present hypocritical pretences and virtuous lies about ourselves.[151]

This statement, though it smacks of Hickey's messianic self-justification, is taken by Sarah as evidence that he has the 'touch of the poet' in him. But he decides to have done with paradox and to resolve his internal conflicts by dedicating himself solely to the pursuit of wealth, convinced that, traced to their origins, all actions derive from self-interest, 'As if at the end of every dream of liberty one did not find the slave, oneself, to whom oneself, the Master, is enslaved.'[152] This becomes the reality on which he structures his life. He accepts a social-Darwinian stance and rejects everything else as illusion. The reality he accepts is that of the subconscious: 'I am alive to life as it is behind our hypocritical pretences and our weak sentimental moral evasions of our natural selves.' This becomes a justification for an antinomian world, for an absurdist conviction that 'our lives are without any meaning whatever – that human life is a silly disappointment, a liar's promise, a perpetual in-bankruptcy for debts we never contracted, a daily appointment with peace and happiness in which we wait day after day, hoping against hope, and when finally the bride or the bridegroom cometh, we discover we are kissing death'.[153] It is a Kafkaesque vision which Simon invokes to validate any action, including murder.

The key to the play and to O'Neill's sense of life as an endless quest for a non-existent solution to the cipher of existence is contained in a fairy-story which Deborah told her son as a boy and which had been a sublimated form of her own life. She tells of a king of a 'happy land' who is dispossessed of his land by an enchantress and banished to wander the world as an unhappy outcast. In a moment of remorse the enchantress offers him a hope that if he finds a magic door he would have his kingdom restored to him. But he is later warned that if he were to open the door he would find only a barren desert and death. As a result he spends the rest of his life standing before the door. As an account of human life it is obviously close to that offered by Kafka in *The Castle*, published in translation for the first time in 1943. The enchantress is simultaneously a God principle, and his mother. Life thus becomes a struggle to return to the womb, to the peace of death. Simon is right in recognising that kingdom of peace as love – unity – but wrong in his desire to restore the kind of love which is pure egotism. He wants the 'mother who loved me alone – who alone I loved'.[154] He has, in effect, never progressed beyond the animistic phase. Finally, his mother tries to save him by passing beyond his grasp, by choosing madness and walking through the door of the summer-house to death. But it is too late for Simon who turns to Sarah's redemptive love but can see in her only the distorted image of his mother. He becomes the evidence for Deborah's assertion that, 'the means always becomes the end – and the end is always oneself'.[155] His pursuit of self leaves him finally as dispossessed of self as his mother.

The restless attempt to end a primal dispossession through possession of externals is futile. So, too, the desire to end all 'separating'. The restlessness is a given, the origin alike of destructive irony and the poetic imagination. It can only be evaded through death or insanity. In a sense meaning can only lie in the search. In John Barth's words, the key to the treasure is the treasure. Or, more importantly, it lies in the love which leads Deborah to sacrifice herself and which makes Sarah accept the burden of her husband's failure. This is the only completion possible: a tension between opposites which involves neither stasis nor capitulation. Simon wishes to be free of one of his two selves, to settle for a single view. But neither his earlier conviction as to man's innate goodness nor his present belief in his utter depravity is an adequate description of a human nature for which these are the two poles, the two extremes within which the individual has to live out his life. To settle for one or other is to remove the dynamic principle from life which derives precisely from the energy generated by the effort to sustain the self in the face of contradiction and paradox. The individual who believes meaning to exist on the other side of the door surrenders the possibility of meaning in the course of his quest. O'Neill's last plays indicate his sense of how that meaning could be generated. Though Simon is unable to escape his childhood, to progress beyond the self, Sarah does transcend an egotism equally destructive on a personal and a public scale.

O'Neill's work is concerned with what Camus called 'the division between the mind that desires and the world that disappoints'. Its spirit is that of his observation: 'The body, compassion, the created world, action, human nobility will...resume their place in this insane world.'[156] It is a paradox which fits exactly O'Neill's ambivalence and indeed the ambivalence inherent in the act of writing, of delineating entropic reality in aesthetic form. Though dramatising characters who live a neurasthenic existence, he balances this with a persistent and even sentimental conviction as to the power of life to generate a response. There was a Sisyphean victory to be won. At times, indeed, there was a frankly bourgeois contentment to be claimed. But for the most part he was concerned with the struggle to make sense out of experience and out of the bewildering tension between a desire for survival and an equally powerful drive towards death.

His characters are, in a way, ascetics, in Pater's sense – 'the sacrifice of one part of human nature to another, that it may live in what survives the more completely' – but what they place as risk by so doing is a crucial membership in the human community. The impurities that they attempt to purge are the impurities which are a part of a full human nature.

The same absoluteness which Camus saw in political totalitarianism, O'Neill saw in a totalitarianism of the self, a narcissism which he saw as epitomised by Con Melody who parades in front of his mirror – a literal mirror but, also, the mirror of other people and of the self. And this is no less true of James Tyrone or Hickey. O'Neill's characters tread the same vertiginous ridge between self-destruction and an acknowledgement of community as do Camus's, and in the end he can offer no more reason for the necessity of resistance than can the French writer. Opposition to despair, and transcendence of a lethal egotism become moral necessities, which must be arbitrary since the basis of morality is destroyed through the acknowledgement of the absurd. But for both, this paradox is inverted. It is the very collapse of any absolute authority for moral value which makes morality a necessary fiction, a contingent truth distinguishable from other fictions only by its utility in sustaining life. Egotism offers mere survival without meaning, like a brain-damaged patient sustained by medical technology. Relationship is inherently ambiguous, but it offers the only real resistance to an insensate world. Indeed, O'Neill occupies essentially the same linguistic world as Camus, who once, in reply to a magazine's request for his ten favourite words, listed: 'world', 'suffering', 'earth', 'mother', 'men', 'desert', 'honor', 'misery', 'summer', and 'sea'.[157]

Like Camus, O'Neill had no very clear social view. His youthful socialism was in effect an aspect of his revolt against materialism and expression of his commitment to relationships which, if the source of despair and a reminder of the gulf from which absurdity was born, were also the basis for the only form of transcendence available. His subject was imperfection and incompletion, social realities but, more disturbingly, metaphysical truths. And this was what he meant by saying that he was more interested in man's relationship to God than man's relationship to man. Far from showing a disregard for such relationships he was stating his conviction that the former determines the latter. Identity might be socially defined but the individual has to choose to submit himself to the social world. Since there is no god in O'Neill's universe, the crucial act of definition derives from the individual's sense of his own meaning – his decision as to whether to capitulate, to avoid the paradox of the absurd by becoming, in effect, inanimate, freezing selfhood into a compacted past, or whether to challenge it by entering the imperfect world of historical time and personal relationships.

By the nature of things this paradox resisted resolution. The fact that so few of his plays end with any sense of real completion is thus a logical expression of a vision which committed the individual to an unending struggle. It was Schopenhauer who had characterised that world:

> For as every body must be regarded as the manifestation of a will, and as will necessarily expresses itself as a struggle, the original condition of every world that is formed into a globe cannot be rest, but motion, a striving forward in boundless space without rest and without end.[158]

And it was Thomas Mann who identified the connection between Schopen-hauer and those other primary influences on O'Neill's imagination, Nietzsche and Freud:

> Schopenhauer, as psychologist of the will, is the father of all modern psychology. From him the line runs, by way of the psychological radicalism of Nietzsche, straight to Freud and the men who built up his psychology of the unconscious and applied it to the mental sciences. Nietzsche's antisocratism and hostility to mind are nothing but the philosophic affirmation and glorification of Schopen-hauer's discovery of the primacy of the will.[159]

For O'Neill the struggle remained a central fact of existence but it became a struggle in which the will could operate as something other than a thirst for power. It became a resistant force, a boundary marking a clear-edged division between man and the absurdity which suffused and defined him but to which he was not obliged to submit. But the temptation was strong as *Hughie* indicated. Typically, if his last plays showed a genuine glimpse of hope they also revealed the depth of suffering and despair with which he wrestled.

For Georg Lukács, 'it is a formal principal of epic and drama that their con-struction be based on a plot'. Questioning whether or not this is merely a formal requirement, he comes to the conclusion that it is not, for 'when we analyse this formal requirement precisely in its formal abstractness, we come to the conclusion that only through plot can the dialectic of human existence and consciousness be expressed, that only through a character's action can the contrast between what he is objectively and what he imagines himself to be, be expressed in a process that the reader can experience'.[160] Otherwise the writer would either be forced to take his characters as they take themselves to be and thus present them from their own limited subjective perspective, or he would have to assert the contrast between their views of themselves and an unproblematic reality and would not be able to make his readers experience that contrast. But for O'Neill, the dialectic is less between self and society than contained within the psyche. The mask is an image of this doubleness. And though many of his plays are heavily plotted, he began his career with plays in which the plot was minimal – more especially in *Moon of the Caribbees* – and ended with a play, *Hughie*, in which the absence of plot becomes a metaphysical assertion. The mask finally constitutes a total account of the real. There is no external world. The individual addresses only himself.

For Lukács, art is an engagement with a public world. For O'Neill the dissonance is of a different order. The character's view of himself is a total truth because the world has become subjective. For Lukács, plot has a central role to play in exposing social process: for O'Neill, process can be conveyed by an image, a tableau. Plot becomes parody. The assumption of a genuine dialectic between inner and outer world, a basic tenet of O'Neill's work, in effect disappears with *Hughie*.

Lenin once remarked that if the appearance and essence of things coincided, then science would not be necessary. The same might be said of culture. So that it is possible to see a play like *Hughie* as an expression of O'Neill's sense of cultural collapse, equally conveyed by writers like Ionesco and Beckett. Appearance and essence coincide. The play also stands as an expression of O'Neill's fear of the final futility of art in that its subject is a story-teller whose stories never communicate. For O'Neill, who had in many ways lost touch with the American public, it was an expression of a genuine fear and a dramatisation of an absurdity which invaded even the art generated to resist it. For a Marxist critic, O'Neill's sense of absurdity would doubtless be linked to his generalised assaults on materialism and the dialectic restored by positing a world whose social and economic determinisms were the prime cause of a deracinated self. But he was not concerned, in *Hughie*, with offering either a slice of life realism or a social critique. In his cosmology the many mansions of heaven have shrunk to the rooms of a seedy hotel, or the solitary cell of the self – an implacable prison not subject to transformation. It was not his last word on man but it did express his sense of an ever-present potential. The two men in this play deaden themselves, destroy all thought, obliterate their humanity. They become mere role-players, elaborating fictions and hoping to evade the absurd by compounding it. Love becomes either simple lust or meaningless domestication. The resistant self has collapsed. It was a view of life to which he was drawn but his final plays, for the most part, do not rest in this mode. He still identified a source of resilience in *A Touch of the Poet* and *Moon for the Misbegotten* or a quality of compassion which went beyond stoicism in *The Iceman Cometh* and *Long Day's Journey*, and these latter remain not merely two of O'Neill's best plays but two of the best plays to have emerged from America.

3 The Theatre Guild and its playwrights

The Washington Square Players were founded in 1915. Their manifesto declared that standards in the American theatre could only be raised by experiment and initiative. Their policy with regard to plays was to produce only those works with 'artistic merit', a platitude which derived its meaning from the depressed state of the American theatre. They survived for four years, during that time producing sixty-two one-act plays and six longer ones. Thirty-eight of these were by American authors. They collapsed under the pressure of the First World War which deprived them of actors and, to an extent, of an audience.

Immediately after the war, however, in December 1918, a meeting was held to discuss the establishment of a new group whose roots were deep in another institution as well. Three of the six directors and several of the playwrights (Philip Barry, Sidney Howard and S. N. Behrman) were products of Professor Baker's Workshop 47. The title Theatre Guild was chosen because it suggested the co-operative organisation and craftsmanship of the medieval trade guilds. It was to be a commercial theatre in so far as it was to be self-supporting, relying substantially on a subscription audience, but its professional standards were to be high and it was to concentrate on plays not likely to secure commercial production. It was hostile to the star system and developed its own actors though not its own acting style – its failure to do so precipitating the establishment of the Group Theatre from its own ranks. Its standards were such, however, as to lead both Bernard Shaw and Eugene O'Neill to entrust it with the production of some of their major works.

The first production, *The Bonds of Interest* by Benavente, opened on 14 April 1919. Its second play, too, was by a non-American, St John Ervine, and was so successful that the group transferred to a larger theatre – a move which, in the eyes of some, suggested a commercial instinct which cast doubts on its claims as an art theatre. And, indeed, the Guild was essentially a production company not especially concerned with fostering American drama but rather with bringing to the American public the best of world drama, past and present. As Walter Pritchard Eaton remarked, in his essay on the first ten years of the Guild:

> they could not experiment with undeveloped native work, however promising, as an amateur group could do, because they were definitely pledged to the subscribers to produce finished entertainment...It was not in their minds, at any time, an experimental theatre in the sense of trying out new, undeveloped work.

It was an experiment in establishing a theatre dedicated to good drama on a permanent basis, and part of their pride in being self-supporting was, and is, based on the belief that by depending on the public for support you keep yourself anchored to the consolidated artistic gains of the present, however much you may reach out toward the future. Accordingly the Guild had to endure more or less in silence the frequent charges that they were 'un-American' and to go ahead proving that good drama, written with distinction and intellectual point, would pay in America, and especially pay in their theatre, hoping that ultimately American authors of capacity would write such drama, and be willing to submit it to them. If you like, their influence was indirect. But it was an influence and a profound one.[1]

One of its principal playwrights, Eugene O'Neill, whose first Guild play was not produced until 1928, had of course been discovered elsewhere, but nonetheless the Guild was to prove responsible over the years for a number of crucial productions of American plays. It spun off one of the most important companies in American theatre history – the Group Theatre – and it remained a constant influence for good on the standards of American production. It built its own theatre by selling bonds and by 1926 was in a position to establish the nucleus of a permanent company. It began to stage productions in other cities so that Lawrence Langner could boast that while

The Washington Square Players, in the year 1914, produced a program of one-act plays in the little Band Box Theatre, seating 299 persons; its direct lineal descendant, the Theatre Guild, in the year 1929, is providing ten of the large cities in the United States with a program of from five to six artistic plays of the kind not ordinarily produced in the commercial theatre, acted by some of the best acting talent available in the country, and running for seasons of from five to fifteen weeks outside New York, to a full season of 30 weeks in New York itself.[2]

The Guild developed no social or aesthetic programme. It staged a propaganda play, Tretyakov's *Roar China*, a political melodrama, Kirchon and Ouspensky's *Red Rust*, but equally it staged Shaw's plays, historical dramas by Maxwell Anderson, and frivolous revues. It discovered few new playwrights and its production methods were frequently bitterly attacked by writers who objected to a committee structure which meant that, even after being accepted for production, plays were likely to be severely criticised by members who had not favoured their acceptance. Eventually, embittered by this, and by the peremptory refusal of some of their plays, a number of writers who had come to think of themselves as Guild playwrights broke away to form their own production company, The Playwrights' Theatre, just as some of the more adventurous directing and acting talent left to form the influential Group Theatre. Strictly speaking, there were no Guild playwrights but a number of American writers were frequently produced by the

12. Theatre Guild production of Tretyakov's *Roar China* at the Martin Beck Theatre, 27 October 1930. Settings and costumes by Lee Simonson. Among the sailors was Clifford Odets.

Guild and benefited greatly from the arena offered by a production company which offered high standards and which, for the most part, rose to the challenge of work which might have had great difficulty securing a Broadway production.

The American theatre was born at a time of crisis. It was the immediate heir to the break-up of the liberal synthesis. The small town had given way to the anonymous city; the independent farmer to the industrial worker. Historicist convictions seemed to have foundered on the reality of geo-political conflict. The spaces, physical and social, which the nineteenth-century theatre in America had celebrated, had now disappeared. The frontier had been closed for a generation. The determinants of contemporary existence made the moral pieties of melodrama manifestly inadequate. Self-sufficiency and ethical independence, which had been national totems, now survived as ironic myths. It was a world without confidence. Truths carried into war had apparently disintegrated in an anarchy which allowed no room for definitional gestures and no time for personal dignity. It was perceived by Hemingway as essentially a non-tragic, indeed an anti-tragic age. The density of characters was attenuated. The novel was full of individuals deploying roles, theatricalising themselves as a protection against the real, as a strategy for resisting that personal commitment which could only precipitate vulnerability and exacerbate a fundamental absurdity. Language became deeply

122

suspect as an expression of reality. If a gulf had manifestly opened up between beauty and truth so it had between reality and truth, between language and essence. For some the only value lay in a self-created world, or in an art which could sustain an order no longer credible in the external world.

There was a pressure to abstract the self from its context, to see the individual outside of history. But for the most part the consequence was a destructive irony, presented as a failure of imagination and morality alike. The theatre likewise displayed characters under pressure. Modernity, once welcomed as a kind of pure energy which could be converted into dynamic motion, into technological marvels or into a sustained pressure against the boundaries of the possible, was now regarded as an entropic force. The old America was dead: on that there was a reasonable unanimity (Saroyan notwithstanding). But the new America struggling 'towards birth was deeply ambiguous. The machine, at first welcomed as a kind of generator of positive energy, was viewed more sceptically. Henry Adams's dynamo gave way to O'Neill's, crucifying its worshippers. Indeed, for O'Neill and for Elmer Rice, the individual not only served the machine, he stood in danger of being changed into it. The forced collision of ideal and reality threatened a genuine collapse of morale.

The dominant image was likely to be the cage, the machine, the drifting ship, the petrified forest, the tenement room, the urban street. In O'Neill's world language itself was in decay. Yet this also seems to have inspired a reactive assertion of the survival of values, though seldom, it must be said, one which was rooted in a practical perception of social realities. Hence Robert Sherwood, a pacifist, can envisage a state of grace but it is one which never really grows into a public posture – never, that is, until another war made it necessary to breathe life into liberal principles which in the immediate aftermath of the First World War he had been happy to consign to the dustbin of history and which thereafter he had left at the level of simple piety. Another world could be imagined, then, but virtually no American playwright could conceive of the necessary mechanism for precipitating out a practical world from a bland moralism. Hence, for Philip Barry and William Saroyan the old varieties had never died, simply been foolishly discarded. Though the former acknowledges a social dislocation ignored by the latter, they both assume the survival of values and assert a social and moral cohesiveness. For Thornton Wilder social dislocations are, anyway, rendered insignificant by a principle of continuity which denies the pressures of the immediate and the actual felt so acutely by some of his contemporaries. For Paul Green and Marc Connelly the harsher realities could be side-stepped through resort to fantasy. Even the committed writers of the 1930s rarely succeeded in shifting from rhetoric to realised action. But they did respond to a basic failure of connectiveness which O'Neill saw as primal and metaphysical and which they were prone to see as practical and social. For O'Neill the sense of loss is expressed in a momentary feeling for the natural world, by a wistful longing for which no objective correlative can be located. It is a world in which the relationship between man and environment had been destroyed – a theme which runs through American drama from O'Neill through Sidney Kingsley and Elmer Rice to Arthur Miller and Tennessee Williams. For the committed writers of the 1930s, however, that loss is seen as a sense of alienation bred by social injustice. No longer concerned, as was O'Neill, with the relationship between man and God, they pursue a more immediate and presumably rectifiable failure of relationship – that between man and man. Hence the transition from a metaphysical to an essentially social drama, though as will become apparent the line between the two is not as sharp as it might appear. The survival of spiritual integrity remains at the heart of both enterprises.

Erich Fromm in his 1942 book, *The Fear of Freedom*, identified this shift of emphasis:

> Primary bonds once severed cannot be mended; once paradise is lost, man cannot return to it. There is only one possible, productive solution for the relationship of individualized man with the world: his active solidarity with all men and his spontaneous activity, love and work, which unite him again with the world, not by primary ties but as a free and independent individual.[3]

This was certainly the path taken by the American theatre of the 1930s. But, disguised as Marxist homilies, these were often attempts to breathe life into familiar American pieties. The social world indeed was an attempt to locate a substitute for the natural world and the language of the one was frequently appropriated by the other. Clifford Odets's encomiums to a vaguely felt sense of human brotherhood, to a renewed sense of commitment, were more spiritual than material. Indeed they were not finally as remote from the images displayed by Thornton Wilder as he would have wished. And certainly there were few writers who acknowledged the special menace, the essential escapism, of their commitments to an ideological position which contained its own threat.

As Erich Fromm remarked,

> if the economic, social and political conditions, on which the whole process of human individuation depends, do not offer a basis for the realization of individuality in the sense just mentioned, while at the same time people have lost those ties which gave them security, this lag makes freedom an unbearable burden. It then becomes identical with doubt, with a kind of life which lacks meaning and direction. Powerful tendencies arise to escape from this kind of freedom into submission or some kind of relationship to man and the world which promises relief from uncertainty, even if it deprives the individual of his freedom.[4]

It was certainly a risk and if few American playwrights became simply servants of an ideology whose absolute demands became an essential part of its attraction, they were drawn to images of communality which could, it seemed, only be sustained through a radical simplification of the sensibility which sought such an absolution. It was an intellectual and perhaps even a moral weakness. It was certainly a dramatic weakness, few of these plays surviving the era which generated them.

It remains true that the central theme of twentieth-century American drama is alienation: man from God, from his environment, from his fellow man and from himself. This could, of course, be taken as an account of the various stages of Eugene O'Neill's career but it is equally a description of the tradition which begins with O'Neill and runs through Odets and Hellman to Miller and Albee. Again, this is a process which Fromm describes with clarity.

> Not only the economic, but also the personal relations between men have this character of alienation; instead of relations between human beings, they assume the character of relations between things. But perhaps the most important and the most devastating instance of this spirit of instrumentality and alienation is the individual's relationship to his own self. Man does not only sell commodities, he sells himself and feels himself to be a commodity...the business man, the physician, the clerical employee, sell their 'personality'...This personality should be pleasing...Thus, the self-confidence, the 'feeling of self', is merely an indication of what others think of the person. It is not *he* who is convinced of his value regardless of popularity and his success on the market. If he is sought after, he is somebody; if he is not popular, he is simply nobody.[5]

This is, of course, essentially the position of Willy Loman, in Miller's *Death of a Salesman*, desperately clinging to the conviction that he is 'well liked' because this is the only valuation which he can accept as having any value. It is a fiat the more absolute for being internalised. But his marginality is so much that of so many other figures in American drama that he becomes paradigmatic. Odets's and even Rice's characters think to neutralise this with the assertion of their participation in a wider struggle. Such declarations carry little conviction, the more especially since both writers are so adept at depicting the implacable economic and social realities which confront their characters. The secularisation of desires clearly opens up an area of guilt which the American dramatist could never believe to be expiated through a simple restoration of social justice, whatever the surface logic of his play.

The American theatre of the 1920s and 30s was a curious amalgam of embittered social analysis and confident moralism, sometimes coexisting in the same play. On the whole, 1920s drama shared that conviction about the collapse of social connectiveness and a sustaining sense of moral or imaginative energy to be found in the novel. The image of sexual impotence operates in both. And there is a clear parallel between Sinclair Lewis's *Babbitt* and Elmer Rice's *The Adding Machine*. But there is a stronger assertion of the survival of values, a more confident insistence on a resistent liberalism than one could find in Dreiser, Fitzgerald, Hemingway or West. And though the Theatre Guild embraced no specific ideological stance its major playwrights expressed this ambivalence as profoundly as most.

ELMER RICE

Elmer Rice was an amazingly prolific writer. Best known for two plays, *The Adding Machine* (1923) and *Street Scene* (1929), he was in fact the author, by his own account, of some fifty full-length plays, four novels and a book about the theatre (*The Living Theatre*), an output attested to by several drawers full of index cards in the Humanities Research Center at Austin, Texas. Rice was stylistically eclectic, but philosophically located himself essentially in the same territory as Clifford Odets. What seemed at times, and particularly in *We, The People* (1933), to be radicalism was in fact a desire for the restoration of American idealism, for liberal principles undermined by urbanism and industrialism. There is, indeed, ample evidence of that nostalgia for a lost world which runs throughout twentieth-century American drama. In Rice's work this constitutes a gravitational pull towards the sentimental which constantly threatens to relax a crucial tension. As he has said explicitly of *We, The People*, it was intended to be 'a panoramic presentation of the economic and social situation in America, an exposé of the forces of reaction which stand in the way of a better life for the masses of the American people and a plea for a return to the principles enunciated in the Declaration of Independence and the Constitution'.[6]

The Adding Machine, a Theatre Guild production, is an expressionistic fantasy about a man pointedly called Mr Zero whose life has added up to nothing. Displaced from his job after twenty-five years by the introduction of mechanical adding machines, he murders his employer, is tried, executed and finds himself in the Elysian Fields. A Babbitt figure, he carries his prejudices with him even here and is dispatched back to earth with the same slave mentality which has apparently characterised him in successive incarnations. He is held to his vacuous existence by a groundless and vague hope, and by a none-too-powerful sexual instinct which reconciles him to his fate. And he is surrounded by figures who are indistinguishable from him in their empty conformity and vapid lives. It is, on the face of it, an absurdist play not remote in spirit from Ionesco's *The Bald Prima Donna*.

But Rice is in fact more of a satirist than an absurdist. He is closer in spirit to Sinclair Lewis than to Beckett, as he made plain in an article which he published in the *New York Times* in 1938:

13. Theatre Guild production of Elmer Rice's *The Adding Machine* at the Garrick Theatre, New York, 1923. Scene 4, with Dudley Digges as Zero.

> What I have been trying to say is simply that there is nothing as important in life as freedom and that the dominant concern not only of every human being, but of all of us as we function as members of society should be with the attainment of freedom of the body and of the mind through liberation from political autocracy, economic slavery, religious superstition, hereditary prejudice and herd psychology and the attainment of freedom of the soul through liberation from fear, jealousy, hatred, possessiveness and self-delusion. Now that I have stated it, I see that I was right in saying that everything I have ever written seriously has had in it no other idea than that.[7]

Clearly this statement says a great deal about the mood of the times but it did adequately describe the essence of his position, which was a liberal humanist revolt against the reductivism of material life. In his book, *The Living Theatre*, Rice singled Lewis out for special mention alongside Harold Stearns's *Civilization in the United States*, in which some thirty critics and specialists had come to the conclusion that 'the most amusing and pathetic fact in the social life of America today is its emotional and aesthetic starvation'.[8] Also influential was Capek's *RUR*, produced by the Theatre Guild only five months previously, which had also presented an image of man as a

14. Elmer Rice's *Street Scene*, New York, 1929. Setting by Joe Mielziner.

social mechanism, but Rice denied the direct influence of German expressionists. His own play was, he said, written in the 'stylized, intensified form loosely known as expressionism, though I had hardly heard the term at the time. It was a compound of comedy, melodrama, fantasy, satire and polemics'.[9] In a memorandum to Dudley Digges, who was to play the part of Mr Zero, Rice wrote:

> What we must convey...is a subjective picture of a man who is at once an individual and a type...In the realistic play, we look at the character from the outside. We see him in terms of action and of actuality. But in the expressionistic play we subordinate and even discard objective reality and seek to express the character in terms of his own inner life. An X-ray photograph bears no resemblance to the object as it presents itself to our vision, but it reveals the inner mechanism of the object as no mere photographic likeness can.[10]

Though acknowledging Theodore Dreiser's *Plays of the Natural and Supernatural* (1916) as a source, Rice claimed for himself an important role, alongside O'Neill and John Howard Lawson, in introducing expressionism to America.

The Adding Machine was produced by the Theatre Guild. Rice had much more trouble finding a producer for *Street Scene*. The play was set in a New York brownstone tenement building but it was no more concerned with slum dwellers than *Awake and Sing* was to be. Rice took as his central characters the same lower middle-class characters, trapped in a seemingly hopeless environment, as Odets was to do. Within the house are an Italian violinist with a German wife, a Russian–Jewish radical whose daughter is a school-teacher and whose son is a law student, an Irish–American stagehand whose daughter works in a real estate office, a shopkeeper with a son who drives a taxi, a Swedish janitor, and so on. In addition, the frame of the drama is filled with minor characters who pass and repass. If, as Rice claimed, the house was itself in some degree to be the central character and the unifying factor, the play was an attempt to capture America, almost in a Whitmanesque way, by sheer inclusiveness. But against this was to be enacted a double drama – an inadequate love-affair between the stagehand's daughter and the radical's son, and a murder committed by the girl's father, who kills his wife and her lover. Both the size of the cast and the conception of the play discouraged backers. Eventually Rice directed the play himself, and it had a considerable critical and popular success.

He aimed at a denseness of events, a profusion of character and collage of plots partly in order to recreate the social texture of the world of the tenement and partly to suggest the degree to which that variousness was homogenised by context. It was not to be simply a realistic play. Indeed Rice resisted the idea of simply copying an existing tenement building in order to create the set. It was a conscious effort to raise that setting to the level of symbol. In an early draft of the play, then called *The Sidewalks of New York*, there was to be no dialogue – simply a series of situations linked by the determining presence of the tenement. And though Rice abandoned this idea, he did claim the play as essentially experimental, explaining that 'instead of unity of action, there was a multitude of varied and seemingly irrelevant incidents'. Blending and arranging these unrelated elements into a patterned mosaic and introducing the many characters in a seemingly natural way posed technical problems of the greatest difficulty. 'The play is,' he asserted, 'the most experimental I have ever attempted, a fact not readily apparent to the reader or spectator, for its construction depends not upon novel or striking technological devices, but upon concealed architectonics.'[11] And indeed it was a play which relied on collage and on a careful orchestration.

Rice was very close in spirit to Odets. Like Jacob in *Awake and Sing*, his radical character is allowed a perception which never moves from language to action. His becomes just one response among many to the circumstances in which he finds himself. Like Odets, Rice was concerned in *Street Scene* with the hyphenated Americans in their struggle to discover the essence of the world to which they wish to assimilate themselves. The young girl, tempted to succumb to the unsubtle sexual advances of her employer, asks a question which could equally have come from any Odets hero or heroine: 'Why must people always be fighting and having troubles, instead of sort of being happy together?'[12] The answer lies in the same bland assurance that self-knowledge is all. As the same girl eventually learns, 'I don't think people ought to belong to anybody but themselves. If you'd only believe in yourself a little more, things wouldn't look nearly so bad. Because once you're sure of yourself, the things that happen to you aren't so important. The way I look at it, it's not what you'll do that matters so much; it's what you are'[13] – a position, of course, which neatly undercuts a radical stance. Her decision to leave New York is equally an evasion as the playwright relaxes the tension implicit in his own central image and permits himself a solution which implies the possibility of escape through simple movement which is a denial of the basic strategy of the play which otherwise ends with a new family moving into newly vacated rooms in the tenement.

Elmer Rice had little time for the Theatre Guild. To his mind it had failed in what should have been its principal objective. In a letter which he wrote to Barrett Clark in January 1930, he said:

> there seems to be no good reason why I or any American playwright should ever submit a play to the Guild. The Guild in its entire career has done nothing whatever to encourage the American playwright nor to help foster a native drama. It has drawn its support from the American public and has consistently refused a hearing to practically every American author of promise. My own case is typical. After the production of The Adding Machine, the Guild refused production to The Subway, Baa, Baa Black Sheep, Life is Real, Helen and John, Street Scene and See Naples and Die. Admitting the imperfections of all these plays, they certainly represent as high a level of achievement as do the dull and piffling European farces and costume plays which for years have represented the Guild's stock-in-trade.
>
> Furthermore, the Guild, in my opinion, no longer has any claim to be called an art theatre. It has become a large scale commercial producing organization, dominated by box-office policies and using all the familiar devices of ballyhoo and high-pressure salesmanship. It has become timid, respectable and conservative.
>
> Considering the Guild, therefore, as a purely commercial producing organization, I find I can sell my wares to better advantage elsewhere. I receive from the so-called Broadway managers, not only more courteous treatment and more prompt action, but much more favourable terms. Consequently, I cannot as I said, see what I have to gain by submitting my plays to the Guild.[14]

It was a complaint which would be repeated and one which did identify a basic ambivalence in the Guild's policies as it did, of course, in the attitude of Rice who complained of the Guild's placing money before art while endorsing those Broadway producers who did likewise. His letter also glosses over the difficulties which he had had over Street Scene while his collaboration in the founding of the Playwrights' Producing Company in 1938 revealed his jaundiced view of the commercial theatre which he here uses to belabour the Theatre Guild. Rice's real view of the Theatre Guild is clear from John Wharton's account of that company, Life Among the Playwrights. The Guild may indeed have proved unadventurous but their production of *The Adding Machine* proved crucial for Rice while, despite his prolific production of plays, he never regained the reputation which had resulted from that production.

PHILIP BARRY

Two of Philip Barry's plays were produced by the Guild, though his reputation had preceded the occasion of the first Guild production. Barry came from an upper middle-class Irish Catholic family. He attended Yale University and subsequently Professor Baker's Workshop 47. He shared with Scott Fitzgerald a fascination with the rich but lacked Fitzgerald's conscience which made him see wealth as a source of corruption, an evidence that the age of the Caesars had arrived. Barry escaped Spengler's influence and filled his plays with wealthy people who for the most part felt no twinge of social guilt and revealed themselves as articulate and witty individuals comfortably immune to the economic necessities and moral conflicts of the poor. At his best in high comedies of manners like *The Philadelphia Story* (1939) and *The Animal Kingdom* (1932), Barry was also drawn to more profoundly speculative pieces like *Hotel Universe* (1930) and *Here Come the Clowns* (1938). His humour was carefully calculated, his characters seldom more than vehicles for his wit or for metaphysical speculation. There was a dark side to his life and his work. His young daughter died and there are traces of the pain that this caused both in the introduction of this fact into his work and in the speculation on human suffering which becomes the intellectual, though hardly the emotional, subject of that work.

In a sense *Hotel Universe*, produced by the Guild in 1930, is built on a cliché – the suggestion that the rich and powerful are ravaged by self-doubt and existential despair. It was not a theme which one would have thought particularly appropriate to the year of its first production, and, indeed, it ran for only eighty-one performances. Today, I think, it seems a little mannered and precious, but it is not without interest in its incorporation of psychodramas, and its implication that the theatre perhaps has a therapeutic function, an Aristotelian argument unconsciously endorsed by much left-wing drama of the decade. Like much of the American theatre of the time it bears the mark of Freud, but here Barry is less interested in individual psychology than he is in a sense of cultural *Angst*. He was immune to the bitter economic realities of his day. Like Hemingway he seemed to feel that he had served his time for democracy (he served as a cipher clerk in the London embassy during the First World War) and felt little obligation to join his voice to those of the committed writers who felt the necessity to offer their talent to the cause of the oppressed. Indeed he wrote *Hotel Universe* in Cannes in 1929.

It is a play about the glittering people, those with whom he never tired of associating. All the characters are described as 'lovely', 'handsome', 'rather pretty' or of 'amiable good looks'. The least of them has a 'certain prettiness'. But they are infected by a sense of unease, a self-questioning prompted by the suicide of a young man who had dived into the sea because 'he's had just enough, that's all'.[15]

They are told that the villa they are living in had formerly been the Hotel de l'Univers, which local rumour suggests is a place in which 'people began to resemble other people and the place itself other places. And time went sort of funny. Their past kept cropping up.' And the play consists of such a series of re-enactments as the characters are made to face their self-doubts, betrayals and fears, reverting to childhood and reliving crucial incidents from the past. It ends with a faith pledged in the future, in new beginnings. As a result of these psychodramas they have been restored to themselves and to their condition and if serenity is not completely re-established at least despair has been sidestepped. Metaphysics defer once more to simple process. The story about the Hotel Universe is revealed as a mistake. The legend in fact applies to another building and they have, therefore, themselves created the cathartic pressures which leave them able to face the idea of death and hence able to confront the fact of life. Whatever has happened is thus less a consequence of magic than of the interaction of characters who have placed themselves under pressure. There is, then, presumably greater authenticity in the state in which they now find themselves.

The play is neatly constructed. The characters are witty. The shift into apparent unreality is accomplished with skill. And yet the total effect is one of inconsequence. It is a dramatic machine wound up for the entertainment of seeing it unwind itself. The psychological model is distressingly simple, like O'Neill's partially digested Freudianism. The characters are rooted in no experience, simply in a milieu. Their social vacuity, lost to the Barry who himself so admired this world, is the guarantee of their inconsequence as characters. Consequently the dramatic attention is thrown on the central conceit which is too insubstantial to bear the weight. *Hotel Universe* is urbane and sophisticated. Its effects are finely controlled but its profundities are signalled too directly, its characters too lightly sketched to sustain interest. Even restored to themselves as a result of their self-inflicted psychotherapy they reveal a shallowness which Barry fails to detect or to criticise. Fitzgerald was attracted to the rich; his saving grace was that he never saw them as simple, as the images which they themselves projected. It is not that Barry was a naturally comic writer who should not have strayed into serious matters but that he lacked the ability to question his own assumptions. The metaphysical was, for him, potentially an evasion.

In *The Philadelphia Story*, the most elegant of his comedies, and another

Theatre Guild production, Barry makes fun equally of radicals and of the rich, but he allows the latter the last laugh. Thus a young man, who calls himself a Jeffersonian democrat (as so many apparent radicals of the 1930s were in fact), suggests that 'the prettiest sight in this fine, pretty world is the Privileged class enjoying its privileges' only to be reminded that Jefferson had himself come from the same class. A stylish play, created as a vehicle for Katharine Hepburn, its moral seems to be that 'in spite of the fact that some- one's up from the bottom, he may be quite a heel. And that even though someone else's born to the purple, he still may be quite a guy.'[16] It was Barry's offhand response to the clichés of the 1930s but beyond that he had few pretensions to social or aesthetic revolt.

In the last resort Barry offered a kind of soft metaphysics – comedies of manners with aspirations to delve equally into the individual psyche and human frailty. But he resisted his own evident concern with a destabilising subconscious. He never permitted himself to question manners which had become values. The uneasy humour of *Hotel Universe* deferred to a wit which he declined to inspect for its social or moral meaning. That wit was very much the currency of the social world in which he moved but he shared the assumptions of that world too much to question its meaning or probe the insecurities which in part generated it. He was never simply a Broadway wit but equally never allowed his more profound concerns to disturb the surface of his work.

WILLIAM SAROYAN

For many writers in the 1930s drama was a pragmatic weapon, a somewhat blunt instrument. It was an intervention made necessary by a state of crisis. It was a moral and educative force which derived its energy from the public world. William Saroyan offers an altogether more patrician and lyrical justification for the harmony of art and politics. For him:

> Art and politics must move closer together. Reflection and action must be equally valid in good men if history is not to take one course and art another. The weakness of art is that great poems do not ennoble politics, as they should, and the trouble with politics is that they inspire poets only to mockery and scorn.... We have always believed that art should be one thing, religion one thing, and so on. This kind of isolation of entities, while convenient, is, I believe, foolish. All things must come together as one, which is man. The functioning of all things should be to the glory of living. Art is answerable to politics, and politics is answerable to religion, and all are answerable to man, so that when there is disgrace in life, as there is now, we are *all* guilty.[17]

Romanticism and existentialism combine. Art must intervene because it cannot abstract itself from the world which shapes it and which it shapes in a reciprocal relationship. And this is a product not of political exigencies but of the nature of art, though it was the pressure of the Second World War which precipitated the statement and which determined the nature of the appeal.

> Intelligence and grace...are the means of concealing disputes, which are un-imaginative *creations*, not realities. Political systems, however deeply and emotionally integrated in the legend and behaviour of a people, are worthless when they can survive only at the cost of the actual lives of the people they claim to protect. And yet we know one political system or another is still necessary for the management of the world. For this reason, art must enter the arena. It must be part of one large thing: the world and its management, life and its instruction. Art must not be a separate and special thing. The intention of art has always been to deepen, extend, elevate, ennoble, strengthen, and refresh the experience of living. It cannot begin to do these things until it accepts part of the management of the *physical* life of man, which is now in the hands of inferior men.[18]

Grace, it seemed, was to replace truth which had become too various and contradictory. It was not an approach likely to appeal to those for whom grace was precisely required to defer to truth. And Saroyan's social position seemed clear in his argument that the masses were committed to regimenta-tion, and resisted 'the kind of individual freedom the poet, for instance, must insist upon'. His argument in favour of 'truly superior men exerting a truly superior influence' smacked of an elitism at odds with the mood of the times. But his conservatism brought him to conclusions about the centrality of art not substantially different from the left-wing writers. The paramount need for Saroyan was 'to restore faith to the mass and integrity to the individual'.[19] It was an Arnoldian model of art. Art begins by being a personal exercise of grace for its creator, who in shaping experience shapes himself. Art 'must entertain as it instructs',[20] he insisted. But its function was not to respond to the immediate issue; it was to speak to the future.

> There are many who believe art cannot do anything about history. I am not one of these. I believe art can do a good deal about history. Art cannot charge with the infantry or roll along with the armoured car units of an army, but there has always been less charging and rolling in history than quietude and conversation; fewer parachute jumps and power dives, less strafing and bombing than poems and the reading of them...War is tentative. Aberration is tentative. Art is not tentative.[21]

Saroyan wrote these words when the war in Europe had been under way for nine months. He was clearly proposing a role for art which was less interventionist than that proposed by many writers of the 1930s. They were, at least ostensibly, interested in the immediate and the practical, in a unity forged out of shared deprivation, a vision of a transformed environment. He was concerned with transcendence, with a lyrical unity of spirit. But the lines intersected in a patent sentimentality. He dedicated his first play, *My Heart's in the Highlands* (1939), a Group Theatre production, to 'the pure in heart', to the 'poet in the world'. The irony is that beneath the realities of the urban environment which they reproduced with such care, this was no less true of Rice and Odets.

Saroyan, with measured assurance, announced that *My Heart's in the Highlands* was 'a classic', and, while admitting that 'it is surely impertinent of me to believe that the greater and truer American theatre shall begin its life after the appearance and influence of this play', confessed that 'God forgive me, that is what I believe.'[22] A slight work, it hardly sustains his claims for its significance. Set in Fresno, California, it concerns an unappreciated poet and his son Johnny, who barely survive on the charity of a local storekeeper of good heart, and on fruit stolen from local farmers. They are joined briefly by an old man who plays a bugle with such beauty and emotional power that the neighbours bring gifts of food. But he is sick and his powers are failing. He chooses to die a free man, however, and runs away from the old people's home where he lives. He expires surrounded by his new friends, speaking fragmented lines from Shakespeare. The play ends with the boy and his father dispossessed, aware that 'something's wrong somewhere', but setting off nonetheless into an indefinite future with spirits unbroken.

The critics were mostly baffled by a play which failed to develop a clear plot, to underline its meaning and to develop characters beyond the simplest of outlines. It was in fact a kind of tone poem, or argument, as he implied in an introduction, 'for integrity and reality, truth and imagination, in art, in living, and in the theatre'.[23] The value of the characters lies in their insistence on being themselves, refusing to concede anything to the values of the world they inhabit. The poet persists in the face of repeated rejections of his poetry; the bugler refuses to surrender his instrument. Their talent is recognised spontaneously by those in touch with the daily struggles of life. Described by virtually all reviewers as experimental, it was a radical break with the heavily plotted plays which preceded it but was close in spirit to Wilder's *Our Town*. It was also patently sentimental and naive. Its concern with the pure in heart lacked Tennessee Williams's acknowledgement of the power of the forces which confronted such individuals. And in that respect it reflected his sense of the European war which in some senses he regarded as a minor aberration. The moral of the play, he insisted, was that 'It is better to be a good human being than a bad one. It is just naturally better.'[24] But there is no attempt to understand what those terms mean. There is no room in the play for ambiguity, for a testing of the moral axes on which it supposedly depends. It is a moral tale drained of a moral sensibility.

If Saroyan thought *My Heart's in the Highlands* a crucial play in terms of the development of American drama he was ready to make a similar claim for the more successful *The Time of your Life* which was also a product of 1939. Like his first play it is about the good in heart. Set in a San Francisco bar it provides a comic counterpart to O'Neill's *The Iceman Cometh*, written in the same year. Gathered in the bar are a group of people who have never made it in the terms which society respects but who, like Steinbeck's lovable derelicts in *Sweet Thursday*, evidence a humanity lacking in the world beyond the swing doors of the bar. Outside America a war is being waged; in the streets strikers and police are clashing, while society makes sporadic efforts to enforce its lifeless standards. It is a world with 'No foundation. All the way down the line.'[25] Yet in Saroyan's eyes, stripped of money and pressed to the margins of society, his social derelicts become mythical heroes re-enacting the essential qualities of America; what in a stage direction he calls the 'sorrowful American music'. Spiritually crippled by a society which has no place for them they battle on, making what they can of life but never becoming, like Tennessee Williams's Kilroy in *Camino Real*, simply victims, patsies made the more pathetic by their lack of self-knowledge. A two-dollar whore refuses to accept this as an adequate description of herself, insisting that she is a former burlesque star as O'Neill's prostitutes, in *The Iceman Cometh*, prefer to be called tarts. But she knows her own falsehoods for what they are. The truth is, however, that the play wallows in sentiment. Lovers are united, the evil are defeated, goodness is triumphant. The play is a vaudeville piece, with cameo performances for song-and-dance men, musicians, comics. For Saroyan, though, these are America's mythic heroes. They are debased forms of the Hemingway hero playing the cards they have been dealt, exhibiting grace under pressure, improvising their lives, pressing experiences to extremes. The sentimentality of such a stance had always been clear in Hemingway. The spare prose style was in part his attempt to neutralise this. Saroyan uses the episodic vaudeville structure to achieve the same effect, as he does a dislocated lexis, a disjointed construction, a gulf between word and action. The comedian introduces comic monologues which are painfully devoid of humour but rich with social observation. A young man's comic pursuit of women conceals a painfully fragile sensibility. The style of the play is almost epileptic. It moves in sudden spasms of energy. It has a neurotic intensity which makes the simplistic foundations on which it rests seem the more deeply suspect. Indeed it seems clear that Saroyan's dismissal of the public world – wilfully excluded by him as it is by his characters – is a means to reject the kind of complexity he wishes to avoid. He is happiest with conventional paradoxes – poor men whose faith in the future surpasses that of the rich, cynical humanists, soiled angels. He is made decidedly uneasy by formulations which do not depend on the distillation of pure thought or emotion.

Evil exists but beyond the threshold of his plays. Where it does enter briefly, as here in the form of Blick, a member of the vice squad, described succinctly in the case as 'a heel', it is with all the subtlety of a morality play. And that indeed is what Saroyan's plays are. The naivety, seen as part of the charm of his characters, and certainly an aspect of their weakness, is a function of this. And his description of the atmosphere in the bar exemplifies equally his approach to character:

> The atmosphere now is one of warm, natural, American ease; every man innocent and good; each doing what he believes he should do, or what he must do. There is deep American naïveté and faith in the behaviour of each person. No one is competing with anyone else. No one hates anyone else. Every man is living, and letting live. Each man is following his destiny as he feels it should be followed; or is abandoning it as he feels it must, by now, be abandoned; or is forgetting it for the moment as he feels he should forget it... Each person belongs to the environment in his own person, as himself.[26]

The model of human nature is not essentially different from that to be found in Odets, Rice or Behrman. Saroyan's contribution is to stress the theatrical dimension of character, its performative quality. His characters discover themselves through acting. They perform themselves. The energy which creates that performance is the energy which Saroyan counterposes to the destructive entropy of the purely material world. But the seductive quality of this energy, displayed with apparent carelessness, evades essential questions. It was, after all, singularly ill-suited to the situation in Europe. It was a view of human nature which few writers felt able to sustain in the post-war world. According to Budd Schulberg, indeed, the war was a personal and artistic blow to Saroyan; he 'couldn't write for it, couldn't write against it, couldn't write in it'. Schulberg, in fact, 'always thought of Bill Saroyan as a conscientious objector in uniform', who on one occasion had told him that, 'We don't belong in this thing at all.... After all, we're not soldiers, we're artists; artists don't belong to any sides of wars.'[27]

The 1930s was a magic decade for Saroyan, and this was precisely the difference between him and the good-hearted, whole-spirited people whom he celebrated but who were themselves grappling with problems more acute and real than he cared to acknowledge. He never recaptured the personal success which that decade had brought him. The death camps of Europe left a legacy with which his work was ill-designed to cope.

The son of an Armenian vineyard worker, he was exuberant. He took pleasure in an American language which was not the native language of his family. His early short stories which, typically, he regarded as the best ever written, appeared in the middle 1930s. For Bud Schulberg their essential theme was that 'the world is our oyster even if we never find a pearl'.[28] He was concerned with celebrating America. A man who believed himself the world's greatest living author was not likely to be overawed by the Depression, for it coincided with his own success as a writer. His commitment was to the pure in heart, to the people, rather than to any ideology or class. Despairing of his apoliticism Schulberg took him to a rally in support of the Loyalist cause in Spain only to be asked by Saroyan 'How can you be on one side or the other when the people are on both sides?'[29]

ROBERT SHERWOOD

Robert Sherwood was a member of the famous Algonquin Round Table (a group of writers who met regularly at the Algonquin Hotel, New York) before he had written a single play. His reputation was established initially as one of the first serious movie critics. He subsequently collaborated in producing scenarios for Hollywood and in 1924 was offered $2500 for rewriting the subtitles of the silent *The Hunchback of Notre Dame*, a modest introduction to the craft of writing dialogue.

His first produced play was *The Road to Rome* (1927), a play about Hannibal which was rejected by the Theatre Guild. Highly successful, it was followed by a series of disappointing works which managed little more than a few weeks' business (*The Love Nest*, 1927, 23 performances; *The Queen's Husband*, 1928, 125 performances; *Waterloo Bridge*, 1930, 64 performances; *This is New York*, 1930, 59 performances). It was not until *Reunion in Vienna* (1931) that he came close to rivalling the success of his first play. This time the Theatre Guild did agree to produce it, but the difficulties which he had adjusting to the committee system, and the virulence, in particular, of Lee Simonson's attacks on his work, led him later to join with other playwrights, equally disenchanted with the Guild's methods, to form the Playwrights' Producing Company.

Reunion in Vienna is a comedy, but the published version is preceded by a preface which is less concerned with identifying the genesis of a comic spirit than with justifying the play's sense of cultural decay. The play is set in Vienna on the one-hundredth birthday of the late Emperor Franz Joseph I. A ragged collection of aristocrats and court flotsam gather to celebrate their past glories. In order to invoke that past more brilliantly, they wish to bring together the wildly egotistical and partly mad Archduke Rudolph Maximilian von Habsburg, now a taxi driver, and Elena, who as Fraulein Verveson was once Rudolph's lover and his consort in wild exuberance, but is now the wife of Anton Krug, a psychoanalyst and one-time revolutionary and pacifist.

The play's humour derives from the tussle between Anton and Rudolph, the former relying on his somewhat dangerous conviction that people can be cured of their romantic attachment to past lovers by exposing them to the reality of those lovers in the present, the latter trusting to his old seductive powers, to the frisson of the illegitimate and the dominance of id over ego. Part of the play's effectiveness lay in Sherwood's refusal to offer a clear resolution. Beneath this level of effective but somewhat banal comedy there was indeed a more serious concern which justified the play's preface, though it hardly surfaced as a dominant theme in the play. For at one level Sherwood was contrasting the old romanticism with the new rationalism. He was setting side by side an effete, decadent culture and one which destroyed the spontaneous and undermined the moral conscience.

The Habsburgs represent an irrationalism which dismisses reality in the name of the senses and arrogates to the self all power and purpose. Anton Krug represents a detachment, a cold analysis, which fails to allow for the needs of the living organism. We are offered on the one hand a dangerous sentimentality and on the other a disturbing scientism. In the play itself this tends to be lost in the humour but the preface is more sober and reveals something of the moralism which grew progressively stronger in Sherwood's work. To his mind his was a generation which occupied a limbo-like interlude between one age and another. He had fought in the First World War and emerged from it a pacifist. He shared the cynicism of the immediate post-war writers but equally felt the insufficiency of such a posture, later accusing himself of complicity in a destructive negativism. Behind him he saw 'the ghastly wreckage of burned bridges' and ahead only the doubtful insights of rationalism or, in Europe, the 'anachronistic attempt to recreate the illusions of nationalism; people drugging themselves with the comforting hope that tomorrow will be a repetition of yesterday'.[30] The Habsburgs were the representatives of this tendency, this desire for the Caesars to return, which became an increasing concern of Sherwood, culminating in *Idiot's Delight*.

In America he found either cynicism or the sentimentalising of cynicism into a pose of aestheticised anguish; for him, Eliot's 'The Hollow Men' became an exemplary text. For a generation raised on the idea that science had replaced any other experience of faith, the betrayal of that faith in war had left them without a coherent and transcending faith. For Sherwood this was most effectively expressed by Joseph Wood Krutch's *The Modern Temper*. This acknowledged precisely that fear of rationalism which Sherwood himself felt. It was, he felt, a threat to the imagination. 'It would seem,' he lamented, 'that the only subjects now available for man's contemplation are his disillusionment with the exposed past and his disinclination to accept the stultifying circumstances of the revealed future.'[31] For many of his fellow writers Marxism constituted a possible resolution to this paradox. It was not an alternative that Sherwood could himself embrace. To him it was the 'ultimate ant-hill'. All that Sherwood could bring himself to endorse was the anarchistic spirit, the impulse, indeed, to be an artist at all in such a period, the impulse, in his play, that leads Elena to indulge in her own mischief-making, her own deliberate disorientation of her husband. Freud joins Marx as an enemy of the unpredictable.

What Sherwood looked for was a life which, in Whitman's words, was 'copious, vehement, spiritual, bold'.[32] Of the play itself he claimed that 'those who may read this play, or see it performed, may rest assured that it does not provide nor even attempt solution of the mess of problems touched upon in its preface. It is intended solely to inspire relieving, if morally un-profitable, contemplation of people who can recreate the semblance of gaiety in lamentably inappropriate circumstances.'[33] In fact the Vienna of the 1930s offered a not inappropriate setting for ideas which provide the context rather than the subject for his play. Like so many of his works it hinted at a serious-ness which it never fully engaged. The prefaces indeed tended to do the work which his plays failed to complete. He never entirely solved the problem of accommodating his increasingly serious philosophical and political views to his comic method. A bias towards caricature sits uneasily with his humanistic stance. Accused of writing sub-Shavian plays he could indeed be criticised for a somewhat unconvincing presentation of political positions.

In the introduction to *There Shall Be No Night* (1940) Sherwood remarked of this preface to *Reunion in Vienna* that 'In it I came closer than ever before to a statement of what I was trying to think and write...It has a considerable bearing on all that I have written since then.'[34] The sentiments to be found fully articulated in that preface, but only sketched in the play, found their way directly into his subsequent work, *The Petrified Forest* (1935) – *Acropolis* (1933) having folded after twelve performances. His argument about the fallibility of rationalism is now put into the mouth of a writer who meets his nemesis in the middle of the Arizona desert. The same character refers to Eliot's 'The Hollow Men'. The play is a dramatisation of Sherwood's con-viction that his was a transitional generation, ironically poised between equally unacceptable possibilities. It is offered as an allegory of the collapse of individualism, the rise of a destructive chauvinism and the distant threat of totalitarianism.

Alan Squier, a wandering writer, arrives at the Black Mesa Filling Station and Bar-B-Q in the desert in eastern Arizona. Here he meets Gabby Maple, a young girl whose romantic ideas are in danger of being crushed by the banality of her setting, by her father's prejudices and by the simple power of biological reality which will deflect her from her desire to escape. He leaves, but is forced to return by Duke Mantee and his gang who arrive, trapping them, together with a passing businessman and his wife. Mantee, like Squier is, as Sherwood indicates in his stage direction, 'condemned'. He is the representative of an America which has effectively died. Together, Mantee and Squier are the last survivors of an age of romantic self-sufficiency, and the petrified forest, which exists further down the same Arizona road, is offered as a patent image of their vestigial existence. As Squier observes in a speech which is singularly ill-suited to his audience of gangsters,

> I'm planning to be buried in the Petrified Forest. I've been evolving a theory about that that would interest you. It's the graveyard of the civilization that's been shot from under us. It's the world of outmoded ideas. Platonism – patriotism – Christianity – romance – the economics of Adam Smith – they're all so many dead stumps in the desert. That's where I belong – and so do you, Duke. For you're the last great apostle of rugged individualism.[35]

The hope for the future clearly does not lie with either of them. They exist in a devastated landscape which Squier relates to Penguin Island, Anatole France's allegorical, capitalist country which is destroyed in a cataclysm. And Sherwood clearly sees no hope in the communism naively endorsed by a passing customer, nor in the mindless jingoism of the Legion members who set out with such enthusiasm to destroy Mantee. The only source of renewal lies with Gabby, whose spirit has not yet been broken. As Squier insists, 'She's the future. She's the renewal of vitality – and courage – and aspiration – all the strength that has gone out of you. Hell – I can't say what she is – but she's essential to me, and the whole damn country, and the whole miserable world.'[36] Accordingly he persuades Mantee to shoot him, having signed over a life-insurance policy to the girl.

The play is simple melodrama, welded none too satisfactorily into a thesis drama which strains credibility. The Villon-reading waitress and the erudite novelist–philosopher coexist uneasily with the earthy Mantee not simply because they emerge from different experiences but because Sherwood manages the laconic language and physical directness of the gangster rather better than he does the rhetoric of Squier or the sentimental longings of the girl. The gulf between the two sets of experience is filled on the one hand by action, and on the other by a series of simple statements that suggest the allegorical overtones of the action. Besides the familiar absurdity of bringing together in a single setting the usual microcosm of individuals representative of different racial and philosophical positions (communists, protofascists, capitalists, criminals, lawmen, the old, the young, the romantic and sentimental, the brutally physical), the play never entirely succeeds in bringing the components into a satisfying relationship.

Sherwood was aware of his own weaknesses. As he confessed, in an interview for the *Herald Tribune*, 'The trouble with me... is that I start with a big message and end up with nothing but good entertainment.' But he was also conscious that in writing for Broadway he was engaged in an ungainly balancing act. 'Do the great run of theatregoers peel off their banknotes to see an Indian fight, a gunman, a millionaire, and an American Legionnaire symbolizing the passing of a world order?' he asked rhetorically. 'In a pig's eye! They come to see two parts of a highly improbable and sentimentalized romance stirred, like a martini, with one part gun-play. They don't want a message and, anyway, perhaps I didn't give it to them as I should have.' He felt, in particular, that he had failed in his intention to establish the young waitress as a legitimate and effective image of a possible future. As he said, 'I lost control of the idea, to a certain extent, just as I lost control of the theme of *Reunion in Vienna*, and made Lynn Fontanne's husband a man instead of a scientist.'[37] But starring Humphrey Bogart as Duke Mantee and Leslie Howard as Squier, the play was a considerable success, running for 197 performances and being sold to Hollywood for $110000.

With his next play he returned to the Theatre Guild. *Idiot's Delight* (1936) was his reaction to the situation in Europe. As a pacifist he found himself in an increasingly difficult position. The rise of fascism was alarming. In a sense it seemed the confirmation of the convictions which he had expressed in his plays. A decadent and ineffectual generation had ceded power to a new brutalism. The cynical withdrawal from idealism, the surrender of any notion of transcendent values, had simply left the arena clear for the unscrupulous and the violent. In fact he was hopelessly confused philosophically and politically. Alarmed at a new rationalism which would destroy all mystery and usurp the imagination he found it hard to conceive of the triumphant irrationalisms of fascism. Convinced of the need to oppose an historical process which seemed wholly destructive, he could conceive of no method of opposition beyond the quixotic gesture, the self-sacrifice which would generate new values. He was indeed unclear as to precisely what those values would be and how they could be realised. Both Squier and Mantee, at the end of *The Petrified Forest*, are defeated by the forces of reaction. It is hard to see how this can be dignified as a sacrifice when the values which they pass on are so fragile, remaining locked up in language and embodied in the person of a girl who believes paradoxically, with Squier and Mantee, that her freedom depends on money.

In *Idiot's Delight* he set himself a more difficult problem. Mussolini had already invaded Ethiopia. Hitler was poised for expansion. But he remained convinced of the necessity for pacifism, insistent on the virtues of the Sermon on the Mount. As he wrote at the time of the play's rehearsal, a comment quoted by John Mason Brown in his book on Sherwood, 'I believe in two things...true Democracy and true Christianity. I hope to God neither of them dies before I do. Certainly nothing can kill them but brutal stupidity... All I want to do do with my life is to go on attacking...betrayers of the human race...and expounding the simple doctrines of the Sermon on the Mount.' *Idiot's Delight* was to show that such a victory could be won with 'calmness, courage and ridicule'.[38] Not surprisingly, therefore, it was a play which, for all its success, is riddled with contradiction and unconscious ambiguity.

A group of people, again offered as a representative cross-section of political and philosophical positions, are stranded – this time in a hotel on the borders of Italy, Austria, Germany and Switzerland. There is a munitions manufacturer, a German doctor working on a cure for cancer, a French radical, some fascist troops and a troupe of American entertainers led by a man, reminiscent of Duke Mantee, whose cynical and detached exterior masks a humane character. The weakness of the play lies precisely in the adequacy of this description. Sherwood wrote of the arms manufacturer:

> I've been thinking about the character of Weber...wondering whether I should make him more sympathetic, more human. The answer is no. I believe that such people are the arch-villains of mortal creation, and since I believe that, why am I so scared to say so? It's just that recent theatrical tradition decrees that villains must be charming. What has clinched my determination is reading in *Time* a quotation from Sir Herbert Laurence of Vickers: 'The sanctity of human life has been exaggerated.' Such men are sons of bitches and should be so represented.[39]

The play is a moral melodrama. The French radical, himself a confused character given a jumble of contradictory views by Sherwood, is abruptly shot for insulting the fascists, a rhetorical gesture which accomplishes nothing. The English are represented by a honeymoon couple, oblivious to the developing situation. Only the American, Harry, ostensibly detached from the situation, identifies and represents a resistant humanity which will redeem the brutality around him. Having acknowledged that 'the precise trouble with the world today' is that, 'We have become a race of drug addicts – hopped up with false beliefs – false fears – false enthusiasms',[40] he expresses his conviction that nonetheless 'above everything else I've found faith. Faith in peace on earth and good will to men'.[41] The distinction between 'false beliefs' and this celebration of human faith in peace on earth is never established. And the insistence that the meek '*will* eventually inherit the earth' seems hopelessly inadequate in the face of the violence conveniently displaced off-stage – a piece of sleight-of-hand which is less a sign of his desire to resist melodrama than a confession that to intrude the realities of fascism would be to place a pressure on his Christian ethic which it would be incapable of sustaining. Harry's conviction that 'with dawn will come again the light of truth'[42] is a piece of vapid rhetoric which is not neutralised by the play's humour. When the arms manufacturer abandons a woman whose moral qualms have made her dangerous Harry puts himself in danger by staying with her. The play ends as bombs explode ever closer to the hotel and Harry and the woman sing 'Onward Christian Soldiers'. The ironies of this are curiously at odds with the play's central theme, and indeed in some ways expose the weakness of a play which, like his previous works, relies on the quixotic gesture and a personal commitment, both of which imply a resolution which the play cannot sustain. Such contradictions are rooted in Sherwood's sensibility, and the result was plays whose simplicities were only redeemed by wit and by a skilful control of structure. In no way innovative, he offered the absolution of moral seriousness in plays which combined sentimental personal drama with portentous allegory.

His ambiguities moved to some kind of resolution with his next play, *Abe Lincoln in Illinois* (1938), which constituted a development of his thinking rather than an abrupt reversal of the kind that Maxwell Anderson's *Key Largo* was to be in the following year. The pressure of events in Europe made equally impossible a pose of cynical detachment and a conviction that platitudes about human resilience could suffice in a world proving remarkably resistant to rhetoric. The story of Lincoln's rise to the presidency, indeed, dramatised as a struggle on Lincoln's part, with a natural pessimism, with a desire to remain uninvolved, was essentially Sherwood's own. In particular the play shows Lincoln, a man who, like Sherwood himself, had been shocked into pacifism by an early experience of violence, being brought to the conclusion that justice and freedom have their price. The first of his plays to be produced by the newly formed Playwrights' Producing Company, indeed the first production of any kind by that group, it could scarcely have appeared at a more appropriate time. For Sherwood's conversion from isolationism was equally an American experience, and his appeal to a national hero was hardly likely to receive anything less than total approval. The play ran for 472 performances and was his most successful play by far. Abraham Lincoln's final speech in the play was offered equally as a public rallying cry and an acknowledgement of a personal transformation:

> when threats of war increase in fierceness from day to day...I have tried to enquire: what great principle or ideal is it that has kept this Union so long together? And I believe that it was not the mere matter of separation of the colonies from the motherland, but that sentiment in the Declaration of Independence which gave liberty to the people of this country and hope to all the world. This sentiment was the fulfilment of an ancient dream, which men have held through all time, that they might one day shake off their chains and find freedom in the brotherhood of life. We gained democracy, and now there is the question whether it is fit to survive. Perhaps we have come to the dreadful day of awakening and the dream is ended...let us believe that it is not true! Let us live to prove that we can cultivate the natural world that is about us, and the intellectual and moral world that is within us, so that we may secure an individual, social and political prosperity, whose course shall be forward, and which, while the earth endures, shall not pass away.[43]

Sherwood followed this with *There Shall Be No Night* (1940), a play in which the central character, a pacifist scientist, comes to realise that appeasement can only result in the extinction of the principles which he values. Like its immediate predecessor it was awarded the Pulitzer prize. In a postscript to *Idiot's Delight* he had written that 'those who shrug and say, "War is inevitable", are false prophets', insisting that 'the world is populated largely by decent people, and decent people don't want war. They fight and die, to be sure – but that is because they have been deluded by their exploiters.' The exploiter could, it seemed, be defeated by 'calmness, courage and ridicule' and a display of those qualities by England, France, the Soviet Union, and the United States 'will defeat Fascism...and will remove the threat of war'.[44] By the time of *There Shall Be No Night* this was no longer a position which he could sustain. Indeed he was widely accused of betraying his long-standing pacifism and denying the experience of *Idiot's Delight*.

In an extensive preface to the published version he denied this, insisting that the new play was more properly seen as a sequel to *Idiot's Delight* rather than a denial of it. In an extended analysis of his moral and philosophic development he recalled an early cynicism for which the moralism of his plays was plainly offered as a form of expiation. But, in particular, he confessed to the bitterness of the moment in which he was forced to recognise the necessity to oppose fascism with force. He now found the basis for his optimism in the new spirit of awakened resistance, insisting that

> I believe that man, in his new-found consciousness, can find the means of his redemption. We are conscious of our past failures. We are conscious of our present perils. We must be conscious of our limitless future opportunities. We are armed with more bitter experience, more profound knowledge, than any generations that ever were in the history of the world. If we can't use this experience and this knowledge then the human story is finished.[45]

His strategy had changed; the tone was the same.

Though he continued to write for the theatre after the war, his career as a dramatist had effectively ended, being superseded by direct involvement in a public world from which his characters had so ostentatiously removed themselves. As the president of the Dramatists' Guild he pressed writers to lend their efforts to the battle against Hitler: 'Words which may originate in the minds of someone here in this room...may be brought to people of all kinds and kindreds who are hungry for them – who may be stimulated by them to a new faith in the brotherhood of life – who may, for all any of us can tell, be saved by them.'[46] He became a member of the Committee to Defend America by Aiding the Allies and on 10 June 1940 drafted an advertisement which appeared in major newspapers and which announced the need to 'Stop Hitler Now.' The advertisement was praised by President Roosevelt and for the next few years he worked as scriptwriter for the President, abandoning the theatrical for the political world.

Sherwood's work was strongly moral. It expressed a nostalgia for the values and for the world which he had first thought destroyed by the First World War. When Lindbergh and Ford campaigned against involvement in the Second World War he reacted against them not simply as appeasers but as worshippers of the machine. His plays tended in some sense to be set outside of time. Though the realities of history were acknowledged, they were kept at arm's length. The Arizona desert, the reception room of a Viennese apartment, a hotel room on the eve of war, were offered as being resistant to process. By degrees he came to feel that the values which he had thought destroyed and to which he paid some kind of homage in the rhetoric, though not in the action, of his plays could be exposed to historical process again, firstly in the safety of a historical drama, *Abe Lincoln in Illinois*, and then in a present in which the realities of warfare made it possible to articulate Jeffersonian principles which were once more declared to be national virtues. As a playwright and as a speechwriter he felt himself to be a spokesman for precisely that idealism which he had once thought to be betrayed by another war. The comedy drained from his work. In the words of the title of one of S. N. Behrman's plays, this was to be *No Time for Comedy*. But without the humour, the didacticism of Sherwood's plays was unrelieved. His work is peppered with overblown rhetoric, with undramatic arias. His situations and characters are frequently contrived, his allegories simplistic and his plots sentimental. He had no time for the experimentalism of O'Neill. He distrusted ideology and his work frequently expresses the contradictions of his philosophical position. At his best when working in a comic mode, he was capable of work with considerable popular and critical appeal, winning three Pulitzer prizes.

This was not a period which produced outstanding drama. Sherwood was not a major talent but he did express, more clearly than most, the conflicting forces in American society and the dilemma of the liberal moving from the bitter disillusionment of the 1920s to the renewed commitment of the late 1930s.

MAXWELL ANDERSON

In a sense Maxwell Anderson can be seen as evidence of a persistent desire to retreat from the modern, to evade the implications of a contemporary experience which seemed to imply discontinuity, social and moral disintegration. Despite an early realist comedy – *What Price Glory* (1924) – he was persistently drawn to the creation of pastiche Shakespeare, creating plays set in Tudor England or in America's past – a world in which he was not forced to confront the complexities of the moral world of the 1920s and 30s. But to him the theatre was essentially a moral force and in his 1947 book, *Off-Broadway*, he insisted on its essential didactic dimension.

> Analyze any play you please which has survived the test of continued favor, and you will find a moral or a rule of social conduct or a rule of thumb which the race has considered valuable enough to learn and pass along. Excellence on the stage is always moral excellence. A struggle on the part of a hero to better his material circumstances is of no interest in a play unless his character is some-how tried in the fire, and unless he comes out of his trial a better man. The moral atmosphere of a play must be healthy. An audience will not endure the triumph of evil on the stage.[47]

It is not an axiom that could be easily applied to his first Theatre Guild play, *Both Your Houses* (1933) but here the moral weight is born less by the plot than it is by Anderson's comic method. The play was an attack not only on the corruptions of the Hoover administration but on the American system of government itself. Through the eyes of a mid-Western idealist it exposed a system built on patronage, graft and corruption in which the national interest, if served at all, is merely a by-product of personal greed and regional avarice. It capitalised on a mood of disillusionment which had been expressed equally in Kaufman and Ryskind's *Of Thee I Sing*, which won the Pulitzer prize for 1931–2, and a movie called *Merry-Go-Round*, which was close enough to the plot of *Both Your Houses* (1933) to necessitate legal agreements to prevent a plagiarism suit before the Theatre Guild would go ahead with the production.

The play was a comedy but was as marked by Anderson's moralism as his more sombre verse tragedies. And Anderson had a genuine comic talent. Some of the funniest scenes of the earlier *What Price Glory*, which he had written with Lawrence Stallings, had been his.

Alan McClean is a college professor, dismissed for protesting at mis-appropriation of funds, who is consequently elected to Congress as a man who will stand up for his beliefs. The world he enters is wholly corrupt and he finds it impossible to operate without dirtying his own hands – a fact which leaves Anderson in a curious ideological position at the end of the play. McClean tries to defeat a 'pork-barrel' bill, firstly by voting it down in committee, and, when this fails, by so inflating it that it will collapse of its own accord. Just before a crucial vote, however, he is told that unless he releases his votes, Simon Gray, the committee chairman, who has tried to do battle with the system from within, will go to jail for corruption in connec-tion with a city bank which will collapse as a direct consequence of the bill's failure. The clash between his principles and his genuine concern for an individual who has remained as honest as possible in the circumstances should be crucial to an understanding of McClean. But Anderson fails to probe the issue, just as he seems deliberately to obscure the liberal congress-men's role in the bill's final passage. Anderson is finally not interested in his characters. They are pegs on which to hang his assault on the new Gilded Age. McClean remains a mystery – a man supposedly devoted to integrity who compromises his values with little compunction. The other congressmen are caricatures, though hardly ciphers. Indeed in the person of Solomon Fitz-maurice he created a figure which in large part accounted for the play's success. A larger-than-life figure, he turns up at his office with a jug of liquor and boasts openly of his corruption, regretting only that his ambitions have never been on a large enough scale: 'the sole business of government,' he explains, 'is graft, special privilege and corruption – with a by-product of order. They have to keep order or they can't make collections...What I'm most wrong about is I don't steal in a big enough way. Steal apples and they put you in jail – steal a nation and the hosts of heaven come down and line up under your banners.'[48]

The play is curious in its failure to have the courage of its own convictions. Its analysis seems to equate corruption with capitalism and to trace its history to origins in a material drive which was as powerful as the spiritual thrust of the early settlers. Hence Solomon explains that 'Brigands built up this nation from the beginning, brigands of a gigantic silurian breed that don't grow in a piddling age like ours! They stole billions and gutted whole states and empires but they dug our oil-wells, built our rail-roads, built up everything we've got and invented prosperity as they went along...Let the behemoths plunder so the rest of us can eat!' To this Anderson's tainted idealist can only reply, 'More people are open-minded nowadays than you'd believe. A lot of them aren't so sure we found the final answer a hundred and fifty years ago. Who knows what's the best kind of government? Maybe they all get rotten after a while and have to be replaced.'[49] The play is offered as a call to arms, as an attack on apathy, but it equivocates both over the nature of the new system which it suggests to be necessary and over the human resources which will facilitate this, since it presents a portrait of human nature as apparently in-eluctably drawn to the corrupt. It is not a subject which his comic method could adequately deal with. The play ends with the word 'Maybe'.

For some critics the play was anachronistic. The Roosevelt administration had already transformed the American political scene and Anderson himself, like Robert Sherwood, eventually became a speechwriter for the new Presi-dent. But it was a popular success and received the Pulitzer prize. Indeed, its sense of America as being on the edge of a new era was reflected in a great deal of 1930s drama which was just as ideologically confused as Anderson's. But, as he remarked, 'Every artist is at a loss in a confused civilization, but the playwright is in the worst plight of all.'[50] The implied 'plague on both your houses' leaves Anderson poised irreproachably outside the corruption which he observes as a social fact but never examines as a human reality. His distrust of government, repeated in his next play, *Valley Forge* (1934), is rooted in a distrust of human nature. And that distrust he seems to have felt able to deal with only in his verse plays, feeling, it seems, the inappropriateness of prose to the job of addressing problems which he chose to acknowledge here only in the immediate form of social corruption. *Both Your Houses* reveals a comic spirit in Anderson's work, equally evident in *What Price Glory*, which was never entirely absent from his work but which was increasingly subordinated to a concern with tragic potential. Like Robert Sherwood he also came increasingly to express the need for a commitment that went beyond vague expressions of the need for abstract values.

It is not hard to see why historical drama proved such a powerful attraction to Anderson. A pacifist and an irrepressible optimist, he was confronted by a reality which encompassed war and the Depression. Like Eliot, he was tempted to turn to a past which offered order, a time when history subordinated itself to the will of the individual, and a lyricism driven to the margin by the pressures of contemporary life. Like Eliot, too, he felt that the natural language of elevated thought was poetry. As he insisted:

> To me it is inescapable that prose is the language of information and poetry the language of emotion. Prose can be stretched to carry emotion and in some cases, as in Synge's and O'Casey's plays, can occasionally rise to poetic heights by substituting the unfamiliar speech rhythms of an untutored people for the rhythms of verse. But under the strain of an emotion the ordinary prose of our stage breaks down into inarticulateness, just as it does in life. Hence the cult of the understatement, hence the realistic drama in which the climax is reached in an eloquent gesture or a moment of meaningful silence.[51]

O'Neill, of course, made that inarticulateness an aesthetic instrument of some subtlety, but Anderson was suspicious of an attachment to the contemporary which he dismissed as simple journalism. To him an obsession with the immediate problems of American society was inimical to the basic function of theatre which was, in a broad sense, religious in so far as it was to concern itself with what he called 'the exaltation of the spirit of man'.[52] He was less interested in what the individual suffered than in what man could aspire to. And since he felt that such profundities were best approached through verse it was to verse tragedy that he looked to revive the theatre and to provoke a sympathetic response from the audience.

Winterset (1935), however, is located in the present, but offered as an attempt to write verse tragedy with a contemporary setting. It was his first real effort in this direction and he was not unaware of the difficulty of persuading an audience of the correctness of his analysis, being all too conscious of the fact that he was less responding to a demand for this kind of theatre than attempting to create such a demand.

I may have been somewhat guilty of this last misapprehension in *Winterset*, for I have a strong and chronic hope that the theatre of this country will outgrow the phase of journalistic social comment and reach occasionally into the upper air of poetic tragedy. I believe with Goethe that dramatic poetry is man's greatest achievement on this earth so far, and I believe with the early Bernard Shaw that the theatre is essentially a cathedral of the spirit, devoted to the exaltation of men.[53]

His resistance was expressed as a reaction against a particular way of perceiving the world but in fact seems to have been an expression of a strong resistance to modernity itself. The historical drama, rather like Thornton Wilder's insistence on the mutuality of past and present, was, in effect, an attempt to claim a principle of continuity, to establish a link between that past and the present which denied the significance of the merely social. It was not for him, as it was for Eliot, a contrast between a past rich with significance, potent, Christian, and a present sterile, debased and secular, though *Winterset* could hardly suggest otherwise. It was an assertion that the poet could not be so casually disinherited, that an intensified modernity, in life and art, ignored the eternal, the unchangeable in human nature. His work implied, in particular, that the essential battle was not between the individual and his society but between the individual and his sense of self. To him it was the social theatre of the 1930s which was guilty of evasion rather than his own plays which by-passed the ephemeral in search of the tragic. And this, he felt, could never be concerned with events which merely provide the context, or constitute the immediate justification, for the essential drama of man's confrontation with his own potential.

Winterset mobilises the familiar iconography of 1930s theatre but does so less because Anderson responded to the immediate social realities implied by his setting than because he wished to assert a continuity between past and present. Though the inspiration undoubtedly lay in the Sacco and Vanzetti case (in which two Italian immigrants were, it was widely felt, falsely accused of robbery and murder and executed, their anarchist connections making them convenient victims), his subject was less the hysterical politics of his own period than the fact of injustice and the eternal struggle to oppose it. The play is set on a river front, underneath a bridgehead. At the rear of the stage is an apartment building, to the right an outcrop of original rock. The set is plainly offered as a correlative of the action rather than simply its context. The familiar claustrophobic world, such a recognisable feature of American drama, stands in contrast to the soaring arch of the bridge which appears to lift over the heads of the audience. Social and psychological determinants are acknowledged, but to Anderson they become simply modern versions of a fate against which the individual must struggle, less to improve his social and political fate than to redeem his soul, to restore a sense of dignity to man. And the mythic origins of the story are repeatedly underlined.

The drama which is enacted in this setting is one of a struggle for justice, denied by the forces of darkness. Mio is the son of a man who had been executed for a crime which he did not commit. Hearing that new evidence has come to light, he endeavours to find a witness. The real killer, recently released from prison, has much the same idea, as does the trial judge, now driven mad by guilt. Mio falls in love with the sister of the man who had witnessed the crime and eventually learns the truth. But the authorities show no interest and he and the girl are shot down by the gangsters. And so they are crushed by their fate, a conclusion anticipated not simply by the play's general setting but more precisely by the cellar apartment in which much of the action takes place: 'A cellar apartment under the apartment buildings, floored with cement and roofed with huge boa-constrictor pipes that run slantwise from left to right, dwarfing the room'. The only light is from a 'low squat window'.[54] But, for Anderson, the challenge is enough. Indeed it is the essence of the tragic struggle:

> this is the glory of earth-born men and women,
> not to cringe, never to yield, but standing,
> take defeat implacable and defiant,
> die unsubmitting...
>   On this star
> in this hard star-adventure, knowing not...
> what the fires mean to right and left, nor whether
> a meaning was intended or presumed,
> men can stand up, and look out blind, and say:
> in all these turning lights I find no clue,
> only a masterless night, and in my blood
> no certain answer, yet is my mind my own,
> yet is my heart a cry toward something dim
> in distance, which is higher than I am
> and makes me emperor of the endless dark
> even in seeking! What odds and ends of life
> men may live otherwise, let them live, and then
> go out...[55]

The play is a curious mixture. On occasion Anderson tries to adapt his verse to street argot, to aim at a deliberately reductive versifying; at others he seems to reach for a pseudo-Shakespearian rhetoric which overbalances his own careful location of character and setting:

> Now all you silent powers
> that make the sleet and dark, and never yet
> have spoken, give us a sign, let the throw be ours
> this once, on this longest night, when the winter sets
> his foot on the threshold leading up to spring.[56]

The times are out of joint. Justice is for sale, along with the old values of honour, virtue and glory. Mio's task is to set things right less by defeating the forces of evil than by showing that resistance is still possible.

For John Mason Brown, reviewing the play in September 1935, it was a failure less because of his resort to verse than because of 'his muddled treatment of a story often as cheaply plotted as it is confused in its thinking' and because the poetics were ill-suited to the crude melodrama. And certainly Anderson permits himself some strange diversions, having Mio discuss the adequacy of the verse form which he himself employs when reciting a requiem for one of the characters. For Brown, Anderson's own verse, though sonorous and alive with modern idioms, was 'strangely inactive in the theatre. It is more contemplative than dramatic, and more difficult to follow than is either good for the story or suitable to it.' He also accuses him of dressing up 'some very indifferent generalities in some extremely gaudy plumage'.[57] When he published this review in book form, however, he revised his opinion, not because he now felt differently about Anderson's verse but because 'the mere melody of language, which has some regard for sound and imagery and rhythm, continues to stir emotions in a way no prose, however eloquent, can hope to do; and that playwriting can still function as the distillation of proud man's spirit'.[58] It was less a reversal than a response to what he felt to be the weakness of the American theatre in the early 1960s, when his book was published, and to a dramatic literature which seemed to stress rather man's essential absurdity, or, at best, his uneasy truce with his nature and his fate. In fact his earlier response was the more accurate. The play has an undeniable power which does not rest solely in the melodramatics of its plot; but this is threatened on the one hand by the bathetic consequence of attempting to accommodate the self-consciously colloquial, and on the other hand by an attempt to reach for a tragic resonance through scattered references to Greek archetypes and through a use of verse which was not so much Shakespearian in form as in the associative power of its language. In the Tudor plays the clever word-play, the mannered speeches, are legitimised by a setting which sustains the pastiche. In *Winterset* the archaisms, the sudden moments of pure eloquence, are earthed by the realism which Anderson cannot bring himself wholly to abandon. Rejected by the Group Theatre, the play was commercially produced bypassing the Theatre Guild, who were interested in it, and was a great success, winning the first New York Drama Critics' Circle award.

Like Robert Sherwood, Maxwell Anderson moved from the witty cynicism of his early work to the point of commitment. And *Key Largo* (1939) is a debate about the nature and extent of that commitment. Written on the eve of the Second World War, it was an attempt to relate the events of the Spanish Civil War to the collapse of moral value in America. The play

begins with a prologue, set in Spain, in which an American, King McCloud,
tries to convince his compatriots of the pointlessness of fighting. The men
have no illusions about those they fight alongside, especially the Communists,
who are less interested in fighting for the freedom of the Spanish than with
establishing their own brand of totalitarianism. But, finally, they have to
believe in some transcendent value or acknowledge their own absurdity. As
Victor D'Alcala, one of these men, observes:

I have to believe
there's something in the world that isn't evil –
I have to believe there's some in the world
that would rather die than accept injustice – something
positive for good – that can't be killed –
or I'll die inside. And now that the sky's found empty
a man has to be his own god for himself –
has to prove to himself that a man can die
for what he believes – if ever the time comes to him
when he's asked to choose.[59]

He is answered by King, who, in an extended speech, expresses the cynicism
which had been the intellectual fashion of the 1920s, a position which Sherwood among others had adopted and for which he was later to blame himself. It is offered here equally as an indictment of Anderson's own self-doubts
and of a pose which had facilitated the events in Europe:

We should know
by this time – we've looked at Europe long enough
to know there's nothing to fight for here – that nothing
you win means freedom or equality
or justice – that all the formulas are false –
and known to be false – democracy, communism
socialism, naziism – dead religions
nobody believes in – or if he does believe
he's quietly made use of by the boys
who long ago learned better, and believe
in nothing but themselves...
I tell you it was a dream,
all a dream we had, in a dream world,
of brothers who put out a helping hand
to brothers, and might save them – Long ago
men found out the sky was empty; it follows
that men are a silly accident, meaningless,
here in the empty sky, like a flag on the moon,
as meaningless as an expedition led
to take possession of it – in the name of Marx –
or maybe democracy – or social justice!
Why should we die here for a dead cause, for a symbol,

on these empty ramparts, where there's nothing to win,
even if you could win it?[60]

As a speech, it is offered as an epitaph for a generation. For King it is, more specifically, his justification for retreat and, since he has in effect acknowledged his absurdity, for defection to Franco's forces. If there are indeed no values, then the distinctions can no longer be sustained.

The rest of the play is offered as a rebuttal. Harassed by guilt, he visits the families whose sons he had betrayed to explain, to justify, and in some sense to expiate what on a fundamental level he acknowledges to be a sin against man if no longer against God. But the situation he meets in America is not substantially different from that which he had encountered in Spain. In Key Largo, Florida, he finds the family of his dead friend Victor being menaced by a local gangster. In league with a corrupt law department this man exploits people through a gambling operation which is sustained by his brutal gang. King is thus offered a second chance to stand up for human values. When the leader, Murilla (whose Spanish name reinforces the connection), announces that he intends to move into the D'Alcala house, and implies thereby his sexual designs on their daughter, King draws a gun but is unable to fire it. When he is falsely accused of one of Murilla's murders, however, he refuses to escape the charge by framing two Indians who have escaped from a nearby work gang. At last sure of himself and of the need to oppose the plainly evil, he shoots Murilla. The man who had earlier said:

by the truth no man can live at all,
even a day. We die when we look at truth.
And one by one the illusions
wear themselves out.[61]

is finally left to confront the truth about himself and the world in which he moves. That truth appears to have no space for transcendence. It is a series of closed doors.

We jump first at the door
with Christ upon it, hanging on the cross,
then the door with Lenin, legislating heaven,
then the emblem of social security, representing
eighteen dollars a week, good luck or bad,
jobs or no jobs – then the door with the girl expectant,
the black triangle door, and they all give meaning
to life and mental sustenance, but then
there comes a day when there's no sustenance,
and you jump and there's nothing you want to buy with money,
and Christ hangs dead on the cross, as all men die,
and Lenin legislates a fake paradise,
and the girl holds out her arms, and she's made of sawdust,
and there's sawdust in your mouth![62]

But for D'Alcala, his dead friend's father, such absurdity is the beginning and not the end of meaning.

> Where this voyage started
> we don't know, nor where it will end, nor whether
> it has a meaning, nor whether there is good
> or evil, whether man has a destiny
> or happened here by chemical accident –
> all this we never know. And that's our challenge –
> to find ourselves in this desert of dead light-years,
> blind, all of us, in a kingdom of the blind,
> living by appetite in a fragile shell
> of dust and water; yet to take this dust
> and water and our range of appetites
> and build them toward some vision of a god
> of beauty and unselfishness and truth...
>
>   perhaps men help
> by setting themselves forever, even to the death,
> against cruelty and arbitrary power,
> for that's the beast...[63]

Belatedly converted to this faith, King dies as the old man claims him as his son.

The play is not wholly alien in mood to *For Whom the Bell Tolls* and certainly the movement from Anderson's early plays to this statement of human values is not unlike the movement in Hemingway's work from *A Farewell to Arms* to this novel, also published in 1939. The idea of a brotherhood which is non-ideological, found equally in *The Grapes of Wrath*, also published in this year, was very much a product of the events in Europe which challenged equally the cynicism and the social comedy which had been so much in vogue. It was a patriotic fervour which grew stronger in Anderson's wartime plays.

Anderson's real claim to attention lay in his efforts to rehabilitate verse drama. It was that 'third voice' which Eliot had identified:

> The first is the voice of the poet talking to himself – or to nobody. The second is the voice of the poet addressing an audience, whether large or small. The third is the voice of the poet when he attempts to create a dramatic character speaking in verse; when he is saying, not what he would say in his own person, but only what he can say within the limits of one imaginary character addressing another imaginary character.[64]

It was not a distinction which Anderson always sustained. The logic of his moral drive frequently led him to apostrophes to human resilience, expressions of his own convictions as to man's potential, and, on occasions, he succumbed to a lyricism at odds with character and setting. Too often what he wrote, in Cocteau's words, was poetry in the theatre rather than poetry of the theatre, in the sense that it was more mannered than organic. The language draws attention to itself, the rhythms become independent of those expressed by character or *mise-en-scène*. Sometimes that dissonance is crucial and deliberate, a comment on a world which has expelled the lyrical, a prosaic world of fact and simple determinism. Sometimes it is expressive of a failure to integrate vision with character. William Archer, reflecting Ibsen's own reaction against his own early verse plays, remarked that in Elizabethan drama 'the established custom of writing in verse, good, bad, or indifferent, enabled and encouraged the dramatists to substitute rhetoric for human speech'.[65] And certainly this was a temptation to which Anderson succumbed rather too often. But his plays were popular with the public. The verse form was taken as an earnest of the profundity of his views.

In his verse drama, it seems, Anderson was trying to create the appurtenances of myth and provide the skeletal framework for epic. The resonances which he sought through the use of verse were precisely those he felt to be absent from his own age. Like Wilder, who, conversely, created a poetry of the theatre rather than in the theatre, he sought to find in the past not primarily a sanction against the present (though the urge to do so was clear in his historical drama) but an assurance that the essential struggles were not immediate and social but eternal and metaphysical. Despite a surface pessimism he was a profound optimist about human nature and his verse was designed to sculpt the seemingly random and inchoate into a form which implied a ritual, a pattern behind the chaos. Verse was a unifier, a creator of structure, of ceremony. It was to suggest a hidden consonance, the contiguousness of language and experience, a rhythm which related the individual to the group and the group to the race. It was a project not without its grandeur for all its weaknesses, its pretensions and, at times, its disturbing naivety.

Philip Barry felt at home in the world on a fundamental level, as did Rice, and Odets and Saroyan. O'Neill had felt the pressure of what Ibsen had called the 'damned compact liberal majority'. Rice, Odets and Barry, along with most other major American dramatists of the period, actually spoke to and for that majority. To be sure, they showed a profound sense of unease. How could they not? Liberalism itself was undergoing a radical reconstruction. But underneath the alarm, below the concern with an oppressive urban environment and the pressures towards social conformity and moral surrender, was a faith in social and metaphysical order which remained curiously untroubled. The real may no longer be adequately conveyed by mere surface representation but it was still recoverable. Barry, Rice, Saroyan, Anderson and Odets were certainly not concerned with metaphysical revolt (Barry's Catholicism, indeed, was vital to his philosophical stance). Nor were they in reality social rebels. They were not exiles in any sense, except from their times. They reached back towards a model of human possibility, of social action and moral responsibility, which was embedded in an American liberal mythology. They regretted the loss of physical space which had given that myth its social credibility, regretted, too, a materialism which had usurped its spiritual justification in a self-improvement which was of the soul and not of the body, but they could not bring themselves to deny the essence of its claims. If physical space was gone, then it had to be recreated by an act of imaginative appropriation. The new world had to be re-created, first in language and then in symbolic form – in the unresolved endings, the dramatic ellipses which became the mark of much American drama. By the same token materialism was to be rejected. Odets's Ralph, in *Awake and Sing*, refuses a legacy as Miller's Biff Loman, in *Death of a Salesman*, was to do. Stripped of worldly goods they become fit figures to re-enter the myths which generate them. Their weakness all too often lies in the poverty of their imagination, which fails to transcend that myth. They are representative men and women. Whitman and Emerson lie behind their claims to an individual self-realisation which is simultaneously an acknowledgement of their participation in the world. But in so far as their language is derivative it is unconvincing. In so far as they accept a world whose determinants are shown to have a shaping if not absolute power that language rings hollow. And this is no less true of Biff Loman than it was of the heroine of *Street Scene*, the protagonist of *Awake and Sing*, or the socially free but metaphysically bound characters of *Hotel Universe*. In rebellion against the naturalists' assumption of total biological, historical and environmental determinism, they reached for some existential freedom which remained no more than an article of faith so long as they could not identify any mechanism for liberating their characters. In fact, few American dramatists were willing to hand the problem over to a revolutionary working class or an autonomous history which would solve the problem once given its head. But they did embrace their own historicism. The present, though it was to be faithfully rendered as an earnest of good faith, was finally seen as a caesura, a brief interruption in the rise of man. Human nature, it seemed, remained resistant. Below the level of contingent event, of economic fiat and immediate circumstance, was a liberal spirit which only awaited the kiss of the poet, the pointed sacrifice, the painful shock, to bring it to life. The ironies which had seemed definitional – romantic yearnings confronted by an unromantic world, spiritual convictions blunted by a material setting, personal aspirations denied by an anonymous environment – are shown to be ultimately subordinate to the will and imagination in alliance. The new world has first to be imagined before it can be inhabited. The weakness of many of these playwrights, however, is precisely one of imagination. The worlds which they invoke, usually in the final uplifting lines of their plays, have no more substance than Lennie's imagined world in *Of Mice and Men*, except that this work allowed a crucial irony to insert itself between dream and reality, an irony which began quickly to appear in the work of Odets whose own imagery began a radical subversion of his work.

The Guild did not cease functioning with the Second World War; but in his book called *The Vintage Years of the Theatre Guild* Roy Waldau makes a persuasive case for the vintage years being essentially those from 1928 to 1939. This was indeed its heyday. It did not discover O'Neill but it played an important role in bringing his work to the American public. It staged plays by Elmer Rice, Susan Glaspell, Maxwell Anderson, Philip Barry, Sidney Kingsley, Sidney Howard, Robert Sherwood, Marc Connelly and S. N. Behrman as well as classics of the European stage. It created its own audience and sustained it with its subscription programme. It developed major acting and directing talents and it took first-class theatre on the road, to cities other than New York. It introduced new developments in theatre; it adopted an eclectic policy which prevented it from becoming merely the mouthpiece of a single ideology or aesthetic orthodoxy. It also spawned the Group Theatre.

On the negative side it increasingly tended to conservatism in its choice of play, as it, of necessity, considered its financial solvency. It abandoned its repertory system and inevitably lost many of its better actors to Hollywood. Its commitment to experimentation gradually weakened and its sense of its own objectives gradually blurred. Nevertheless it was the Guild which first recognised the potential of Tennessee Williams and it continued to be a force in the post-war theatre. But its crucial period was in the inter-war years during which it fostered the career of a group of writers who, if they could not compare with the best that the European theatre had to offer, were nevertheless a testimony to the new vigour of the American theatre and its commitment to engaging the reality of the private and public world.

4 The Group Theatre and Clifford Odets

Harold Clurman grew up in an America in which the theatre had suddenly come into its own. The Theatre Guild had begun to operate along with the Provincetown Players. While in Paris, where he lived from 1921 to 1924, he had written a thesis about French drama, attended Copeau's productions and gone to lectures at Copeau's school at the Théâtre du Vieux Colombier, but he felt disenchanted with that theatre, feeling the absence of the contemporary and a true human significance. On his return to America he worked as an actor for the Provincetown Players and then for the Theatre Guild where he met another aspiring actor, Lee Strasberg, a student of Boleslavsky and Ouspenskaya at the American Laboratory Theatre where the techniques of Stanislavsky were taught. Clurman himself enrolled in the course, preferring this to playing in John Howard Lawson's *Loud Speaker* (1927) for the Playwrights' Theatre. It was here that he met Stella Adler, his future wife and collaborator, along with Strasberg, in the creation of the Group Theatre.

Early in 1928 a first effort was made by Clurman, along with the young actors Morris Carnovsky and Sanford Meisner, to establish a group which would work together on a new work, with no precise production plan but with the intention of broadening their experiences as actors and examining the full potential of the play. The effort foundered, but provided the model for the Group Theatre.

By now Clurman was working for the Theatre Guild, where he met Cheryl Crawford, then casting director, and it was at this time that a group once again began to meet together to discuss ways in which they could personally develop as writers and the theatre could be made more responsive to the needs of its audience. The first meeting of this unofficial group was held in November 1930, in Cheryl Crawford's apartment, and it continued meeting until May 1931. The members then approached the Theatre Guild, who employed its principal members, and asked it to release the option which it held on Paul Green's play, *The House of Connelly* (1931). The Guild agreed, also releasing two of its actors, Franchot Tone and Morris Carnovsky, and offered $1000 towards the expense of rehearsing the play during the approaching summer. So was born the Group Theatre, which, with the much more ambitious but shorter-lived Federal Theatre, was the most influential production group operating in the 1930s.

Cheryl Crawford, Lee Strasberg and Harold Clurman were to be the directors and, with money raised from well-wishers, including Maxwell

Anderson and Edna Ferber, they secured a summer home at Brookfield Centre, Connecticut, where they invited twenty-eight actors. Clurman and Strasberg were complementary to one another. The former was primarily concerned with the need to analyse both the play and its connection with the social world which generated it, to which it referred, and in which it operated; the latter was committed to advancing the craft of acting, to using the process of rehearsal as a means to develop the actor and his skills.

There was a symbolic relevance to their own situation in the choice of the play, which was concerned with the battle between the old and new orders in the south. Their principal methods in actor training, the use of improvisation and of exercises in affective memory (a Stanislavsky technique whereby the actor recalls an experience from his own past in order to recreate through that emotional authenticity a psychologically convincing action) were both steps towards a 'truth' which the Group saw as their aim – a truth which did not lead them, as it did many of the Marxist groups of the 1930s, to a desire simply to expose the realities of Depression America but which did charge their work with a social as well as artistic commitment. Theirs was not merely to be a new theatre, it was to be a celebratory theatre. According to Clurman they believed in 'the perfectibility of man, or at least the inevitability of the struggle against evil'.[1] Accordingly they persuaded Green to change the ending of his play to make it less 'pessimistic'. Clurman's faith was rather more mystical than political. The 1929 Wall Street Crash meant very little to him, though he lost some money in it; neither did the political meaning of a Soviet play, The Man with the Portfolio, which he rehearsed along with The House of Connelly during the first summer.

The Theatre Guild had reservations about the production of The House of Connelly but eventually agreed to put up the money for its production and to sponsor it, provided the original ending was reinstated. When this offer was declined the Guild offered only half the production expenses. The Group eventually raised the remaining finance from the play's publisher and from Eugene O'Neill. Announcing themselves as The Group Theatre, 'an organization of actors and directors formed with the ultimate aim of creating a permanent acting company to maintain regular New York seasons',[2] they staged their first public performance on 23 September 1931. It was an immediate critical success and much to their delight the reviews included the words which had dominated their own vocabulary. It was described as 'true', 'consecrated...ensemble work'.

Though the Group survived for a decade, at a time when others were collapsing, it failed in one of its principal objectives. It never established the kind of financial independence which would enable it to plan an entirely coherent strategy. It was forced into precisely that situation which it had sought to avoid, namely raising its funds in the normal way of Broadway productions by seeking backers for every venture rather than by establishing the company itself as a viable concern with a consequent freedom of action.

In the programme for the Group's second production, a play about unemployment by Claire and Paul Sifton, called *1931*, Clurman explained their aims: 'the development of playwrights, actors, repertory and the rest are important only as they lead to the creation of a tradition of common values, an active consciousness of a common way of looking at and dealing with life. A theatre in our country today should aim to create an Audience.'[3] Despite the failure of this production, in retrospect Clurman saw evidence of the emergence of this audience which was to be the basis of so much theatre work in the 1930s.

Waldo Frank, in an address to the librarians of New York in 1932, made clear the rather vague, visionary dimension of the Group's world – a social and artistic vision implied in their choice of plays. 'I suppose,' Frank said,

> the reason why I believe in the Group is because I am primarily interested in what I might call the creating of a new world. I am not alone – I am sure – in a belief that there must be a new society, a new humanity in the moral and spiritual as well as the economic sense. A new humanity must be created – literally made up of human beings who have different values, who have a different vision and a different sense of the dignity of life, who have a different loyalty to the truth, and a different technique in expressing this truth than most of us have today...There must be a group of conscious people patiently devoted, because of these positive impulses, to the ideal. They must be organized to work toward the creating of a new world. The one method whereby the new society may slowly and laboriously be created is a new alliance in place of the alliance of the intellectuals with the money class, an alliance of the men of mind, of vision, the artists, with the People, consciously working toward this creative end.[4]

In 1932, Cheryl Crawford and Harold Clurman broke with the Theatre Guild, and the Group Theatre became an independent organisation. It never adopted a coherent political position. It certainly resisted co-option as a simple theatre of the Left, and yet, as the various statements make clear, it was animated by a social vision, a sense that the theatre needed to respond to human needs. But it was also committed to the development of the skills of the theatre. The two objectives were not easily reconcilable nor were the available plays always such as to justify the work which went into them. The company was thus not particularly proud of one of the few commercial successes of its early years, Sidney Kingsley's *Men in White* (1933), which won the Pulitzer prize but which was in essence a contrived melodrama whose gestures towards social commitment were somewhat arbitrary. Set in a hospital, the play was noted for its attention to the mechanical details of medicine, but despite its run of 351 performances the company was not happy that it had been living up to its own ideals, no matter how vaguely these ideals were expressed. It was aware that downtown Theatre Union had staged *Peace on Earth* (1933), an anti-war play, and was about to produce *Stevedore* (1934), which tackled the race problem.

Despite the achievement of Provincetown and the Theatre Guild, the American theatre was not self-confident. It was aware that innovation in actor training and in production originated in Europe. In Russia, for example, where art and social action seemed to have found a symbiotic relationship, art was accorded a significance which it simply lacked in America. Stanislavsky seemed to have brought an honesty, an authenticity to the Russian theatre which was lacking in the American, while the fact of the Russian Revolution seemed to charge the Soviet approach with an authority plainly absent in an American theatre which was still largely perceived as simple entertainment. And the Group Theatre, producing on Broadway, was caught up in this ambiguity. For all its claims, it was not, as were the Communist Party's amateur theatre groups, genuinely going in search of new audiences. It was concerned with converting the existing audience. Clurman and Strasberg were especially ambiguous, responding to the fervour of Russian theatre and to the potency of its methods but distrustful of its ideology. Clurman, in particular, was sympathetic to the notion of theatre as an ideologically cemented collective but wished to translate this into a less severely prescriptive form. He was aware that behind the terminology of the new Russian theatre 'was the authority of a great historical event – a Revolution – the brilliant example of a theatre carried on in days of upheaval and starvation, and, above all, something that seemed very strong and definite compared with our de-based incantations'.[5] But when he asked himself what ideology cemented his own collective he had to confess that it was something vague, even mystical, and the more so because it lacked any historical authentication.

Some of the Group Theatre's actors went to the early meetings of the Theatre Collective and the Theatre Union. Indeed Clurman himself attended but felt uneasy with the language of those for whom the theatre was to be wholly subordinated to other objectives. A product of a liberal, middle-class background, he lacked the biting anger of Clifford Odets. But he shared the feeling that their activities, 'Unknown figures', as they were, 'in a backward art practised in a tiny corner of our land',[6] were magnified by the social upheavals of the age. It was not simply that there was an iconographic similarity between the stage and the political platform but that every activity was politicised by the times and that the theatre had elsewhere assumed a central significance. And yet, as Clurman himself was all too aware, 'The Theatre Union was on the firing line on Fourteenth Street, charging no more than $1.50 for the best seat, while we were 'safe' on Broadway with the contemptible carriage-trade price of $3.30.'[7] But there was an aesthetic as well as a social distance between the two theatres. The Group Theatre, through its attachment to Stanislavsky, was concerned with penetrating the psychological truth of individuals, with tapping emotional verities rather than with subordinating character to action, the individual to the type, private anguish to public meaning.

A visit to the Soviet Union by Stella Adler and Clurman did little to resolve these issues, but it did have a considerable influence on the Group. Clurman, exposed to the variety of Soviet theatre styles, felt liberated, no longer dominated by Strasberg's version of Stanislavsky. Adler, like Clurman, met Stanislavsky in Paris and came to feel that Strasberg was misapplying his work. On her return she challenged his version. Later, Strasberg was to comment, 'She was always over-emotional... Then she went to Stanislavsky. *Of course*, he said that this was a misuse of the Method, and that was all she wanted to hear. She came back and told the Group we were misinterpreting. But the results were right. You can't be doing it wrong if the results are right.'[8] This split later became the basis for two of America's principal acting schools. In 1947, Crawford, Kazan and Bobby Lewis founded the Actors Studio, of which Strasberg became director in the following year. In 1949, Stella Adler founded the Stella Adler Theatre Studio.

Strasberg also visited the Soviet Union at this time and when he returned he did so full of enthusiasm for Meyerhold, incorporating his concern with movement into his own directing style. Meanwhile a number of actors were showing increasing signs of social commitment, publicly supporting radical causes and urging other members of the group to do so. And this coincided with the emergence of a committed writer of considerable power from among their own ranks – Clifford Odets. To some degree thereafter the fate of the company and of this writer were entwined. It was the success of his plays in 1935 which cemented the success of the company and it was the gradual disengagement of the company from his 1941 play, *Clash by Night*, which marked its dissolution. The latter was to have been produced under the auspices of the Group Theatre but commercial pressures slowly dislodged it. For Clurman this was paradigmatic. And in an article published in the *New York Times* in 1940 he looked back on the brief history of the Group as a continuous struggle to develop a serious and consistent acting style and an attempt to foster intelligent and effective native drama in a context which made it almost impossible. For the Group's central failure was its inability to secure the kind of financial independence which would have given it artistic independence. For ten years a major influence in the development of the American theatre, it foundered for the very reasons which had led to its creation. For Clurman, the cardinal fact was that:

it had to operate all these years on the hit-or-miss system that characterizes Broadway. For a theatrical enterprize which has any other view outside the necessary one of making money, it is utterly destructive at every point...the habit of judging plays from the standpoint of their immediate box-office draw spreads insidiously from the backer to the producer to the company to the critics and finally to the audience, whose tastes and minds are thus unconsciously but progressively debauched and then made indifferent to the theatre generally ...If we fail to carry out to the full what is still our real program, the failure will be as much the failure of our theatrical environment as the fault of our abilities.[9]

The Group Theatre succumbed, but its influence on American acting and production styles remained, while its stress on native playwriting talent did much to secure the future of America drama.

Clifford Odets wrote the first two acts of *I Got the Blues*, subsequently re-named *Awake and Sing*, in the winter of 1932–3. A single act was played by the company at Green Mansions, a holiday camp where the Group summered in 1933, but the play, which Strasberg disliked, was not produced until 1935 when it was selected partly as a means of keeping the Group together beyond its short season. According to Harold Clurman rehearsals for the play had already been under way for ten days before *Waiting for Lefty* (see pp. 200–2) had its historic première. The latter opened on 5 January 1935 and a series of benefit performances of the play were given at the Civic Repertory before the Press were invited. Their enthusiasm made a Broadway production in-evitable and in March, a month after the opening of *Awake and Sing*, the Group Theatre staged it, together with another one-act play, *Till the Day I Die*.

Described by Clurman as one of the first serious anti-Nazi plays to reach Broadway, *Till the Day I Die* (1935) was a melodramatic celebration of the human spirit and a painfully naive endorsement of the move towards consensus left-wing politics. Set in Nazi Germany, it concerns a small group of committed Party members who take on the new German state with mimeographed newspapers and Hitler joke books. Somewhat astonishingly Odets seems not to feel any sense of disproportion in the battle. His characters are naive and romantic; their organisation is easily penetrated by the security forces. But Odets seems unwilling to accept the implications of his own plot, balancing the incompetence of the young Communist with an equally naive police force, easily placated with implausible stories. The naivety, in other words, is not merely the characters', it is also the playwright's.

The play dwells on the sadistic nature of the Brownshirts, the simple-mindedness of Nazi Party members and their agents, and the heroism of Jew and Communist. By a particularly casual act of displacement, the political conflict is dramatised on a sexual level. A love-affair between two Party members leads to a pregnancy which comes to stand for the future towards which they are working, while a particularly vindictive and anti-semitic Nazi captain is portrayed as a homosexual.

Ernst, a violin player, has his hand crushed by Captain Schlegel who is given the deliberately reductive but unbelievable line, 'Hitler is lonely too. So is God.'[10] Schlegel is then killed by Major Dehring, a Nazi officer with a Jewish background who commits suicide, having done what he can to help the cause. The play climaxes with the suicide of Ernst, suspected by his colleagues of informing but in fact a heroic Party member. It then dissolves into a simplistic plea for the united front, an endorsement for which there is no justification in terms of the play's action except in the solidarity of the Jewish officer, a hesitant ally despite his clear self-interest. The Major dies with a speech neatly divided between self-accusation and political exhortation: 'I am so slimed over with rottenness...."Red Front" I can't say to you... But "United Front" – I say that. In every capitalist country in the world this day let them work for a united front.'[11] When Ernst staggers to his lover with a broken body and tortured mind, she offers him only the consolation of a few hours sleep before an obligatory dose of propaganda: 'Sleep, Ernst, sleep. Tomorrow you can read the full report on the united front. L'Humanité came through with several copies.' Instead of rebelling, Ernst cries out with joy, 'Our work is bearing fruit? In that beautiful classic country. The united front? Oh, Tilly, oh, Tilly.'[12] He dies announcing an imminent new world, 'we live in the joy of a great people!...soon all the desolate places of the world must flourish with human genius. Brothers will live in the soviets of the world!'[13] But contained within the play is an implicit justification for its simplicities. Ernst's brother poses a central question for the committed theatre when he asks, 'Mozart – is there time for music today?'[14] This statement follows the Party Secretary's announcement that 'Three new theatre-of-action groups have been formed in the last week. They are now functioning regularly throughout the city.'[15] The assumption that the theatre is indeed a mechanism for social transformation is unquestioned, while subtlety is proposed as an approach which cannot be afforded.

It is true that the play, like *Waiting for Lefty*, was unconvincing in its psychology, that it substituted situation for character and subordinated plot to ideology. But in this respect it scarcely differed from many other such works which were offered primarily as moral homilies, as dramas of situation. Jean-Paul Sartre, writing in 1947, called for just such a theatre, asserting that:

> if it's true that man is free in a given situation and that in and through that situation he chooses to be what he will be, then what we have to show in the theatre are simple and human situations and free individuals in these situations choosing what they will be. The character comes later, after the curtain has

fallen. The most moving thing the theatre can show is a character creating himself the moment of choice, of the free decision which commits him to a moral code and a whole way of life. The situation is an appeal: it surrounds us, offering us solutions which it's up to us to choose. And in order for the decision to be deeply human, in order for it to bring the whole man into play, we have to stage limit situations, that is situations which present alternatives one of which leads to death...It is through particular situations that each age grasps the human situation and the enigmas human freedom must confront.[16]

Odets presents just such 'limit situations' in which characters choose themselves, in which they lose themselves in order to affirm themselves. Indeed the final lines of the play, delivered by the man whose brother is committing suicide, are 'Let him die...Let him live.'[17] His death is precisely a sacrifice which gives his life meaning. The weakness of the play, however, derives from his failure to engage the human reality of his characters in such a way as to give any political force or existential reality to their decisions; it lies in his unwillingness to acknowledge any complexity in the moral or political world which can make such decisions any more than self-evident.

Its companion piece, *Awake and Sing* (1935), however, represents a move away from the methods and assumptions of *Waiting for Lefty* and the simplicities of *Till the Day I Die*. Since it predates both plays it constituted another pole in Odets's work, an opposing approach to the agit-prop sketch and the episodic or collage plays of the Left. These had stood as revolts against bourgeois realism. They had sought to reduce the gap between life and art not merely by the choice of subject matter, nor even by the use of street theatre, the pursuit of new audiences, the creation of a collective protagonist or a collectivist approach, but by foregrounding theatricality, by undermining illusionism, by insisting on the factitious nature of the theatrical moment.

Distrustful of their own articulateness, fearful of stressing the individual component of experience, left-wing groups, particularly in the early 1930s, saw some virtue and integrity in a flight from realism. But in *Literature and Revolution* (1924) Leon Trotsky defended both the need for art and the necessity for retaining realism.

Art, it is said, is not a mirror, but a hammer: it does not reflect, it shapes... But...If one cannot get along without a mirror, even in shaving oneself, how can one reconstruct oneself or one's life, without seeing oneself in the 'mirror' of literature?

He distrusted the abandonment of a psychological drama, asking

What does it mean to 'deny experiences', that is, deny individual psychology, in literature and on the stage?

replying that

This is a late and long outlived protest of the Left wing of the intelligentzia against the passive realism of the Chekhov school and against dreamy symbolisms.

But, he insisted,

If the experiences of Uncle Vanya have lost a little of their freshness – and this sin has actually taken place – it is none the less true that Uncle Vanya is not the only one with an inner life. In what way, on what grounds, and in the name of what, can art turn its back on the inner life of present-day man who is building a new external world, and thereby rebuilding himself? If art will not help this new man to educate himself, to strengthen and redefine himself, then what is it for? And how can it organize the inner life, if it does not penetrate it and reproduce it?[18]

Odets's Berger family is trapped, in a mental no less than a physical world. The limits are partly those imposed by an urban setting which itself has been shaped by a history of speculation and exploitation, and partly by a mental geography which they regard as implacable as a physical terrain. Most of the family accept as unyielding what is mutable, constructing their own prisons out of economic fiats to which they give metaphysical authority. The primary space which they surrender is the crucial territory within which the self defines its own possibilities. Dreams are mistaken for visions and vice versa. The harsh realities of economic life are allowed to deform the moral imagination. The falsehoods of public mythology become the falsehoods of private life. The social lie, which proposes the inevitability of success and which accounts for failure by locating it in the weakness of the individual or the incorrigible wilfulness of a particular group, becomes the private lie, which demeans by forcing the individual to respect externalities, to allow a dangerous gap to open up between appearance and reality. The Berger family are on the verge of the middle class and as such are especially vulnerable. To deny the reality of the American dream is ostensibly to condemn themselves to permanent deprivation. The constant image is one of flight, escape. They look to escape the reality of their situation through marriage, through luck, through a desperate commitment to political or social myths, through a sardonic humour, through self-deceit, or even, most desperately, through suicide, albeit a suicide which, like that which was to send Willy Loman to his death in *Death of a Salesman*, is designed to liberate the next generation.

All the material is there for a social play which indicts a brutal and brutalising system. Certainly it is possible to make money. Bessie Berger's brother does so by dint of caring nothing for anyone, remaining blandly unaware of others' suffering and evidencing the crudest intolerance. Otherwise, it is really only the gambler and the cynic who can survive, and they do so by taking society on its own terms. But Odets is less interested in offering an indictment of capitalism than he is with asserting the need for a morally improved world, for the individual to wake up to a failure which is as much private as public. Odets was now a Communist Party member, but the mood of *Awake and Sing* is much closer to Roosevelt than to Marx. The awakening with which the play climaxes is very much that moral regeneration for which Roosevelt had called and which he was to continue to call for in his Second Inaugural, where he was to assert that:

> Old Truths have been relearned; untruths have been unlearned…We are beginning to wipe out the line that divides the practical from the ideal; and in so doing we are fashioning an instrument of unimagined power for the establishment of a morally better world. This new understanding undermines the old admiration of worldly success as such. We are beginning to abandon our tolerance of the abuse of power by those who betray for profit the elementary decencies of life…Shall we pause now and turn our back upon the road that lies ahead? Shall we call this the promised land? Or, shall we continue on our way? For 'each age is a dream that is dying, or one that is coming to birth'.[19]

Awake and Sing recounts the personal growth to a kind of maturity of Ralph Berger and, ostensibly, of his sister Hennie. Condemned to play their required roles in the social drama which their mother has formulated from shreds of American pietism and capitalist propaganda, wedded to the lower middle-class insecurities of immigrant life, they are caught between her pretensions and the constraining power of their far from genteel poverty. Having failed to win her own place in the sun, she relies on her children to justify her and is implacable in the zeal with which she seeks to mould them. By the end of the play they have apparently learnt the need to break free, though the suicide of their grandfather offers an exemplary warning of the futility of a commitment and a vision not rooted in practical action.

Clifford Odets is an urban writer. The pressure which his characters feel is that of the city. The collapse of personal space, the closing off of social possibilities, the erosion of familial cohesion, the betrayal of moral values, the loss of transcendent vision, are the product of a world which is seen as essentially urban. The Bergers live in a tenement building. Their dog is exercised on the roof; their son sleeps in the living room; the different generations are crowded together, making the ironies of lost lives inescapable. Lost opportunities, denied hopes, frustrated plans, are ruthlessly exposed. Nothing can be concealed. The loss of space is the loss, too, of privacy, the exposure of failure and weakness. The transformation of this circumstance by simple ideological shift is not credible nor presented as such by Odets. Jacob's communism is a fantasy, rooted neither in knowledge nor action, while Ralph's personal liberation is drained of ideological content. Indeed that lack of ideological content emphasises the individual nature of that transformation, and its slender foundation. The ambiguity of this conversion is an indication of some of the play's more disabling contradictions. Odets delineates with

168

15. Group Theatre production of Clifford Odet's *Awake and Sing*, New York, 1935. Direction by Harold Clurman, setting by Boris Aronson.

care the pressures which destroy personal relations, individual conscience and communal values; he is less capable of identifying the source of regeneration which survives in language but not in action. Hennie's pursuit of personal fulfilment at the expense of her child, whom she abandons at the end of the play, is ostensibly endorsed by Ralph, suggesting a concern for self at the heart of his own bid for freedom which stains it with an egotism at odds with his language, and with the logic of the play which suggests a movement towards a self-realisation linked to national recovery.

Odets's is a world in which language is warped by circumstance. The language of familiarity cloaks a fundamental estrangement. The pressure of the city erodes the word, insinuates a space between language and meaning. Jacob's romantic radicalism is born out of a desire to bring word and referent into some kind of dialectical relationship, to close the space opened up by time and the loss of an environment in which such a relationship would be possible. The pathos of Jacob is clear. He dies without closing that space and, worse than that, he dies with a kind of betrayal. In plunging to the sidewalk from the rooftop he offers his life to buy his grandson a future by leaving him $3000. It is a gesture which denies the life that he has constructed in his mind. It is a bribe offered to the world he thinks he holds in contempt. It is a gift which will taint the young man; which, if accepted, will pull him down into the material world, which will locate him with the forces he affects to despise. Like Willy Loman, in *Death of a Salesman*, he offers a dubious inheritance. The proof of Ralph's maturity lies, like Biff's, in his realisation that it is an inheritance which has to be refused. But where Willy Loman prides himself, no matter how self-deceivingly, on his success, desperately trying to relate to the public myths of America, Jacob consoles himself for his failure by con-

169

demning that society. In doing so, he inevitably defuses Odets's own indictment of the system. In both cases the weakness lies as much in the indivdiual, wilfully self-blinding, vacillating, visionary without cogent perception, as it does in society. It is a weakness which blunts the social critique.

By the same token Ralph's decision to hand the money over to his mother and stay in the tenement leaves him in a social world unreconstructed except by his new version of a world which he now believes, without any evidence, to be susceptible to his transforming imagination. But that imagination is too insubstantially rooted to carry conviction. The density of the city, the accumulated evidence of loss, betrayal and surrender, is too great for his new perception to sustain the weight which Odets would place on it. What is presented as a triumph, as perception transmuted into action, is invaded by an irony generated less by his own weaknesses, though these are plain, than by the subversive power of a social world whose force lies more in its demeaning materialism than in the capitalist injustice. The play's action implies a determinism scarcely neutralised by a quixotic gesture, a commitment to transformation pushed not simply into the future and hence untested in action, but into a spiritual world which is perhaps indistinguishable from the fantasy which had animated his grandfather.

In the context of *Awake and Sing*, in which disillusionment, the blunting of aspirations and the slow depletion of energy are demonstrable facts of personal and public life, there is a terrible symmetry in Ralph's decision. The naive enthusiasm which he feels in the closing moments of the play is indistinguishable from that with which Moe Axelrod had gone off to war, Bessie had married her now dispirited husband and Jacob had responded to the images of human solidarity which had filled him with sufficient energy to purchase, but not read, a library of radical texts. There is a logic established which cannot be neutralised by simple rhetoric. He exchanges one dream for another; the vaguely-felt social commitment which now engages him. As he puts down the telephone, following the ending of a brief, but apparently passionately-felt affair, he announces, 'No girl means anything to me until... Till I can take care of her. Till we don't look out on an air shaft. Till we can take the world in two hands and polish off the dirt.'[20] The extent of the rationalisation seems clear, though it threatens the integrity of his new commitment. Indeed his failure to sustain that personal relationship in the face of opposition, the collapse of will which leads him to sacrifice her to her vindictive relatives, is of a kind with his sister's willing sacrifice of her child, abandoned so that she can seek happiness unencumbered. It cannot be viewed unambiguously and it must be presumed to have implications for his new faith, which is expressed with precisely that enthusiasm which he had previously reserved for his private world.

And the risk clearly exists that for Ralph the future will become a kind of crystalline myth, as the past does for his father. Teddy Roosevelt and Valentino define the parameters of his fantasy world, as Marx and Lenin do those of Jacob. The present is evacuated. It contains the threat of uncontrolled emotion; it demands a human response. It is Jacob who is described by Odets as being 'a sentimental idealist with no power to turn ideal into action' but it is not clear why this should not also prove an adequate description of Ralph.

For Odets, the change in the lives of Ralph and Hennie, at least, though minor in origin and in immediate effect, was to be a public act. To newspaper interviewers he asserted that 'The play represents an adjustment in the lives of the characters, not an adjustment of environment...just a minor family turmoil, an awakening to life of the characters, a change in attitude...But today the truth followed to its logical conclusions is inevitably revolutionary. No special pleading is necessary in a play which says that people should have full and richer lives.'[21] When Jacob is particularly depressed or harassed he plays a recording of Caruso singing 'O Paradiso' and explains that 'a big explorer comes on a new land – "O Paradiso"... You hear? Oh paradise! Oh paradise on earth!'[22] This, presumably, is the America, now destroyed by greed, which must be redeemed.

The family, central to American mythology, becomes, if not the source of corruption, then its most obvious evidence. Jacob's comment, 'Marx said it – abolish such families', is a genuine reference to the Communist manifesto, which does indeed assert that the bourgeoisie have made the family relationship into a financial relationship. This is exemplified here not merely by Bessie's willing sacrifice of moral value to financial security but also by the legacy left by Jacob. It is a temptation which has to be resisted. And yet the family is not to be abandoned, or, as in Hennie's case, not to be abandoned without moving into a dubious moral world. It is to be transformed by changing the nature of the society in which it is located. But this merely serves to underline the inadequacy of Ralph to the task which he wishes to take on. 'Get teams together all over. Spit on your hands and get to work,' he insists, 'And with enough teams together maybe we'll get steam in the warehouse so our fingers don't freeze off. Maybe we'll fix it so life won't be printed on dollar bills.'[23] But the agency for this transformation, the process whereby he will move from perception to action, is unclear.

The play's final speech signals his private rebirth in his own mind, but the link between that and a public act of reconstruction is dubious while the tone of the speech is scarcely different from that in which he had earlier announced his love-affair. At the beginning of the play he had explained that 'I'm telling you I could sing...We just walked along like that, see, without a word, see. I never was so happy in all my life...She looked at me...right in the eyes... "I love you," she says, "Ralph." I took her home...I wanted to cry. That's how I felt.'[24] At the end of the play it is an abstract cause rather than a girl, but the tone and indeed the language are the same: 'My days won't be for nothing...I'm twenty-two and kickin'! I'll get along. Did Jake die for us to fight about nickels? No. "Awake and sing," he said...The night he died, I saw it like a thunderbolt! I saw he was dead and I was born! I swear to God, I'm one week old! I want the whole city to hear it – fresh blood, arms. We got 'em. We're glad we're living.'[25] For Odets, his was an affirmative voice, just as below what he acknowledged to be the 'dirty lie' implicit in Hennie and Moe's escape to Cuba he could bring himself to assert that 'I do believe that, as the daughter in the family does, she can make a break with the groundling lies of her life, and try to find happiness by walking off with a man not her husband.'[26] The flouting of convention is offered as itself adequate evidence of rebellion, but it is difficult to sustain this interpretation given Hennie's weakness and her casual abandonment of her child, and given Moe's strategy of neutralising the crude immorality of society with his own homeopathic corruption. Marx did not propose adultery as a solution to capitalism, nor the exchange of one failed capitalist paradise for another. But the confusion does not only operate in Odets's mind; it is endemic in the play. A drama of praxis requires both the possibility of change and characters capable of imagining and sustaining that change. Neither Hennie nor Moe has this imagination. They gamble on the future, on a radical change in Moe's personality for which there is no evidence; on the existence and desirability of a static world of romantic delight which will make no demands on their sensibilities or their consciences. Odets is caught between a social play of public revolt and a private drama of personal rebellion. The two are never successfully welded together except at the level of language.

There is perhaps an explanation of sorts in the fact that *Awake and Sing* had originally been deeply pessimistic. Indeed Clurman had called it 'almost masochistically pessimistic'. In an early version Moe is arrested before his proposition to Hennie; Bessie is a cruder figure, drained of what sympathy attaches itself to her in the final version. The changes may explain something of the obvious tensions in a play whose realism of dialogue and character was not matched by a coherent dramatic or social vision. Clurman described Odets's work well when he said:

> There was in it a fervor that derived from the hope and expectation of change and the desire for it. But there was rarely any expression of political consciousness in it, no deep commitment to a coherent philosophy of life, no pleading for a panacea. 'A tendril of revolt' runs through all of Odets's work, but that is not the same thing as a consistent revolutionary conviction. Odets's work is not even proletarian in the sense that Gorky's work is. Rather it is profoundly of the lower middle class with all its vacillation, dual allegiance, fears, groping, self-distrust, dejection, spurts of energy, hosannas, vows of conversion and prayers for release. The 'enlightenment' of the thirties, its efforts to come to a

clearer understanding of and control over the anarchy of our society brought Odets a new mental perspective, but it is his emotional experience, not his thought, that gives his plays their special expressiveness and significance. His thought, the product chiefly of his four years with the Group and the new channels they led to, furnished Odets with the more conscious bits of his vocabulary, with an occasional epithet or slogan that were never fully integrated in his work. The feel of middle-class (and perhaps universal) disquiet in Odets's plays is sharp and specific; the ideas are general and hortatory. The Left movement provided Odets with a platform and a loud-speaker; the music that came through was that of a vast population of restive souls, unaware of its own mind, seeking help. To this Odets added the determination of youth. The quality of his plays is young, lyrical, yearning – as of someone on the threshold of life.[27]

Paradise Lost (1935), begun in 1933 and completed when the play was already in rehearsal two years later, was designed to be a work in which 'The hero... is the entire American middle class of liberal tendency.'[28] It is certainly concerned with indicting a group whom he wished to accuse of complicity in the collapse of the very moral values to which they had historically laid claim. Clurman responded to it because it reflected his own sense of a disintegrating social and moral world. Returning from a Soviet Union in which he had been impressed by the sanity of the people whom he had met, he was struck by the fact that

> Wherever I went it seemed to me I observed an inner chaos. People hankered for things they didn't need or really want, belied their own best impulses, became miserable over trivialities, were ambitious to achieve ends they didn't respect, struggled over mirages, wandered about it in a maze where nothing was altogether real for them. *Paradise Lost* seemed to me to reflect this almost dream-like unreality and, in a measure, to explain it.[29]

The play, presented in December 1935, takes place in the home of Leo and Clare Gordon. Leo is the somewhat vague and idealistic partner of Sam Katz. Together they run a small business manufacturing handbags, which Leo designs and Sam makes. But times are bad. Unbeknown to Leo, his partner has been systematically defrauding him, and at one point proposes that they should employ a gangster to burn their business down so that they can claim on the insurance. Under the pressure of a deteriorating financial situation criminality is presented as a constant temptation. Leo's son, Ben, an Olympic runner who discovers that public success as a sportsman is of no value to him in the job market, turns gangster and dies in a hail of police bullets. Another son, Julie, is dying, while a daughter, Pearl, abandoned by her lover, plays a piano all day long, finding that musical accomplishment is of no practical use to her. And the same mark of disaster is apparent in virtually all of the play's characters. A delegation of workers protest the inhuman wages and conditions to which they have been subjected by Sam. Leo's daughter-in-law is an empty-headed nymphomaniac. Through the Gordon apartment troop homeless men, corrupt politicians, bored newspapermen. Odets crams his stage with evidence of collapse and decay.

The characters are all dreamers. Pearl looks for a concert career. Ben confidently, and with no justification, expects 'a swell berth' in Wall Street. Like Biff, in Miller's *Death of a Salesman*, he believes that athletic success necessarily leads to business success – that achievement is a matter of personal magnetism. And where for Miller the symbol of Biff's delusive dreams is the golden football helmet, for Ben it is a gold athletic figurine. And lest the significance of this should be lost on the audience Odets has Clare recount the story of the making of the golden calf, the false idol which the Israelites preferred to the worship of the true God. And this is a play about false gods, about the pre-eminence of money, the failure to distinguish between the real and the ersatz, about the betrayal of basic human values, about the collapse of American idealism into pragmatism. In other words, in many respects it is another version of *Awake and Sing*, but Odets attempts to paint a broader canvas.

It is a sprawling mess of a play, with a series of cameo portraits which suffer from the violence which he does to character. But beneath the level of melodramatic action, of trite plot, of painful caricatures, there is a real sense of pain and of an abandonment which goes considerably beyond the fact of financial collapse. His targets are various but indefinite. They are those who betray themselves for money, the system which has failed everyone, the distant fascists, and those, closer to home, who seem to be preparing the way for a new war. They are the persistent failure to learn from experience, the capitulation to despair and the reaching for dreams which are dangerous in their power to distract from a real world of human need and positive action. As Leo remarks, 'We cancel our experience. This is an American habit.'[30]

But there is an attempt to root these views in character no matter how much character itself is seen as a product of social reification. Thus Mr Pike, the furnace man, is given a speech which is ostensibly concerned with denouncing warmongers (a woman on the radio is heard celebrating Armistice Day by pledging American motherhood to sacrifice another generation for the maintenance of a system exposed by the rest of the play as fraudulent and deeply inhuman) but which, in its incoherences, offers a striking and even lyrical sense of a man reaching for a language which can contain experiences which can only be diminished by that language:

> PIKE:...they have taken our sons and mangled them to death! They have left
> us lonely in our old age. The belly-robbers have taken clothes from our
> backs. We slept in subway toilets here. In Arkansas we picked fruit. I followed
> the crops north and dreamed of a warmer sun. We lived on and hoped. We

lived in garbage dumps. Two of us found canned prunes, ate them and were poisoned for weeks. One died. Now I can't die. But we gave up to despair and life took quiet years. We worked a little. Nights I drank myself insensible. Punched my own mouth. Yes, first American ancestors and me. The circle's complete. Running away, stealing away to stick the ostrich head in sand. Living on a boat as night watchman, tied to shore, not here nor there! The American jitters! Idealism! (*Punches himself violently*) There's for idealism! For those blue-bellied Yankee Doodle bastards are making other wars while we sleep. . No logic. .

LEO: But what is to be done?

PIKE: I don't know...I mean I don't know...

LEO: I will find out how to do as I think.

GUS (*drinking and laughing*): We're decayin', fallin' apart minute by minute.

PIKE: All these years one thing kept me sane: I looked at the telegraph poles. 'All those wires are going some place,' I told myself. Our country is the biggest and best pigsty in the world.'[32]

The Pike who speaks of the solitary, piano-playing Pearl as 'alone in her room with the piano – the white keys banked up like lilies and she suckin' at her own breast'[32] is not the simple radical the others would wish to make him. He represents not only the need to work for the transformation of his society – a need in which he is himself deficient – but also the necessity to create space for beauty. He is, in a sense, an expression of Odets's own amalgam of romanticism and radicalism.

It is once again clear who the enemy is. The local democratic politician is concerned only with votes, and when the Gordon family is dispossessed and their furniture placed on the street outside, his only thought is to have it removed lest it interfere with the 'prosperity party' which he wishes to hold. In the face of sixteen million unemployed the politicians are presented as powerless and self-contained. But again all that Odets has to offer is the need to abandon fantasy, a world in which 'in the end nothing is real. Nothing is left but our memory of life',[33] and to wake up to the reality of a world which is no longer susceptible to pieties derived from an American idealism negated by the present realities of unemployment, corruption and despair. Again the whole weight of Odets's faith rests on the play's final speech in which Leo, content up to this time to remain uninvolved, declares his conviction that the time has come to take a stand, to abandon illusion and acknowledge responsibility.

There is more to life than this!...the past was a dream. But this is real! To know from this that something must be done. That is real...we searched; we were confused! But we searched, and now the search is ended. For the truth has found us...Everywhere now men are rising from their sleep. Men, men are understanding the bitter black total of their lives? Their whispers are growing to shouts! They become an ocean of understanding. *No man fights alone.* Oh, if you could only see with the greatness of man. I tremble like a bride to see when they'll use it...I tell you the whole world is for men to possess. Heartbreak and terror are not the heritage of mankind!...the world is in its morning...and *no man fights alone*! Let us have air...Open the windows.[34]

In the context of the play such a speech should be ironic. It is clearly not offered as such. Brecht was amazed that Odets apparently saw such middle-class businessmen as worthy of sympathy, but this is a characteristic of Odets's plays. The bourgeoisie may have been in some respects the heart of the problem but to Odets they were also the class capable of articulating the dilemma; they were the class with its roots in American idealism.

Odets presents his capitalists as sexually impotent. Indeed the play transposes the social into a sexual dimension. The embezzler is impotent. The children of his partner are denied sexual relations (Pearl loses her lover; Ben is cuckolded). Kewpie, the gangster, is sexually as well as financially avaricious. It is a familiar conceit. Hemingway, Fitzgerald and West each offered a sexual correlative for their sense of a lost harmony between the self and society. But here, as in Hemingway's *To Have and Have Not*, it is rather too casual a gesture to sustain conviction. The symbol becomes an alternative to analysis.

In common with others Odets's imagination was caught by the forces which so manifestly press on the sensibility and physical existence of individuals for whom individuality had become problematic. Liberalism itself had undergone a profound redefinition. The novel had registered a collapse of faith in liberal individualism which was a product, in part, of the shocks of late nineteenth-century life – the determinism engendered by urbanism, industrialisation, the disturbing new realities exposed by Darwin and Freud – and in part of the bewildering brutalities of the First World War. For Hemingway, liberal language and the abstract virtues had been destroyed by an ineluctable facticity; for Fitzgerald liberal individualism was inherently ambiguous, dangerously allied to romantic egotism. The old liberal virtues – individualism, self-improvement, laissez-faire economics – had effectively been taken over by conservatism. Politically, liberalism re-emerged as a corporate reformist philosophy. For many the logic of that was that this line should be projected in the direction of Marxism. But in the case of many Americans, more especially writers, the Marxism they embraced was less ideological than spiritual – it was an image of human unity, a conviction that capitalism had run its course (by which, more often than not, they seem to have meant that money should no longer be a defining factor, that war was simply a product of capitalist imperialism). But in truth the model which Odets, no less than Steinbeck, treasured was closer to that embodied in Jefferson. What they looked for was a sense of spiritual and moral renewal. The rhetoric was often Marxist, the content essentially concerned with the need to restore an idealism which was recognisably American. They were against a life 'printed on dollar bills', saw business as potentially a form of gangsterism, proposed a model of history with clear edges, saw America as waking up to its own betrayals. It was to be a new Great Awakening.

The realist texture of Odets's work itself implies rejection – a rejection of fantasy and dream. His characters have to be weaned from their self-conceits, from the myths to which they pledge their lives, because, ostensibly at any rate, it is that tactile world which has to be reforged, shaped so as to contain the freedom they would claim. And yet there is a problem here for Odets in so far as he is himself a visionary. He rejects the myths with which society has sought to validate greed and self-concern, but wishes to endose the potential sentimentality of love and to parade his own visionary ideas. It remains true that for him the crucial transformation is within, a conversion which will radiate outwards from the self to the context within which it operates. If realism, as René Wellek implies, was a polemical weapon against romanticism, for Odets this opposition was only of limited validity. Certainly he saw himself as opposing the dangerous and facile illusions paraded by society (the glory of war, the significance of externals, the value of status) but he was drawn to the romantics' view of art as a central moral force, as in some senses an expression of a rebellious sensibility as well as of a visionary experience. And if he clearly replaces one romanticism with another, then Wellek was prone to do much the same.

The vagueness of the commitments to which his protagonists awake is striking. They turn their backs on poverty, injustice and violence, to be sure, but the world to which they turn their faces is a simple blur of light. It is negatively defined; it is everything the old world was not. And yet the characters who set out towards that light as the curtain falls are themselves imperfect – if the plays' action is to mean anything. They have learned the need for conversion but there is no agency for that conversion, no object of worship, no regulated life for the convert, no creed (beyond the brotherhood of man), no sacraments, no icons, no mechanism to turn the moment of conversion into a dedicated life. The Party, which for many provided all this, is for the most part nowhere to be seen. They are apparently reconverted to American idealism but an idealism historically stained, subverted by time and by human nature which Odets had presented as implacable but now wishes to believe is redeemable. Against all evidence, perfection is proposed as a realisable objective in *Awake and Sing* and in *Paradise Lost*. Dealing in absolutes he thus had nowhere to go in *Golden Boy* and *The Big Knife*, when he was forced to acknowledge the inadequacy of his characters to the task which they glimpsed. The irony is that the real energy of the plays is not contained in the unlocked fire, the spiritual regeneration, but in the cluttered plot, the dense human matter, the wit, the overlapping, energetic self-displays. This may be the energy of a culture in decline but it is compelling in a way that the new world which he welcomes at the end of the play is not. The debate between the rights of the individual and those of the collective are contained in the form of the plays which pitch the resistant self against the density of social experience and the sheer volume of incident. This is the central strategy of Odets's work.

Clurman characterised the period from the opening of *Paradise Lost* to the fall of 1937 as one of 'floundering' for the Group Theatre. Piscator's version of Theodore Dreiser's *An American Tragedy*, though well received by reviewers, did not impress Clurman, who found it schematic. Paul Green and Kurt Weill's *Johnny Johnson* suffered a series of appalling previews, being in Clurman's view wholly unsuited to the large theatre which was the only Broadway house they could secure. Though the play, a gentle anti-war drama, was kept going for nine weeks, it was the cause of considerable discontent within the Group, with the actors complaining about the nature of the production. Odets's *Silent Partner*, a strike play with allegorical overtones, was put into rehearsal but abandoned as incomplete. The Group had reached crisis point. A revolt of the actors led to a lengthy and detailed critique of the three directors. The actors called for reforms, more especially with respect to the Group's financial arrangements, which had, in their view, pauperised a number of them. The three directors resigned but agreed to join a committee to discuss future plans. Though Clurman announced in the *New York Times* in January 1937 that the Group would continue, the production of *Silent Partner* was finally abandoned and Clurman left for a period in Hollywood without making any arrangements for the future.

In Hollywood he was engaged to direct a film for which Odets was writing the script, though he was subsequently replaced by John Howard Lawson. In addition a number of Group actors were placed under contract. In April 1937, Cheryl Crawford and Lee Strasberg resigned. Prodded by Elia Kazan, who had also gone to Hollywood (where he resisted an invitation to change his name to Cézanne, despite a Studio assertion that any confusion with another person of the same name would be obviated because 'You just make one good picture, and nobody will even remember the other guy.')[35] but who returned to the East, Clurman announced that the Group would start work again. And Odets was to provide a new play for the occasion.

It was, indeed, a critical moment. The Theatre Union had folded. The Group had lost two founder directors. The Federal Theatre had occupied territory which they had previously considered their own.

Golden Boy (1937) could almost be Odets's *mea culpa* for his desertion to Hollywood. For the Group, Hollywood had always constituted a threat. They themselves operated on minimal salaries, surviving from production to production. The continuity of personnel, the personal commitment, indeed even the ascetic life-style forced on them by circumstances became essential elements, or at least distinguishing characteristics, of their approach. Hollywood, with its flamboyance, its wealth, its frank acknowledgement of itself as an industry producing commercial products, was the antithesis of this. To opt for Hollywood was thus more than a simple decision to experiment in a different medium. It had its element of betrayal and Clurman was not beyond capitalising on this, calling on both Franchot Tone and Clifford Odets for financial support for Group productions.

In the case of Odets the feeling was exaggerated by his central importance to the Group. He was the single most important writer they had discovered. He was also one of their own. The production of his four plays in 1935 had in a sense put the seal on their success as a production unit, while the social commitment in his work was of a kind which made it seem central to the concerns of the decade. In the period of his absence in Hollywood, moreover, the fortunes of the Group flagged. There were signs of a possible break-up, and *Golden Boy* was written in some degree to prevent this. And in its theme of a man who sells his talent for immediate success, who abandons art for money and fame, it contains, perhaps, more than an element of self-accusation. As Clurman said, for Odets, Hollywood was sin and the higher the pay the greater the sin. His first stint there, which lasted less than three months at the turn of the year 1935–6, netted him $20000. In the year of *Men in White* the Group was paying its actors a top salary of $200 a week. Worse than that, Odets was actually married to a movie star, Luise Rainer. He did infiltrate radical statement into his film scripts, but for the most part Hollywood exaggerated an element already endemic in his work – a melodramatic tendency, a sentimental attachment to redemptive love, usually thwarted by the forces of history or reaction, but occasionally sustaining.

Called before the House Un-American Activities Committee as a 'friendly witness' in the early 1950s, Odets claimed to have been a member of the Party for less than a year, leaving it some time in the middle of 1935. Certainly in 1935 he was responsible for two other brief committed plays, the monologue *I Can't Sleep*, which was an extended self-accusation by a member of the proletariat who has abandoned the working class, and *Remember*, about the need not to be demoralised by the fact of living on relief payments.

Clifford Odets was a man who saw in the Communist Party and the Group Theatre alike a sense of community which he desperately needed. He was far less concerned with ideology than he was with the need to find some animating myth, some shared experience which could neutralise his sense of abandonment. In many ways he was singularly ill-equipped to deal with his paradoxical fate – to be a writer whose financial success was built on his achievement as a radical playwright. The Group offered absolution of a kind. It was equally committed to a vague radicalism and to artistic development

179

but nevertheless frowned on careerism. Its ascetic life-style was well-suited to both causes. And yet, like Scott Fitzgerald, Odets was drawn to the world which he wished to denounce. To go to Hollywood and marry a movie star was thus simultaneously the height of his ambition and the depths of corruption. The consequence was a series of plays that condemn the artist who betrays his talent, and that denounce the mores of a society which has made money the only locus of values.

Odets was in many senses a sentimentalist. Love, assaulted by cynicism, menaced by corruption, usually defeated by the brutal force of materialism, is a central force. It represents life, not merely a biological drive which stands in contrast to the mechanical rhythms of the social world, but the source of spiritual renewal. It may, as in *Awake and Sing*, have to be deferred until the world is made a fit place for such personal concerns, but it remains a prime reason for effecting that social transformation. And yet the plays contain no transcendence, no real vision. It is clear what they are against: poverty, oppression, the corruption of the pure in heart. It is less clear what they are for. Purged of its inequities and injustices Odets's ideal society would seem to consist only of loving couples, of artists practising an art whose lyricism need no longer be coarsened by utilitarianism, of an organic community of like-minded people. He is able to imagine the moment of conversion, the moment in which his central characters perceive the paramount need for transformation; he is less able to show that transformation at work. So they see the need to strike, to awake and sing, to 'find some city where poverty's no shame – where music is no crime!'[36] but never test that new conviction in action. Indeed, with every successive play that declaration becomes more desperate, more subverted by a social world whose momentum is increasingly seen as detached from human concerns, as implacable not simply because it has the authority of power and money but because it has the authority of a human nature which is no less ineluctable for not being examined. Joe Bonaparte, in *Golden Boy*, abandons the violin for the boxing ring because he feels the pressure of the public world on him; he needs to assert his own independence and strength, paradoxically, by submitting to its values. But Odets never questions that impulse, never really asks why the individual should be willing to grant such authority to public myths.

Golden Boy is concerned with the battle for the soul of Joe Bonaparte, a young man who is torn between a career as a violinist and the quick success which he can earn as a boxer. His whole life has in some sense been a struggle to compensate for what he takes to be his own deficiencies – symbolised by an astigmatism.

His brother, Frank, is an organiser for the Congress of Industrial Organisations (CIO), and this establishes a subdued but constant point of reference. It is a commitment which Joe never considers, being locked inside a private struggle the social implications of which never penetrate his consciousness. To him music represents both an escape and a sense of that harmony which is otherwise missing from his life – the kind of hold on life for which O'Neill's characters had always been reaching. 'Playing music...that's like saying, "I am man. I belong here." '[37] But this does battle with another impulse. As he explains, 'People have hurt my feelings for years. I never forget. You can't get even with people by playing the fiddle. If music shot bullets I'd like it better – artists and people like that are freaks today. The world moves fast and they sit around like forgotten dopes.'[38] It is not that he wishes to wield art as a weapon in a social cause, it is that he holds a grudge against the world, that he wishes to demonstrate his significance in a world which places no value on art. Like Dostoevsky's man from underground, he feels the need to run full tilt into the social world in order to prove his existence.

To Joe, Lorna, his manager's lover, is amoral and spiritually dead. But her cynical wit and her worldly-wise pose barely conceal a sentimental attitude. She responds to those who have been wounded, who are vulnerable, shifting her allegiance accordingly. Indeed a principal weakness of the play lies in the mannerism with which Odets establishes this amalgam of sentiment and cynicism as a defining character mode. The fight game, it seems, is full of gentle romantics, even if it is threatened by the hoodlum Eddie Fuseli, who represents the cruder forces of the business world. But even Eddie proves remarkably vulnerable. A homosexual, he is attracted to Joe, and while his gentleness has a sinister dimension he, too, seems to consist of warring forces. And so the battle between the artist and the boxer, the spiritual and the material, is internalised and becomes not only a basic motif of the play but a fundamental character trait, and the basis of his dramatic strategy. Thus Lorna, Moody (Joe's manager), Fuseli, Joe and his brother-in-law Siggie are all expressions of this dualism. By the same token Joe's paranoia is shared by others, in particular by Lorna who is drawn to Moody because 'He loved me in a world of enemies.'[39] She has killed all real emotions in herself because emotional commitment has only made her more vulnerable. This is a lesson learned also by Fuseli, who compensates for his sexual vulnerability with the same bitter violence as Joe. The problem is that this paranoia, this sense of life as an assault on the sensibility, as loss, as corruption, is not deeply-enough rooted in a coherent social vision. Indeed Joe and Fuseli suffer from a sense of exclusion and victimisation which is not at all social in origin. Odets may find in the fight game a perfect image for capitalist society, but he never establishes its validity as such. Man may be turned against man for profit, to the extent that Joe even kills a man in the ring, but the parallel is assumed rather than demonstrated.

As Lorna observes, Joe is 'an island', trapped in a world of 'me, myself, and I'. His knowledge of the world comes from reading the *Encyclopaedia*

Britannica from cover to cover. What he lacks is any insight into himself or others. Indeed his recurrent dream is to sit in a speeding car where 'nobody gets me'.⁴⁰ He is in flight from commitment, from acknowledging his own identity. In turning to boxing he is not so much looking for fame and fortune, though this is the reason he gives, as denying part of his identity which disturbs him, which cannot be reduced to the wholly knowable. Thus, when he breaks his hands in the ring, this seals his new identity as a fighter, but his exultant cry, 'Hallelujah!! It's the beginning of the world!'⁴¹ is offered as simple irony, more especially to those who recalled Ralph's similarly exultant speech at the end of *Awake and Sing:* 'I swear to God, I'm one week old!...We're glad we're living.'⁴²

It is perhaps too fanciful to see a potential homosexuality in Joe, despite his obvious attraction to Fuseli. But it is certainly the gentler aspects of his character which he sees as despised by his society. And, like Fuseli, he feels it necessary to develop a hard exterior, a shell, in order to function. And yet in his father we are offered the portrait of a man who feels no such need. He is an immigrant whose values transcend those of his setting. Apart from anything else Joe is learning the business of being an American and, Odets implies, this involves a process of loss. It is a country which, like prize-fighting, is simply not built on the principle that 'the meek'll inherit the earth'.⁴³ Just as Joe is accused of being 'half a man', so his is a society which has seemingly suppressed its idealism and its transcendent values. It is a society which pays a thousand dollars to a boxer but leaves its violinists on the street corner (a contrast, incidentally, which remains unexamined). As a social analysis this leaves something to be desired, but in 1937 there was a real sense of alarm about American values and a play which proposed a polarisation between genuine values and the merely expedient was likely to have an authenticity which has been undermined by time.

Joe's coloured silk shirts, like Gatsby's, are offered as an indication that he fails to see beyond the surface, that he mistakes the image for the thing itself. He has something of Gatsby's naivety, but it is hard to accept him as anything more than a dramatic construct, a convenient device. On the one hand we are told that his skill as a boxer comes from his intellectual ability to analyse his opponents' weaknesses; on the other his is presented as a wholly unoriginal mind, deriving its knowledge in a programmatic manner. Where Gatsby is, from the beginning, a self-created myth, Joe exists only in terms of functional dualisms which serve Odets's dramatic purposes at the cost of a credible character. There is a fundamental lack of confidence in Odets's work which leads to a destructive explicitness. Meaning has to discharge itself completely. Language is not problematic. Thus when Joe kills an opponent in the ring the event is not allowed to speak for itself. For Odets it only becomes real when it is fully discharged in words:

JOE: I see what I did. I murdered myself, too! I've been running around in circles. Now I'm smashed! That's the truth. Yes. I was a real sparrow, and I wanted to be a fake eagle!

LORNA:...You wanted to conquer the world –
JOE: Yes.
LORNA: But it's not the kings and dictators who do it – it's that kid in the park –
JOE: Yes, that boy who might have said, 'I have myself; I am what I want to be!'[44]

The irony lies not in this apprehension, which clearly carries the burden of the play's existential logic, but in the fact that this perception seems valueless in a society which will not allow this kind of self-knowledge to function. And this is an assumption which drives his characters through perception into myth, as it does his own work through realism to an uneasy symbolism. So, Lorna announces to Joe Bonaparte, who has just acknowledged the need to face the reality of his character and the world, 'We have each other! Somewhere there must be happy boys and girls who can teach each other the way of life! We'll find some city where poverty's no shame...Where a man is glad to be himself, to live and make his woman herself.' Joe replies to this by exultantly opting for the world of the speeding automobile in which, apparently, there are no consequences. 'That's it – speed! We're off the earth – unconnected! We don't have to think!! That's what speed's for, an easy way to live!'[45] The insight is rejected out of fear.

But, of course, Odets had always found it as difficult as Joe to actualise the world which he describes and which he, too, is liable to displace into myth or into a future which has all the appearance of a myth. Joe and Lorna are dispatched into their mythological world by means of a car crash, leaving Joe's brother, Frank, to point an ambiguous moral. For Frank, as a union organiser, bears the scars of his social commitment. Although he can boast the virtue of living in a real world, of acknowledging his identity and his circumstance, he does so in a language which, on the one hand is as visionary as Joe's, and on the other hand seems to embrace a disturbing determinism. He acclaims the 'pleasure of acting as you think! The satisfaction of staying where you belong, being what you are...at harmony with millions of others!'[46] But since we see virtually nothing of this character it is impossible to know what value to give to such a statement, while the model of identity offered is disturbingly simplistic. A suggestion that one should be 'what you are' is likely to seem distressingly banal after a play which has attempted to emphasise the problem of arriving at a satisfactory sense of the self and its potential. By the same token the passivity of his suggestion that one should stay 'where you belong' is a doubtful proposition in a play in which this character is charged with representing the possibilities of change, of social reconstruction.

183

Like Fitzgerald in *Tender is the Night*, he seems to take as his protagonist in *Golden Boy* the spoiled priest, the man who is tainted, tempted by a warped sense of pride. Cynicism may be the defence displayed by his characters; it is also, in a sense, the defence which he himself deploys. Hollywood was so antithetical to everything he stood for, it was as though that became the one place he had to go. He placed himself in the maximum possible danger.

Odets's strength as a writer lay partly in his humour, in the skill with which he rendered the defensive wise-cracking of characters who sought to shore up their collapsing world with jokes, and partly in an unashamed sentimentalism kept just under control, in his best plays, by the counter-balance of a faithfully rendered sense of moral and physical constraint. His characters often want to escape, to opt for speed, for wide open spaces, for fantasy, for an indefinite future. He is at his best when he opposes to that the tactile, physical, three-dimensionality of a present not so easily evaded. His weakness as a writer lies in his willingness to relax that tension, for ideological reasons as in *Awake and Sing*, for melodramatic reasons as in *Golden Boy*, or for sentimental reasons as in *Night Music* (1940). A rhetorical gesture, a dramatic convenience are simply not adequate to the density of the world which at times he creates. His was a melodramatic imagination. He tended to push things to extremes. In the case of *Waiting for Lefty* the mood of the moment redeemed this, though by the same token it is no longer possible to take it entirely seriously. In the case of *Golden Boy* he created a cliché, an opposition between the spiritual and the material, between a transcendent art and the hard fact of capitalist society, which was too obvious to be credible. In many ways Hollywood was Odets's natural home. And so he lived there, arguing ferociously for the significance of the group which he had abandoned.

Odets's next play for the Group Theatre was *Rocket to the Moon* (1938). It was, as Clurman noted, different from his earlier work. Its theme was the redemption through love of a weak man and a shallow-spirited woman. Love, destroyed by circumstances in all of his previous plays, was to prove redemptive. It was a transformation badly mishandled by Odets and one which came as a surprise to the actors who received the final act only ten days before opening. A girl who, earlier in the play, had been presented as un-educated, self-deceiving and trivial becomes an articulate spokesman for a new life, while the man, a dentist, whose will had formerly been dominated by his wife, is given one of Odets's final curtain speeches about the new life which is opening up. *Rocket to the Moon* received mixed notices, and the ensuing post-mortem did little for the morale of the company which now began to show signs of the tensions which would contribute to its decline.

The social convictions which had given a certain force to Odets's earlier work were now virtually absent. A gesture is made in the direction of his former self. In some ill-defined way social conditions are undermining human relations but in essence the central need is for individuals to awake and sing. The language is the same, but the meaning is undercut by the violence which Odets does to character and by his failure to imagine the world which is placing his characters under such pressure. The play's speeches are entirely familiar. The woman asks the question all Odets's characters are fated to ask: 'Don't you think there's a world of joyful men and women? Must all men live afraid to laugh and sing? Can't we sing at work and love our work? It's getting late. It's getting late to play at life; I want to *live* it.'[47] She receives the answer all Odets's characters are fated to receive: 'I insist this is a beginning... I saw myself clearly, realized who or what I was. Isn't that a beginning?... Yes, I, who sat here in this prison office, closed off from the world...for the first time in years I looked out on the world and saw things as they really are.'[48] The indictment of Odets was that he neither saw nor dramatised things as they were any more. He was a huckster for love, like Steinbeck, and like him he could offer nothing but a lyrical language and a patent symbol.

As Clurman insisted, Odets was the voice of his day. He expressed the curious contradictions of a society which was experiencing the most profound challenge to its values which it had ever experienced outside the Civil War. For a few critical years the whole direction of The Great Experiment was in the balance. A socialist rhetoric, which had been regarded as fundamentally alien, now emanated from the White House. The Constitution seemed a positive hindrance to radical solutions which not only the poor regarded as necessary. The pressures in the society were considerable, and in a sense it was these pressures which Odets tapped. They gave his work a resonance which it might otherwise have lacked. They charged the theatre, too, with an energy which had hardly characterised it before by moving it to the centre of concerns which no American could afford to ignore. Odets's melodramatic tendencies found an echo and a response in the social melodrama of ruined lives, starved children, a dispossessed bourgeoisie and a radically disaffected working class. But for a playwright this was also a liability, not simply in the sense that he became tied to a particular moment but to the degree that he was seen as a writer who drew his energy from a narrow range of experience. Leaving the Group was a forbidding necessity for him but it was one which left him with a clear residue of guilt.

There is little evidence that Odets was concerned with pressing the limits of drama, with testing the potential of theatre. He was most at home with realism, with a form which could render the moral dilemmas of the age as he saw them. His work emerged out of the press of events, out of the individual's struggle to relate to public myths and private visions. The density of the social world, which he felt obliged to render in detail and with a straining for authenticity of tone and texture, was itself the source of tensions born in the individual and magnified by social inequity and the false gods of materialism. His social conscience was real but sentimental. Despite his membership of the Party he seems never to have grasped the essence of its ideological beliefs and certainly never to have embodied those beliefs in his work. What we have instead is the poetic spirit struggling to emerge in an apparently irredeemably material world. The implied longing is for an organic society, a restored sense of community. Class plays little or no role in his work at a dramatic or moral level. What he yearns for is what O'Neill yearned for, a restored relationship between man and his environment. Odets saw society as a boxing ring, a tenement building, an embattled union hall. His characters long for space but have to reconcile themselves with a world in which that space has apparently been irrevocably annihilated. And it can, it seems, only be recreated in the imagination – that is certainly where we tend to be left at the end of his plays. We are offered a vision, a dream, a renewed commitment, a wistful regret, a confident assertion; but we are left at the brink, on the margin, pressed, still, to the edge of life. The visions never have the sharpness of the tenement building, the dreams never have the authentic power and the truth of the practical realities which commanded his dramatic imagination and which he captured so purely in the languages of America. The visionary rhetoric rings false; the verbal small change of daily life rings true even when carefully sculpted to accommodate the aphorism and the one line gag. And that was the ambiguity of his work – the social no less than the dramatic ambiguity. The sentimentality, always strong in his work, becomes progressively stronger until in his final Group Theatre play, *Night Music*, his social commitment has become deflected into the purest kitsch. And Odets's usual curtain-speech call for renewal becomes a celebration of love and domestication. George Washington's language is appropriated to endorse a simple celebration of private relations in a world conveniently transformed by his version of a Dickensian Cheerybleness: 'remember this,' says an avuncular detective, '"The preservation of the sacred fire of liberty...is in the hands of the people." Washington said that – It's on the statue. You are the people. Whatever you want to say, say it! Whatever has to be changed, change it! Who told you to make a new political party? Make it and call it "Party-to-Marry-My Girl".'[49]

The gravitational pull towards stereotype in his work was only in part an expression of his sense of the reductive power of environment. His work lacks subtlety, prefers dualism to ambiguity and offers a distressingly simplistic model of psychological and social truth. The times made demands upon his sensibility which he felt obliged to answer with a drama which denied itself opacity and paradox. Perhaps they were beyond him anyway. His people are all masked, emotionally scarred, but they battle on clinging to whatever imaginative driftwood they can find. The passage of time has created an ironic undertow which tends to pull *Waiting for Lefty* in the direction of *Waiting for Godot* and *Awake and Sing* towards *Happy Days*, not because this was an irony which he could ever bring himself to face (though there is a suggestion of it in *Golden Boy*) but because the confidence of those plays did not so much come from the works themselves as from the context of their presentation. That context, changed, a fundamental pessimism seems to remain, a sense that the individual cannot free himself of his immediate determinants nor of a human nature which dooms him to see his assertions frustrated and his dreams denied.

Golden Boy was a considerable success, running for 250 performances and selling to Hollywood. Financially it was the most successful of all the Group Theatre's productions. It made enough to keep them going for two years. The film version was rewritten so as to have a happy ending. It was symptomatic. Compromise, acknowledged or not, was an inevitable consequence of a precarious financial situation and of the conflicting objectives and motivations of the Group members.

The success of the play engendered a spurt of activity on the part of the Group. But it was to prove misleading. Its slow demise, indeed, coincided with these years of financial security and when the buffer of these profits was removed, finance became an increasing problem. The Group's very success in certain directions inspired a sense of frustration that it had not achieved more, that it had not, for example, become a permanent repertory company, that it had failed to become a major influence on world theatre. This failure was indeed in large part a consequence of long-term financial problems, but it was also a product of personal tensions and a result of the absence of major playwriting talent. But most of all, in Clurman's opinion, those involved in the Group Theatre were victims of the nature of theatre in America. That is, they were hopelessly divided between a desire to serve the interests of theatre and a desire to further their careers; a belief in the moral power of drama and the need to achieve success in the eyes of the public. Their ambivalence was very much that of their principal writer, Odets, which may, indeed, account for the close relationship which they sustained in the latter half of the 1930s, despite, or perhaps because of, the guilt which he felt following his defection to Hollywood. Thus, Harold Clurman, in describing the death of the Group, remarked that

> There was a desire for anonymity in the Group and eventually a desire for personal aggrandisement. There was a desire for freedom and a desire for a discipline imposed from without to silence the devils that the freedom might set loose. There was a realization of the time needed to produce anything real and complete in the theatre, and there was a bitter impatience with anything less than the 'just right', though created in short order under hazardous

circumstances. There was a desire for humility, for tolerance, and there was a suspicion of almost everyone's defects.[50]

As a group it was caught in the familiar problem of raising its cash on a commercial basis for plays which were to be produced for reasons having little to do with their commercial viability. Beginning with a confidence in its own objectives which made public production itself not a necessary consequence of its work, it moved, perhaps inevitably, to weighing its success by the criteria of friendly reviews and long runs. Believing initially that it could play its part in transforming society in such a way and to such an extent that its own work could be seen as central, it found itself increasingly isolated. And the public mood had changed. The artist could no longer regard himself as the cutting-edge of history. The mood in America had shifted towards a bland consensus politics. Left-wing theatre groups had collapsed. The Federal Theatre had been killed. And the siren voices of Hollywood remained strong, attracting not only Odets, Tone and Lee J. Cobb, but, subsequently, Clurman, Adler, Strasberg and Kazan.

5 Left-wing theatre

In *Literature and Revolution* Leon Trotsky describes how in 1918 and 1919 it was not uncommon to meet at the front a military division, with cavalry at the head, and wagons carrying actors, actresses and stage sets at the rear, this being an image, he explained, of the fact that in general the place of art is in the rear of historic advance. However, in the turmoil of war, he implied, that order might be momentarily inverted.

For Michael Gold, writing at the beginning of the 1920s, the class war had indeed long since been declared, and art potentially had a leading role, an art forged out of the experience of the working class by the proletariat itself. So it was that in 1921, under the name Irwin Granich, he wrote:

> In blood, in tears, in chaos and wild thunderous clouds of fear the old economic order is dying. We are not appalled or startled by that giant apocalypse before us. We know the horror that is passing away with this long winter of the world. We know, too, the bright forms that stir at the heart of all this confusion, and that shall rise out of the debris and cover the ruins of capitalism with beauty.

This formed part of his famous essay, 'Towards proletarian art'. It was offered as a manifesto of the new cultural order. 'We are prepared,' he observed:

> for the economic revolution of the world, but what shakes us with terror and doubt is the cultural upheaval that must come. We rebel instinctively against this change. We have been bred in the old capitalist planet, and its stuff is in our very bones. Its ideals, mutilated and poor, were yet the precious stays of our lives. Its art, its science, its philosophy and metaphysics are deeper in us than logic or will. They are deeper than the reach of the knife in our social passion. We cannot consent to the suicide of our souls. We cling to the old culture, and fight for it against ourselves. But it must die. The old ideals must die. But let us not fear. Let us fling all we are into the cauldron of the Revolution.[1]

Gold was charting a path into Whitman's 'new territory', a world for which travel maps were 'yet unmade'. He was a revolutionary first and a writer second. His first plays were produced by the Provincetown Players but his sensibility was formed by an unemployment demonstration in Union Square in 1914. He was a natural radical in politics and art. In his essay he hailed Whitman as the 'heroic spiritual grandfather of our generation in America',[2] insisting that Walt 'dwelt among the masses' and knew them 'too well to believe that any individual could rise in intrinsic value above them'.

189

Accordingly he quoted approvingly Whitman's observations in *Democratic Vistas:* 'I say that democracy can never prove itself beyond cavil, until it founds and luxuriantly grows its own forms of art, poems, schools, theology, displacing all that exists, or has been produced anywhere in the past under opposite influences.' But, for Gold, the model was no longer to be America. The lesson was now offered elsewhere. It was in Russia, a country which, with Whitman, believed 'that the spiritual cement of a literature and art is needed to bind together a new order. The *Prolet-Kult*' he asserted, 'is their conscious effort toward this. It is the first effort of historic Man towards such a culture.'[3]

The question was whether this could be recreated in America, whether a workers' art could be forged that would go beyond 'the obsessions and fears that haunted the brains of the solitary artist'. Accordingly he looked for a 'drama group of the workers in every factory'.[4] He looked for an optimism to neutralise the 'sad and spiritually sterile' world of the 'priests of art'.[5] In the age of the common man and of revolution tragedy was dead. He looked for an art of the people which would escape the 'solitary pain, confusions, doubts and complexities'. It was a view tainted with a profound sentimentalism. It was, indeed, one rooted in a romantic sensibility. He asserted 'the deep need of the masses for the old primitive group life'.[6] His views were, indeed, not untouched by mysticism and his language anticipated that of the 1930s in its proposing of a secular religion. 'The Revolution,' he asserted, 'in its secular manifestations of strike, boycott, mass-meeting, imprisonment, sacrifice, agitation, martyrdom, organization, is thereby worthy of the religious devotion of the artist.'[7]

The Party was indeed to demand of its converts a discipline and an obedience which many responded to with religious zeal. The greater the sacrifice demanded, the greater the feeling of grace. And one of the principal sacrifices was evidently to be that of dramatic subtlety. Gold's attacks on 'confusions, doubts and complexities' suggested a model for art which left no space for the ambiguous, which sought, indeed, to close social and aesthetic spaces, which reached for a language which voiced itself completely, which left no residual meaning unprobed, no potential unrealised. Appearance and essence must be made to coincide. Symbol was to be exchanged for substance. The energies of this new art were to come from outside art; they were to emerge from the kinetic difference between classes, levels of income and experience. The crudity of this work was in some sense to be the guarantee of its authenticity. It followed that articulateness was liable to be in some senses ambiguous, a potential class betrayal. So that action was to stand in for language. But communication remained at a premium. As Jean-Paul Sartre was to say, 'I distrust the incommunicable; it is the source of all violence. When it seems impossible to get others to share the certainties which we enjoy, the only thing left is to fight, or burn, or to hang.'[8] It was a prescription for an energetic art, one whose power derived from its directness, from its exposure of the hidden. This is an art whose imagery is one of resistance, friction, a tensing of physical and moral muscles. It is likely to shun silence, to fill space with action, to crowd moment on moment, event on event. Its social model is likely to be one of a clear causality. Private life is likely to exist only as an expression of social truths; the self to exist only in relation to the group. Human nature is likely to be assumed, on the one hand, to be relentless, implacable, in so far as the cruelty of the class enemy seems to be irremediable, while on the other hand it is likely to be shown as courageously resisting encroachments on its space. And certainly this paradox was never fully inspected in 1930s drama.

Gold's manifesto was ahead of its times and when a left-wing theatre did emerge it did not, for the most part, rise spontaneously from the masses as Gold had hoped. Nor, indeed, was it a wholly realistic art. But it was the socially committed theatre which provided a principal interest for more than a decade.

Trotsky had himself doubted the possibility of a proletarian culture emerging, suggesting that the energy of the proletariat must necessarily be deflected elsewhere, into the more immediate problems of the class struggle and the radical reconstruction of society. Indeed he insisted that

> The formless talk about proletarian culture, in antithesis to bourgeois culture, feeds on the extremely uncritical identification of the historic destinies of the proletariat with those of the bourgeoisie. A shallow and purely liberal method of making analogies of historic forms has nothing in common with Marxism. There is no real analogy between the historic development of the bourgeoisie and of the working class.[9]

But it was just such an analogy which Gold, himself of petty-bourgeois origins, was asserting.

For Trotsky, the whole debate was at an unsophisticated stage. He resisted the reductiveness of those who sought to base their aesthetic on the crudely forceful political homily, derived from writers able to deploy irreproachable class credentials, and unconcerned with form. But he also resisted a model of art which would abstract it from its social origins. Where for Shklovsky art was always 'free of life' and, while 'its color never reflected the color of the flag which waved over the fortress of the city',[10] content being a simple by-product of form, the committed writer had to deny autonomy to the word. And yet there was, of course, a classic problem. For both language and artistic form are the product of cultural tradition. They are infiltrated with the values which the radical writer would wish to deny. Trotsky himself had

191

asked how it was possible to build a new society with the aid of an old science and the old morals; he might well have focussed on the problem of subverting language. But he knew that science was not so easily subverted, that its own internal logic was not necessarily susceptible to ideological perception and that art, too, had its own sustaining structures. What he did insist upon was that 'one cannot turn the concept of culture into the small change of individual daily living and determine the success of a class culture by the proletarian passports of individual inventors or poets'.[11] In other words, in calling for a proletarian literature Gold was in danger of side-stepping the nature of the culture of which the literature would be an expression. Trotsky had no time for honest expressions of proletarian feelings if they did not acknowledge that in choosing to express themselves in literary form they were perforce acknowledging the existence of certain disciplines and constraints: 'weak and, what is more, illiterate poems do not make up proletarian poetry, because they do not make up poetry at all'.[12] Crudity of conception, slackness of form, weakness in technique were, for him, no guarantee of authenticity. This was not Marxism but 'reactionary populism'.[13] 'Proletarian art should not be second-rate art.'[14]

And this, of course, was the great temptation. If content is perceived as being of paramount importance, as too often it was by critics of the Party press, if ideological orthodoxy was to be considered as a prime objective, then the risk was that proletarian art would be stillborn, would become a coterie art locked in a closed world of aesthetic and political timidity. And this risk proved a real one in the committed drama of the American 1930s and more especially in the small, amateur, Communist drama groups. Trotsky's warning was a timely and prescient one. 'Such terms as "proletarian literature",' he warned, 'and "proletarian culture" are dangerous, because they erroneously compress the culture of the future into the narrow limits of the present day. They falsify perspectives, they violate proportions, they distort standards and they cultivate the arrogance of small circles which is most dangerous.'[15] All too many of the attempts to create workers' theatres in the 1930s in America foundered for just such reasons. But, in so far as they were concerned, in Sartre's words, 'to project for the audience an enlarged and enhanced image of its own sufferings'[16] they did sharpen a social and political consciousness which was born outside of art in the real conditions of social and economic collapse which that audience experienced. The effect of the 1930s was, in the telling phrase which Trotsky applied to the radical publicist Belinsky, 'to open up a breathing hole into social life by means of literature'.[17]

The theatrical revolt of the early decades of the twentieth century was largely a product of what was called the little-theatre movement. Its audience was drawn from a somewhat restricted social group; its supporters were interested in the development of theatre but uncertain as to the role of that theatre in human affairs. In a society which George Jean Nathan characterised as 'amusement mad to the point of insanity',[18] the theatre was either given over to escapist entertainment or to an art so pure as to exclude its potential as a political force and a social irritant. At least this was how it seemed to John Dos Passos, who returned from Paris excited by the energy and iconoclasm of modernism but remained anxious to direct its generalised revolt into a more clearly political direction. The struggle to create a committed theatre of the Left, though principally a product of the 1930s, was indeed born out of the excitement of European political theatre in the immediate post-war years and reached America in an organised form first in the short-lived Workers' Drama League and then in the almost equally short-lived New Playwrights' Theatre.

The theatre was to be stripped for action: reduced, like the Russian and German theatres, to its essentials. It was to lose its embellishments, its romantic posturing, its excessive concentration on the individual, its reassuring separation of audience and performer. Michael Gold, a founder of the New Playwrights' Theatre (along with John Dos Passos, John Howard Lawson, Em Jo Basshe and Francis Edward Faragah), returned from Russia enthusiastic for the vitality and innovatory pressure of a theatre which was concerned with catering for a new audience no longer socially or artistically containable:

> Acrobatic actors race up and down a dozen planes of action. The drawing-room play has been thrown on the junk-pile of history. Things happen – broad, bold, physical things, as in the workers' lives. There are dangers and the feel of elementals...Machinery had been made a character in the drama. City rhythms, the blare of modernism, the iron shouts of industrialism, these are actors.[19]

For O'Neill, as for Elmer Rice, the machine was a threat; for Gold, as for the futurists whom he admired, it was, at first, the image of the modern. Thus, what had struck him about Meyerhold's theatre was

> His bare, immense stage...stripped for action, like a steel mill or a factory... Intricate structures, like huge machines created for a function, furnish the scaffold on which actors race and leap and walk from plane to plane. All that was static in the old theatre has been stamped out. This is the theatre of dynamics. This theatre is the battle-field of life; it is a trench, a factory, the deck of a ship in a storm.[20]

Dos Passos and Basshe were more suspicious of this mechanism, choosing to celebrate a resistant human spirit.

In 1929, Michael Gold attempted to create a workers' theatre, called the Workers' Drama League, which included Ida Rauh, former secretary of the Provincetown, and, technically, John Howard Lawson and Jasper Deeter (neither attended meetings). It was not a success, quickly collapsing in disarray, but it was swiftly followed by a better-organised attempt.

The New Playwrights' Theatre was founded in 1926. The money for the new venture was put up by Otto Kahn, the same friendly banker who had supported both the Provincetown and the Guild, and who offered thirty thousand dollars despite the declared political objectives of the group. It brought together a number of writers who not only shared left-wing views but had also been exposed to European experimentalism. John Howard Lawson, indeed, had written both *Roger Bloomer* (1923) and *Processional* (1925) while living in Paris. The former was produced by the Actors' Theatre, a fragile creation of Actors' Equity, the latter by the Theatre Guild. *Roger Bloomer*, about a young man's struggle in a materialistic world, consisted of a series of brief scenes culminating in a Diaghilev-influenced 'Freudian dream-ballet'. *Processional* was a 'jazz symphony', a 'conception of the stream of American life carried along on a current of vaudeville patter and jazz noises'.[21] Another member, Em Jo Basshe, had been a member of the Provincetown theatre, as was Michael Gold who was by now an editor of *New Masses*.

In an article in *New Masses* in 1927, Dos Passos explained his idea of revolutionary theatre: 'By revolutionary I mean that such a theatre must break with the present theatrical tradition...it must draw its life and ideas from the conscious section of the industrial and white-collar working classes which are out to get control of the great flabby mass of capitalist society and mould it to their own purpose.'[22] It was an extravagant claim, inaccurate in its assessment of the state of working-class consciousness and wholly disproportionate to any likely achievement for their small-scale venture. Certainly the New Playwrights' Theatre did little either to revolutionise theatre or society. A Greenwich Village group, they rarely came close to the working class, while they drew a consistently bad press. Yearning for the national significance of an Abbey Theatre or the Theatre of the Revolution in Moscow, they sought to create an 'American mass myth'[23] (an objective which immediately made clear the gap between their own situation and that in Ireland and Russia, neither of which needed quite so mechanical an approach to myth). And there was an air of desperation about Dos Passos's statement that 'If you can make a god of a Workers' Theatre and attract an audience and hammer into them some valuable truths the result will be a first-rate theatre probably.'[24] Probably, indeed.

For John Howard Lawson, the New Playwrights' Theatre, which staged its first production in the spring of 1927, was, the Workers' Drama League aside, the first attempt to build a theatre on a social foundation in America. The earlier experimental theatres, the Provincetown and the Washington Square Players, had been concerned with affirming individualism, with a new approach to theatre which failed nonetheless to identify a new audience. But Dos Passos's 'probably' proved more disabling than he would have wished, so that, looking back from the perspective of 1937, Lawson was forced to concede that 'No such audience was visible in 1927, but the *need* for it determined the activity of the New Playwrights.'[25] The 'Revolt of Fifty Second Street' (the heading of their manifesto) proved if not abortive then remarkably contained within the limits of Fifty Second Street. But though the critics were almost unanimously hostile, a number of the Theatre's productions genuinely tried to break new aesthetic as well as social ground.

Indeed, it would be a mistake to imagine that these plays were all realistic accounts of strikes, of gallant workers in rebellion against the forces of reaction. Just as the revolutionary theatre in Russia had at first responded enthusiastically to social revolt by creating an art commensurate with that revolt, expressive of the liberated energies released by the collapse of an old system, so, for a while at least, American writers responded in similar vein. Lawson, Dos Passos, Basshe and Gold all created plays which were celebratory rather than analytic and which attempted to find some form which would reflect the confident social and aesthetic modernity of their views. Thus, Dos Passos called *The Garbage Man* (1925), a 'parade with shouting', while Mike Gold submitted *Hoboken Blues* (1928), 'A Modern Negro Fantasia on an Old American Theme' and included in it a parade of giraffes, elephants, lions, monkeys and clowns as well as a full orchestra.

The stage set for *Hoboken Blues* was 'a futurist composition suggesting a corner of Harlem twenty-five years ago'.[26] It was dominated by bright colours suggestive of 'peasant gaudiness'. The scene was to be 'dynamic, yet with an old-fashioned peasant touch. A child's composition. It would,' Gold indicated, 'be a calamity to treat the scenes in the play realistically. They must be done by an intelligent futurist like Arthur Dove, Covarrubias, Demuth or Hugo Gellert...At times scenes will...overlap slightly – there will be an effect of simultaneous planes of action – as in some futurist paintings.' But, lest this seem too purely modernist, dangerously detached from the world it pictured, Gold insisted that 'There is nothing esoteric about all this, however.'[27]

The stage, in Gold's play, is full of sound, from the banjo music and orchestral version of the cake-walk, to the shouted ecstasies of the store-front church. But it also flirts perilously with racial stereotypes. Sam Pickens, a black layabout, is hounded by his wife who wants him to get a job and religion. In despair he goes to Hoboken, where he has been told everything will be available. Caught between his own instinctive hedonism and the brutal realities of American life he plunges into a fantasy which dramatises his dilemma. And the set itself is offered as an extension of this action. So the stage direction indicates that a part of the design is to consist of 'an African jungle, with huge, monstrous vegetation and palm trees. Great American sunflowers. A park bench. Symbols of modern industrialism, wheels, pulleys, machine designs. Dollar marks. Musical notes. Question marks. African masks. Coney Island. Circus. Advertisements. A battle of jungle and industrialism.'[28] There follows a series of pantomime scenes in which Sam is humiliated in the various jobs offered to him: waiter, bootblack, 'hit-the-nigger' side-show attractions. The only other jobs available involve heavy labouring. The play then lurches further into fantasy: he is beaten by four white-faced policemen; a series of caricatures of white leaders (a businessman, a minister and the president of a women's club) are paraded along with Christopher Columbus and George Washington, while a chorus chants 'Law and order must rule the day / America first; hip, hip, hooray!'[29] Against this are offered only the pieties of a black angel, an idealised form of his wife, who kisses him and tells him, 'Forget everything, Black Man – poor black man – forget the rape, the tar and feathers, the flames of the hitching post. Forget the cold sneers and cruel laughters of the world. Forget the past and sing only the deep music of the melodious future.'[30]

What follows is a mock trial in which he is found guilty 'of being poor... of being lazy and musical...of every other crime possible to persons who can't afford to hire lawyers' and sentenced to 'life imprisonment in a factory'. There follows an expressionist scene in which the workers 'fall into machine dance motions' inside a cage to the accompaniment of a 'frothy Broadway musical comedy tune' which gradually dominates a 'monotonous machine music'.[31] But the workers rebel and elect Sam as President of Hoboken. He then returns to Harlem, to a set which is 'vastly more angular, confusing, colorful and jazzy...Industrialism rampant', and to 'futurist city music in the style of Edgar Varèse.'[32] He returns only to realise that his time in Hoboken had been an illusion, a consequence of a police beating. But the play ends with his appeal: 'But folks why can't there be a place for de poor man, black and white, where birds sing sweet, and every house is full of music, and dere's sunflowers round the factory door? Where no one is hungry, where no one is lynched, where dere's no money or bosses, and men are brudders?'[33]

It is a curious play. The piety with which it ends is in perfect harmony with the fantasy tone but at odds with the social realities which inspired the work and with his own satirical style. As in so much committed theatre of the next decade and more the concluding optimism is threatened by the accuracy of its social observation.

Both *The Garbage Man*, first produced by the Harvard Dramatic Club in 1925 under the title *The Moon is a Gong*, and Em Jo Basshe's *The Centuries* (1927) contrast the machine world with the individual's struggle for survival. In *The Garbage Man*, a young couple struggle with a mechanical existence which denies them freedom. As the girl remarks, 'Machine's spinning, weaving steel webs, cold steel splinters sharp as razors, and nothing but our bare hands to lay hold of that, our naked bodies to fight all that, to conquer all that.'[34] For much of the play they are defeated and destroyed but, as with Gold's play, with a final flourish the young man announces, 'Voice of the machine, voice of the machine, I defy you.'[35] Together they face the world of possibility 'with nothing but the whirl of space in our faces'.[36] The play employs an entire orchestra and contrasts its sentimentalised version of reality with the harsh sounds of machinery and the desperate poetry of the individuals. The stage is cluttered with representative and symbolic figures. It is a moral tale of human resistance but one whose moral force is undermined by its own sentimentalities.

In *The Centuries*, Em Jo Basshe attempts a similar contrapuntal arrangement of machine and human voice in a play which offers a conventional image of the committed theatre of the 1920s and 30s. Again the stage is packed with characters: Jewish immigrants newly arrived in America. It is part celebration, part denunciation of the American economic and political system. The crowded stage is an attempt to engage a whole society. Like *Hoboken Blues* and *The Garbage Man*, *The Centuries* offers itself as an image of social process. Like the Russian theatre it was an attempt to capture the dynamic energies of the social scene, to celebrate the resistant spirit. But its analysis was not profound, the drama tended to be over-extended and the characters predictable. Nonetheless these were plays which were prepared to challenge the orthodoxies of realist art which increasingly came to typify left-wing theatre.

In 1927 the New Playwrights' manifesto had sounded somewhat strange. Certainly it made large claims for the theatre artist. Published in the *New York Times* in February 1927, it had asserted that:

> He stands shoulder to shoulder with the mentors of our age: the Einsteins, Gothals, Curles, Michelsons, Edisons. He is their historian, their toastmaster and very often their clown. He accepts the clay and the model they have ready for him. He accepts their nuts, bolts, cranes; he listens to the tune played by their acetylene torches, cutting through steel, rock, bone; he trembles as the earth trembles when their showy engines shriek and pound away...Throw rotten eggs at the dynamo. The show will go on. We are in the presence of the present.[37]

It was not at first entirely clear that the theatre was to be radical in a strictly political sense. The constructivist set for *Loud Speaker* dominated the production, and though the play offered a jaundiced view of the American political process it was rather more concerned with staging American vitality than prophesying the collapse of the system. It was, as Karen Taylor has suggested, and as John Howard Lawson has asserted, the execution of

Sacco and Vanzetti which clarified this question for the group: 'There's no doubt that the execution of Sacco and Vanzetti (and our trial that followed which we won*) had an effect in making the NPT more openly revolutionary. But this was a basic tendency in the culture of the time.'[38]

The latter was not, of course, entirely true in an American context. Political revolution by no means typified American culture of the late 1920s which was, rather, in a state of withdrawal, declaring a 'separate peace', lamenting the collapse or the simple inefficacy of liberal values, proposing art as itself a value to counterpose to an entropic reality. The truth was that for rather mixed motives and in a somewhat confused way the dramatists of the New Playwrights wished to inject an element which was strong, for good historical and political reasons, in the European theatre but which had no such roots in the American one. This, indeed, was a crucial difference and the source of an important problem for left-wing playwrights in America. The First World War – of fundamental importance in Germany and Russia – had not been a shared experience for the American masses, though its significance for the American intellectual, as fact and symbol, was considerable. Political revolution was equally meaningless in America while it, and the art which it generated, was a fundamental fact of recent history and a continuing point of reference in the countries to which these playwrights looked as models. The American radical playwright operated in a profoundly different context from his European counterpart.

Karen Taylor makes exaggerated claims for the plays of the New Playwrights, both directly and by implication. To suggest that the structural antecedents of Em Jo Basshe's *The Centuries* are in Elizabethan drama, 'the last time in which plot was clearly subordinated to theme', is plainly unhelpful and untrue. But these plays were clearly written out of a desire to stake out new territory, political and aesthetic. Their failure was partly a failure of production, a failure fully to integrate all the elements of their eclectic style, and partly a failure of writing. When Dos Passos offered his epitaph for the group in 1929 he began with a quotation from Piscator, commenting on the failure of the Volksbühne in Berlin, but immediately admitted its failure on a political level, blaming this on 'the American mind of all classes and denominations'.[39] But, having assailed both radicals and revolutionaries for failing to understand that the revolutionary theatre needed new tools, he offered a rather more limited but accurate admission, coupled with a prophecy more appropriate than his rather wild swings at his critics:

> I think the New Playwrights' Theatre failed, in the first place, because authors are largely too preoccupied with their own works to make good producers, and secondly because the problems involved were not seen clearly enough in

* They had been arrested for picketing the Massachusetts State House.

the beginning. But the fact that it existed makes the next attempt in the same direction that much easier. One thing is certain: the time for half measures in ideas or methods is gone, if indeed it ever was.[40]

This article appeared in *New Masses* in August 1929. Two months later the stock-market collapsed and those who had been predicting and working for the overthrow of capitalism suddenly found themselves confronted with the ostensible fulfilment of their prophecies. The small, radical theatre groups were boosted by this apparent evidence that history was indeed squarely on their side. Certainly left-wing theatre now moved more clearly to the centre of affairs.

Many of these groups saw themselves unambiguously as adjuncts of the revolution, as instruments in the class war. A spokesman for the Workers' Laboratory Theatre, founded in 1930, insisted that such a group

> must be organized in such a manner that dramatic troupes may be developed thruout [sic] the country; traveling groups must be evolved, ready one day to go to strike meetings to cheer up the strikers, just as ready another day to accompany a demonstration to inspire the workers; it must be a theatre where the worker may be inspired to fight for his liberation; a theatre of the class struggle – a theatre of the workers, by the workers, for the workers.[41]

One such group was the Proletbühne (Proletarian Stage), a German-speaking group, formed in 1925, but regrouped in 1928, which very consciously modelled itself on the committed theatre of Europe. Indeed, though securing small audiences, these groups did act as a main conduit through which European models of committed theatre entered America.

In 1934, the Workers' Laboratory Theatre became the Theatre of Action. It abandoned the agit-prop outdoor drama of its early period for social realism performed on a professional basis. More significantly, it modified its political and aesthetic stance in such a way as to broaden its appeal and its support. As the Communist Party moved towards a policy of a united front of all progressive forces, so the theatre reflected this. Theatre of Action's Advisory Council included both Moss Hart and Lee Strasberg as well as Party personnel, while Elia Kazan directed two of its plays. John Howard Lawson, by now a Party member, was on the Executive Board. But the group lasted only two more years, having transferred its activities to a Broadway which was not ready to support its still somewhat crude work.

The Theatre Collective, a branch of the Workers' Laboratory Theatre, proved equally fragile, surviving a bare four years, from 1932 to 1936, during which time it performed only four plays. Nor did the League of Workers' Theatres, formed in 1932, do much to remedy this situation. The problem lay basically in the failure of these groups to produce drama which was anything but formulaic, or to transform Party zealots into actors. But, rechristened the New Theatre League in 1935, it came out more clearly for a united front which would be more catholic ideologically, uniting only around a broadly liberal leftist position, hostility towards fascism, and a belief that the theatre had a primary social function, more especially in a time of clear political, economic and social crisis. And this new grouping did at last discover a play which could work both theatrically and socially – Clifford Odets's *Waiting for Lefty* (1935).

In the autumn of 1934 *New Theatre* and *New Masses* had jointly offered fifty dollars for the best revolutionary play in any form. When nothing worth even fifty dollars was forthcoming, they offered to declare Odets the winner following the publication of his play in the February edition of *New Theatre*. Odets had himself joined the Party in 1934.

Waiting for Lefty was a play which negotiated a middle ground between extended agit-prop sketch and realistic play. Concerned with the possibility of a taxi-drivers' strike, which is also a tussle for control of the union, it integrates familiar caricatures with brief flashback scenes which attempt to establish the human reality behind the action. The taxi drivers turn out to be a veritable army of moral heroes, having come to cab driving from every walk of life except the priesthood. One is a chemist, who would rather drive a taxi than manufacture poison gas. Another is an intern dismissed from his hospital because he is Jewish. Another is an actor who becomes a taxi driver for ideological reasons, probably the only person to do so in the history of the profession. In other words *Waiting for Lefty* is not without its absurdities. It remains to account for its undoubted success.

Harold Clurman in *The Fervent Years* has commented that, 'The first scene of *Lefty* had not played two minutes when a shock of delighted recognition struck the audience like a tidal wave. Deep laughter, hot assent, a kind of joyous fervour seemed to sweep the audience toward the stage.' To Clurman it was an event of major significance in the development of American drama. The audience's responsive cry of 'Strike! Strike!' was, he suggested:

> the birth of the thirties. Our youth had found its voice. It was a call to join the good fight for a greater measure of life in a world free of economic fear, falsehood, and craven servitude to stupidity and greed. 'Strike!' was *Lefty's* lyric message, not alone for a few extra pennies of wages or for shorter hours of work, strike for greater dignity, strike for a bolder humanity, strike for the full stature of man.[42]

Published in the immediate aftermath of the Second World War this description doubtless combines immediate post-war optimism with the remembered enthusiasms of the mid 1930s. Clurman, as the man who had encouraged Odets to write the play, was, anyway, scarcely a disinterested source. Nonetheless his view was not really challenged.

Odets conceived of the play as being modelled in part on the minstrel show, at least in so far as individuals would step forward in order to present their acts against the background of an ensemble. It was a play which centred on American life. There were no appeals to support the international working class or the struggle of the Soviet Union, although the refusal of the young chemist to work on chemical warfare and the charges of anti-semitism were clearly designed to indicate the larger context. One scene in which the actor is advised to read the Communist manifesto, though included in the first production, was dropped from the version published in 1939.

The subject matter seemed to give the play an immediate relevance. There had indeed been a taxi strike in New York the previous year, though Odets was, unconvincingly, to deny all knowledge of this when called before the House Un-American Activities Committee – always a healthy aid to forget-fulness. Doubtless some of the attraction of the play lay in the apparent authenticity of its dialogue, as in the rather more subtle interplay of private and public worlds than was normally true of such productions. But none-theless it was clearly a committed document, designed to serve the interest of the Party to which he was such a recent convert. The play closes with a clear call to action by the cab drivers' new leader, Agate, who, pointedly, is not a Party member but who is therefore ideally placed to offer a wholly un-prejudiced endorsement of it.

> These slick slobs stand here telling us about bogeymen. That's a new one for the kids – the reds is bogeymen! But the man who got me food in 1932, he called me comrade! The one who picked me up where I bled – he called me Comrade too! What are we waiting for...Don't wait for Lefty! He might never come ...Hell, listen to me! Coast to coast! HELLO AMERICA! HELLO. WE'RE STORM-BIRDS OF THE WORKING CLASS. WORKERS OF THE WORLD...OUR BONES AND OUR BLOOD! And when we die they'll know what we did to make a new world! Christ, cut us up to little pieces. We'll die for what is right.[43]

This co-option of Christian symbolism was a basic strategy of 1930s writing. Man was to be his own God. The solution lay in the hands of the martyrs of a new secular religion, as it was to do in Steinbeck's *The Grapes of Wrath*. And this play is no clearer than Steinbeck's novel about the means of translat-ing rhetoric into action. It is a call to arms, to spiritual renewal, but the way in which that renewal is to express itself is left unexamined, displaced into a language of brotherhood and a symbol of solidarity which is sustained on the fragile premise of a strike for more money.

The play ends with a call, in which the audience joins, to 'STRIKE! STRIKE! STRIKE!!!' But as a solution to the problems identified in the play, a strike is itself more than a little irrelevant. What it did offer was a reassuring feeling of solidarity of a kind which the American government itself was trying to foster and which, on a personal level, Clifford Odets himself yearned for.

Harold Clurman recalls him talking about his state of mind and the feelings which the times evoked in him. 'He wanted comradeship; he wanted to belong to the largest possible group of humble, struggling men prepared to make a great common effort to build a better world. Without this, life for him would be lonely and hopeless.'[44] If this explains something of his motive in writing the play it also, perhaps, explains something of its reception.

Waiting for Lefty suffered from the same deficiencies as much committed theatre of the 1930s, in that while aesthetically open – inviting the involvement and commitment of the working-class audience to which it was addressed, assuming a permeable membrane between audience and performer – it remained ideologically closed. It begins with its conclusions. Sartre, indeed, once attacked the French Communist Party for its tendency to exhibit 'so complete and superb a conviction that from the very start it places itself above debate, casts its spell, and ends by becoming contagious; the opponent is never answered; he is discredited; he belongs to the police, to the Intelligence Service; he's a fascist.'[45] To make the businessman a simple exploiter, the industrialist only a destroyer of the human spirit, is to borrow a tactic from the forces it would engage. In so far as it is assaulting not simply historic injustice and inveterate class diabolism but the reductive process whereby entire classes are dismissed as wholly knowable and hence wholly ignorable, it becomes guilty of the same offence. But its power was undeniable. It was the first left-wing drama which could claim a genuinely popular appeal. And if its proletarian ethic was grafted somewhat uncomfortably onto bourgeois characters, this was not the moment to inspect too closely the ideological purity or, indeed, the aesthetic consistency of a play acclaimed equally by the politically committed and the patrons of the Group Theatre.

Waiting for Lefty opened on 6 January 1935. Though sponsored by the League, it was acted by members of the Group Theatre which in March staged its own production of the play. By June the play had been presented in fifty cities and had the distinction of being banned in a number of them, Boston performing its usual function of endorsement by censorship. It achieved what so much other Party drama had failed to achieve; it attracted audiences from the widespread world which supposedly constituted the united front. Some unease was felt by the Left, but it was hard to argue with their first real success.

A year later the League produced another success in the form of Irwin Shaw's *Bury the Dead* (1936), a play which was set in 'The second year of the war that is to begin tomorrow night.' The shift to a united front policy had, apparently, both opened up a new dramatic vein and located a new audience. Beginning as an apparently realistic play, in which an army burial detail goes about its job, it lurches suddenly into a wholly different style as the dead

16. Clifford Odets's *Waiting for Lefty*, a Group Theatre production, New York, 1935. Directed by Clifford Odets and Sanford Meisner.

bodies refuse to be buried, further evidence that the principal achievement of American left-wing theatre in the 1930s did not lie in realist art.

The stage is suitably bare and stark. There is no scenery and there are no properties apart from some scattered sandbags. Lighting becomes the source of dramatic effect, as the action is lit by the flashes of gunfire or by sudden spotlights. The premise of the play is contained in a speech by a middle-aged soldier who observes that

> Kids shouldn't be dead... That's what they musta figured when the dirt started fallin' in on 'em. What the hell are they doin' dead? Did they get anything out of it? Did anybody ask them? Did they want to be standin' there when the lead poured in? They're just kids or guys with wives and young kids of their own. They wanted to be home readin' a book or teaching their kid c–a–t spells cat or takin' a woman out into the country in an open car with the wind blowin'... That's the way it musta come to them, when the dirt smacked on their faces, dead or no dead.[46]

The play's subversions were not without their dangerous relevance to the ideological group which staged them, like the comment by one of the corpses that 'Men, even the men who die for Pharaoh and Caesar and Rome, must, in the end, before all hope is gone, discover that a man can die happy and be contentedly buried only when he dies for himself or for a cause that is his own and not Pharaoh's or Caesar's or Rome's.'[47] But there were few Party members in the mid 1930s who were yet prepared to detect the potential irony of those lines. The play was welcomed as an anti-war drama which had incorporated the agit-prop sketch and the episodic method into a coherent and original dramatic vision.

When the wives are persuaded to confront their young dead husbands *Bury the Dead* has something of the emotional and even the sentimental impact of Wilder's *Our Town*. In a series of cameos their lives together are recreated, lives which stand in stark contrast to the literally fatal experiences into which they have been betrayed. The play is a paean to life. As the leader of the dead soldiers says,

> The fight's never over. I got things to say to people now – to the people who nurse big machines and the people who swing shovels and the people whose babies die with big bellies and rotten bones. I got things to say to the people who leave their lives behind them and pick up guns to fight in somebody else's war. Important things. Big things. Big enough to lift me out of the grave right back on to the earth...I got another religion. I got a religion that wants to take heaven out of the clouds and plant it right here on earth.[48]

But where a few years earlier he would have been expected to spell out the nature of that heaven and to invoke its Soviet model, now it rests as a general commitment to a secular religion which was such a common feature of writing in the 1930s. It is, strictly speaking, not simply an anti-war play. It is about the need for the dead in spirit to awake and sing. In the words of an anonymous Voice, 'Mankind is standing up and climbing out of its grave.'[49] 'The dead have arisen, now let the living rise, singing.'[50] The play ends with a chorus of voices denying the silence of the grave as the corpses leave first their graves and then the stage. It is, in other words, a natural companion-piece to Odets's work. Indeed the parallel between them is clear.

Like Odets, Shaw moved on to the commercial theatre. Indeed the prospect of a commercial production of the play led to its being withheld from the affiliates of the League of Workers' Theatres and, as Morgan Himelstein has shown, in *Drama Was a Weapon*, the failure of the League to retain its play-wrights contributed to its decline. Though it continued to operate until 1941 it did so with ever-decreasing effectiveness. It failed to locate or generate scripts, even advising its affiliates to consult the listings of the newly-created Federal Theatre; and the effort to create a Communist-dominated chain of theatre companies ultimately collapsed in disarray.

Another shorter-lived but significant theatre of the Left was Theatre Union. Formed in 1933, it was created to give currency to plays of the Left which otherwise would founder under the impact of the commercialism of Broadway or the amateurism of radical theatre groups. It announced that

> We produce plays that deal boldly with the deep-going social conflicts, the economic, emotional and cultural problems that confront the majority of the people. Our plays speak directly to this majority, whose lives usually are

caricatured or ignored on the stage. We do not expect that these plays will fall into the accepted social patterns. This is a new kind of professional theatre, based on the interests and hopes of the great mass of working people.[51]

The idea was to give fully professional performances of these plays. It had the usual uneasy relationship with the Communist Party, which was happy with united front operations only if behind the facade they were ultimately committed to Party policies. Theatre Union was not. In 1934 it re-stated its policy:

> *The Theatre Union is not agit-prop theatre.* It is a united front theatre organized to produce plays that all honest militant workers and middle-class sympathisers can support; plays that, without compromise on questions of principle, will appeal particularly to unorganized workers who are not yet class-conscious... Like other organizations which maintain a united front policy, such as the League Against War and Fascism, we stick to specific and limited tasks, functioning as a theatre, not as a political party.[52]

If this was a virtue it was also a vice. The Theatre Union was intent on attracting two potentially incompatible audiences: the 'not yet class-conscious' members of the working class, and the conventional Broadway theatregoer, to which end free tickets went on the one hand to the unemployed and on the other to regular theatre reviewers. They made strange bedfellows. And though Clifford Odets and Irwin Shaw had shown that it was possible to bridge the gap, Theatre Union never really succeeded, though its first two plays were moderately successful.

Peace on Earth, by George Sklar and Albert Maltz, concerned the conversion of a middle-class professor into a martyr for the cause of organised labour. By presenting him as supporting workers who are striking as a means of protesting against the sale of weapons to foreign countries, Sklar and Maltz manage to combine a number of favourite themes of 1930s drama. Thus the play is pro-union, anti-war and suspicious of technology and those who control it. It implicitly calls for an alliance between workers and intellectuals, and insists on the impossibility of remaining detached and objective. While one Broadway reviewer objected that far from being martyred, university professors, under Roosevelt, were now actually running the country, the choice of a middle-class protagonist was finely calculated to appeal to the Theatre's double audience. But it was true that the issues tackled were in effect those being taken on in some degree by the New Deal itself: the National Recovery Act actually reversed the downward trend in union membership by securing legal protection for organised labour, though, as Karen Taylor points out,[53] the NRA Board was less than scrupulous in enforcing its terms. The play ran for 125 performances, a success only rivalled by *Stevedore*, which dealt with the delicate issue of race relations that O'Neill had pioneered. But where O'Neill had attempted to expose the effects of racism on the psychology of blacks and whites, the subtle corrosions effectuated by destructive myths, Peters and Sklar see racism as simply a product of capitalism, and they see it, moreover, only in its most obvious public form. In what is essentially a melodrama they propose that familiar alliance of blacks and organised white unions pictured by Richard Wright in *Uncle Tom's Children* which was in fact something of a rarity in 1930s America, and they create a revolutionary dramatic logic which is historically dubious.

Lonnie Thompson, a black stevedore, is falsely accused of raping a white woman: a charge for which there is no evidence, but which serves the interests of his white employer for whom Lonnie is simply the root of trouble, demanding justice over wages. When he is assaulted by a lynch mob and hunted by white police, it is the white union-organiser who comes to his assistance. The play ends with Lonnie, the 'Black Jesus' as he is called, shot dead by a white racist, a martyr to the cause, while his fellow blacks and white trade unionists fight off and defeat the racists, a blatant piece of wishful thinking remote from the truth of race relations in the 1930s and dramatically as simple as it is socially inaccurate.

The Theatre Union produced a number of plays in its short life, most of them realistic (George Sklar and Albert Maltz's *Peace on Earth*, Paul Peters and George Sklar's *Stevedore*, Friedrich Wolf's *The Sailors of Cattaro*, Albert Maltz's *Black Pit*, Victor Wolfson's *Bitter Stream* and John Howard Lawson's *Marching Song*). Indeed, its commitment to realism even extended to a treatment of Brecht's *Mother*, a production which stimulated a virulent attack by the author. It finally collapsed in 1937, killed largely by its failure to generate an audience for plays which offered a simple model of human affairs, but also by the existence of the Federal Theatre which offered professionalism and theatrical innovation at prices which could be afforded by those hit by the Depression. Theatre Union had the low prices but not the financial strength to sustain them or the theatrical inventiveness to attract large audiences.

The Party, moreover, was faced from the early 1930s onwards by an ideological dilemma in the form of the New Deal, which in its pragmatism, its social energy, its genuine attempt to tackle the principle causes of discontent, occupied territory which the Party had regarded as its own. The New Deal also undermined the rhetoric of the Left, counterposing rational political action to the public myths of working-class solidarity. The popular front policy was partly a response to this, as it was to wider political developments in the world. But though it did generate a number of plays which engaged practical social realities it did not for the most part command the popular support which was to have been its justification and its strength.

Left-wing drama in the 1930s contributed little to the long-term development of the theatre. Indeed its objectives were immediate and to some degree not entirely to do with the future of theatre. Nonetheless it did provide a stage, briefly, for Clifford Odets, and others who were more clearly drawn to the theatre by their political convictions. It also left a strong imprint on American drama in its insistence on seeing the individual primarily in a social context, in relating psychological to economic reality. The theatre group as a social as well as aesthetic unit remained a feature of American life. The melo-dramatic nature of left-wing theatre left its mark, as did a certain strain of sentimentalism, a tendency to press action and character to extremes, to seek meaning in excess and rhetoric. In the form of its effect on the Federal Theatre it also contributed to one of the most exciting periods in American dramatic history.

In a sense the language of theatre stands at another extreme from the language of action. The framing of that language by the context of the stage is a protection against the consequences of its own meaning. Art is utopian. It is pulled towards a world in which language is end as well as means. Michel Beaujour has gone so far as to say that 'If the poem can address itself to all men, it is evidently because it cannot command any specific action.'[54] Both art and revolution are intent on the creation of new worlds, but these worlds do not necessarily occupy the same space. An act of translation is required, a transposition which involves more than literal enactment. Each accuses the other of utopianism, relying for purity of line, clarity of purpose, on a model of action and of being which is threatened as well as confirmed by articula-tion. But the impotence of art is an essential part of its implied contract – more especially with theatre, which presents the real with the assurance of its un-reality. The audience may indeed have sprung to their feet at the end of *Waiting for Lefty*, calling out 'Strike! Strike! Strike!', but the gesture remained a theatrical one. The theatre and the real join only in what Beaujour calls the 'anti world' – the apocalyptic day when rhetoric will be transformed into action, the 'tomorrow' which haunted and lured O'Neill's characters in *The Iceman Cometh*. Sartre speaks of the poet cleansing language, 'just as the revolutionary, *so to speak*, can envisage cleansing society'. But Beaujour asks 'Can the Word have magical power? Can its action be analogical and sub-stantial? Is it enough, as Confucians claim, to speak rigorously in order to remake (to cleanse) society?'[55] Certainly the playwrights of the 1930s came close to believing this to be true. The theatre was ideally placed to expose the lie. It could juxtapose language to action. And yet its scepticism was not directed at language as such, which had to be preserved, presumed to be a rational instrument, a clear glass through which to see the real. Communica-tion became a moral necessity. What was at stake was not simply the presenta-tion of a private vision but the elaboration of a social model. And in that context language was action.

Whatever revolution they were concerned with, it did not involve a revolt against the word. In France in 1936, Artaud published *The Theatre and its Double* in which he advocated the subordination of language to the physical dimensions of theatre. But for the revolutionary artist the word is central and without ambiguity. Language was to be honed to a sharp edge. It was to be wielded with the weight of history behind it – though the playwright was not, for the most part, ready to deal with the fact that it was also subverted by that history. For there was a destructive irony in parading the old clichés, pieties and sentimentalities as a means of precipitating a new world. Odets's work in particular suffers from this contradiction. His radicalism never extends to language. Announcing a new world, he is contained by the theatrical tropes of the old.

If this was a theatre of revolt, there were clear limits to that revolt. Dedicated to a social revolution which would adjust life to man these radical writers displayed nothing of Artaud's sense of metaphysical rebellion. Artaud had denounced the surrealists who turned to Marx. 'They believe that they can laugh at me when I write about metamorphosis of the inner state of the soul, as if I had the same vile notion of the soul that they do, and, as if from any absolute viewpoint it could be of the slightest interest to change the social structure of the world or to transfer power from the bourgeoisie to the proletariat.'[56] But theirs was, of course, a drama which was concerned with the writer's struggle to escape incarceration in literature. The theatre potentially offers such an escape. For the committed writer, however, it must subordinate itself to the world. It takes on the burden of history or the freedom of creating it.

The avant-garde and the politically revolutionary coexist uneasily. Perhaps the suicides of Esenin and Mayakovsky sealed off some kind of possibility which has never really been realised since. For art reaches for a utopianism which is different in kind from that attempted by the political revolutionary. As Michel Beaujour has remarked, 'poetry is the incarnation of man's permanent aspiration as a speaking being to a *beyond* which only language, whose code is shaken by the poet, can offer him.'[57] Theatre is held in a paradoxical position. The social circumstance of performance constitutes a gravitational pull which holds it back from this beyond. It is in a state of tension, at its best. In a purely social theatre that tension is relaxed, is sacrificed. The utopian dimension is distrusted as simple evasion. This was the essence of Sartre's attack on Camus whom he denounced for refusing to pay his dues to history and to the pressure of the fact. Sartre was particularly struck by Camus's lament, in his *Letter to a German Friend*, that 'For so many years now, you tried to *make me enter into History*' (Sartre's italics) and by his later comment: 'You did what you had to do, *we entered History*. And for five years, it was no longer possible to enjoy the birds' singing.'[58] The moral world and the aesthetic world are held apart in an act of bad faith. For Camus the act of revolt was crucial, but it was not primarily a social act. 'Man must affirm justice to struggle against eternal injustice, create happiness to protest against the universe of unhappiness.'[59] The origin of injustice thus lies in an indifferent universe, a God whose final joke was not to dominate existence but to absent himself. Man is thus wrenched from his historicity. It is a world without progress but with a transcendent understanding, and art becomes the essence of that understanding. The fundamental act of resistance is thus contained and defined by the imagination. It was a position which distinguished some of O'Neill's and Glaspell's best work. But for Sartre, it is a stance adopted independently of experience. It refuses history without inspecting it. It becomes a kind of religious stance which needs take no account of time. It was a stance most obviously undermined by the war, which gave evidence of the power of history to press its demands; but for Camus this was simply a tithe to be paid in order to retreat into metaphysics. For Sartre such a retreat was an ultimate betrayal; a failure of knowledge but a failure, too, of morality. For the war was not different in kind. History was not an occasional volcanic eruption, to be grudgingly acknowledged. It was a primary reality. Injustice was not a plague visited on the earth; it was a social construction. 'You revolted against death,' he wrote to Camus, 'but in the iron belts which surround cities, other men revolted against social conditions which raised the toll of mortality.'[60]

For the American playwright, as for many novelists of the 1920s and 30s, history asserted its primacy with the same insistent stridency as it did for Camus during the war. But the gulf between man and the natural world was more of a shock to an America in which their close relationship had been part of a central and animating myth. The full force of this was perhaps not felt in the 1920s, but the 1930s revealed the centrality of the social, and the power of historical process.

For Sartre, man 'makes himself historical in order to undertake the eternal, and discovers universal values in the concrete action that he undertakes in view of a specific result. If you say that this world is unjust, you have already lost the game. You are already outside, in the act of comparing a world without justice to a justice without content.'[61] This was ostensibly the stance of a writer like Odets, but in fact the practical and the immediate are constantly subverted by a vague universalising impulse. What surfaces as a persistent sentimentality in so much American drama of the inter-war years is a failure to engage the practical world which is its ostensible object. Its reputation, not without justification, is that of an irredeemably social theatre, but in truth the constant temptation was to press through the social to the universal. The soft metaphysics of Saroyan and Barry are there in only a slightly disguised form in Elmer Rice, in Maxwell Anderson, Paul Green and Clifford Odets.

Sartre accused Camus of presuming that every defendant was, before the fact, a guilty man; the assumption of these writers is the opposite and thus essentially the same. They all proclaim a natural innocence, an essential goodness which resists the pressure of history and the closure of social possibilities. For Saroyan this must be clearly stated, but for the others it is a basic assumption which may account for a version of history which is hard to accept and whose naivety constantly threatens to dissolve into simple sentiment. Their tendency is to turn the social world into an object. They aestheticise it. While they purport to show process, in fact they create a series of tableaux vivants. There is thus no exchange between history and the individual who observes it, announces his wish to transform it, but seldom does so. Morality turns into moralism for them, as Sartre said it did for Camus. And American drama is a very moralising drama; humanistic, pious, innocent and committed to declaring man's innocence. That innocence was the source of a vitality which was mistaken for a life generated by the text. But in truth it lay outside it, indeed was at odds with the sombre setting – graveyard, tenement room, crowded street – which appealed to a nascent social conscience. The failure was a failure of thought, an analysis which failed to strike through the pasteboard mask, failed to ask crucial questions about the human nature which their own logic presumed would triumphantly survive the environment which they simultaneously wished to regard as implacable. Love, presented as social responsibility but in fact deeply romantic and redemptive, was the key. A generalised love to be sure, a sudden shared experience of being; platonic, transforming, and wholly unbelievable as a solution to problems presented with such a flourish, even if they became vague, generalised, symbolic in the telling. American drama was discovering itself, and its central theme was self-discovery. The resources, it implied, were already to hand. All that was necessary was to awake and sing. What that song should be and how mere consciousness was to transform experience was less clear. If the failure of these American writers was in part one of thought, it was also one of imagination, of vision.

Their model of human nature was surprisingly static. What was necessary, apparently, was to acknowledge the self, to free it of the pressures external to that self. Odets in particular has his characters move through a social world towards a self which survives its apparent determinants, awaiting only the moment of revelation which renders the past inoperative, neutralises history and leaves the self free to enter the new world. It was a piety generated by the times, but it was a piety which threatened equally the political ability and the dramatic integrity of his work. One can say no less of most of those writers who, thinking themselves to be offering an objective account of social reality, in fact presented an art in which the real existed to be transformed by a human spirit which remained paradoxically free of the world which ostensibly determined it.

6 The Federal Theatre and the Living Newspaper

Among George Pierce Baker's students at Harvard in 1923–4 was a young woman called Hallie Flanagan who went on to produce plays in the experimental theatres at Grinnel and Vassar Colleges. Hallie Flanagan was a student of theatre. In 1926–7 she was granted a Guggenheim fellowship to study comparative methods of production in England, Ireland, Scandinavia, France, Austria, Italy, Germany, Russia, Czechoslovakia and Hungary. In 1934 she added Africa and Greece.

In Russia she saw for herself the work of Stanislavsky, of Meyerhold and Taïrov. She was especially struck by Meyerhold, who had broken away from the techniques and objectives of his former teacher, Stanislavsky, choosing to work with minimal facilities, to communicate a sense of theatrical energy directly to a new audience. She responded both to his audacity and to the boldness of his gestures, his willingness to work against tradition, even the relatively new tradition of the Moscow Art Theatre.

Unsurprisingly, the result was not only a considerable knowledge of drama practice in a wide range of countries but also a studied eclecticism, an empirical faith in adapting methods to individual scripts, which she practised as director at Vassar. It was this conviction which she carried with her into a larger context when in 1935 she was telephoned by Harry Hopkins, Works Progress Administrator in the Roosevelt administration, and asked to assume the direction of the Federal Theatre, which rapidly grew to be the largest state-financed theatre in the world outside of Russia, before being dismantled, for political reasons, in 1939.

The acting profession had suffered not only from the effects of the Depression but from the rise of radio and the movies. In her book, *Arena*, Hallie Flanagan described the nature of this impact;

> In 1932, according to the *Motion Picture Almanac*, 14,000 movie houses were wired for sound and were attracting 70,000,000 admissions a week. Theatre after theatre closed its doors to the living actor and set up a screen on the stage. Road companies were stranded all over the country. Stock [repertory theatre] declined and died. Vaudeville, which held top billing at the Palace until 1933, was forced to retreat before the exclusive film policy of the movie-house chains. Loews, as one typical instance, had, previously to 1930, regularly scheduled stage shows with forty to fifty weeks' employment for the vaudevillian in thirty-six theatres; in 1932, it gave stage shows in twelve houses, in 1933–4 in three houses...stagehands and technicians were no longer needed.[1]

The economics of theatre had collapsed. In 1933 half of New York's theatres were closed and more than half of the actors unemployed.[2] This was the context in which Hallie Flanagan took the oath of office in August 1935, swearing to defend the Constitution of the United States against all enemies foreign and domestic, an oath which was later invoked against her.

The new organisation was to be a federal rather than a national theatre: that is to say its activities were not to be focussed on a single building or even a single city. Its prime objective was relief. It was to provide work for unemployed theatre personnel across America on a non-discriminatory basis. But, as Hallie Flanagan suggested, in an address to the assembled regional directors, it was also to be an opportunity for theatre to reflect more directly the transformations of society, to reach a broader cross-section of people than ever before by responding to the contemporary not merely as subject but as informing presence.

> We live in a changing world, [she insisted] man is whispering through space, soaring to the stars in ships, flinging miles of steel and glass into the air. Shall the theatre continue to huddle in the confines of a painted box set? The movies, in their kaleidoscopic speed and juxtaposition of external objects and internal emotions, are seeking to find visible and audible expression for the tempo and the psychology of our time. The stage too must experiment with ideas, with psychological relationship of man and woman, with speech and rhythmic forms, with dance and movement, with color and light – or it must and should become a museum product.[3]

The Federal Theatre was organised on a federal basis, but the largest unit was New York. This in turn was subdivided into five main divisions: the living newspaper; the popular-price theatre, presenting new plays by new authors; the experimental theatre; the Negro theatre; and the try-out theatre, which was to be a co-operative venture with commercial management. A number of these divisions were then duplicated nationwide, the Negro unit, for example, operating in Seattle, Hartford, Philadelphia, Newark, Los Angeles, Boston, Birmingham, Raleigh, San Francisco and Chicago, employing 851 Negro personnel in the lifetime of the theatre and producing seventy plays.[4] But New York operated as a service centre. It was here that the *Federal Theatre Magazine* was produced, here, too, that playreading and bibliographical services were centred, though there were regional play bureaux, Susan Glaspell being director of the mid-western one. Yet while each regional theatre organisation attempted to adapt its own needs and capacities to the general schema, drawing on its own traditions and personnel, the simultaneous production of Sinclair Lewis's *It Can't Happen Here*, in twenty-one theatres in seventeen states on the night of 27 October 1936, was a symbol of the national pretensions of a theatre which did indeed see itself as playing an important role in national self-recovery and in the re-establishment of national morale. The script was the same in each theatre (except for the Yiddish production, and minor alterations in the Negro version in Seattle), the production strikingly different. In New York City alone the play was seen by 300 000 people.

As an agency of government the Federal Theatre was bound to become the focus of political debate. Though its productions ranged widely, there was an inevitable pressure to address the social conditions which had given rise to its own creation. If Roosevelt, in his Second Inaugural address, had spoken of the 'one-third of a nation ill housed, ill clad, ill nourished', this was in large part their audience. It was this fact which determined their pricing policy; it was from this group that they were obliged to recruit. And in their attempts to tackle contemporary issues they had the support of Harry Hopkins on the one hand, and that of Burns Mantle, the drama critic, on the other.

The dangers, however, were clear. Tied so directly to the New Deal programme its fate was ineluctably linked to that of the Roosevelt Administration. America was no more used to the idea of sponsoring the theatre than it was to the notion of pouring large sums of money into public works, and the Federal Theatre had to adjust itself to the foibles of local officials as ultimately it had to bow to the power of national representatives. But it was unavoidably a social theatre. Though many of its productions were bereft of political content, the sheer fact of their origins in the WPA (Works Progress Administration) charged them with political significance. The mere existence of Negro units was itself seen as a provocation by some. To the usual complexities of theatrical production were added the problems of negotiating with those who exercised political and bureaucratic control. It was an experiment not merely in theatre but in institutional modes. Where previously the American theatre had been largely bifurcated between the commercial theatre and the often arcane little-theatre movement, now, for the first time, experimentation could be conducted on a large scale. Minority concerns breached economic and social barriers previously thought to be absolute. And, encouraged by this, both Shaw and O'Neill released their plays for production by the Federal Theatre for a simple fifty dollars' weekly rental.

Admission to Federal Theatre productions was free or at very low rates (10¢, 25¢ and 50¢, never to cost more than $1.10). Its audience averaged five hundred thousand a week and during the four years of its operation its productions were seen by over thirty million people. 65 per cent of audiences were attending a play for the first time and 'trades' and 'office workers' constituted 25 per cent of audiences. Audience surveys demonstrated that the preferred plays were straight plays, vaudeville, circus, children's theatre, puppets. Theatre was taken to the people in the form of social dramas which addressed the problems of this new audience. These were performed in parks,

213

camps, public halls, hospitals, anywhere an audience could be attracted or identified. In four years the Federal Theatre could claim to have made the theatre a popular art to a degree which had simply never been true before in America.

Perhaps the single most original contribution which this theatre made was the Living Newspaper. And it was doubtless this, more than anything, which paved the way for the congressional assaults which eventually destroyed it. The Living Newspaper was born out of a desire to find a format which would employ the largest number of actors. According to Hallie Flanagan, the idea came to her in September 1935. In trying to convince Elmer Rice that he should become the director of the New York project, she proposed the idea of dramatising the news, using the minimum of scenery and relying on music, light and the large cast itself to secure effect. She had attempted something similar when at Vassar. *Can You Hear Their Voices?* was based on Whittaker Chambers's account of families who had suffered in a drought in Arkansas. The Journalism Department at Vassar had conducted the basic research, and Hallie Flanagan and her students had written the play in ten days. Premièred in 1931, it was subsequently widely performed and reviewed.[5] Elmer Rice, however, believed that he had conceived the idea as a consequence of discussions with the head of the Newspaper Guild who was concerned with the plight of unemployed newspaper men. The model for him was the *March of Time* movie series which was a staple product of the American cinema. But there is a clear line which links the Living Newspaper to European theatre, and more specifically to the theatre which had been born out of the social pressures and vivid theatrical innovations of the Russian Revolution two decades earlier.

Nikolai Gorchakov notes the creation of the *Zhivaya Gazeta* (Living Newspaper) during the civil war. This consisted of performances in which extracts from newspaper accounts were read out, together with a commentary. This was followed in 1920 by the 'Blue Blouses', founded by students and supported in 1923 by the Institute of Journalists. Described in a book on *The New Spirit in the Russian Theatre 1917–1928* by Huntly Carter, which was published in 1929 and hence was available to Hallie Flanagan, who had herself just returned from Russia, it was an organisation consisting of between five and six thousand troupes, comprising ten thousand players, whose object was to perform the newspaper in villages and small towns. It derived its name from the workmen's blue blouses worn by the actors. The performances combined current news with films and slides in a format close to that of the political cabaret.

One of the ironies of this period (1922–8) was that while the West was fascinated by the experiments of the Russian theatre, a fascination deepened by the cultural exchanges which blossomed for a while, those involved in the

Russian theatre were equally interested in America and in the artistic movements of the West. Though American decadence was fiercely denounced, America itself was the source of central images and ideas. The Russian avant-garde admired American films, jazz and its urban culture. Far from seeing America itself as spiritually exhausted and effete, they admired its dynamism and energy. Meyerhold, indeed, wished to blend the new technological world of radio and cinema with circus, music hall and sport, to create a new art of the people commensurate with the modern world. And doubtless this symbiosis between Russian revolutionary fervour and American modernity facilitated theatrical influence.

The Theatres of Working Youth (TRAM in Russian) were concerned with staging plays about the political and social realities of the moment, but as Marc Slonim has pointed out they employed the techniques of the avant-garde.[6] In 1923 Mayakovsky and others announced in their magazine *LEF* (*The Left Front of the Arts*) that art should be functional, that it should aim at reportage, that it should model itself to some degree on journalism, that truth lay in a vitalised documentary. This, inevitably, in the Russian context, was part of the assault on realism and the notion of art as an icon which led equally to a revolution in styles of acting and production. For a while, at least, the circus and the music hall were proposed as models of theatricality, and the physical precision and strength of ensemble display were seen as a principal means of reflecting and celebrating a technology which was regarded less as threat than liberation, and as a principal image of that collective solidarity which was both method and subject for the new socialist theatre. And something of this objective lay behind the Federal Theatre's projects in the United States, which equally found in the collective enterprise a strength which was simultaneously dramatic and social strategy. The method whereby the Living Newspaper was created itself proposed a model which could equally apply to the exigencies of public life. It theatricalised not merely society but its own methods.

As Douglas McDermott has pointed out, however, in an article in *Modern Drama*, the Federal Theatre's Living Newspaper also had its American predecessors, though these too had their roots in the political theatre of Europe: 'The first record of one was a letter in *New Masses* for 1931 about the activities of a Hungarian-language drama group called *Uj Elore*. The second notice was a one-act script printed in *Workers Theatre*, March 1933. It was called *Learned Judge, a Sketch for a Living Newspaper*, and was based on a recent news story which was printed with.'[7] As he indicates, the connection between the Federal Theatre and those various forerunners in the field of Living Newspaper productions is clear. Not merely had Hallie Flanagan seen the Blue Blouses at work and described this in her 1928 book, *Shifting Scenes in the European Theatre*, but several of her Federal Theatre personnel concerned with

Living Newspaper productions (Joseph Losey, Brett Warren and Alfred Saxe) had been associated with workers' groups which had themselves responded enthusiastically to the Russian model and to its German imitators. She had also staged two agit-prop plays, *Miners Are Striking* and *We Demand*, at Vassar, plays which had originally been presented by Communist groups in New York City.

The process of creating a living-newspaper production was described in detail in the *Federal Theatre Magazine* of April 1936:

> How is this newspaper published? Its publishing staff is organized like that of a large city daily. The editor-in-chief, or producer has under him a managing editor, and he under him a city editor, who in turn directs the work of thirty-five reporters, fourteen copy-readers, seven research specialists and ten rewrite men. This staff produces the newspaper – i.e. the script which is acted out by Federal Theatre actors on the stage of the Biltmore.
>
> The script differs from a conventional play in that it is not 'written' as a play is written; it is reported. The imaginative dramatist invents and arranges his scenes to create a chosen effect. The reporters of the Living Newspaper are not permitted to invent anything, or arrange any sequence. They cannot choose a climax or a mood. They take the news exactly as it is and prepare it for the stage.
>
> Preparing news for the stage is not so different as one might suppose from preparing news for the press. The craft of the reporter in both cases lies in seeing the essential news value in the event and stating it simply. . .
>
> The theme is chosen by the managing producer and the Federal Theatre director of New York City, in consultation with the national director. It then goes into round-table discussion, much as a board of editors would discuss the layout of a national news story for tomorrow's edition. The managing editor, who is also the head dramatist, then breaks down a subject into scenes, indicating as specifically as possible the treatment he has in mind for each scene, and passes this on to the city editor in charge of the research and editing staff. This scenario is then parcelled out as assignments to the research men with a deadline of two or three days to get the material required.
>
> The mass of material which is presently brought in by the thirty-five reporters is sufficient to make fifty evenings at the Biltmore. It must be sifted, selected, cut, organized. Somewhere in the process the headlines begin to emerge. These indicate the trend of the story and suggest the key scenes in which it is to be told. The managing editor makes a scene scheme – the logical sequence of the story. From this the production scene is worked out: the dramatic sequence translated to terms of the stage, the characters planned and the action plotted.
>
> The scenes are now assigned to the sixteen rewrite men to put into dialogue. These are experienced dramatists. But they are bound by the newspaper rules of brevity, simplicity, clear grasp of essentials. . . .
>
> Then again all the dialogue must be submitted to the project's lawyer, to be

read for possible libel action. Many of the scenes represent living persons, and although they present only objective fact, still literal truth does not in itself guarantee against action for slander.

When the script has at last received tentative approval, it is still far from final form. It must be translated into 'theatre' by the dramatists, the scene and costume designers, the light man, the sound man, the stage manager who will eventually have to see that the scenes are shifted instantaneously...All these specialized workers are equally subject to the newspaper rules – brevity, simplicity, clearness. Scenes and impressions must follow in rapid succession and must get an instantaneous effect. Scenery must be very simple because it must not distract attention for a split second from the action.

...The process here described...must generally be completed within four weeks.[8]

Useful as a simple account of process, this clearly represents a naive description of the theatrical and political realities of the Living Newspaper. Notions of taking the news 'exactly as it is', of presenting 'objective fact', suggest a model which is no more sustainable in the world of newspapers than it is in the world of theatre. And this was a lesson swiftly learned, as the first such production, *Ethiopia*, was summarily banned by the Washington office of the WPA, despite Harry Hopkins's assurances that the Federal Theatre was to be free, adult and uncensored. Elmer Rice, persuaded with difficulty to take on the New York project, immediately resigned, and though the Living Newspaper as a form continued, the fiction of its neutrality could scarcely be sustained.

In many ways *Ethiopia* laid the groundwork for the productions that were to follow. The notion of using a teletype across the top of the proscenium arch was abandoned in favour of a loudspeaker voice, which became a feature of subsequent plays. The strict causality, the simplified model of social action and reaction, was established. Released from a pure narrative drive the creators of living-newspaper productions created a technique which was in some senses cinematic. Its principal structural devices were montage and episode. Scenes were frequently short, with jump-cuts and voice-overs. Indeed stills and movies were themselves projected. Inevitably the technique itself had a flattening effect on character, an attempt being made to counterbalance this by means of the dramatised incidents in which public policies were shown operating on the lives of individual characters.

For Hallie Flanagan, the Living Newspaper was to be a means of placing the individual in possession of himself by locating his personal struggles in terms of social change. It was a theatre which transcended the merely psychological and which offered an epic sense of private and public destiny. Writing in the National Service Bureau of the Federal Theatre Project, she outlined the objectives of the Living Newspaper as being the desire

217

to make [theatre] out of everyday factual materials; to dramatize the struggle not of two men for one woman, not of one psychological trait against another psychological trait in a man's soul, not of one social class against another social class. All these struggles are important for the theatre, but the Living Newspaper seeks to dramatize a new struggle – the search of the average American today for knowledge about his country and his world; to dramatize his struggle to turn the great natural and economic and social forces of our time toward a better life for more people.[9]

Her objective was the 'birth of a politically and economically literate theatre in America',[10] willing to experiment with a 'rapid, simplified, vivid form of stage expression'.[11]

As I have already said, the first living-newspaper production almost immediately ran into trouble. *Ethiopia* was chosen, as Hallie Flanagan has explained, partly because it was a subject in the news, and partly because one of the first groups of unemployed actors sent to the new Federal Theatre organisation was a troupe of African actors who spoke no English. Later, aliens would be banned from benefiting under WPA programmes but now they were an embarrassing responsibility. Originally *Ethiopia* was merely to be the featured story in a succession of news stories but Arthur Arent's fifteen-minute treatment convinced Elmer Rice that this should become the basis for the entire show. It quickly became evident, however, that this was a sensitive issue. To begin with, it involved America's relations with another power, and when it became clear that the play involved not merely quotation from contemporary documents but the impersonation of foreign leaders and government personnel, pressure from Washington became apparent. The opening was delayed for five days because the government purchasing office had failed to complete arrangements for the purchase of lighting equipment. Then, on 18 January 1936, a memo was received from Jacob Baker, who was in charge of the white-collar division of the WPA and sympathetic to the objectives of the Federal Theatre and who, incidentally, had, together with Harry Hopkins, been instrumental in persuading Hallie Flanagan to accept the directorship of the Federal Theatre some eight months earlier. The message was straightforward:

> This will direct that no issue of the living newspaper shall contain any representation of the head or one of the ministers or the cabinet of a foreign state unless such representation shall have been approved in advance by the Department of State. In view of the impracticality of getting advance approval in sufficient time to give timeliness to the performances of the living newspaper, it seems to me that it is necessary that there not be included any representations of such persons.

Hallie Flanagan persuaded Mrs Roosevelt to intercede with her husband, and arranged for Jacob Baker to see a rehearsal of *Ethiopia*. The result was a concession. On 23 January, Baker sent another note:

This will modify my memorandum of January 18 as to the performance of *Ethiopia*. No one impersonating a ruler or cabinet officer shall actually appear on the stage. If it is useful for you to do so, the words of such persons may be quoted by others.[12]

It was a compromise which Hallie Flanagan was willing to accept, but Elmer Rice, suspicious from the start, felt obliged to resign and his resignation was willingly accepted by Baker. In the end, the first living-newspaper production received only one performance, a private viewing for the Press. To Rice this was proof that Washington was only prepared to support 'pap for babes and octogenarians'.[13] This was a view shared by the *New York Times*. Certainly this and the suppression in Chicago, at the Mayor's insistence, of *Model Tenement*, a play about a rent strike, hardly boded well for a theatre which was to be free, adult and uncensored. But Hallie Flanagan took some encouragement from the controversy that these two events stirred up, accepting only that future living-newspaper productions would concentrate on domestic issues – a decision which eventually led to the closing of the entire project, the sensibility of domestic politicians proving far more lethal than those of foreign leaders and dignitaries.

Ethiopia was written by Arthur Arent. He was also the principal author of *Power* and *One Third of a Nation* (1938) and was the co-author of *Triple A Plowed Under* (1935), and *Injunction Granted* (1936). A graduate of New York University, he was the first writer to respond to requests for playwrights.

Ethiopia consists of fourteen scenes, some extremely brief and containing no dialogue, others quoting extensively from political leaders, including Mussolini, whom the State Department had been so anxious to avoid offending. Plainly, the effect depends in large part on the pressures of the moment, on the *frisson* which derives from the congruence between theatre and life. The shaping of history and the dramatic event are complementary acts. Rather than focussing political realities through an individual sensibility, the stage becomes a prism breaking down historical process into a spectrum of moments, relying on the audience's historical location to refocus those moments into a clear form. Offering, as it does, a radically simplified version of history, it also generates its theatrical effects from a series of radical simplifications: tribal rituals and rhythms disrupted by the staccato modernity of machine guns, women falling injured by bomb fragments, self-seeking and self-betraying individuals revealing their treacheries in a few casual sentences, political debates reduced to simple terms and staged as confrontations. Historical events are assumed to render up their meaning under the pressure of scrutiny; the deceits of language are presumed to become apparent through juxtaposition with actions whose historical and dramatic meanings are supposedly clear. Juxtaposition, indeed, becomes a theatrical and political tactic assumed to produce truth. Meaning generates plot as, more conventionally, plot is assumed to generate meaning.

219

The Living Newspaper inevitably offers a naive model of historical process. Reliance on the public document seals off both private reality and the secret motives and processes of history except as paranoid paradigm. What is offered, for the most part, and especially so in *Ethiopia*, is a compilation of public positions. The editorial hand is revealed in the process of selection and in the voice of the people for which there is no precise documentary validation.

Like the Proletcult theatre in the Soviet Union the Living Newspaper was, in effect if not in intent, producing a collectivist view of history. Events were seen as having a curious momentum of their own and, though suffered individually, were generated, and ultimately were to be understood, at a level other than the personal. There was, in short, a view of history implied in the Living Newspaper, and a dramatic reaction against the individualism of bourgeois drama – a reaction partly pragmatic and partly ideological. They were produced at a time of crisis in America, and America was ineluctably, perhaps, the central character – but an America seen very much as divided between the people and the interest groups who are presented as being responsible for the entropic turn of history.

In the Soviet Union, the Mass Theatre of Meyerhold and Evreinov, the Living Newspapers of *Zhivaya Gazeta* and the Blue Blouses, the documentary thrust advocated by *LEF* were all directed at a single objective: the need to theatricalise life. A catch-phrase of the moment was 'Live theatrically! Act your daily life!' The mass re-enactment of the storming of the Winter Palace three years after the actual event, in the same location and with a cast of thousands, was a means of seeing the dramatic content of the original event. The extension of this to issues of a more immediate kind in the Living Newspapers, and in the documentary plays which tackled local concerns, charged these events, too, with an epic quality, integrated them into a drama and a history which gave them dimension, significance and dignity. The theatricalising of life gives everyone a role. In the Soviet Union, for a time, this became quite literal, as it had been in medieval drama. In the case of the Federal Theatre it was more symbolic than actual, though the immediate relevance of the material to the audience was likely to have much the same effect. It was not simply that many more people saw theatre than ever before in America, but that many people came to see the dramatic dimension of their own times and lives. They were themselves theatricalised, saw themselves as actors in a national drama rather than simply victims of process, the refuse of economic and historical forces, and, increasingly, were represented in the living-newspaper productions by figures who stood for themselves.

For Hallie Flanagan, the Living Newspaper was 'as American as Walt Disney, the *March of Time*, and the *Congressional Record*, to all of which American institutions it is indebted. The living newspaper,' she insisted, was 'factual and formal, musical and acrobatic, abstract and concrete, visual and

NOW AT **AIR CONDITIONED** CIVIC THEATRE
WACKER DRIVE at WASHINGTON ∴ Phone State 7887

| LIVING DRAMA | **The Living Newspaper** | SPOT NEWS |

Vol. I. No. 1.   GREAT NORTHERN THEATRE   Opened July 6, 1936

"TRIPLE A PLOWED UNDER"

SILHOUETTE

One of the Many Spectacular Scenes in "Triple A Plowed Under"
Now Playing at the Great Northern Theatre.

DRAMATIZED NEWS NOW OFFERED IN FAMOUS PLAY

An entirely new form of theatrical production, live news enacted by living actors, is being given for the first time in Chicago, by the presentation at the Great Northern of the New York success "Triple A Plowed Under," under the auspices of the Federal Theatre. This production marks a unique and spectacular departure for the stage by offering a thrilling series of dramatized news events, with a large cast of actors in a series of swiftly moving scenes.

A good description of this new stage form is conveyed by its secondary title, The Living Newspaper. To achieve it, the abilities of many newspaper men and women, dramatists, actors, directors, scenic designers and other stage technicians were employed. In all, the work of 200 persons, including 100 actors and actresses, has gone into the production, with the staging being done by H. Gordon Graham, who also staged the New York edition of the same play.

One of the biggest jobs connected with producing the show was the editing. The first step was to choose which of thousands of news events to present on the stage.

News Subjects Sifted

Preliminary scanning of newspaper files resulted in the choice of about 100 events as of sufficient importance and lending themselves to dramatization. From these the editors of THE LIVING NEWSPAPER finally selected the most important connected with the main subject,—that of Triple A.

The forty research workers, for the most part experienced newspaper workers, on the staff of THE LIVING NEWSPAPER were then sent out to gather material on the selected subjects. Their reports were voluminous, in some instances running to more than 5,000 words on a single subject.

With this material the editors went to work again. They picked out about 30 events that could be presented vividly on the stage. They also kept in mind that the production should be balanced; that as wide as possible a variety of subjects should be included.

Still More Sifting

When the dramatic versions of the remaining happenings were turned in by the fifteen dramatists on the project there was more editing. The technical difficulties of staging some of the episodes made their presentation impractical. Some were too long. The show was not to run for more than an hour.

Even after the rehearsals were started, various scenes were re-written—often several times—or were discarded and replaced by others. Those who saw the early rehearsals scarcely recognize the production as it is now presented.

In this way "Triple A Plowed Under" finally took form and after weeks of rehearsing was ready to make its bow to the public.

Draw of Federal Theatre
Goes Over Best Expectations

Results Prove Public Is Eager For Plays

New York City. . . .
Fed Shows Do Top Biz!

Which is the way that our theatrical neighbor, "Variety," might hint at the fact that a handful of WPA Federal Theatre productions in New York recently played to more customers than many commercial productions on Broadway.

This is neither a boast nor idle fancy. It does not prove that the Federal Theatre is undermining commercial production, for the box-office scale, from 25 to 55 cents, can hardly be considered important money competition for the commercial managers. Moreover, about twenty per cent of the audiences have occupied free seats, since certain nights are free to WPA workers and persons on relief—and they make the most of it!

What it does indicate is that the recent batch of New York WPA productions has offered superb entertainment meriting a high degree of public acceptance. That it has kept a body of actors, writers and theatre workers constructively busy is almost too obvious to note.

Fine Record

Here is the record. From its opening on March 14, "Triple A Plowed Under," THE LIVING NEWSPAPER'S first production, played to over 40,000 people in 85 perform-ances—two a night—in a small theatre.

"Murder in the Cathedral," at the Manhattan, served an even larger number of playgoers, in a week's less run with one performance a night, 38 curtains in all. "Murder" topped them all in audiences and money business, and was a sellout when reluctantly closed on May 2.

And so it goes. The Experimental Theatre's "Chalk Dust," first to open and showing for eight weeks, the longest run of any, brought 21,000 persons to Daly's Theatre in its 51 performances.

The Bard a Hit

"Macbeth," the Negro Theatre's amazing hit at the Lafayette in Harlem, proved consistent in doing capacity business of 7,400 seats a week in the early part of its run. With the Lafayette having a slight edge on the Manhattan Theatre in seating capacity, Shakespeare topped T. S. Eliot in attendance (both were sell-outs) and drew

(Continued on Page 3)

> Don't forget! "Triple A" is given twice nightly, at 8:30 and 9:40 p. m. sharp. Be prompt so as not to miss any of the twenty-five exciting scenes. There are no matinees and no Sunday performances.

17. Publicity for *Triple A Plowed Under.*

aural, psychological, economic and social. . .a dramatic form in the beginning stage, a form capable of infinite extension.'[14] Like the newspaper, it was to be 'varied as to medium, including not only news but history, economics, the human-interest story, the signed article, the chart and graph, the statistical survey, the cartoon, and the columnist's comment'. Also, like the newspaper, 'its juxtapositions are important, as are its headlining, composition and set-up'.[15] It was not a mode with which actors felt an instinctive sympathy. Its mixture of forms was confusing, the anonymity it pressed on the actor was alien. And there was a problem on this score with the first production to follow *Ethiopia*, *Triple A Plowed Under*. Inspired by the Supreme Court's finding that the New Deal's Agricultural Adjustment Act was unconstitutional, it concentrated on the special plight of the farmer caught between the Depression and drought. It was not a subject, the actors felt, to which New Yorkers would feel instinctively drawn.

Nor was it a play entirely without ideological confusions. For while it takes a clear stance in opposition to the Supreme Court and ends with the clear suggestion that a farm-labour party should be formed (itself a proposal being touted by the American Communist Party), its analysis of the situation of the farmer is far from clear. In particular it takes an ambiguous stance on the subject of falling production, which on the one hand it deplores, but which on the other it sees as potentially ameliorating the situation of the share-cropper if only the blatant injustices and illegalities of the owners can be obviated. Nor were those newspapers which assailed the Federal Theatre for producing propaganda without justification. For the play ends with the un-employed and the farmers coming together while the voice of the loud-speaker offers newsflashes of events to do with the farm-labour party. But the furore demonstrated that for the moment, at least, the Federal Theatre was not cowed by its early experience of censorship nor yet vulnerable to the attacks which inevitably came from a number of quarters.

Triple A Plowed Under consists of twenty-five scenes and, as a production note makes clear, is modelled on the production scheme of a musical revue. 'The scenery consists almost entirely of combinations of a unit set of plat-forms and ramps. Properties, costumes and painted scenery are negligible.'[16] The play was designed to utilise different playing levels and selective lighting to create a fast-moving sequence that would forge the link between private experience and public policy which was the play's central premise. Music was to be used both as cover to bridge any gaps, and to underscore and comment ironically upon the action. The play begins in 1917 with a series of exhorta-tions to farmers to increase their acreage as a part of the war effort. It then traces the consequence of this through the 1920s as speculators turn their attention elsewhere and banks begin the process of foreclosure. In particular it attempts to establish the economic connection between the collapse of the farming economy and that of the industrial economy. The villains are the middle men, taking huge profits, and the speculators, who are concerned only with personal gain. The consequence is a series of strikes, with the farmers attacking those who try to blackleg. In one scene a truckload of milk is turned over, the effect deriving from a skilful use of sound and light and from an ominous background music designed to underscore the emotional content. As in *Ethiopia*, slide and movie projections were used, while actual recordings of official speeches were employed. But this authenticity was balanced by a deliberate stylising of other scenes, a conscious mechanising of individuals in the Chicago Wheat Pit, for example, which was designed to underscore the surrender of human to commercial values, of a personal world of suffering to the soulless, mechanical world of speculation.

> The scene is a stylized representation of the Chicago Wheat Pit. Two ramps, their large ends set upstage, are joined by two four-foot platforms. Behind the platforms, elevated so that they can be seen over the small ends of the ramps, are open telephone booths. A large clock is next to the blackboard right. Instead of numerals it depicts the months of the year. It has only one hand. This hand revolves slowly through the playing of the scene. Left of the blackboard is a large thermometer – to indicate increasing heat... There is a man at each of the four telephones, and several runners between them and the men in the Pit. The Wheat Pit is filled with 30 traders. These traders are divided into groups, left and right, one buying and one selling. At rise there is a din of voices. Immediately after rise a loud gong rings. The two groups of traders speak in unison, those buying speak first, and those selling right after. Their movements are also in unison – a movement which should be divided on count of two beats to a measure of four beats to a measure... building tempo and volume of scene consistently until end.[17]

Such manifestly expressionist scenes alternate with brief snatches of realistic dialogue, as caricatured social leeches are juxtaposed to individualised farmers. In short, a series of entirely familiar devices were deployed. They were novel really only in their combination, in the attempt to yoke them all together in a single vision. But that was, after all, the essence of the Living Newspaper for, as Hallie Flanagan herself said, 'Theatrical expression of elements so diverse makes for confusion unless held in a unified pattern. Subject matter in the best living newspapers dictated such a form...the basic necessity was synchronization.'[18] A clear objective was the key to this, the one production which lacked such a spine, *Highlights of 1935*, being in her judgement a failure.

The Living Newspaper required a mixture of acting styles as it rested on different modes of production. This did not always prove easy. The manuscript of *Triple A Plowed Under*, for example, contains a note that one scene, between a Negro farmer and a sheriff, was not used because 'it was impossible to get actors to play it with the necessary simplicity. The scene is conceived to be played...with vaudeville technique, but not to be played up or plugged.'[19]

Despite the clearly propagandist dimension of *Triple A Plowed Under*, Hallie Flanagan felt more favourably disposed towards it than she did to the subsequent *Injunction Granted*. Indeed she characterised that production as 'bad journalism and hysterical theatre', writing to the director, Joseph Losey, that 'To show the history of labor in the courts is appropriate. If the struggle now going on within the ranks of labor itself were made clear, if the AAA, NRA, and the Coal Act were fully explained, the end could possibly give the stand of each political party.'[20] In response to a rejoinder from Morris Watson, production supervisor, she insisted that, 'I will not have the Federal Theatre used politically.'[21] The production, in her mind, was 'special pleading, biased, an editorial, not a news issue'. Moreover it was not politically effective:

> The production, in my opinion, lacks a proper climax, falling back on the old cliché of calling labor to unite in the approved agit-prop manner...[The] production uses too many devices, too much hysteria of acting...the production is historical drama and hence, by reason of compression, is open to the charge of superficiality. I think we should consider whether history should not rather be used, as it is in *Triple A*, to illuminate the present, not lead up to it in the chronological manner.[22]

So angry was she with Losey and Watson that she considered them 'both through'. Critics were hostile, and there was some discussion of discontinuing the living-newspaper project. But it was, of course, likely from the beginning that a play about organised labour would take a clear political position, not merely because of the known commitments of its creators and the context of of its creation but because a reconstructed history of the labour movement was likely to generate its own political logic.

Flanagan's complaints were largely justified. Certainly the play was some considerable distance from the supposedly objective reportage proposed as the model in the Federal Theatre's own publication, even allowing for the unreality of that model. Neither did *Injunction Granted* focus on the contemporary moment. It offered a history of the labour movement in America from the seventeenth century to the present, including Bacon's Rebellion of 1676, a strike of Philadelphia shoemakers in 1806, the Molly Maguires of 1875, the Haymarket riot of 1886, and various legal tussles of the twentieth century. The roles are indeed stereotyped. The law is a simple agent of money and power; labour, a series of honest working men and women seeking alliance to secure sheer survival. The ambiguities of the closed shop are passed over without comment; representatives of labour alone are seen in a private context, outside of the roles acknowledged by history. Much of the material is not derived from documentary sources, despite the bibliography

18. *Injunction Granted*, written by the Living Newspaper staff under the direction of Arthur Arent. Staged by Joseph Losey.

which precedes the text and which is clearly offered as part of the text, as a validating principle.

Rather less justified were Hallie Flanagan's comments on the dramatic strategy. Its weakness lay in its conventionality rather than its nervous eclecticism. It was for the most part a series of brief scenes juxtaposing invented dialogue with public documents and speeches. One novel feature, however, was the introduction of the figure of the Clown, who appears in fourteen out of the play's twenty-eight scenes. The Clown does not speak, but acts as an ironic commentary on the action, which he subverts by his own irreverent person and by the signs which he displays. In the first scene, the lyrical description of America offered by landowners looking for indentured labour is undercut by the Clown who 'swings a tomahawk...and lets out a blood-curdling shriek. ARC picks HIM up as HE turns toward audience with scalp.'[23] In the thirteenth scene, in which a series of anti-labour judgements are handed down by the judiciary, to the accompaniment of an ironic and reductive musical commentary, the clown holds up a sign which reads: 'The interests of the Workingmen are not affected...Grimms Fairy Tales.'[24] This dimension of the play is stylistically incorporated in the eighteenth scene, in which a Demagogue adroitly combines appeals to both sides of the industrial divide, his dubiety symbolised by his carnivalesque appearance. 'He is dressed in an outfit split up the middle, the side facing Capital being a striped trouser, half a cutaway, slick hair and a half mustache. The side facing Labor...consisting of an overall leg, half a blue shirt, rumpled hair, and one horn-rimmed glass.'[25] This scene is presented as a circus performance, with the Clown as ringmaster.

225

Indeed the play is marked by a humour largely lacking from its predecessors, a dimension not remarked on by Hallie Flanagan. Various scenes are clearly modelled on vaudeville sketches, particularly one between two down-and-outs, called Mopey Dick and The Duke, while another transforms the battle between William Randolph Hearst and Dean Jennings of the Newspaper Guild into a boxing match. John D. Rockefeller Jr and Howard Heinz end their serious perorations on the state of labour relations by dancing off the stage to ironic music from the orchestra. This was clearly the strength of the production, which sustained its popularity with the public not simply, as Hallie Flanagan believed, through the support of organised labour but because its propaganda message was delivered with humour. It was closer than most living-newspaper productions to the political cabarets of Europe.

For Arthur Arent a central weakness of *Injunction Granted* lay in its reliance, in the first act, on pure montage: 'the scenes were skeletonized and flowed into one another without pause, building up to the act curtain. The act as a result was dull and repetitious.'[26] Its strength lay in its subsequent reliance on an episodic method which was, to his mind, patterned closely on the revue, allowing for comic disjunctions and variety. The play also revealed a further development of a central device as the Voice of the Living Newspaper became distinct from the loudspeaker which was simply a neutral voice of the news. The Living Newspaper Voice now became a clearer character, with an editorial opinion.

If Hallie Flanagan objected to *Injunction Granted* because of its clear political bias she can have had little time for the unproduced *The South*, which is dated March 1936. *The South* is a virulent denunciation of the entire southern region, dealing directly with the Scottsboro case, in which nine black teenagers were falsely accused of rape, and with the Angelo Herndon case, in which a black Communist was charged with incitement to insurrection under an 1861 law. The play also deals with the suppression of the share-croppers' union, the flogging and murder of Tampa citizens by the police, the corrupt government and assassination of Huey Long in Louisiana and the Southern filibuster of the Wagner anti-lynching bill in 1935. It itemises the discrepancy between money set aside for black and white education in the South, quotes Governor Talmadge of Georgia praising Hitler and pokes fun at Senator Bilbo of Mississippi. The play is very much concerned with contemporary events, several scenes being left blank so as to include stop-press news on current developments. It is mentioned neither by Hallie Flanagan in *Arena* nor by Jane Mathews in *The Federal Theatre*. It was a crude form of living newspaper, but closer to the model described in the *Federal Theatre Magazine* than most of those which were actually produced. The Voice of the Living Newspaper does not appear, but the teletype is used extensively as the source of statistical information and news developments. In its contemporaneity it fulfilled the objectives of the project more fully than did *Injunction Granted*. But from a dramatic point of view it was unadventurous, relying on the assumed power of the fact, deformed by editorial selection. Perhaps with figures like Huey Long, Talmadge, Bilbo and the assembled grotesques of Southern justice any embellishment would have become redundant. It was anyway evidently too violently anti-Southern to launch as a product of the Federal Theatre which had instead sent a touring production of *Jefferson Davis* through the South at the request of the Daughters of the Confederacy. It was not a decision or a production in which Hallie Flanagan took any pride, but her response to *Injunction Granted* makes it plain that she was not willing to risk the future of the project by what she regarded as pointless provocations.

Much the same logic doubtless applied to another unproduced script which, like *The South*, survives only as a single copy in the Federal Theatre Archive at George Mason University. This is an unashamed celebration of the Russian Revolution. The script was apparently never completed, one note delightfully observing, 'Conquest of Winter Palace (5 minutes) Being re-written.' Since Mayakovsky staged the same event with the aid of several thousand actors, not to mention free access to the armed forces of the Soviet state, this was likely to give pause for thought even to the Federal Theatre staff. Otherwise the script is reasonably complete and reveals precisely that tendency towards theatrical hysteria which Hallie Flanagan had objected to in *Injunction Granted*. A series of set pieces (Bloody Sunday on the Nevsky Prospect, in which hundreds of workers are killed by Cossacks; the death of Lenin) stress the melodramatic nature of Revolutionary Russia, while public speeches are offered as an adequate rendering of experience. The play moves towards a climax in which, surrounded by various groups of workers and others, a speaker intones:

> Out of the East the dawn is rising. Out of the night the day appears. The Russian people have cast behind them three centuries of Tsarist oppression. They have established an advanced form of democracy, based on a co-operative effort for the common good. They have cast aside the false idols of secret diplomacy and imperialism, and have abolished exploitation of every kind. They have made great progress...Factory workers forward...Land workers forward...Pioneers forward!...Metro guards forward!...Bus drivers forward...Athletes forward! Honored artists of the republic forward!... Soldiers forward![27]

With the music growing to a crescendo, this is an entirely apt conclusion to a play which is indistinguishable from the Marxist historical dramas of the period. But, belatedly mindful of their own status as members of the Federal Theatre, the anonymous authors surrender their climax to a bathetic voice-over speech by Senator Robert M. La Follette who offers the American view that 'The Russian people are struggling to establish the sort of government they want. It may not be the kind of government we would prefer. But it is not our job to determine that question for Russia.'[28] There then follows the hopeful remark, 'Appropriate finale fanfare', an attempt to replace musically what has just been destroyed dramatically. The non-appearance of *Russia* was scarcely surprising.

In his article in *Modern Drama* Douglas McDermott suggests that there were thirty-eight living-newspaper manuscripts produced in America. The Federal Theatre Archive has thirty-two, only nine of which were produced. The living-newspaper scripts represent, as Hallie Flanagan has said, 'the major playwriting done by project playwrights on project time'.[29] They were, in other words, the principal contribution which the Federal Theatre made to American drama, as opposed to the general, vivifying effect which it had on the American theatre at large. Some of the scripts are indeed crude. Their creators were, after all, trying to create a form which was new to most of those involved, whatever its European forebears, and they were also concerned with testing the extent of their own freedom to operate, the relationship between writer, artist and government agency being a completely novel one in the American context.

At its worst the Living Newspaper was a crude device, importing its effects from outside the theatre, substituting the sentimentality and melodrama of fact for that of fiction. Its panoply of innocent victims and ruthless exploiters was liable to be both politically and dramatically reductive, its rationalist and positivist account of historical process displacing questions of value onto a material level and hence problems of dramatic concern onto externals. Individuals are not merely presented as existing *primarily* as political beings but wholly so. History becomes an account of adversary politics; life a process of challenging a system of laws and prejudices. It was a public theatre not merely in the origin of its funding and in its desire to reach a broad audience but in its assumption that the public world is the true arena, the primary and legitimate sphere of human activity. Personal relationships exist in the interstices of public events or more usually not at all. Taken collectively, these plays dramatise the battle of the human spirit against privilege, wealth, corrupt government, prejudice, injustice, poverty and human cruelty. They never question the origins of those evils, never debate the question of human nature or examine the private origins of public positions. They never question their own historicism, never probe, like Ibsen, the ambivalences of the idealist. The world which they describe expresses its truths. Its bigots freely declare their bigotry – as, to be sure, they did on occasion in reality. When this cannot be done credibly then, as in *One Third of a Nation*, a theatrical convention is established whereby it becomes possible for individuals to expose truths which, psychologically speaking, they might

19. *One Third of a Nation*, written by Arthur Arent. Originally staged at Vassar College, it opened in New York in January 1938. Design by Howard Bay.

well conceal even from themselves. The effect is to engage the problem at its most immediate and obvious level. It is to create a drama in which the playwright confines his characters to their economic and social existence with every bit as much rigour as the forces which they wish to indict.

But such an approach was by no means disabling as was apparent in the best of the living-newspaper productions, *One Third of a Nation*. This play was produced under circumstances substantially different from those of the other Living Newspapers. It grew out of a six-week summer session, held at Vassar College, of directors, actors, designers and techniques gathered from the Federal Theatre project throughout America. As usual the research for the play was conducted in New York, and Arthur Arent produced a script. The music, costumes and staging were all worked out in the course of the summer session itself.

The play was concerned with the history and reality of slum life in America. The title was based on Roosevelt's observations in his Second Inaugural address that he saw 'one-third of a nation ill housed, ill clad, ill nourished'. It was centred on New York but was subsequently adapted to meet the

229

circumstances of the various cities which staged it. By the same token the staging itself differed from place to place, the New York production opting for an elaborate set, others offering a more simplified setting.

The production was more thoroughly researched, more coherently developed and more consistently plotted than its predecessors. The bibliography issued by the National Service Bureau ran to eight pages, with over 350 entries, and the press edition of the play was footnoted throughout, the originals of fictional characters being carefully identified.

The play begins with a fire in a tenement block, followed by a commission of enquiry which establishes nothing beyond the fact that if a tenement is old enough it is subject to virtually no housing legislation. This precipitates an enquiry into the history of land speculation and the whole process whereby fortunes were made through the ownership and renting of propetry while the ordinary citizen became trapped in deteriorating housing without sanitation or services.

The principal device of the play is the use of a character called Little Man, supposedly a member of the audience, who is himself a tenant in a slum tenement and who has come to the show in order to understand the reason for his plight ('I went down to see the Tenement House Commissioner. He gave me a bunch of pamphlets and told me the Living Newspaper was doing a show on Housing and I ought to see it...So here I am').[30] Throughout the play he interrupts to ask questions and is guided through the past and present of New York, being shown the squalor and the disease, the connection between poor housing, crime, illness and despair. In the process a series of cameos are presented, micro-dramas of family life. The skeletal framework of the tenement which dominates the stage becomes a hive of small stages, rooms, in which these entropic dramas are acted out. Indeed in some degree the set, with these exposed tenement rooms, becomes an image of the play's episodic strategy – the episodes being contained within a clearer framework than in earlier productions. The factual material is incorporated into the text and the action, where in other living-newspaper plays it had been detached from it and used simply to underline the action and to comment ironically on it.

A superficial attempt is made to justify the position of the landlord, to provide something of that political balance which Hallie Flanagan had looked for. It is made plain that he too is to some extent a victim of the system, that the profit motive which drives him equally drives those on whose services he relies. But the sub-text is clear. What the play is attacking is capitalism. When a judge strikes down a Board of Health ruling that minimal health requirements should be enforced in slum tenements, he does so with the observation that, 'A conclusion contrary to the present decision would involve that species of Socialism under the regime of which the individual disappears and is absorbed by a collective being called "The State"...a principle utterly repugnant to the political system, and necessarily fatal to our form of liberty.'³¹ And when the problems of the landlord have been dutifully rehearsed, the voice of the loudspeaker interrupts the action to insist on a solution which is precisely that shunned by the judge.

> Wait a minute! Hold it! Don't blackout on that yet! Bring those lights up – full! That's better. This scene isn't over yet! Now, Mister Landlord, we know that the conditions you showed us exist. They were a little exaggerated perhaps, but they exist...But we can't just let it go at that. We can't let people walk out of this theatre, knowing the disease is there, but believing there's no cure. *There is a cure!...Government Housing!* You see, everyone of those people who had his hand in your pocket while you were building that house, was inspired by the profit motive – The Landowner, the Broker, the Building Supply Man, the Contractor, and you, too, you were all out to get yours...But there's one thing you've got to stop taking profits on – and that's human misery! *If you can't build cheap houses...then let somebody do it who can – and I mean the United States Government.*³²

The play is clearly pro-New Deal, and ends by attacking the watering-down of the Wagner–Steagall Act which set out to make one thousand million dollars available for public housing but which was attacked and whittled down to half that sum. The play concludes with a denunciation of defence appropriations, a suggestion of further crime and disease, and the recurrence of the fire with which the play had started, a warning and a prophecy.

While provoking a predictable assault from those Southern congressmen who had opposed the bill, and setting Hallie Flanagan her usual political problems, the play was well received by the critics and one of the great successes of the New York Federal Theatre. It ran from January to October 1938 and was seen by 217458 people in that city alone.

Eight months later an act of Congress closed the Federal Theatre. Though the Senate voted to save it, the House of Representatives refused to compromise. Belief as to its Communist penetration was firmly established. Before the Dies Committee, Hallie Flanagan had even found herself having to deny the Communist affiliations of Christopher Marlowe.

Hallie Flanagan took special pride in the social utility of the Federal Theatre, in its success at rescuing people from unemployment, in its reaction against prejudice and intolerance of every kind. 'It strove,' she remarked, 'for a more dramatic statement and a better understanding of the great forces of our life today; it fought for a free theatre as one of the many expressions of a civilized, informed and vigorous life.'³³ In other words it potentially moved the theatre to a central position in the arts and in society. Certainly, in its various forms it introduced whole sections of the American public to the theatre and established the viability and relevance of drama outside of Broadway and the little-theatre movement. It patently strengthened regionalism as it did the growth of ethnic theatre. In fostering dramatic talent, however briefly, it went some way towards laying the groundwork for the post-war theatre. Arthur Miller's first plays were submitted to the Federal Theatre (they were rejected) in its dying months, while Tennessee Williams's early plays were written in a theatrical context partly defined by that theatre.

On the negative side, I suspect that the purely social drive of much of the Federal Theatre's work, more especially the living-newspaper productions, may have had something to do with the shallowness of much American drama, with a failure to press issues beyond an immediate social dimension (the weakness, for example, of *All My Sons*), with a tendency to paint with broad strokes, to substitute sentimentality for sentiment, melodrama for a subtle probing of motive and morale, public issues for private anguish, language for silence. The living-newspaper productions were characterised by a raw energy, a rational analysis of events, an external view of behaviour and a sense of determinism to be neutralised only by the collectivity. It was a powerful epic drama, but it traded its effects for a subtle appreciation of individual psychology and a more sophisticated model of social action and historical process.

Nonetheless its impact was considerable, and by no means simply as a challenging political fact and cultural phenomenon. There was no doubt that it saw its principal role as exposing the nature of the national experience, dramatising in the most literal way the public and private tensions which had eventually led to its own creation. Hence, writing in the *Federal Theatre Magazine*, Michael Garnett urged that Federal Theatre playwrights should deal with 'the most poignant problems of individual and collective judgement ever faced by mankind...Born out of the sternest of all realities – necessity – our theatre should be an instrument for disseminating knowledge of reality.'[34] The 1936 prospectus for the Play Bureau similarly called for 'Plays by young playwrights of promise who have something to say... writing honest plays which are alive to the problems of today's world'. But this was to be combined with a commitment to experimentation: 'We believe in an experimental theatre of ideas, forms and technical expression, as the only experimental theatre worthy of the name.'[35] And, despite its European predecessors, the Living Newspaper in particular was innovatory, if only in an American context, while the sheer range of the Federal Theatre's activities, the number of new writers, directors and actors which it sponsored, had an impact on the American theatre which has never been equalled. For four brief years it created an unprecedented market for new plays in America. The necessities of touring theatre on the one hand, and working to limited budgets on the other, also led to a re-examination of production methods, and in particular to a stress on simplified staging and the imaginative use of lighting which was an extension of a movement in the theatre in which Hallie Flanagan had herself participated at Vassar. Indeed in January 1938, she wrote a letter to Federal-Theatre personnel urging them to substitute light and dynamic movement for cumbersome scenery: 'but even more important than that,' she insisted,

> the elimination of realistic sets was necessary because plays now began to look, in their limited horizontality, like inferior movies. The cinema had beaten realism at its own game; instead of showing only a few rooms or exteriors, it could flash kaleidoscopically in and out of the house with countless camera shots. Consequently the stage should not try to compete, but rather to develop the asset which the movie does not have: the living body of the actor, emphasized by light, seen from as many angles, massed with other bodies in as many formations as possible. Stage forms affording playing space and emphasizing theme should stress the fact that a stage is a stage and not a flat-surface movie. Like architecture, the stage should emphasize its own special materials – three-dimensional movement of three-dimensional bodies; voice, individual and choric; light and its effect on both movement and sound; and an audience with which a connection can and must be made.[36]

This notion of a non-illusionist stage, this concern with the foregrounding of technique, the emphasis on sound and movement, on a redefinition of the relationship between audience and performers, was immediately rejected by some members of the Federal Theatre, but in many ways anticipated a movement in the American theatre which dominated the 1960s and in some ways paralleled the theories of Artaud, though clearly in Hallie Flanagan's case the line went more directly back to a Russian source, sharing as she did the Russians' belief in the social power of theatre. While Howard Bay, who had designed the set for *One Third of A Nation*, insisted that 'A creative compilation of real recognisable objects is the only guarantee of communication of a theme with a controlled, unmistakable application to life outside the theatre',[37] she saw no conflict between a desire to engage the real and a non-realistic presentation.

Speaking of epic theatre, Erwin Piscator remarked that 'Styles are born out of necessity...out of the characteristic modes of expression of an era; they are man-made, yes, but made for the mores and customs and social conditions of the moment.'[38] Much the same could have been said of the Living Newspaper, which owed a good deal to Piscator and his experiments but which resonated to a social awareness that sounded throughout society.

As with the Russian theatre, it was entirely appropriate that German drama should have provided part of the model for the enterprise for in Germany too America played a crucial symbolic role. It was the image of the new, the excitingly technological, the innovatory. But it was not the American theatre which sparked European interest, it was America itself. As Maria Ley-Piscator has said of her husband's group,

> It invented 'America'. Everything that was useful, effective, expedient, operative, performing properly and instrumented for production, was called America. Even time had an American tempo and was valued as such...They admired what seemed real to them: the objective existence of the land of plenty, its material genius, with its prosperity, its sloganism and the great god – the machine. It is impossible to understand the complexity of Epic Theatre without taking into account this capture of the imagination by America.[39]

Ironically in many ways, it is possible to reverse the sentiment, looking to the German as to the Russian theatre for the inspiration of the Living Newspaper, whatever the pragmatics of its development in America.

Piscator pioneered the agit-prop material which was used by his own Proletarisches Theater and, increasingly in the 1920s, by agit-prop troupes throughout Germany. Short sketches with stereotyped characters, these were designed to deliver a simple political message to working-class audiences. In terms of drama, his theatre was concerned with subordinating the writer to the material and in particular learning to make use of 'trivial forms which have the merit of being clear and easily understood by all'. This theatre was to become 'the flint on which the writer's desire for truth will ignite'.[40] The objective was clarity and intellectual stimulation rather than emotional provocation. At the Volksbühne in Berlin he further refined his techniques. His production of *Flags*, a play by Alfons Paquet, a writer who had himself seen Meyerhold's work in Moscow in 1919, employed two projection screens which used slides to comment on or expand the action ('blackboards for purposes of reporting, and documentation'). According to Hugh Rorrison, he was to have used movie film as well, while newspaper cuttings and telegrams were projected. The subject of the play was the campaign for the eight-hour day by immigrant groups in Chicago that led to the Haymarket affair which features in *Injunction Granted*. Piscator later described the play as a kind of dramatic comic strip which justified its subtitle 'An Epic Drama'. Indeed it was in some respects akin to revue of the kind which he subsequently perfected. In the *Red Revue*, which he wrote with Felix Gasbarra, the series of sketches included one called 'The Electoral Boxing Match' in which two politicians spar with one another, a device subsequently also used in *Injunction Granted*. The virtue of this form from Piscator's perspective was that it left nothing unclear or ambiguous. The political moral was clear. For these revues he developed a style requiring no scenery and using ramps and platforms of different levels with slides and film projections – precisely the style which was employed by the Living Newspapers. Meyerhold had worked in a similar way, but Piscator denied any direct knowledge of this. To Piscator the matter of priority was of no importance. 'It would merely prove that this was no superficial game with technical effects, but a new, emergent form of theatre based on the philosophy of historical material-ism.'

The Living Newspaper was equally rooted in a notion of historical materialism, at least to the degree that it was, like Piscator's Documentary Theatre, an attempt to get 'beyond the purely individual aspect of the characters and the fortuitous nature of their fates' showing, as Piscator insisted, 'the link between events on the stage and the great forces active in history. It is not by chance' then 'that the factual substance becomes the main thing in each play. It is only from the facts themselves that the constraints and the constant mechanisms of life emerge, giving a deeper meaning to our private fates.'[41] His description of Documentary Theatre could equally be that of the Living Newspaper: 'a montage of authentic speeches, essays, newspaper cuttings, appeals, pamphlets, photographs, and film'.[42] If to Piscator it was the First World War which had buried bourgeois individual-ism, for the creators of the Living Newspapers it was the economic crisis of the 1930s. Where O'Neill had declared his interest in man's relationship to God, Piscator and the Living Newspaper reversed this: 'man portrayed on the stage is significant as a social function. It is not his relationship to himself, nor his relationship to God, but his relationship to society which is central.'[43] It is not theatre which makes man political; it is society. It is this same fact which drives theatre beyond a concern with fictions, beyond dissembling to take steps to destroy or erode the membrane between performer and audience, stage and life. All of these pressures are observable in the Federal Theatre. The community impulse was strong. It was a social, even a political, theatre in origin and never likely to be less than that in fact. Even a children's play about beavers set in an imaginary world turned out to be a political allegory which led to its being cited in a congressional debate. The freedom and emphasis given to black theatre was not without its subversive dimension while, censorship notwithstanding, it engaged the contemporary world with avidity, projecting its own community methods as a paradigm of social organisation.

Hallie Flanagan's constant references to the number of people who had seen Federal Theatre productions was, to be sure, a purely pragmatic attempt to demonstrate its utility. But beyond that, I suspect, there was something of that bias for the epic potential of theatre stressed by Meyerhold and Piscator in their different ways. The simultaneous production of *It Can't Happen Here* offered something of that *frisson* which had been experienced in the Russian and German theatre. The collective nature of the enterprise was more than the chance by-product of a relief agency. It implied an approach to theatre and to society. The summer session which produced *One Third of a Nation* was, apart from anything else, an experiment in the full integration of all elements of theatre and in a co-operative methodology directly related to the play's central theme. Hallie Flanagan's anger at the cheap theatricality of *Injunction Granted* was a response to an emotionalism which she, like Piscator, wished to subordinate to 'a mutual exchange of problems and experiences with the audience'. And if her enthusiasm for experiment did not derive from an attachment to modernity in its own right, she shared what Maria Ley-Piscator called her husband's 'particular bias for technical innovation, drawing upon other arts and other civilizations'.[44] Maria Ley-Piscator's sense of the German generation of the 1920s as being 'artists astride history' was clearly felt by American writers and artists of the 1930s, and though in her eyes, with a few exceptions, the militant theatre advanced neither the cause of social theatre nor the cause of world theatre, there can be little doubt of the impact of Hallie Flanagan and the Federal Theatre.

In *Arena*, Hallie Flanagan lists over three hundred plays or adaptations given their first professional production in the United States by the Federal Theatre. The Negro unit alone was responsible for forty-one productions. The range of the theatre was considerable. It staged vaudeville and musical revues, had a dance unit, a children's theatre unit, a puppet unit, a Yiddish theatre unit. It produced Shakespeare in the parks three decades before Joe Papp, toured circus along the Atlantic seaboard (including a young trapeze artist called Burt Lancaster). Its radio division produced some 2000 programmes a year, released through commercial stations. It was, in short, a unique experiment. As Hallie Flanagan boasted, in five years its audiences represented one-quarter of the entire population of the United States.

7 Black drama

The theatre is a public art. It is a shared experience, operating in a present tense which gives it not merely the illusion of immediacy but the effect of community. It is ineluctably a social experience, a ceremony with the power to reinforce or challenge values. The Yiddish theatre in New York, for example, acted as a mechanism of cultural reinforcement. It acknowledged the legitimacy of a language and an experience. And that language resisted assimilation; indeed in some ways it stood as a sign of that act of primary resistance.

For the black writer the situation was more problematic. Language had always been a primary mechanism of social control. To become fluent in that language was thus a fundamentally ambiguous act, necessary but in some ways a denial of cultural identity. Indeed, the theatre itself like other institutions was an expression of a society whose cultural life had for the most part reinforced rather than challenged its prejudices. Certainly racism was entrenched in its social operation, audiences being rigidly segregated. Meanwhile the black experience itself was seen less as offering its own legitimation than as a source of exoticism, of a child-like naivety and lyricism, or the source of simple melodrama. And this was, on the whole, how it was used by white writers such as Ridgely Torrence, Marc Connelly, Paul Green and, to some extent, O'Neill.

Ridgely Torrence, whose *Three Plays for a Negro Theatre* opened on Broadway on 5 April 1917, was a pioneer in using materials of Negro life:

> It was not [he explained] only the capacity of the Negro as an actor...that I wished to exploit. It was also the extraordinary dramatic richness of his daily life. The Negro has been a race apart and usually a race in subjection...its life under slavery with its intense but seemingly hopeless longing for liberty produced in it a certain epic spirit, unconscious of course.[1]

For all its ambiguities, this was a crucial production. As James Weldon Johnson remarked,

> We do not know how many colored people of greater New York realize that April, 1917, marks an epoch for the Negro on the stage. Mrs. Emilie Hapgood has given the American Negro his first opportunity in serious legitimate drama. It is amazing how Mr. Torrence, a white man, could write plays of Negro life with such intimate knowledge, with such deep insight and sympathy.[2]

Not only did Torrence make the Negro the subject of his drama but by so doing he was acknowledging that the black American was back on the national agenda. For the first time, in fact, Negroes were actually allowed into the New York theatres. And yet there is a considerable irony in the fact that the black theatre in America should effectively have been launched by a white man. Indeed, ten years later, when Alain Locke published his *Plays of Negro Life* at the height of the Harlem Renaissance, the better-known playwrights still remained white. Only the previous year Paul Green's racial melodrama, *In Abraham's Bosom*, had been awarded the Pulitzer prize, and David Belasco staged Charles MacArthur and Edward Sheldon's lurid play of black street-life, *My Lulu Belle*. And in 1927 this was followed by Mike Gold's *Hoboken Blues* and Du Bose Heyward and Dorothy Heyward's *Porgy*, while three years later Marc Connelly's 'folk' drama, *The Green Pastures*, was staged on Broadway.

The black experience, indeed, proved a fruitful area for white writers. For the black writer, however, things were by no means as simple. As Langston Hughes once remarked, 'Sometimes I think whites are more appreciative of our uniqueness than we are ourselves. The white "black" artists dealing in Negro material have certainly been financially more successful than any of us real Negroes have ever been.'[3]

The black writer was faced with a genuine dilemma. As James Weldon Johnson observed in 1928, 'The moment a Negro writer picks up his pen and sits down to his typewriter he is immediately called upon to solve, consciously or unconsciously, this problem of the double audience. To whom shall he address himself, to his own black group or to white America? Many a Negro writer has fallen down as it were, between these two stools.'[4] For the poet and novelist, at a time when the Negro literacy rate was low, this was perhaps especially acute, more especially since access to the black audience lay through white publishers (the impact of this latter fact on the career of Paul Lawrence Dunbar being a prime example of this). The dramatist, however, was faced with problems of equal magnitude. It was not for nothing that Broadway was known as the 'Great White Way'. The theatre involves a process of mediation more complex than that which faces the novelist. Nor was serious theatregoing an established part of black cultural life. There was, however, a strong tradition of musical entertainment, and some of the most successful works by Negro authors of this period were musical revues like Flournoy Miller and Aubrey Lyles's *Shuffle Along*, a successor to the earlier *Darktown Follies* (1913) which played in Washington and Philadelphia and subsequently, to great acclaim, New York. This in turn became the model for a number of other highly successful revues, such as Noble Sissle and Eubie Blake's *Chocolate Dandies*, starring Josephine Baker, which opened on Broadway in September 1924, and *Blackbirds* of 1928.

The first serious play by a black writer to appear on Broadway was Willis

Richardson's *The Chipwoman's Fortune* (1923), which had originally opened at the Lafayette Theatre in Harlem before moving downtown. A very slight piece, it contrasts poorly with the work of white authors. A brief moral tale, it recounts the story of Silas Green, who loses his job because he fails to keep up his credit payments on a Victrola. He is saved by the intercession of Aunt Nancy, an apparently poor black woman who has been saving her money for her ex-convict son. Released from prison, somewhat incredibly he hands over enough cash to save the situation and everything ends conveniently. The characters are caricatures, the plot simplistic, the moral banal. But it was a breakthrough for the black writer – the staking out of a territory.

Garland Anderson's *Appearances* (1925) was a more substantial work but so suffused with its author's belief in so-called 'New Thought' that its plot lacks credibility. Anderson subsequently became a minister in the delightfully named Seattle Center of Constructive Thinking. Though the play deals with a false accusation of assault, a charge levelled against a Negro bell-hop, it nervously retreats from its own seriousness by taking refuge in humour, and finally and most demeaningly, in the discovery that the complainant is not after all a white woman but a mulatto passing as white. But Anderson was operating in a white theatre and fully conscious of doing so. In a newspaper interview, indeed, he even went so far as to condone racial prejudice. 'I don't resent the prejudice that white men have against the Negro. Not anymore, that is. Before I studied these matters, the white man's antipathy to the Negro got under my skin. Now, I don't think that anybody should be forced to accept a race. They should judge the individual, not the race.'[5] Nothing, perhaps, could more eloquently express the delicate balancing act required of the black writer on Broadway.

To some degree *Appearances* depends on comic stereotypes. Rufus Jones, hired as a hotel porter, is the familiar caricature, slow of speech but quick of wits. Indeed the play attempts to combine humour with a serious moral point. To Anderson it stood as evidence of the validity of its own theme: that positive thinking can transcend circumstance. Hence it opens and closes with framing scenes in which the theatricality of the work is foregrounded, in which the fact of the play is adduced as evidence of the utility of Anderson's personal philosophy. Himself a bell-hop, he places such a figure at the centre of his play and in his achievement finds an embodiment of the success which the playwright himself sought through his work. As his protagonist observes, 'If a black bell-boy with not much schooling could imagine himself a playwright; that by believing and working he could write a play that was interesting and entertaining enough to hold an audience, it would prove to the world beyond the shadow of a doubt that anyone can do what he desires to do, can become anything he desires to be. For you see you are all characters I have dreamt.'[6]

Wallace Thurman, collaborating with the white William Jourdan Rapp, could be accused of evasion in *Harlem* (1929), choosing rather to combine what purported to be a realistic picture of black urban life with simple melodrama. As a consequence he fell foul of black critics who wished to charge the black writer with a social and racial responsibility with which the white writer was not encumbered. To be a black playwright was an ambiguous exercise. On the one hand success on Broadway made it less possible to dismiss black culture; on the other hand that success threatened to reinforce a stereotype which white critics took for realism. So it was that George Jean Nathan said of *Harlem*, 'it has all the actuality of an untouched-up photograph ...a dozen and one vivid hints of niggerdom at its realest'.[7] It is not hard to see the dangerous social and moral ground on which the black playwright was required to tread.

In his introduction to *Plays of Negro Life: A Sourcebook of Native American Drama* (1927), Alain Locke suggested that the Negro experience was charged with dramatic potential. And indeed as the focus of a national, historical, moral and psychological drama, the black American was forced to live at extremes and to examine the nature of private and public truths as they shaped themselves under the pressure of event, of social hostility and personal tension. He existed on the margin of society but came to feel that cultural definition depended precisely on locating with precision the position of that boundary. And it clearly was a crucial task, for the black outcast and the white American alike. For if to the one it held the clue to simple selfhood and social possibility, to the other it constituted the extent of his moral being, the limits to a cultural identity which saw itself precisely in terms of freedom and of inclusiveness. The fate of the Negro, as Melville had suggested, was finally tied to the fate of the American. Neither could know himself without acknowledging the other. Hence black drama in America has had twin goals. On the one hand it has always had the crucial objective of presenting the Negro to himself, of reflecting not so much the public being, forced to wear the abstracting mask shaped by an implacable white hostility, but the private self whose resources lie partly in an historical experience and partly in a shared present. On the other hand it has set itself the task of testing American principles, of exposing a gulf between spiritual ideals and practical politics. In holding the mirror up to black life it has held the mirror up to a potentially fatal flaw in the fabric and substance of American life.

And so, for the black dramatist, personal and cultural identity are of primary significance and, by the nature of American society and history, were likely to be a product of conflict. The ironic contrast between public roles and private experience was never greater than it was for that individual invited to secure access to American myths and realities by accepting and enacting stereotypes which implicitly denied the value of those myths and emphasised the ambiguous nature of those realities. As Locke observed:

> The Negro experience has been inherently dramatic: surely the substance of great drama is there. No group in America has plumbed greater depths, or passed so dramatically through more levels of life or caught up into itself more of those elements of social conflict and complication in which the modern dramatist must find the only tragedy that our realistic, scientific philosophy of life allows us. Indeed the essential, elemental forces of great drama in all time – epic turns of experience, tragic intensity of life, discipline and refinement of the emotions, have been accumulating, like underground well-springs, for generations in Negro life, and now are beginning to seek artistic vent and find free-flowing expression.
>
> Certainly the vitalizing spirit of drama is there also. Generations of enforced buffoonery and caricature have not completely stifled the dramatic endowment of the Negro; his temperament still moves natively and spontaneously in the world of make-believe with the primitive power of imaginative abandon and emotional conviction. It is agreed that, as actor and as audience, the Negro temperament promises to bring back to a jaded, sceptical stage some of the renewing, elemental moods and powers of early drama. If to these unpurchasable things are added, as seems likely now, a worthwhile medium of serious dramatic expression and a seasoned, intelligent contact with the arts of the theatre, the future appears most promising both for the Negro drama and for the Negro actor.

His remarks about the Negro temperament clearly move the debate into a dangerous area. This was after all perilously close to that role which had long been pressed on the Negro: the paradigm of emotionalism, of irrationality and of sexual vitality. For the moment Locke saw the black experience as a resource available to black and white alike, the latter less by virtue of its immediacy and passionate reality than because of superior skills and, more dubiously, 'his more natural objectivity'. But eventually, Locke suggested, 'The Negro playwright will claim his natural advantage of greater intimacy of knowledge and feeling', and perhaps more dubiously, capitalise on his instinctive lyricism and naive spontaneity.

Thus, for Locke, the future lay not so much with protest plays as with folk drama, 'the uncurdled, almost naive reflection of the poetry and folk feeling of a people who have after all a different soul and temperament from that of the smug, unimaginative industrialist and the self-righteous and inhibited Puritan'. As ever, Locke tried to walk a difficult path between asserting the unique nature of the black experience and the availability of that experience as in some way a paradigm of human experience. Hence, he looked for a time when black drama would be 'more universal even in sounding its most racial notes'.[8]

20. Hall Johnson's *Run Little Chillun*. A joint production of the Music Project and the Negro Unit of the Federal Theatre in Los Angeles.

In fact the plays by Negro authors in the collection which he edited ranged from folk dramas, like Willis Richardson's *The Broken Banjo* (1925) and Jean Toomer's *Balo* (1924) to Eulalie Spence's 'Comedy of Harlem Life' called *The Starter* (1927) and Willis Richardson's play about escaping slaves, *The Flight of the Natives* (1927). Though they were plainly not in the same league as O'Neill's work, they did constitute a bid for some kind of hegemony over black experience. They were the beginnings of an attempt at self-definition and dramatic independence.

In terms of Broadway, Hall Johnson's *Run Little Chillun* proved a successful début. It opened on Broadway in 1933 and ran for three months, being subsequently revived by the Federal Theatre. But it, too, trod potentially dangerous ground, running the risk of endorsing the primitive image of the Negro popular with white writers. A folk play, which gave scope for Johnson to make full use of his choir (he was responsible for popularising a number of spirituals), it was concerned with the battle for the soul of the Reverend Jones, pastor of Hope Baptist Church. He is faced on the one hand with the forces of respectability, as represented by the severe strictures of the Church, and on the other with a sensuous paganism, represented by Sulami, a young girl at the heart of a new cult rooted in African experience. It was in essence presented as a struggle between two traditions, two myths, and, perhaps unsurprisingly, it ends with the struggle unresolved. A certain scepticism is implied as to both these alternatives, but there is no middle ground and the play risked reinforcing the popular stereotype which presented the Negro as natural victim of superstition and an avatar of sexuality. But it was highly

21. A drawing of Langston Hughes by Rinold Reiss.

successful. Revived by the California section of the Federal Theatre, as a joint product of the Music Project and the Negro unit, it secured a monthly audience of nearly thirty thousand and ran for more than a year.

But the most successful Broadway production by a black writer in the 1930s was Langston Hughes's *Mulatto* (1935). Hughes was a major talent. A

243

leading figure of the Harlem Renaissance, he was in turn a poet, a novelist, a short-story writer, a dramatist and a journalist. *Mulatto* was a melodrama set in the South. It concerned the dilemma of the mulatto, poised uneasily between two cultures. Faced either with acquiescence or with self- destructive revolt, the principal character destroys himself. A brutal play, resting uneasily on familiar figures from literary tradition and public myth, it established a record run for a black play on Broadway not rivalled for twenty-four years. And if it did little to advance the cause of drama, it did constitute an assertion of the role of the theatre in literally dramatising a primary moral issue of the day. There are no concessions offered to Locke's notion of folk drama; no concessions either to his desire for universalism except in so far as, beneath the mutual incomprehensions and self-destructive violence of racial myths, he hints at a baffled insecurity, a desire to escape both from history and from a personal psychology forged by that history. It was a theme he did not develop, indeed a theme muted less by his own elaboration of crucial ambiguities than by the simple brutalities he feels obliged to document.

And the 1930s clearly did generate their own melodrama, a polarised world of capitalists and workers, exploiters and exploited. For the black American the contrast between black and white was an all too obvious fact of social life and the framing of nine Negro boys in Scottsboro, Alabama, simply offered further evidence of this. Hughes himself wrote *Scottsboro Limited* (1932), a one-act play and four poems which protested at the injustice. But the black writer found himself caught in a dilemma which was not essentially different from that of the Communist Party to which some of them belonged. The Party proposed two mutually contradictory policies which suggested that the Negro was simultaneously a colonial subject, and hence a victim of a racism which was a by-product of capitalism, and a member of an international working class to whom race was of no consequence. In other words race was simultaneously everything and nothing. So, too, the Negro writer wished both to celebrate his cultural identity and to lay claim to the very racial co-operation which was equally a product of the 1930s and evidenced in the new access to the stage which he was experiencing. It was a dilemma which is clear in the work of Richard Wright and equally that of Langston Hughes. *Mulatto* is, for the most part, unambiguous. It is a denunciation of racism. But in his poetry Hughes often claimed the possibility of transcending such imperatives, as in 'Union':

> Not me alone
> I know now –
> But all the whole oppressed
> Poor world,
> White and black
> Must put their hands with mine

To shake the pillars of those temples
Wherein the false gods dwell
And worn out altars stand
Too well defended,
And the rule of greed's upheld
That must be ended.⁹

For all this he was clearly aware of the threat to his cultural identity in such a proposition and even more so in the appropriation of black experience by a theatre which wished to capitalise on that experience while draining it of all meaning. As he observed in 'Notes on Commercial Theatre', published in *The Crisis* in March 1940, making his position clear:

You've taken my blues and gone –
You sing 'em on Broadway
And you sing 'em in the Hollywood Bowl,
And you mix 'em up with symphonies
And you fixed 'em
So they don't sound like me –
Yep, you done taken my blues and gone.
You also took my spirituals and gone.
You put me in Macbeth and Carmen Jones
And all kinds of Swing Mikados
And in everything but what's about me –
But someday somebody'll
Stand up and talk about me,
And write about me –
Black and beautiful –¹⁰

The attack was clearly not simply aimed only at the commercial theatre, however. It was also an assault on the work of the new Federal Theatre, though Hughes submitted a script to that theatre which was never produced. *Angelo Herndon Jones*, later produced by the New York Theatre League, was a brief play set in a black slum which advocated an alliance of the poor, black and white, and extolled the virtues of the black radical leader, Angelo Herndon. But, like *Mulatto*, it offered nothing which could be seen as justifying such confidence in inter-racial co-operation. The dilemma, it seems, was not to be so easily resolved.

There is no doubt that the most famous products of the Negro units of the Federal Theatre were indeed the black *Macbeth* and the *Swing Mikado* to which Hughes objected. The former was essentially the product of John Houseman and the twenty-year-old Orson Welles. It was an exotic affair, 'giant tropic fronds...architecture from the dreams of Toussaint L'Ouverture... costumes – Emperor Jones gone beautifully mad . . sepia male witches stripped

22. *The Black Macbeth*, April 1936, produced by John Houseman and directed by the twenty-year-old Orson Welles.

23. The *Swing Mikado* which opened in Chicago in September 1938.

to the waist against the world's largest skeletal arch'.[11] With a reported ten thousand people crowding the street outside the theatre and an audience for the touring version of one hundred thousand, it placed the Negro at the centre of attention. Much the same could be said of the *Swing Mikado* (1938), a product of the Chicago unit which was so successful that two hundred and fifty thousand people saw it in the first five months. This success prompted Mike Todd to open a commercial version in New York which was a rival to the Federal Theatre's own New York production.

But the fact remains that, as Hughes had implied, such productions could be accused of exploiting the Negro's supposed exoticism. They did little to express Negro life and little to develop a Negro theatre expressive of the special needs and cultural dilemmas of the black American. But according to Hallie Flanagan, the policy of placing such units under the direction of whites was deliberate and a step taken on the advice of Rose McClendon, a black actress and leading figure in the black theatre: 'I asked whether it would not be advisable to have the designing and direction of their project by members of their own race; Miss McClendon felt that since Negroes had always been performers and had no previous means of learning direction and design, they would prefer to start under more experienced direction.'[12] But the Negro units did produce a number of plays by black writers, chief among which were William Dubois's *Haiti* and Theodore Ward's *Big White Fog*, which were evidence of the increasing sophistication of black writing.

Haiti is a fluent and skilfully wrought play about the defeat of the French at the hands of the black Christopher. Despite a reliance on a somewhat archaic machinery of hidden passages, overheard conversations and concealed identities, it was a powerfully polemical work, though inevitably it was praised by critics for its vitality and exoticism. For Arthur Pollack it was 'Beautifully staged, full of movement, sound and fury, a lusty show...vivid stuff', while for Brooks Atkinson 'Nothing so good has exploded in Harlem since the racy nights of *Macbeth*.' For John Anderson it revealed 'Gaudy material bright with the sheen of the tropics'.[13] The exotic, it seems, existed less in the life of the Negro than in the minds of the critics. In fact the play was a highly articulate attempt to dramatise an act of rebellion which proved definitional for black and white alike. The irony is that the critics should have struggled so hard to encyst the black actors and the play's production-style in those very stereotypes which the play itself was concerned with challenging.

Big White Fog, which opened in Chicago in 1938, was a product of the Chicago unit of the Federal Theatre. It was a naturalistic play about Negro life, beginning with the brittle enthusiasms of Marcus Garvey's Universal Negro Improvement Association (an all-black organisation through which Garvey advocated his back-to-Africa policies) and ending, in the year of the play's production, with the attempted eviction of a black family.

24. Playbill for William Dubois's *Haiti*. 1932.

Victor Mason is a Garveyite leader. Having travelled north in search of freedom and prosperity and encountered only white hostility, he turns to Garvey and his back-to-Africa policy as providing a possible escape from indignity. His family is less convinced. A cynical brother-in-law tries to persuade him to join him in buying up property to convert into apartments. His son Les plans to go to college. His daughter Wanda is drawn to the tawdry glamour of the nightclub, having little interest in the deferred hopes of her brother and father. By degrees these dreams collapse. Les is refused a promised scholarship when the college discovers his race. His father invests the family savings in the stock of Garvey's Black Star Shipping Line precisely at the moment when the Garvey empire begins to collapse. Under pressure of the Depression Les turns to radical politics and Wanda is tempted to sell her body to sustain the family. The pressure increases. Bitter at her husband's foolishness, Victor's wife taunts him with his colour, a caste consciousness which parallels the class consciousness with which the play concludes. But stereotypes are created only in order to be neutralised. Hence a caricatured Jewish second-hand furniture dealer is balanced by the young Jewish radical who finally comes to their aid.

The play ends as Victor is shot down by the police when he resists the bailiffs who have come to evict him, and the Communist Party comes to his aid – the final image of black and white solidarity, so much at odds with the mood of much of the play, offering an epiphany which is fundamentally unconvincing.

Big White Fog is a powerful play. It compares more than favourably with Lorraine Hansberry's *A Raisin in the Sun* based in the Chicago of twenty-seven years later. Indeed the scope of Ward's play is considerably greater, as it tries to explore the strategies open to the Negro: the myths of black nationalism, of communism, the attraction of education as a means of escaping prejudice, the temptations of the street and of exploitation. The debate is real; the language is direct. Victor attacks his brother-in-law for using his intelligence to cheat his fellow blacks: 'Your education is like a pair of knee pads, which enables you to crawl through the slime of white prejudice without the least sense of pain or dishonor.'[14] The weakness lies in the melodramatic climax and in a concluding radicalism which is unexamined, which remains, indeed, a simple piety. It was also a radicalism which for a while looked as though it might threaten the play's production. Writing in 1970, Theodore Ward explained:

> There was considerable opposition to the play being produced because it seemed to advocate communism, when, despite my own political outlook at the time, in writing the play I had only sought to present the objective reality as an alternative to the situation and conditions of Victor Mason and his family – happily, Mrs. Hallie Flanagan supported my aim for artistic integrity, so that

the play was finally produced...without adverse criticism from the press. Incidentally, despite the fact that the Chicago production continued to show large profit at the box office, the local officials of *the* Federal Theatre transferred the play to a local high school under the guise of making it more available to the Negro public, for four performances, after which it was closed. Thus, I take it that the play never had a chance on its merits.[15]

The play ran for ten weeks. When it was revived by the Negro Playwrights' Company in 1940 its radicalism was undercut by the fact of the Hitler–Stalin pact.

Ward is more than a little disingenuous in suggesting that the play only presented an objective reality. It is true that the incident in which the interracial Communist forces mass in support of the dying Victor is a kind of coda; the sudden emergence from a series of possible approaches, each judged and to some degree found wanting, of the one effective way of challenging prejudice and economic injustice. But this is the basis of the structural weakness of a final scene which is less a logical or moral consequence of the 'objective reality' which he has exposed than a desperate assertion of the need for one avenue not hopelessly tainted with irony. However, for the most part the play does attempt a sympathetic portrait of people trapped by public and private myths, by history, by their own psychology and by the seemingly inescapable forces of economic determinism. The Garvey movement is a case in point. It was not without its absurdities, and Theodore Ward underlines the pathos of Victor Mason's pretensions as he wears the gaudy clothes of that movement in the increasingly squalid Deerborn apartment house. But, while stressing the dangerous illusions of Garvey and his followers, Ward treats both Victor and the movement which he serves with a compassionate understanding which is a distinguishing feature of the play and which enables him to come closer to rendering the painful ambiguities of black life in the 1920s and 30s than any other playwright, black or white. The slow disintegration of the Mason family is offered as cultural fact and dramatic strategy. And it is precisely his refusal to judge his characters, even in their brief outbursts of prejudice, which raises the play above the simple celebration of Negro folk life or the bitter articulation of anger, the shaping of social suffering into dramatic parable.

For Langston Hughes, indeed, *Big White Fog* was 'the greatest encompassing play on Negro life that has ever been written. If it isn't liked by people, it is because they are not ready for it, not because it isn't a great play.'[16]

The unique problem of the black American in the theatre was perceived early. Seen by whites as a potent image of the irrational, as a symbol of unrepressed sexuality and an unsublimated violence, he was reinvented to serve the interests of dramatic convenience and an exuberant theatricality. He was

25. Playbill for Theodore Ward's *Big White Fog*, Chicago, 1938.

seen as the essence of an exoticism excluded from white puritan existence but also as a means of dissecting the psychopathology of a culture. In other words he was turned into a literary figure, a device. An experience which had been shaped by history, or more precisely by economic circumstances and social pressures which were themselves a product of white prejudice, was now compounded by the appropriation of that experience for the entertainment of essentially white audiences. It was not a neutral gesture. Paul Green's *In Abraham's Bosom* and Marc Connelly's *Green Pastures* perpetuated an image of the Negro as childlike, touching in his naivety and hence, in some senses, outside of history. Such a stance was not without its implications for the black American, struggling towards a self-image which could sustain him. Likewise, O'Neill's suggestion of an ineluctable atavism menaced a new sense of black achievement.

The solution lay, to some degree, in the black American's assertion of his cultural independence and in the creation of an audience which did not necessitate social and artistic compromise. The Federal Theatre was clearly a help in this respect, but the final objective was either a black theatre written and performed by blacks or a social world so transformed as to relieve the pressure to confirm the stereotype or to create a new model defined by the necessity to revolt.

The attempt to create a black theatre in America began early. In terms of the twentieth century it was Montgomery Gregory, the organiser of the Howard Players, and their director from 1919 to 1924, who wrote:

> Our ideal is a national Negro Theatre where the Negro playwright, musician, actor, dancer, and artist in concert shall fashion a drama that will merit the respect and admiration of America. Such an institution must come from the Negro himself, as he alone can truly express the soul of his people. The race must surrender that childish self-consciousness that refuses to face the facts of its own life in the arts... The only avenue of genuine achievement in American drama for the Negro lies in the development of the rich veins of folk tradition of the past and in the portrayals of the authentic life of the Negro masses of to-day. The older leadership still cling to the false gods of servile reflection of the more or less unfamiliar life of an alien race. The 'New Negro'... places his faith in the potentialities of his own people.[17]

Nonetheless their first programme still began with the work of a white writer, Ridgley Torrence's *Simon the Cyrenian*, though they did subsequently produce work by Willis Richardson.

It is true that the main achievement of the Harlem Renaissance lay in poetry, but these efforts to establish an independent black theatre were an expression of a new mood in the black community. So, W.E.B. DuBois organised the Kwigwa Players, in connection with *The Crisis* magazine, which was the official publication of the NAACP (National Association for the Advancement of Colored People), and in 1928 the Harlem Experimental Theatre was founded, to be followed by the Negro Art Theatre, which opened in 1929.

Nearly a decade later, Langston Hughes created the Harlem Suitcase Theatre. This initially performed above a restaurant in the hall of the International Workers' Order, an appropriate enough venue for the play which opened that theatre – *Don't You Want to be Free?* (1936). Hughes wrote the piece in a single night, partly because he incorporated some of the poems which he had already published, together with a number of spirituals and blues. The continuity is provided by a Young Man whose experiences are those of the Negro from slavery through to the Depression. The loose structure made a virtue of the necessities of the Suitcase Theatre, which had virtually no props and little space. As the Young Man indicates in his opening speech,

> Listen, folks! I'm one of the members of this group, and I want to tell you about our theatre. This is it right here! We haven't got any scenery or painted curtains, because we haven't got any money to buy them. But we've got something you can't buy with money, anyway. We've got faith in ourselves. And in you. So we're going to put on a show. Maybe you'll like it because it's about you, and about us. This show is for you. And you can act in it, too, if you want to. This is your show, as well as ours. Now I'll tell you what this show is about. It's about me, except that it's not just about me now standing here talking to you – but it's about me, yesterday, and about tomorrow. I'm colored! I guess you can see that. Well, this show is about what it means to be colored in America.[18]

The play details black suffering and ends with the conventional black/white solidarity which was so much a cliché of the 1930s. A White Worker looks to the immediate future when 'there won't be no hard lines. And no color line', because 'labor with a white skin'll never be free as long as labor with a black skin's enslaved'.[19] An effective combination of verse, music and prose, the play stands out from some of the more simplistic protest works of the period but, like *Big White Fog*, has difficulty in justifying a final inter-racial optimism so much at odds with the catalogue of racial abuse detailed in the rest of the play. It ran for 135 performances to audiences which were reportedly 75 per cent black and who paid only thirty-five cents admission. Playing only at weekends, it ran for a year but, after transferring to the 135th Street Library, the company folded in 1939.

But in that same year the Rose McClendon Players were founded. Though this group foundered with the outbreak of the Second World War, in its brief life it launched the career of a number of people who subsequently became the basis for a post-war revival of black theatre. The same could be said of two other organisations founded at this time: the American Negro

Theatre and the Negro Playwrights' Company. The former was established in 1939 and began production the following year; the latter was founded in 1940.

The manifesto of the Negro Playwrights' Company, quoted by Doris Abramson, makes plain the degree to which the image of the Negro presented on Broadway had been the source of genuine dismay and anger in the black community. It was an attack on commercialism in the theatre but, more than that, it constituted an attempt to regain control over black experience:

> These new writers recognize that they live in a real society...they will be writers worthy of the name only if they remain independent of the forces which have reduced brain to a commodity and driven weaklings and panderers to the practice of falsifying truth in order to make it conform to accepted beliefs and the tastes of those who tend to regard the Negro people as children or slaves placed in the world for their own exploitation or amusement.[20]

The company opened at the Lincoln Theatre on 135th Street with Theodore Ward's *Big White Fog*. It was the company's only production. It closed after sixty-four performances.

The American Negro Theatre (ANT) proved more durable. It was housed in the same 135th Street Library Theatre as the Kwigwa Players had been. Founded by Abram Hill and Frederick O'Neal it survived into the mid 1940s, being effectively destroyed by the success of its production of Philip Yordan's *Anna Lucasta* (1944) which transferred to Broadway along with its cast. In terms of the development of black drama this production was not without its ironies. Originally written as a play about a Polish–American family it was rewritten for the ANT.

The short lives of most of these groups can be traced to a number of sources. Firstly, they shared with other such enterprises in the theatre the conventional problems of finance. But on top of this they were faced with the problem of generating an audience for their work and with locating black theatrical talent. The rights of black Americans had not yet been effectively acknowledged at a national or local level and the struggle for cultural independence was wedded to the struggle for political and social recognition. As became increasingly apparent in the 1950s and 60s, they were two sides of the same coin. In the inter-war years the black American's contribution to drama was slight. It could hardly have been anything else. On the other hand the American theatre itself was in a state of flux. It too was struggling towards a form and a language adequate to its aspirations. And in its own attempt to dramatise the situation of the Negro it perhaps exposed its own weaknesses more clearly than at other times. The stereotype, the melodramatic incident, the radical simplification of experience, the casual romanticising of reality, revealed a theatre not yet entirely free of the conventions which had dominated it only two decades before. For the black American, however, there was more at stake than the development of drama. The theatre enacted a cultural dilemma all too real on a private and public level.

8 Thornton Wilder

As Sigmund Freud once observed, Thornton Wilder was more a poet than a storyteller. Since Freud was at the time seeking to marry off his daughter Anna to the now middle-aged Wilder this was perhaps offered as a calculated compliment, but it went straight to the heart of the writer's strengths and weaknesses. He was indeed a poet manqué who always searched for the lyrical insight, the transcendent moment, the religious experience, the eternal truth. He was not, as he was accused of being, contemptuous of a contemporary factuality but he was always drawn to reach for the universal through the immediate and the actual.

A teacher of French at a famous private school, he came to public attention with the publication of his first novel, *The Cabala* (1926). And when he followed this with an international success, *The Bridge of San Luis Rey* (1927), he was seen as a leading literary figure. But with the onset of the Depression and the publication of his third novel, *The Woman of Andros*, he found himself suddenly attacked as little more than an effete product of, and court jester to, an intellectual, philosophical and social coterie whose other-worldly stance was an affront to those struggling with a world whose manifest injustices required something more than the thin gruel of speculative fiction. He was presented as evidence of a kind of late-romantic recrudescence.

Leading the attack was Mike Gold, who, in the *New Republic* in October 1930, also identified him as a poet, though this time using the term pejoratively. Wilder was

> the poet of a small sophisticated class...our genteel bourgoisie...Wilder is the perfect flower of the new prosperity...he has...the air of good breeding, the decorum, priestliness, glossy high finish as against intrinsic qualities, conspicuous inutility, caste feeling, love of the archaic...This Emily Post of culture will never remind [the parvenue class] of Pittsburgh or the breadlines. He is always in perfect taste.[1]

For a writer who could speak of nothing but Pittsburgh (or its counterpart) or the breadline, whose own works eschewed style in the belief that roughness was a guarantee of authenticity and who made utility a prime requirement of art, the choice of target was understandable. But beneath the fatuity of the assault there was a tincture of truth.

Wilder was certainly a product of a much more rarified atmosphere than was Mike Gold but he also embraced values and expressed a spiritual concern which was more a product of the immediate pre-war world than of the post-war cynicism of Hemingway (though the two, surprisingly, were good friends) or the social urgencies of the 1930s. His imagination was captured by the romantic exoticism of the past, of the foreign setting; his mind was engaged with the struggle of sensitive individuals to relate not only to other individuals but to profounder and less easily articulated truths. If he had eschewed the practical immediacies of America this was perhaps fortuitous, though Mike Gold suggested that if he had not done so 'all his fundamental silliness and superficiality'[2] would have been exposed. But he did prefer settings which suggested mythical resonances. Taken by Gold as a modern exemplar of the New Humanists' stance he was to some degree caught in the crossfire, but Gold was correct in identifying a religious undertow in his work, a concern for the ineffable contained in the real and a preference for the purely imaginative over the practical and the prosaic.

And this is particularly clear in his first commercially published plays, collected under the title of one of them, *The Angel that Troubled the Waters*. So-called 'three-minute plays', because they were all extremely brief and required little more than three minutes to read, these were brief sketches begun in 1915, when he was only eighteen, and finished shortly before publication in 1928. As he explained in the introduction, 'Almost all the plays in this book are religious, but religious in that dilute fashion that is a believer's concession to a contemporary standard of good manners.' He was also not unaware that 'there has seldom been an age in literature when such a vein was less welcome and less understood' but expressed the hope that he could 'discover the spirit that is not unequal to the elevation of the great religious themes, yet which does not fall into a repellent didacticism'.[3] Beyond logic, he relied on beauty as the agent of persuasion. For him the failure of religion to engage the modern mind stemmed from a failure of language.

It is not hard to see what made him such an apt target for Gold's assaults. And the plays themselves do little to redeem the schoolmasterly tone (the introduction was signed from Davis House, Lawrenceville), the highbrow moralism or the spiritual smugness of the introduction. Virtually none of them is stageable. Brief moral tales or striking images, they seem like vivid pictures, miniatures. Indeed this is underlined in the stage direction of one of the plays, *Nascuntur Poetae* (a title which itself suggests something of the sensibility and the presumptions of the author):

> We are gazing into some comprehensible painting of Piero di Cosimo; in a world of pale blues and greens; of abrupt peaks in agate and of walled cities; of flying red stags with hounds at their throats; and of lions in tears beside their crowns. On the road are seen travelling companies, in no haste and often lost in contemplation of the sky. A boy sits on a rock in the foreground. He is listening to the words of a woman dressed in a chlamys that takes on the colour of the objects about her.[4]

The settings are virtually all exotic. The action takes place in Heaven, in the middle of the Mediterranean, in Venice, in the past, in myth. They are for the most part conceits, poetic fantasies, closer in spirit to Browning's monologues than to stageable dramatic pieces. They are self-indulgent and impractical. Their publication was clearly an attempt to cash in on the popularity of a new writer rather than a recognition of their value or of the significance of the form in which he was working. What was clear, however, was that he had no interest in conforming to any model of drama then available. He was from the beginning concerned with forging his own forms and exploring his own territory. Though the influence of other writers is clear, it is not that of the three writers whose imprint was so marked on American writers like O'Neill, Hellman, Miller and Williams, namely Chekhov, Ibsen and Strindberg. It was Pirandello, Dreiser and Stein.

In 1916, Theodore Dreiser published a collection called *Plays Natural and Supernatural*, which were reportedly influential with the young Wilder. Certainly there is a considerable similarity between Dreiser's unstageable visionary plays and Wilder's first published collection. Though Dreiser's plays were not three-minute affairs they were equally drawn to the exotic, the spiritual, the speculative and the bizarre. Both drew on the same suggestive vocabulary. Dreiser's 'Darkness and illimitable space'[5] became Wilder's 'profound shade'.[6] Both sought to dramatise a spiritual world, Dreiser, in *Phantasmagoria*, initiating a debate between the Lord of the Universe and Beauty, and Wilder one between Christ and Satan in *Hast Thou Considered My Servant Job?* It is not difficult to see a connection between three of Dreiser's plays, *The Blue Sphere*, *Laughing Gas* and *The Spring Recital* and Wilder's *Our Town* in so far as the first offers a cinematic cutting between different connected events and the latter two an engagement with the notion of transcendent spirits and their calm observation of the living. They propose precisely that timelessness, that experience of linking individual experience with a continuing human experience, which was at the heart of Wilder's concern.

Wilder's second collection, *The Long Christmas Dinner and Other Plays* (1931), similarly anticipated some of the thematic concerns and dramatic methods of his best known play. *The Long Christmas Dinner* compresses the family events of ninety years into a matter of minutes, situating their trivial concerns against the backdrop of life and death. *Pullman Car Hiawatha* introduces the device of the Stage Manager, derived doubtless from Pirandello, and develops his notion of a stage devoid of scenery. The play takes place on a pullman car called Hiawatha, whose outline the Stage Manager marks out with chalk. The various berths are improvised with chairs. As he explained in the introduction to *Our Town*, the stage was to be virtually devoid of scenery because the naturalistic urge 'fixes and narrows the action to one moment in time and space'.[7] And to him the establishment of place was inevitably the establishment of time and hence a denial of the theatre's power to exist in a permanent present.

As the train supposedly makes its way across the country so the characters act out the minor dramas of the journey, interspersed with reminiscences and occasional arias which celebrate the establishment of the railroad line and the nature of the country through which it is passing. Sometimes the Stage Manager acts as a director and sometimes he substitutes for individual characters, like Pirandello's figure having to deal with minor rebellions from the characters. As the play progresses so it moves closer to abstraction as the characters are augmented by actors representing the weather, the hours, the minutes and the planets, as well as two archangels. The model is fundamentally a musical one – each element sounding individually and then gradually being brought into a fundamental harmony, the representative of a small town called Grovers Corners, Ohio (clearly an anticipation of Grovers Corners, New Hampshire, in *Our Town*) thus being seen in fundamental harmony with the universe – a proposition which equally lies at the heart of *Our Town*.

The experiments of *The Happy Journey to Trenton and Camden*, *The Long Christmas Dinner* and *Pullman Car Hiawatha* had established the viability of Wilder's methods. Indeed he suggested that *The Happy Journey* was at one time to have been a part of what was then called *Our Village*. In a letter to Alexander Woollcott, in June 1937, he wrote, 'I always think of *Our Village* as yours. It is intended to give you pleasure. *The Happy Journey* is no longer part of it.'[8]

The Happy Journey to Trenton and Camden, which was published in 1931, was an account of a family visit to a married daughter who had lost a baby and nearly died herself in childbirth. Concerned with celebrating the simple pleasures and pains of family life and those who deal with profound loss by a combination of habit, cliché and genuine affection, it was an understated piece, a character study, an impressionistic sketch. Its interest lay less in the shock of recognition, the platonic 'recollection' of which he spoke in the preface to the *Three Plays* (the sense which an audience has that 'This is the way things are. I have always known it without being fully aware that I knew it.'), though this clearly lay behind the expression of provincial pieties and the familiar banalities of family life which he recreated so skilfully, than in the innovatory nature of the staging. The principal character is the Stage Manager who reads all the minor parts and on one occasion steps into the action, lays aside his script and enters fully into his role. The play has no scenery, relying on pantomime for its effects. These elements were all developed more fully in *Our Town*.

In justifying its technique Wilder cited Chinese drama and the Japanese Noh theatre, both of which dispense with realistic sets and actions. He did not mention Pirandello, but Wilder's central device of the Stage Manager who establishes the scene and becomes a central figure, sometimes entering the action and sometimes simply commenting on it, obviously owes something to *Six Characters in Search of an Author*, the première of which Wilder had actually attended in Italy. But Wilder's figure is more flexible. He plays more roles, occupies at once a more detached and a more involved position alternately, both observing and participating in the action. Where Pirandello argues the question of artistic reality, Wilder is more content to allow these issues to remain subdued. His Stage Manager is not challenged for his supremacy. His manipulative control is not threatened. He sculpts the action and elicits the moral purpose.

Our Town (1938) is simply one of the most effective and affecting American plays. Deceptively simple in construction, it is unashamed in its emotional directness but reaches for a universal perspective which will neutralise its own sentimentalities. Wilder, in other words, is particularly adept at having his cake and eating it. Few American plays have been performed as frequently; few have succeeded so well in appealing to such a wide range of audiences. In a sense it answers Mike Gold's challenge to engage American realities, but does so in such a way as effectively to deny the significance of ideological presumptions or the immediate practicalities of 1930s America. It is pre-eminently Wilder the poet at work. Some of the early passages of the play are actually set out in a kind of free-verse form, while its central theme – the location of individual experience against the background of passing time, of universals – suggests both a conscious mythicism, a sense of life as ritual, and an attempt to insist on a spiritual continuity. There are echoes here of the New Humanism. Yet it also shares something of Whitman's presumption of the existence of the universal in the particular, and the consequent need to savour the moment, to appreciate its full significance.

At one stage in the play the actors planted in the audience are invited to ask questions, and it is tempting to see that asked by a character identified as the Belligerent Man as Wilder's parody of Mike Gold's simplistic position. 'Is there no one in town aware of social injustice and industrial inequality?' he asks, so missing the point of a play which attempts to place such concerns in the context of questions of a metaphysical nature. The reply is deliberately reductive: 'I guess we're all hunting like everybody else for a way the diligent and sensible can rise to the top and the lazy and quarrelsome can sink to the bottom. But it ain't easy to find. Meanwhile, we do all we can to help those that can't help themselves and those that can we leave alone.'[9] This was, of course, precisely the kind of cracker-barrel philosophy which had so irritated Gold, but Wilder was aware that it was closer to the sensibility of the average American than Gold's shrill politicism and the play was an attempt to write about the American experience in a way which was more accurate and more true to that experience than Gold's urban homilies. The cracker-barrel philosophy, in other words, had authenticity precisely because it was rooted in a folk experience, in a sense of continuity, which made Gold's utilitarianism seem to Wilder to be so provincial and limited. Gold was interested in immediate change and in the exigencies of the moment; Wilder was interested in continuities and in relating present experience to timeless perception. Gold was obsessed with the closing of social spaces; Wilder with the opening of metaphysical ones.

Wilder is extremely lucid about his objectives in the preface to *Three Plays*, published in 1958, and it is worth quoting from this at some length. He had always been interested in the theatre. Even when his reputation as a novelist was newly established and he went to the University of Chicago to teach creative writing, he, in common with all but one of his students, confessed to finding the theatre false to experience. The reason lay, he believed, in a middle-class arrogance, an insensitivity which generated a theatre that would not challenge its principal assumptions:

> They distrusted the passions and tried to deny them. Their questions about the nature of life seemed to be sufficiently answered by the demonstration of financial status and by conformity to some clearly established rules of decorum. These were precarious positions; abysses yawned on either side. The air was loud with questions that must not be asked. These audiences fashioned a theatre which could not disturb them.[10]

It was a comment which only made sense in terms of English-language theatre and which even then ignored the strength of the kind of work produced by O'Neill and Glaspell. But his fundamental point was that the theatre was treated as a phenomenon remote from the experience of those who watched it, a fact exacerbated by the box-set stage which codified this, and a realistic tradition which in reaching for verisimilitude succeeded only in destroying the flexibility of the stage and, in its specificity, undermining a vital dimension. As he explained:

> Every action has taken place – every thought, every emotion – has taken place only once, at one moment in time and place. 'I love you', 'I rejoice', 'I suffer', have been said and felt many billions of times, and never twice the same. Every person who has ever lived has lived an unbroken succession of unique occasions. Yet the more one is aware of this individuality in experience (innumerable! innumerable!) the more one becomes attentive to what these disparate moments have in common, to repetitive patterns. As an artist (or listener or beholder) which 'truth' do you prefer – that of the isolated occasion, or that which includes and resumes the innumerable? Which truth is the more telling...? The theatre is admirably fitted to tell both truths. It has one foot planted firmly in the particular, since each actor before us (even when he wears a mask!) is

indubitably a living, breathing 'one'; yet it tends and strains to exhibit a general truth since its relation to a specific 'realistic' truth is confused and undermined by the fact that it is an accumulation of untruths, pretences and fiction. The novel is pre-eminently the vehicle of the unique occasion, the theatre of the generalized one. It is through the theatre's power to raise the exhibited individual action into the realm of idea and type and universal that it is able to evoke our belief.[11]

This was a point to be made by one of Iris Murdoch's characters in *The Sea, The Sea:*

> the theatre, even at its most 'realistic', is connected with the level at which, and the methods by which, we tell our everyday lies...Drama must create a factitious spell-binding present moment and imprison the spectator in it. The theatre apes the profound truth that we are extended beings who yet can only exist in the present. It is a factitious present because it lacks the free aura of personal reflection and contains its own secret limits and conclusions. Thus life is comic, but though it may be terrible it is not tragic.[12]

This is precisely the argument which lies behind *Our Town* and which leads Wilder to deny its tragic potential.

Our Town is an account of life in a small New Hampshire town called Grovers Corners. In particular it concentrates on two families, the Gibbses and the Webbs. It traces the growing relationship between George Gibbs and Emily Webb as they fall in love and marry. But with the final act Emily dies in childbirth and as her husband mourns her loss she joins the dead in the local graveyard, thereby passing into a state in which her life in Grovers Corners is seen in the perspective of eternity. Allowed briefly to revisit her former existence, she appreciates the extent to which people fail to value their lives moment by moment and the degree to which each event, though apprehended individually, is a part of a continuing human experience.

There is no denying the emotional power of the old romantic theme of young love destroyed by death, of a beautiful girl claimed by the grave, the more especially because it is so clearly located in a small-town America which is an essential part of a national myth. There is no denying, either, the pleasure which Wilder took in his ability to touch such an exposed nerve. He recognised the harrowing nature of the last act and wrote, in a letter from Boston dated 27 January 1938, just five days after the play's opening, of the 'nose-blowing and sobs' in the matinée audience and of the 'lady who called for a friend at five o'clock' only to see 'emerging a crowd of red eyes, swollen faces and mascara stains'.[13] But the essence of the play is designed precisely to deny the justification for such a reaction and Wilder deliberately plays against the more sentimental tendencies of his own text. The characters are summoned forth by the Stage Manager God to play their roles, at times showing a full awareness that they are simply players acting themselves.

26. *Our Town* at Henry Miller's Theatre, New York. The funeral scene.

Characters are planted in the audience, drawing attention to the meta-theatrical nature of the play. Indeed the Stage Manager himself foregrounds the theatrical nature of the event, self-consciously framing the action and underscoring its dramatic procedures. The town is located not merely in terms of the familiar emotional experiences, the recognisable prejudices and assumptions which make it both a typical New England town (typical, at least, in terms of popular and literary myth) and a recognisable human microcosm, but by brief lectures on its history, its geological formations and its sociology. Grovers Corners is, in other words, a theatrical event whose theatricality is a vital and inescapable aspect of its function. The social presentation of the self is in fact contrasted with that self abstracted from the elements which give it its social definition, just as the lectures and the interjections from the audience are included, much as the etymology section of *Moby Dick* is, precisely to show their insignificance as definitional tools except in so far as they establish a series of infinite resonances. The play's method of juxtaposing incidents, telescoping time, building significance from an aggregation of insignificant incidents is a reflection and an enactment of its central theme.

Wilder, however, never presses these concerns to the lengths that Pirandello does, though he had shown signs of doing so in *Pullman Car Hiawatha*. The theatricality of the play is indeed both emphasised and to a degree mitigated, the audience's empathy, ostensibly alienated, being actually encouraged because the play is a parable, a moral homily rather than an intellectual conceit. Where Pirandello sees the space between actor and character as an indication that in many ways fantasy is more real than reality ('The six characters... must not appear as phantoms, but as "created realities". Immutable creatures

263

of fantasy', because 'They are more real and consistent than the voluble actors.')[14] Wilder sees the gap between the characters and the roles which they play at the direction of the Stage Manager as indicative of the existence of an archetypal reality, a spiritual experience which is not more real than individually perceived reality but suggestive of a reality more expansive and significant than that which terminates in the self or the self's mirror image in drama. Pirandello is fascinated by the eternal life to which art can aspire ('He who has the fortune to be born a character can afford to jeer even at death, for he will never die.'[15]). Wilder is interested in the eternal life which the individual attains through his participation in an unfolding and continuous human experience, inexpressible and sublime, which lies beyond language.

In the preface he explained that:

> Our Town is not offered as a picture of life in a New Hampshire village; or as a speculation about the conditions of life after death (that element I merely took from Dante's Purgatory). It is an attempt to find a value above all price for the smallest events in our daily life...Each individual's assertion to an absolute reality can only be inner, very inner. And here the method of staging finds its justification – in the first two acts there are at least a few chairs and tables; but when she revisits the earth and the kitchen to which she descended on her twelfth birthday, the very chairs and tables are gone. Our claim, our hope, our despair are in the mind – not in things, not in 'scenery'.

It was decidedly not to be a genre play, a small-town drama. Thus though Wilder wrote at the time of the play's production that 'the subject of the play is: homely, humorous, touching aspects of a village life', in the same note, a reaction to Jed Harris's production, he insisted that 'The subject of the play I wrote is: The trivial details of human life in reference to a vast perspective of time, of social history and of religious ideas.' It was not, he insisted, to be regarded as 'a picture of rural manners'.[16] This perspective had been precisely that attempted by Dreiser in his so-called 'supernatural plays' which had equally tried to place immediate experience in a spiritual and timeless context. But where Dreiser's plays invoked spirits called up by anaesthetic dreams, ghosts spawned by violence or priestly beings from myth or from a distant past, Wilder's is determinedly prosaic. His spirit world is, it seems, as parochial as his realistic town. The eternal verities are established less through the provenance of the dead than through a rhetoric which attempts to locate action against the context of history – a history which in its domestic simplicities provides a bridge linking past and present and hence proposing the existence of an eternal human experience. Continuity becomes a central premise, continuity between different times and different levels of experience.

The problem for me is that Wilder resists acknowledging the artistic issues which his own methodology provokes. He engages questions of reality at a mundane level. The presumed audience is allowed a superior perspective but not a superior intelligence. The play's rhetoric is that of its characters, which is why the dead appear as provincial as the living. The deliberate foregrounding of theatricality suggests different levels of reality, different perspectives and even different levels of experience, but these are all accommodated to a folksy philosophy, a homogenised rhetoric of transcendence which denies the transcendent dimensions it wishes to invoke. Pirandello's characters resist their manipulation, their accommodation to the conventionalities of the author's mind or to those of social presumption or dramatic convenience; Wilder's embrace those conventionalities. His characters are offered as types and hence as pathways to archetype, but stereotype does not open access to archetype. Hence the professor of the State University turns out to be a parody of such a figure, a literary creation. Wilder complained that Jed Harris's production had turned the professor into a stereotype but that stereotype already existed in the text. The drunken misanthropist likewise remains nothing more nor less than that. As Pirandello's Father insists, 'Human beings are ever changeable and their reality changes from to-day to to-morrow, and on they pass and die away, but the character created by the artist's imagination has its life fixed within immutable bounds.'[17] His characters struggle to resist this fact, no matter how paradoxically. This is, however, a paradox which never enters Wilder's world because he is essentially dealing with figures who are never meant to transcend their fictionality. On one level this is because they too readily allow themselves to become mere role-players; they accede to models; they fictionalise themselves. They live un-examined lives. This is, after all, the point of Emily's brief return to the world of the living. But on another level there is, I think, evidence of some equi-vocation by Wilder. There is a seductiveness about the myth itself to which he succumbs. He ought, after all, to have been profoundly disturbed by the tears which his play provoked. Instead he revelled in them, and by so doing cast doubt on the resolve with which he called upon his audience to re-examine their lives. That is, they were responding essentially to a familiar literary formula.

He may not have intended his work to become a genre play but it comes perilously close to being so. Pirandello's characters lament that, being trapped in literature, they are denied the diversity of life. 'We believe ourselves one person, but it is true to say that we are many persons, many according to the possibilities of being which exist within us. We are one for this and another for that person – always diverse and yet filled with the illusion that our personality is always the same for all.'[18] This is an irony which never obtrudes itself on Wilder, for while it is true that his characters could be seen as collaborating in their own reduction to type, in the scene in the graveyard (when they no longer control their personality, when submission is a prime requirement and natural condition) they seem so locked in that character as to suggest that it is less their creation than Wilder's.

This is not to say that I am indicting Wilder for failing to be Pirandello, but that *Our Town* is a play which insufficiently questions its own presumptions, which shows evidence of a compromise in which its author collaborates. When in his preface he states his preference for a concern with reality over verisimilitude he promises more than he delivers. He rightly says that he is not interested in offering simply a picture of a New Hampshire village but rather in attempting to find a transcendent value in the minutiae of life. But he never raises the question of 'reality' at a sufficiently sophisticated level to give validity to the universal truths which he offers and which, without that acknowledgement of moral and metaphysical complexity, become little more than hand-me-down wisdom, moral mottoes, philosophical aphorisms, delivered in the same tone of voice and with the same air of innocent confidence as the folksy advice offered in the play by father to son on the morning of his marriage.

Grovers Corners is essentially a literary conceit. Its origins lie less in New Hampshire than in a platonic world of literary paradigms. The figures self-consciously play dramatic roles at the direction of the Stage Manager because they are in origin as well as fact literary creations, and Grovers Corners a product of popular myth, sanitised, morally and socially simplified. Frank Capra's *Mr Deeds Goes to Town* (1936), which was on release while Wilder was writing *Our Town*, drew on much the same images of natural innocence and faith in a natural and invincible human resilience. In the late 1930s such a philosophy was a natural resort for those who could find little evidence for the efficacy of any more programmatic stance. The somewhat desperate conclusion of *The Grapes of Wrath* falls back on a transposition from the literal to the symbolic as well as a move to the archetypal. In *Our Town* it appears a confident move and perhaps it is, Wilder being, as Gold implied, less sensitive than Steinbeck to the economic forces then assailing the Grovers Corners of America; but it is not a transition effected with any conviction. The play's weakness lies essentially in a third act which fails to find a way of moving from the daily details of human life to a vision of that life charged with a new significance. The need to respond to those minutiae as the key to transcendence is diminished by his failure to find a rhetoric appropriate to them.

Wilder suggested, in a letter which he wrote to Gertrude Stein and Alice Toklas,[19] that the third act of *Our Town* was based on Stein's aesthetic and philosophic ideas. He was indeed a friend of Stein who wrote her first play in 1913. Her theory of drama was based on a conviction that the theatre should not concern itself with narrative:

Something is always happening...Anybody knows a quantity of stories of people's lives that are always happening, there are always plenty for the newspapers and there are always plenty in private life. Everybody knows so many stories and what is the use of telling a story. What is the point of telling a story there are so many and everybody knows so many and tells so many.[20]

Since Wilder asserted that 'The dramatist must be by instinct a storyteller... The theatre is more exacting than the novel in regard to this faculty',[21] it is difficult to take his acknowledgement of her influence entirely at face value. But it is perhaps possible to see some connection between Stein's belief that the dramatist should attempt to capture the tempo and tone of an occasion without recounting the events which constitute that occasion and his own approach. She wished to 'tell what could be told if one did not tell anything'.[22] Though such an approach, which turned her plays into cubist exercises, dense poetic works which commanded little interest (*Four Saints in Three Acts* being an exception), was not one to which Wilder was likely to respond, there is some evidence of influence in his concern with capturing the texture and mood of Grovers Corners without recourse to any substantial incidents – the marriage and the death, the two principal events, both occur off-stage.

Woollcott had objected at one stage that the play reminded him of Edgar Lee Masters's *Spoon River Anthology*, but Wilder was able to write to him in June 1937 and assure him that it would no longer do so, that nobody told their life story as they did in *Spoon River* and as they had done in severely abbreviated form in *Pullman Car Hiawatha*. The alternation between a private, domestic, emotional and a cosmic perspective was of the very essence. The two 'lectures' in the first scene (Editor Webb's account of the sociology of Grovers Corners he thought of as a 'miniature Middletown' sequence, after the sociological study called *Middletown* conducted by the Lynds in the 1920s) he referred to in a letter as 'columns, pillars, set there throwing lights of "cosmic reference" on to the surrounding scenes'. For Jed Harris, those 'interrupt the affectionate interest we have in the family lives before us'; for Wilder, of course, 'that's the central intention of the play. And it is picked up everywhere.' He would, he insisted, as he fought with Harris for 'the restoration of lines and for the removal of Jed's happy interpolations of New Jersey–New Hampshire', rather have it die on the road than come into New York 'as an aimless series of little jokes, with a painful last act'.[23] It was not a good start. A one-night stand in Princeton, New Jersey, was not a success and neither was a preview in Boston which had to be cut short by a week. Even the New York opening was not unanimously well received. Indeed John Steinbeck's *Of Mice and Men* was preferred by the Drama Critics' Circle for their annual award. But *Our Town* did then receive the Pulitzer prize for 1938 and so restored Wilder's dwindling reputation.

The play ran for over a year on Broadway and on tour, Wilder even playing the role of Stage Manager for a two-week period.

For Wilder the factitious nature of the theatre was of the essence. Virtually all of his plays draw attention to their own processes. In an essay entitled 'Some thoughts on playwriting', which appeared in 1941, he insisted that 'in its greatest ages the stage employed the greatest number of conventions'.[24] To him the theatre, being fundamentally pretence, thrives on an acceptance of that fact, both because it thereby compels the collaborative involvement of the audience and, more importantly, because it raises the action from the specific to the general. 'The stage continually strains to tell the generalized truth and it is the element of pretence that reinforces it. Out of the lie, the pretence, of the theatre proceeds a truth more compelling than the novel can attain, for the novel by its own laws is constrained to tell of an action that "once happened" – "once upon a time".' And this connection between the specific and the general was, of course, at the heart of *Our Town*.

Wilder's is an anti-tragic stance. As Karl Jaspers has said,

> Life and death, the cycle of blossoming and withering away, the facts of transitoriness, do not yet establish in themselves any tragic atmosphere. The on-looker can calmly contemplate the process in which he is himself included and by which he is sheltered. The tragic atmosphere arises as the strange and sinister fate to which we have been abandoned. There is something alien that threatens us, something we cannot escape.[25]

Wilder domesticates the metaphysical, reconciles the individual to his fate, closes the gap between spirit and fact. His is not a drama which engages the notion of revolt on any level. Gold had accused him of shunning social revolt. He equally shunned metaphysical rebellion. There is no resistance in Wilder's work. Where the tragic spirit regrets the victory of the timeless and the universal over the individual, Wilder celebrates it, finding in this the justification for that individual, the key to his significance. His work celebrates the group rather than the individual. There is no individual sensibility which focusses the moral action. It is a drama without conflict. His characters struggle neither with fate nor with history. They transgress no code and hence are required to offer no atonement. The arbitrary is effortlessly accommodated. Submission is presented as a primary virtue. *Our Town* establishes a model of social and metaphysical benignity no less unquestioned than that in *The Merchant of Yonkers* whose comic presumption of order is naturally unchallenged. Character is destiny in such a way as to deny the responsibility which might have created social tension or spiritual rebellion. And though the tragic spirit expresses the conviction that the individual is, as Jaspers suggested, the bearer of something that reaches beyond individual existence, the meaning is generated through experiencing life at its limits, through a full consciousness which is equally his burden and his glory. Wilder's characters are never seen experiencing these limits, nor are they aware of the paradoxes which stem from testing the extent of their freedom or challenging the terms of their fate. In *Pullman Car Hiawatha*, *Our Town* and *The Skin Of Our Teeth* they are perceived as a unit, as representative men and women, whose primary task is to experience the present and acknowledge their responsibility to a process which they are not expected to understand but simply to enact. The fatalism of his characters is equally his own and it is perhaps his untroubled view of human affairs which made his work so appealing, more especially at a time when such a reassurance was desperately needed.

The Matchmaker is a slightly revised version of *The Merchant of Yonkers* (1938). It was based on *Einen Jux will es sich machen* (1842) by Johann Nestroy, which in turn was based on John Oxenford's *A Day Well Spent* (1835). In its original form it opened in December 1938, first at Boston and then at the Guild Theatre in New York. It was not successful, though, revised, it had a respectable run in 1954 in London and the following year in America. The musical version *Hello Dolly*! finally completed the transformation of flop into smash hit. Virtually all of Wilder's plays reveal a sense of humour at odds with his public image as over-serious schoolmaster and philosophical novelist, and *The Matchmaker* was no exception. Indeed it was a conventional farce in which the self-conscious theatricality of his other plays is turned into a comic device as the audience is addressed directly by characters whose conscious play-acting is the standard recourse of the form.

Wilder has insisted that the play parodies rather than utilises the conventions. 'One way to shake off the nonsense of the nineteenth-century staging is to make fun of it. This play parodies the stock-company plays that I used to see at Ye Liberty Theatre, Oakland, California, when I was a boy.'[26] Less a parody than a celebration, *The Matchmaker* was an accomplished work but one of no great significance. Wilder's reputation as a dramatist rests less on this than it does on *Our Town* and the play which finally opened in October 1942 after considerable production difficulties – *The Skin Of Our Teeth*. This was, as he explained, 'written on the eve of our entry into the war and under strong emotion'.[27] In the preface to *Three Plays* he confessed that it was deeply indebted to Joyce's *Finnegans Wake*, which he had been reading at the time – a suggestion which, if made more forthrightly at the time, might have saved Wilder the misdirected accusations of plagiarism which robbed him of the New York Drama Critics' Circle award (though the play did receive the Pulitzer prize), and which for a time detracted from the success of the play. There are clear parallels between the two works. Wilder's Antrobuses are obvious kin to Joyce's Earwickers. Lily Sabina is clearly Wilder's version of

Lily Kinsella. And both works move their characters through different historical periods. But this was less plagiarism than homage, and *The Skin of our Teeth* was scarcely the only one of Wilder's plays to insist on a fluid notion of time, on relating the history of the individual to that of the race.

While writing it, Wilder thought of it as a comic-strip play. It is an attempt to condense the history of man through the mechanism of a middle-class American family who simultaneously enact their conventional suburban reality and an allegorical account of the physical and moral equivocation of the human race. The first act is apparently set at the time of the Ice Age, a menace which stands for any crisis in human history. Mr Antrobus is Man, inventor of the wheel, deviser of the alphabet, creator of mathematics. His wife is the practical helpmate, protective of her young, suspicious of her husband's outgoing manner and instinctive generosity which might threaten the survival of her own offspring. Their son, Henry, plays Cain to their Adam and Eve. He is the moral chancre, as their maid Sabina will develop into the seductress, Lilith. Together with a number of refugees – Homer, Moses and the nine Muses – they reveal an indomitable will in the face of the impending crisis.

In the second act the scene moves on in time and switches to Atlantic City. Society has now elaborated its own social and political organisation along with the egotism, jealousy, greed and destructive habit which are apparently to be seen as their inevitable accompaniment. The act ends with the Flood. The third act takes place following a war. In the aftermath of a destructive convulsion, the characters feel their way towards a new confidence, a new morality. Once again, it was a conclusion in harmony with the times, and it is perhaps not surprising that it was so well received in Germany in the immediate aftermath of the Second World War when rebuilding was the order of the day and confidence in the human spirit a daunting necessity. In a letter to Sibyl Colefax, quoted by Richard Goldstone in his study of Wilder, he described the work as a slapstick account of mankind stumbling childlike, hard-pressed, absurd, and sublime, surviving ice ages, floods and the jungles within his own breast, murder and self-murder.[28]

In 1939, Wilder attempted an adaptation of Pirandello's *Six Characters in Search of an Author* and its influence seems clear in *The Skin of Our Teeth*, though Wilder himself claimed *Hellzapoppin'* as the real inspiration. Indeed, it was Pirandello who observed that the real maidservant of his art was fantasy, a claim which Wilder might have made with equal force. *The Skin of Our Teeth* seems to combine the pieties of *Our Town* with the broad farce of *The Merchant of Yonkers*, locating this within a parodic version of domestic drama. As in *Hellzapoppin'* and *Six Characters*, much of the play's effect lies in its deliberate violation of the frame, its ironic treatment of its own form. Characters resist their roles, as they had failed to do in *Our Town*. Sabina in

particular repeatedly steps out of character, editing out portions of the play
not to her liking and having arguments with the Stage Manager. In the third
act, ostensibly as a result of food poisoning, seven of the actors have to be
replaced by stand-ins. The audience is repeatedly addressed directly. But
once again, where in Pirandello's work this is inherent in the play's theme,
here it is offered simply as a strategy of parodic method and a correlative of
the absurdity of human behaviour.

But beneath the theatricality are the familiar pieties. In the second act Mrs
Antrobus, against character, insists that 'We're not what you're all told and
what you think you are: We're ourselves.'[29] In the third, Antrobus challenges
his son's 'strong unreconciled evil', and asks

> How can you make a world for people to live in, unless you've first put order
> in yourself? Mark my words: I shall continue fighting you until my last breath
> as long as you mix up your idea of liberty with your idea of hogging everything
> for yourself. I shall have no pity on you. Shall pursue you to the far corners of
> the earth. You and I want the same thing; but until you think of it as something
> that everyone has a right to, you are my deadly enemy and I will destroy you.[30]

Though the play literally ends with a return to the opening scene, an assurance that the process continues, it effectively concludes with Antrobus's
rhetoric, which is apparently offered without irony:

> living is struggle. I know that every good and excellent thing in the world
> stands moment by moment on the razor edge of danger and must be fought for
> – whether it's a field, or a home, or a country. All I ask is the chance to build
> new worlds and God has always given us that. And has given us voices to guide
> us; and the memory of our mistakes to warn us.[31]

There then follows a series of excerpts from the Christian philosophical
tradition in a scene reminiscent of *Pullman Car Hiawatha*.

Wilder might have done well to pay attention to Pirandello's observation,
in his essay on *Six Characters in Search of an Author*, that

> I hate symbolic art in which the presentation loses all spontaneous movement in
> order to become a machine, an allegory – a vain and misconceived effort
> because the very fact of giving an allegorical sense to a presentation clearly
> shows that we have to do with a fable which by itself has no truth either
> fantastic or direct; it was made for the demonstration of some moral truth.[32]

Though Wilder resisted such reductivism by the anarchic energy of his
presentation, this scarcely concealed the allegorical insistence of a text whose
moralism slowly overwhelmed the freedom and vitality which, for Pirandello, was the necessary prerequisite for the dramatic image.

Wilder wrote for the theatre on two further occasions. *The Alcestiad*, under
the title *A Life in the Sun*, was produced at Edinburgh in 1955 and then again,

three years later, in a German version in Hamburg. In 1962 three of his one-act plays (*Someone from Assisi, Infancy and Childhood* from a projected cycle, *The Seven Deadly Sins*) were produced under the title *Plays for Bleeker Street*.

Wilder insisted that he was not an innovator. Interviewed in 1955, he suggested that 'I borrow from other writers, *shamelessly*! I can only say in my defense, like the woman brought before the judge on a charge of klepto-mania, "I do steal, but, your Honor, only from the very best stores."'[33] The irony was clear. Though the influence of Pirandello was marked, and that of Dreiser and Stein at least detectable, he created from this a theatre which was less concerned with ontological and epistemological questions than with moral and metaphysical ones. Not unlike Stein, he saw the American experience as offering a classic model of man's attempt to create himself against a landscape which implied a sense of continuity. Less scarred by the specifics of history, the American becomes a representative man. It was perhaps a view rooted in a sentimental perception. He certainly ignored the demeaning realities of city life which so obsessed his contemporaries, offering instead a determinedly white, Anglo-Saxon, Protestant version of American history and myth. In reaching for the permanent and the constant he chose to ignore the immediate and the tendentious. His characters are, on the whole, well fed, invulnerable to the economic realities which determined the con-tours of possibility for so many Americans. Where for Beckett such realities were rendered absurd by the fact of biological process, for Wilder they were transfigured by a faith in the harmonics of that process. Where Beckett sees irony, Wilder sees transcendence.

The family, for him, was not an ambiguous fact of capitalist existence, the source of social and psychological tensions. It was a symbol of a wider family, not defined by history. It was at the heart equally of American mythology and human development. And it was these verities which he chose to celebrate. And in doing so he created a drama which clearly appealed to a basic need. The alienating theatricality proved no barrier to those who responded to his optimism, to his encomiums to the human spirit and to his celebration of an American myth. His work proved remarkably resistant to criticism. Carefully contrived, rooted in an intellectual appreciation of the accomplishment of classical drama and a modernist theatricality alike, he created plays which perhaps paradoxically have the appearance and effect of folk drama. Certainly in *Our Town* he wrote a play which for many was the clearest dramatic statement of American values. As he said in the preface to his plays:

> The theatre has lagged behind the other arts in finding the 'new ways' to express how men and women think and feel in our time. I am not one of the

new dramatists we are looking for, I wish I were. I hope I have played a part in preparing the way for them. I am not an innovator but a rediscoverer of forgotten goods and I hope a remover of obstructive bric-a-brac. And as I view the work of my contemporaries I seem to feel that I am exceptional in one thing – I give (don't I) the impression of having enormously enjoyed it.[34]

9 Lillian Hellman

The tone of Lillian Hellman's autobiographical books (*An Unfinished Woman, Pentimento, Scoundrel Time*) is one of ironic self-deprecation. She reproves herself for a repeated failure to appreciate the value of her experiences. There is a sense of moral reproof for a frivolity which was partly a public posture and partly an actual failure of humanity on her part. These books are a catalogue of wasted lives, of people who failed to value things of real importance because they had been taught to distrust them. To a degree this is the pose of a woman who wishes to disavow her own mistakes. It is the conventional posture of the autobiographer whose present command of experience is underlined by an ability to see the past in a clear perspective. But it also reflects a genuine sense of moral affront. She grew up in a time when personal and sexual emancipation were to be underscored by the withholding of real commitment. Her own experience of abortion is described as being regarded as a kind of badge of distinction, as primary evidence of a life which was to be lived without consequences. Love in particular was to be treated with deep distrust. Hers was a generation influenced by Freud on the one hand, and Hemingway on the other; that is, sexuality was an instinct to be deferred to, but also a game to be played for what it was worth. Martha's bitter denunciation of the woman who is ruining her life, in *The Children's Hour* (1934): 'Try to understand this: you're not playing with paper dolls. We're human beings, see? It's our lives you're fooling with. *Our* lives. That's serious business',[1] is in part an attack on her own failure and that of her generation. The hard causalities of her first play, indeed, are an assertion of the inadequacy of the stance which she and those around her had adopted. The failure of love, the ironic inversions of affection, the deforming power of the amoral, now become matters of real concern.

For Hemingway the attenuation of sexual relationships and the existence of a threatening homosexuality stood as images of a sterile world, an ironic collapse of order. For Hellman too there is a sense of fatalism, a feeling that private experience is vulnerable to public pressures. But it is not simply that. The failures which she indicts in *The Children's Hour* are pre-eminently personal moral failures, failures of perception, compassion, imagination and understanding. These are not for the most part sensibilities in recoil from public anarchy; they are individuals who place self before moral value and who are incapable of distinguishing the truth from the lie. And yet part of the play's strength lies in the ambiguity it is prepared to concede to that truth.

Lillian Hellman's moral drive was central but the source of weakness. 'I am a moral writer, often too moral a writer, and I cannot avoid, it seems, that last summing up. I think that is only a mistake when it fails to achieve its purpose, and I would rather make the attempt, and fail, than fail to make the attempt.'[2] It was indeed a weakness, a drive towards the explicit, an insistence on pressing through action to language which on occasion closed her work too tightly against ambiguity.

Lillian Hellman's first and in many ways best play was *The Children's Hour*. It concerns the fate of two women, Karen and Martha, who run a private boarding-school. Their lives and their livelihood are destroyed when a young girl maliciously claims that they are lesbian lovers. The child's grandmother, blinded by an affection not wholly drained of egotism, chooses to believe her and persuades other parents to withdraw their children, thus ruining the school. In the ensuing court-case a vain and foolish aunt, whose careless reference to the 'unnatural' desire of Martha to discourage her friend's marriage had provided the ammunition for the vindictive young girl, fails to turn up to vindicate them. The court-case is lost but, worse than this, Karen's fiancé, while standing by her, himself has doubts which poison their relationship. And at the end of the play Martha does indeed confess that she had loved her friend with something more than the affection of a friend. She kills herself, leaving Karen alone with a repentant old woman who has belatedly, and a shade too conveniently, discovered her granddaughter's dishonesty and even inveterate evil.

The play's third act is crucial in that it turns the play from a sub-Ibsen account of integrity assailed by private and public self-interest into a drama about the repression of truth on a number of levels. The collapse of the play into simple melodrama thus becomes a more disturbing betrayal. It conventionalises the play but, more alarmingly, its ironic reductivism (an echo of the endings of *The Sun Also Rises* and *A Farewell to Arms*) is a piece of calculated posing of the kind which Hellman was learning to distrust. On a naturalistic level it is hard to believe either in the convenience of the old woman's repentance, which brings her to the school on cue, moments after the death of the schoolteacher, or the calm acceptance of the dead body in an adjacent room manifested by all the characters. On a moral level it is hard to reconcile this response (even of an emotionally drained woman such as Karen) with the deeply concerned character so carefully established earlier in the play. Everything which she values has been destroyed, and while shock and the sheer accumulation of personal disaster may in some degree account for her response, the manner in which the final scene is contrived works against such a conclusion. Lillian Hellman later admitted that 'The play probably should have been ended with Martha's suicide' though this was because 'the last scene is large and overburdened'.[3] This is not really the essence of the problem. The failure relates more directly to an inability to sustain tension rather than its casual exploitation.

The Children's Hour is concerned in part with the degree to which behaviour is a consequence of the individual's desire to see him or herself in the best light; that is, it is concern with an egotism which may disguise itself in many forms, not least, as Ibsen observed, in the form of a self-righteous idealism. Hence, Karen assails the old woman, who now wishes to right the wrong she has done them, by observing that 'You want to be "just", don't you...You want to be a "good" woman again...You told us that night you had to do what you did. Now you "have" to do this. A public apology and money paid, and you can sleep again and eat again.'[4] It is not primarily a play about the power of society to enforce its moral norms, a warning against the witch-hunt; it is more concerned with the destructive effects of insisting on one's innocence at all costs. It has more than a touch of The Wild Duck about it.

The relationship between the two women is drawn with sympathy, its understatement being an important aspect of its achievement. And though it is usual to disavow any connection between Lillian Hellman and her characters, her story of Julia, a childhood friend, contained in Pentimento (1974) – a story which she had found herself unable to tell until then – suggests the origins of this friendship which trembles on the brink of something else. 'In those years, and the years after Julia's death,' she explains, 'I have had plenty of time to think about the love I had for her, too strong and too complicated to be defined as only the sexual yearnings of one girl for another. And yet certainly that was there. I don't know, I never cared, and it is now an aimless guessing game. It doesn't prove much that we never kissed each other.'[5] Like her characters in The Children's Hour, she too had been accused in public of having such a relationship. The point is, of course, not that there was a definable source for the play, but that in The Children's Hour the 'aimless guessing game' carries much of the play's tension and that that tension is to some degree discharged by too explicit an announcement of that passion by Martha. Her death may follow precisely from her own realisation of what she had formerly suppressed, but the clear articulation of that knowledge is required neither by the play's dramatic strategy nor by her own development as a character.

There is a parallel too for the portrait of simple malignity which is represented by the young girl, Mary; but that malignity functions rather too unambiguously in the play, a malevolence which exists, not so much as a psychological truth, as an image of implacable hostility which is then compounded by those incapable of conceiving the existence of pure evil. When the play was revived in 1952, Hellman wrote in an article in the Sunday New York Times that 'On the stage a person is twice as villainous as say in a novel.

When I read that story I thought of the child as neurotic, sly, but not the utterly malignant creature which playgoers see in her. I never see characters as monstrously as the audience do.'[6] It is hard to see this as anything less than a confession of her own dissatisfaction with a character whose 'story' she had first read in a book by William Roughead called *Bad Companions*.

Though in large part a psychological study, there is more than a trace of radicalism, or at least of liberal concern, in the play. The struggling school-teachers are ruined by an old, rich woman, whose high tone conceals a basic failure of humanity. As Hellman commented in *Pentimento:* 'Style is mighty pleasant for those who benefit from it, but maybe not always rewarding for those who make and live by its necessarily strict rules.'[7] And so here, the old woman is able to enforce what she takes to be the proprieties irrespective of truth or humanity because her personal values are socially enforceable. This was not, however, a dimension which she was yet ready to pursue. But, discontented by the romantic rebellion of the writers of the 1920s, she responded to the growing radicalism of the early 1930s with some enthusiasm:

> The rebels of the Twenties, the generation before mine, now seemed rebels only in the Scott Fitzgerald sense: they had wasted their blood, blind to the future they could have smelled if the odor of booze hadn't been so strong... the 1920s rebels had always seemed strange to me: without charity I thought most of them were no more than a classy lot of brilliant comics, performing at low fees for the society rich. The new radicalism was what I had always been looking for.[8]

And that radicalism found its way quickly into her work.

Her next play, *Days to Come* (1936), was not a success. On the first night she vomited at the back of the theatre, and having changed her clothes returned to the theatre in time to see William Randolph Hearst leading his guests out in the middle of the second act. She has confessed to having a fondness for the play: 'it is crowded and overwrought, but it is a good report of rich liberals in the 1930s, of a labor leader who saw through them, of a modern lost lady, and has in it a correct prediction of how conservative the American labor movement was to become'.[9] It is hard to say much more for it. Certainly Lillian Hellman's moral concerns are obscured by a more immediate social imperative, while its characters stand as a simple concession to the conventionalities of the committed theatre.

Days to Come was Hellman's strike play. The family brush-making factory is in a state of crisis. Competitive wage-cutting has forced Andrew Rodman, a liberal employer, to mortgage his business and to propose a wage-cut which precipitates a strike. Persuaded against his better judgement to call in strike-breakers he provokes events which he cannot control. Violence breaks out. A striker's child is murdered. The strike collapses. Lacking any real moral resources of his own, Andrew has simply compounded the brutalities of the system which he had hoped to humanise.

As an image of the future it is bleak, but Hellman is less concerned with indicting a corrupt and unjust political and economic system than she is with identifying a moral failure in the class from which she herself derived. Granted, she offers a portrait of a naively docile workman and a knowing and effective labour leader, but the emphasis is on the family who operate the business and whose welfare is the central consideration.

In the figure of Cora, Andrew's sister, Hellman offers a version of Regina in *The Little Foxes* (1939) and a reprise of the self-concerned aunt in her first play. She is a woman for whom self is the central and motivating force. But Hellman is far more interested in the two other family members: Andrew and his wife Julie. It is through these characters that the play rises momentarily above the conventionalities of the strike drama. For Julie is precisely that kind of figure whose sensibility had been forged in the 1920s, whom she herself had denounced elsewhere and whom she herself had represented. She contracts a loveless marriage and drifts aimlessly, indulging in extra-marital affairs because she inhabits a world with no values of any kind. As she explains, 'We belonged to the time when talk was part of the marriage ceremony. Such cynical, smooth talk, about marriage and life and freedom.'[10] Her husband, on the other hand, still clings to the liberal virtues but does so in an abstract way, protected by his money from the harsh causalities of life. As he belatedly realises, he has been 'The delicate prince in his ivory tower... carefully protected from the dust and din of battle.'[11] His liberal vacillation has been the cause of the collapse of the world he fondly imagined himself to inhabit. And this is no sudden failure of will and imagination. Lillian Hellman's point is that it is a self-deceit of long standing which has merely been exposed by the brutal realities of the 1930s. Neither Andrew nor his wife has been in touch with the real world at any time in their lives. Born to wealth, they have been disabled by the presumptions of power, but also by the empty posturings of a decade in which morality was conceived as a private testing of the sensibility or that pursuit of the ineffable ideal, with its underside of self-deceiving or corrupting violence, which Fitzgerald had described in *The Great Gatsby*. Indeed it is a play best seen in the context of a book like *Tender is the Night* rather than in that provided by the strike plays blossoming in the American theatre of the time. For its real concern is with the spoiled priest Andrew Rodman, who believed that the world could be sustained by his own moral imagination, that he could play the game of wealth without being corrupted, and that his wife's desperate sense of alienation could be controlled by his own sense of moral purpose. The inadequacy of such a stance, the incubus of anarchy concealed beneath apparent order, is symbolised here, as in Fitzgerald's book, by the wife's adultery; and he is left at the end of the play discarded by history, and displaced from the comfortable world he had imagined himself to inhabit, like Fitzgerald's Dick Diver. The weakness of the play is that this moral tale is contained within the pieties of a sub-genre – the strike play – which Hellman handled with less assurance. The noble workman whose child is killed by vicious strike-breakers, the intelligent and courageous union leader, the corrupt and scheming lawyer, the single-mindedly grasping capitalist shareholder are all off-the-peg characters who parade clichés as truth. She was simultaneously writing two distinct plays. The two proved incompatible.

She herself detected something of this while claiming a factual basis for her portraits. In the introduction to *Four Plays* she wrote that she had made the conventional mistake of trying to pack everything she knew into the play.

> I knew a woman like Cora and I hated her, and *that* hate had to go in the play; I knew a woman like Julie, I pitied her, and *that* pity had to go in the play; I had been raised with the Ellicotts of the world, and what I felt about them had to go in the play, too; I knew Leo Whalen and I wanted to say how much I respected men who work for other men. I wanted to say too much.[12]

The point, of course, is not whether these characters have their counterpart in reality but how they operate in the play; and here they combine to create a simplistic social parable and, more destructively, distract from what might have been a more rewarding concern with the failure of the moral sensibility. It was a buried theme which she herself hinted at when she said that the play was to have been a 'study of innocent people on both sides who are drawn into conflicts and events far beyond their comprehension'.[13] But the nature and origins of that innocence are never examined except as a class inheritance, or, in Julie's case, a product of a cynical posturing. More crucially, the attempt to link the two elements within the play is unconvincing and graceless. Hence Julie, who has already had an affair with Ellicott, Rodman's lawyer, now makes a play for Whalen, the union organiser. This is credible neither in terms of the play's action nor in terms of the function which Julie, somewhat anomalously, adopts as her husband's moral mentor, calling him to his duty, urging him to resist his own tendency to betray himself and his ideals.

The play was poorly received and Hellman returned to Hollywood where she had the job of writing the screenplay for Sidney Kingsley's *Dead End* before leaving for a trip to Russia and then to Spain, where she saw something of the brutality of the Spanish Civil War.

Like Faulkner's Snopes trilogy, her next play, *The Little Foxes*, deals with the transition from an old to a new South. The bourbon tradition has become enfeebled. Its self-deceiving ways have made it easy prey to the amoralism of the new capitalism. Its own materialism had been cloaked in a myth which eventually insulated it from process. Denying historicism, it turned history itself into an icon, seeking, like Faulkner's Quentin or the mentally damaged Benjy in *The Sound and the Fury*, to stop time. But to deny time is to risk personal and cultural infantilism, a precocity which is inseparable from vulnerability. And so it proves. The new generation, unhampered by cavalier myths, takes a vindictive pleasure in the destruction and parodying of the old values, appropriating the public forms of a decaying system as conscious cover for rapacity. For Tennessee Williams the process is more direct and is transposed into sexual terms. For Faulkner and Hellman, power is a substitute for sexuality; for if the old aristocracy are denied a present by their fixation on the past, the new bourgeois capitalists can conceive of the present only in terms which deny it any human component and hence any real future.

The Hubbard family, Ben, Oscar and Regina, like the Snopeses, have appropriated the wealth of the old aristocracy through marriage. As Ben explains to a northern industrialist in a rather too explicit expository passage, the old plantation had been ruined partly by the American Civil War but partly because 'the Southern aristocrat can adapt himself to nothing. Too high tone to try'.[14] By contrast the Hubbards have proved infinitely adaptable. '*Our* grandfather and *our* father learned the new ways and learned to make them pay. *They* were in trade. Hubbard Sons, Merchandise...Twenty years ago we took over their land, their cotton, and their daughter.'[15] Birdie, Oscar Hubbard's wife, is the cowed symbol of that defeated aristocracy, a diminishing asset in the Hubbard drive for wealth and influence, a trophy of their inexorable rise. Regina Hubbard has also married money by allying herself to Horace Giddens, a local banker, but this is a bargain on which she has swiftly reneged, withdrawing her sexual favours some ten years before the play's action. Her own growing callousness had coincided with his increasing success. Now he has realised his mistake and, knowing himself to be dying from a heart condition, has come to recognise some of the danger which the Hubbards represent. Accordingly he refuses to collaborate with them in a scheme to bring a textile factory to the South, thus preventing his wife from sharing in the expected profits and endangering the project. But he is out-manoeuvred by Oscar's son Leo, a spendthrift and worthless product of the new order, who appropriates the bonds which Horace keeps in his bank safe deposit box. When he discovers this, but before he can make use of the information, he has a heart-attack. His wife looks coldly on as he begs for his medicine and crawls up the stairs only to die before he can reach it.

In many ways, as this summary makes clear, the play is a melodrama. The characters are painted in primary colours. The young Leo has no redeeming features. He steals, consorts with whores, beats his horses, lacks both grace and intelligence, substituting only a low cunning. His father Oscar is allowed no motives and no thoughts which do not bubble to the surface in language. Regina is willing to bargain away her daughter's future happiness, effectively to murder her husband and, in all probability, seduce their Northern partner. Birdie Hubbard is totally ineffective, a fluttering birdlike creature, wholly cowed by her husband. The neat turn of the plot, depending, as it does, on the theft of the bonds and the convenient discovery of that fact a few days later, suggests a weakness in Hellman's work which is characteristic. But beyond the level of melodramatic encounter is a play whose moral scope extends beyond that of a simple clash between greed and virtue and whose concerns go beyond the simplicities of the mechanical plotting.

On one level it is a Chekhovian account of a culture caught in a moment of transition. Power has decisively shifted already, but the moral world is still in a state of some flux. Like Chekhov, Hellman has little sympathy for the world which has been displaced. Its moral failures were simply too great; though, again like Chekhov, she was not immune to the civilities with which it surrounded itself. Beauty is not destroyed by its proximity to decay. Indeed the risk is that it will be enhanced. But where Chekhov saw a certain honest vigour in the world which would replace the old, Hellman recoils with horror. Apart from the Negro characters, in whose conventionalisation the playwright shares responsibility with the society which she wishes to indict, the only character who stands aside from the corruption is Regina's daughter, Alexandra. She is given the crucial insight, but neither the strength of character nor the means to enforce it. Her father has proved inadequate to the task of defeating the Hubbards and there is nothing to suggest that Alexandra will prove any more capable. Indeed that failure is at the heart of the play's concern. For as the Negro servant remarks, 'there are people who eat the earth and eat all the people on it like in the Bible with the locusts. And other people who stand and watch them eat it. Sometimes I think it ain't right to stand and watch them do it.'[16] This view is echoed by Alexandra at the end of the play. But the irony lies in the play's date. It takes place at the turn of the century. The characters' future is thus the audience's present and the failure of Alexandra becomes apparent in that implied world. As Ben Hubbard remarks, 'The century's turning, the world is open. Open for people like you and me. Ready for us, waiting for us. After all this is just the beginning. There are hundreds of Hubbards sitting in rooms like this throughout the country. All their homes aren't Hubbard, but they are all Hubbards and they will own the country someday.'[17] Alexandra's understanding of the meaning of this underscores Lillian Hellman's commitment to oppose such reductivism. That it lacks conviction is in part a consequence of her failure to imagine and create a character with the strength for such a fight, who is not coarsened by that strength or rendered insipid, as is Alexandra, by the weight of her moral sense. And in part it is a consequence of the vigour with which she presents the opposing forces. Regina is simply too vivid and vital a character for us to believe that at the end of the play she succumbs to fear and defers to her daughter.

In an interview in the *Paris Review* many years later Lillian Hellman said that *The Little Foxes* was to have been the first part of a trilogy, and that Alexandra 'was to have become maybe a spinsterish social worker, disappointed, another angry woman'.[18] Indeed she expressed surprise that critics could have supposed that she had a chance of defeating the forces which she had come to recognise as the enemy. 'I mean her to leave,' she explained, 'But to my great surprise, the ending of the play was taken to be a statement of faith in Alexandra, in her denial of her family. I never meant it that way. She did have courage enough to leave, but she would never have the force and vigour of her mother's family. That's what I meant. Or maybe I made it up afterward.'[19] The last remark is revealing, for the clear logic of the play suggests that Alexandra, in leaving, is to bear the burden of a necessary transformation. The failure to establish the credibility of this is a structural weakness.

The Little Foxes was produced at the end of a committed decade in which the writer was pressed to declare his or her allegiance in ideological terms. Despite the subsequent attempt by the House Un-American Activities Committee to turn her into an ideologue, however, and despite the more simplistic assumptions of *Days to Come*, Hellman was never that. Indeed she took some pride in her refusal to bend her art to the immediate cause. Her model, in that respect, as in others, was Chekhov. In an introduction to a collection of his letters, she praised his balance in a way which sounds very like a justification of her own position in a decade in which balance was not regarded as a primary virtue.

> While many of his contemporaries were jabbering out the dark days and boozing away the white nights, turning revolutionary for Christmas and police spy for Easter, attacking too loudly here and worshipping too loudly there, wasting youth and talent in futile revolt against anything and everything with little thought and no selection, Anton Chekhov was a man of balance, a man of sense.[20]

And yet he was 'a man of deep social ideals and an uncommon sense of social responsibility' and 'This has been true of almost every good writer who ever lived.' It was one thing to disavow pragmatic politics, it was clearly quite another to have no moral vision. Thus she quotes approvingly Chekhov's observation that:

> Writers who are immortal or just plain good... have one very important trait in common: they are going somewhere and they call you with them... Some

of them, according to how great they are, have aims that concern their own times more closely, such as the abolition of serfdom, the liberation of their country, politics, beauty, or simply vodka. Others have more remote aims, such as God, life beyond the grave, human happiness and so on. [In] the best of them...every line is permeated, as with juice, by a consciousness of an aim, you feel in addition to life as it is, also life as it should be...he who wants nothing, hopes for nothing and fears nothing cannot be an artist.[21]

He doubted his own position in this respect as Hellman doubted hers. But this moral drive was crucial to her work. Like Chekhov, she believed that the agent of transformation was likely to be the individual, but found it, if anything, more difficult than he did to imagine the kind of individual who could sustain the burden of inventing the future.

The Little Foxes is in many senses close to The Cherry Orchard. Both plays are concerned with dispossession, with the collapse of old myths and the denial of supposed verities. Both are set in a cotton-growing area some time after the freeing of the slaves but at a time when the transformation of slave into domestic servant had not yet softened the guilt and the suffering which had been the underpinning of gentility and cultural life. Both plays bring the old and new worlds into confrontation by the simple device of having the former plebeians displace the aristocrat from his own home. Thus Ben announces that he had bought Lionet, the family plantation, and taken over 'their land, their cotton, and their daughter', just as Lopahkin, in Chekhov's play, had announced that he had 'bought the very estate where my father and grandfather were serfs, where they weren't even admitted to the kitchen!'[22] But where Lopahkin is an ambiguous figure, willing to destroy the old cherry orchard in order to build villas for the rising bourgeoisie, but showing respect and compassion for those he is displacing, Hellman's Hubbards are single-mindedly cruel. The ambiguity with which the two plays conclude is fundamentally different. In Chekhov's case it lies in a recognition of the native energy and wit of the new class, allied to a pragmatism which can sacrifice the valuable with the worthless; in Hellman's case it derives from a simple failure to establish the potential and capacity of Alexandra who, besides the minor Negro characters, is the only figure to show any humanity. In other words, for Chekhov it is a willed ambiguity, a doubt born in the self and expanding to a cultural fact; for Hellman it is a consequence of a sensibility which presses character to extremes, which precipitates out evil and good until neither carry real conviction. It is a difference which enables Chekhov to call his play a comedy but which makes Hellman's a melodrama. To be sure, Chekhov had said, 'It is the duty of the judge to put the questions to the jury correctly...and it is for members of the jury to make up their minds, each according to his taste',[23] but the case which he presented was more finely balanced, less prejudiced (though in the person of Natasha in

Three Sisters, he showed that he, too, was capable of conceiving the purely evil), less dependent on a view of history as moral decay. It is as though Chekhov doubted that truth could be seized whole by any individual or class. Lillian Hellman's contempt for the Hubbards is total, and though she attacks those who allow such evil to operate it is by no means clear who she means by this, or who in the play is in a position to oppose them and fails to do so. Certainly the dying Horace is not a fit candidate. And so her cry that something should be done goes unanswered, not because there is no one with the will to answer but because she herself fails to imagine what such a person would be.

It is true that Chekhov himself had a melodramatic imagination, that he too offered expository speeches and had a weakness for the clarifying act of violence. If his work was in any way a model, therefore, it would hardly be surprising if these faults were reflected and even magnified in her own. But if this influence was strong it remains clear that Lillian Hellman's world is recognisably American and, in particular, recognisably Southern. The constant intersection of past and present, myth and history, social custom and sexual behaviour, is definitional. Sensual brio and financial rapacity are compounded. But the control is too clear and too tight. The mechanics of the play, ruthlessly insisted upon, weaken that slow unravelling of process which is the essence of Faulkner's work – the truth never completely told because never completely known. For Lillian Hellman, time is the enemy. Hidden motives and desires have to be rushed to the surface and displayed, and in the process they lose their power to disturb. The urge to expose is indulged at the expense of dramatic tension, which then has to be recreated by other means. She lacks confidence in her own power to create character which has no need to spill itself quite so carelessly in words. Evil which is so ready to expose its own inner contents loses something of its power as evil.

And her desire to create a closed world of greed is such that we are required to believe that the brothers would be unwilling to raise the necessary $75 000 outside the family, even though to do so would save them considerable expense, would obviate a destructive clash, and by their own calculations would be a short-term loan easily repayable – a loan against the collateral of the factory. In other words the exigencies of plot seem to win out over the practical details.

And her own misjudgement of the response of critics and audiences was indicative of a failure to control the tone of a play which, thirty-five years later, she was still insisting was not what it seemed. 'I had meant,' she said, 'to half mock my own youthful high-class innocence in Alexandra...I had meant people to smile at, and to sympathize with, the sad, weak Birdie...I had meant the audience to recognize some part of themselves in the money-dominated Hubbards; I had not meant people to think of them as villains to whom they had no connection.'[24] Based in part on her own family, the play had been an attempt at 'angry comedy', but the comedy is lost in the vehemence of the moral perspective as its general application is lost in the implacable specifics of the Hubbards' villainy.

Seven years after *The Little Foxes* she returned to the Hubbard family, producing *Another Part of the Forest* (1951), which is set in 1880. As she has said, 'I believed that I could now make clear that I had meant the first play as a kind of satire', but once again was forced to concede that 'What I had thought was bite they thought sad, touching, or plotty and melodramatic.'[25] And, indeed, the weaknesses of the former play are exaggerated in this one, which locates the Hubbards at an earlier stage but which does not come any closer to explaining the origin of their destructive egotism or to situating it in terms of an historical process.

The two plays are not entirely consistent in their details. The Hubbard money, willed to Ben and Oscar on their father's death in the first play, is shown in the second to have been prised from his unwilling grasp while he was still alive. Only one of Birdie's brothers apparently survives the American Civil War. Horace, only referred to in the second play, nonetheless becomes an economically more attractive catch, while Regina's proposed marriage to him is presented as a cynical plot by her brother Ben. But consistency was no more of the essence for Hellman than it was for Faulkner. The principal weakness of *Another Part of the Forest* lies in the dominant significance of the plot, in the reduction of character to role, and in the subservience of all elements to a simplistic moral about an obsessive and unexamined materialism, a greed simply assumed and certainly not presented as an aspect of individual psychology, of class presumption or corrosive national myth. The family members only exist through their plots. All relationships are considered simply for their financial implications. Where love does exist it is corrupted by a natural machiavellianism which is simply postulated and not inspected for its origin in human nature, in personal or social behaviour. This time, there is, indeed, no Alexandra. The only signs of humanity are exhibited either by the black servants, who are, of course, incapable of intervening in history, or the enfeebled and mentally etiolated aristocracy. The Hubbards are irredeemably evil. Marcus, who, somewhat unbelievably, has struggled to acquire the trappings of cultural life, has founded the family fortunes on wartime profiteering, a trade which led to the death of twenty-seven men in a confederate training camp. And this piece of suppressed information becomes a central part of the play's dramatic strategy – hinted at throughout and then flourished at a critical moment.

Again, Lillian Hellman holds no brief for the aristocracy. They are presented as inept and immoral. Their cultivation is based on the corrupting fact of slavery. Theirs is, indeed, a death-centred culture. Birdie's brother can think of nothing better to do than fight for pro-slavery forces in Brazil. Marcus is right to describe him as 'an empty man from an idiot world...A man who believes in nothing, and never will. A man in space...'[26] But by the same token the Hubbards believe in nothing but money. As Ben says, 'I don't think anybody in this family can love.' The play is, then, a great deal bleaker than its predecessor.

Lillian Hellman did not propose a model of lyricism replaced by realism, a moral world voided of its meaning by the pressure of the modern. She, like Faulkner or Penn Warren, and later Tennessee Williams, knew all too clearly the corruption hidden by neo-classical façades and romantic lies. But she does tend to sentimentalise evil, insisting on its unambiguous outline and thereby falsifying the real nature of the world struggling towards birth in the late nineteenth century. Of course the woman who had worked for the Loyalist cause in Spain was likely to be drawn to a Manichaean view, likely to dread the totalitarian spirit and hence to insist on its diabolism. And certainly the events of that war did little to suggest that this was not an adequate account of the real. But evil remains so distressingly unexamined in her work that it becomes a literary conceit. It simply exists.

The fact is that in reality the broken spirit of the old South has a history. It is rooted in a recoverable experience. The connection between the drive for wealth and power and the surrender of conscience was genuinely complex. It involved self-deceit which had its own historiography. The New South, which fascinated her more, she understood, if anything, less; and lacked the objectivity therefore to see it in the comic light which she wished. Greed and egotism raised to the level of social strategy were things that she had observed at close quarters but never penetrated. They remain simple facts, stated baldly but never located in a private or public history. As far as one can see, the Hubbards were born with their cruelties already perfectly formed. Hence the structure of the play is not concerned with uncovering a set of experiences or perceptions which would explain their character and their actions but simply with exposing a hidden past which can be utilised to shift the balance of power. Marcus attacks the old aristocracy for 'getting in the way of history',[27] but in fact he sees history not as process but as artifact – something to appreciate.

What we see in Hellman is, in a sense, a Southern version of O'Neill's New England alarm at a new generation detached from time, from a natural world and from any notion of human continuity and community. The internecine battles of the Hubbards share something with those of O'Neill's Tyrones, though even more with Faulkner's Snopeses. Their world becomes hermetic. They become one another's hell. The context is one of change. The old South gives way to the new. But the real centre of the plays is the absence, the void, the space where the committed individual, the human relationship, the sensitised conscience should be, the moral basis for such a resistance having been betrayed by history. As Edgar Allan Poe had suggested:

A voice from out the future cries
'On, on!' – but o'er the Past
(Dim gulf!) my spirit hovering lies
Mute, motionless, aghast![28]

In January 1940, Lillian Hellman spoke at the Book and Author Lunch at the Hotel Astor. 'I am,' she said, 'a writer and also a Jew. I want to be sure I can continue to say what I wish without being branded by the malice of people making a living by that malice.'[29] The Second World War clearly made a special demand on a Jewish writer watching from a distance the struggle for survival and dignity in Europe. It was a demand which she responded to in part by a visit to the Soviet Union and in part by a more rigorous inspection of her own position and the public failures which had led to holocaust. The war, of course, posed the writer with a classic dilemma: tempted on the one hand to engage the world directly, to abandon the word for the act, and on the other to retreat from the immediate pressure of the event in order to see more clearly, to observe a pattern invisible to those involved in the flux of a lived history. Dashiell Hammett, with whom she lived and who was her severest and most sensitive critic, opted for involvement. Despite having suffered from tuberculosis in his youth he enlisted as a private in the army. Lillian Hellman chose to mobilise her art for the cause. The effect was socially admirable but dramatically disappointing.

Her own contribution to the times consisted of two plays, *Watch on the Rhine* and *A Searching Wind*. The former, which opened on Broadway in 1941, was an attempt to import the politics of Europe to a domestic American setting. It was also offered as an anxious debate about the utility of art at moments of social crisis. Hence she has one of her characters insist that there is 'Too much talk. By this time all of us know where we are and what we have to do. It's an indulgence to sit in a room and discuss your beliefs as if they were the afternoon's golf game.'[30] It is a speech which suggests a degree of insecurity on Hellman's part which is increasingly translated into a strident and desperate rhetoric.

Watch on the Rhine is an improbable story about the betrayal of a resistance worker by a cynical German exile. He is presented as an effete German aristocrat and is offered as representative of those who had seen Hitler's rise as offering an opportunity for their own aggrandisement. It was a plot which encouraged Hellman's worst instincts for melodrama. The characters converse in clichés. And though some of these are put into the mouths of children, thereby suggesting a level at which Hellman was aware of the need to undercut her own rhetoric, the context of the play hardly allows room for such self-deprecating irony. However simplistic the statements, they are spoken with a half-embarrassed compulsion: 'Anger is protest. And so you must direct it to the proper channels and then harness it for the good of other men;'[31] 'I remember Luther: Here I stand. I can do nothing else. God help me. Amen:'[32] 'For every man who lives without freedom, the rest of us must face the guilt;'[33] 'In every town and every village and every mud hut in the world there is a man who might fight to make a good world.'[34] The implicit or actual quotation marks around such speeches are an indication of Hellman's attempt to have her political cake and eat it. She wishes both to show that she is aware of the inflated rhetoric and simultaneously to claim its essential truth.

The play is, in effect, an assertion that it is impossible to remain uncommitted. It ends with a murder, the resistance hero killing his would-be betrayer. This is presented as a necessary act of violence and as such is a challenge to the liberal values of the family in which he finds himself. But while berating liberals she was herself clearly one of them, and while urging the need for commitment felt the need to express her sense of dilemma in a language whose falsities perhaps exposed her own doubts. Hence when Kurt, the resistance hero, explains to his children that 'I have a great hate for the violent. They are the sick of the world. (*Softly*) Maybe I am sick now, too', he expresses a level of self-doubt which has more to do with American liberal *Angst* than with the character of a man who has been systematically tortured and who is returning to Germany in order to save his friends from a similar fate. The language contains a doubt which the play's action and logic excludes. Indeed a predominant weakness of the play lies in that simplification of forces which had undermined her earlier work. While Teck the betrayer is implicitly attacked for seeing Nazism as a natural and unavoidable fate, Sarah, the wife of the resistance worker, insists that he is 'not difficult to understand'.[35] The truth is, indeed, that Hellman treats evil as an implacable but easily perceivable fact. She chooses to engage it at the level of fact, of action and simplistic motive (he betrays for money). The more profound aspects of a presumed evil never engage her attention any more than do the subtleties that lie behind the act of resistance. Her Manichaean imagination denies her the insight which would make the play something more than a morality play in which goodness challenges and defeats evil.

Violence is brought into the American stage living-room for the best of motives. It is to be an honest recognition of the fact that opposition to evil means an inevitable flirtation with its principles and methods; but since these principles and methods, and the nature of the human behaviour in which they are rooted, remain largely unexamined it becomes an empty gesture, dramatically enfeebled and theatrically dishonest. But the political scene seemed to justify such moral absolutism, and the rhetoric of her play was scarcely different in kind to that being deployed on public platforms. The weakness of the play lay in its refusal to examine the constituents of that rhetoric, to probe beyond the public conflict between self-evident forces.

But there was a level at which the commitment which she seemed to be urging on others was a commitment which she herself had resisted. As she said of herself in *An Unfinished Woman*, describing her relationship with Dashiell Hammett, 'a woman who was never to be committed was facing a man who already was'.[36] She was convinced that, 'during the war in Spain, Hitler and Mussolini could have been stopped, the bumblers and the villains led us into this'.[37] This was, after all, essentially the view expressed in both *Watch on the Rhine* and *The Searching Wind*. But she was herself not immune to this criticism. She had, to be sure, been to Spain, signed documents and spoken out; but earlier in her career she had resisted calls to turn her art into a weapon, to make it a force in the world, and this bred a guilt which, along with the new pressures of the public world, now destabilised her work.

The play won the New York Drama Critics' award. It ran for 378 performances. Lillian Hellman herself worked to raise funds for the anti-fascist movement and a specially bound edition of the play was issued by the Joint Anti-Fascist Refugee Committee. But she dismissed many of these activities as 'idle lady stuff' and has confessed to being jealous of Hammett's positive action, feeling 'lonely and useless, jealous of his ability to take a modest road to what he wanted'.[38] *The Searching Wind* (1944) was another product of this dissatisfaction and guilt.

The Searching Wind (1944) was an attempt to analyse the moral failures which had led to war, the liberal equivocations, the self-concerned tolerance for the intolerable. It was her attempt to establish a connection between private and public morality. It was also another stage in her self-accusation and in her self-justification as a writer. Her principal character, Alexander Hazen, is a diplomat who, like the writer, has a perfect excuse for non-involvement. The play is set at crucial moments in the history of the rise of fascism: in Rome, in 1922, at the time of Mussolini's take-over in Italy; in Berlin, in 1923, as the first signs of Hitler's rise becomes apparent; in Paris, on the eve of Chamberlain's appeasement. Despite the accumulating evidence of crisis, Alexander remains convinced that things are not as bad as they seem. And when what Hellman sees as the betrayal of appeasement is imminent, despite his now clearer view of what is happening and despite his aroused conscience, he sends a report back to his government offering equivocal support for appeasement. He defends himself against his conscience by insisting that the individual cannot hope to deflect the course of history. And since he chooses not to deflect it he is seen by Lillian Hellman as compounding it. So that when his own son is injured, it is clear that responsibility for this is to be laid at his own feet and at the feet of those, like him, who, beginning with the liberal failures of Wilsonian policy a generation before, had connived in a process which created its own inevitability. And the same betrayal of natural instinct operates on a private level. He turns his back on a passionate love-affair and marries a woman who derives her pleasure from consorting with those very businessmen and politicians who had facilitated the rise of the forces which eventually wound her own son. It is a thesis relentlessly advanced and repeatedly underscored with an insistence which weakens both characters and dramatic intensity. Thus Alexander acknowledges to his son a fact which has by this time become abundantly evident: 'You mean that if people like me had seen it straight, maybe you wouldn't have had to be there twenty-two years later.'[39]

The play was also offered as Hellman's defence of her own portraits of unalloyed evil, for part of Alexander's failure of perception lies precisely in the fact that, as he says, 'I can't believe in villainy. I can't. I always want to laugh when somebody else believes in it.'[40] The play was a mechanical thesis drama. Its characters were simple exemplars dragged from one historical nodal point to another. It lacked both conviction and force.

In *Pentimento* Lillian Hellman observed that 'In my case, I think, the mixture of commitment and no-commitment came from Bohemia as it bumped into Calvin: in Hammett's it came from never believing in any kind of permanence and a mind that rejected absolutes.'[41] It was a perceptive remark. Her work expressed a profound suspicion of those who apparently compounded the anti-human drift of history, either by positive manipulation or, more often, by liberal temporising or a high-toned concern for style over content, manners before morality. Yet in adopting herself a pose of moral detachment, of an observer contemptuous of the values of those who directed the nature of public forms and action, she was potentially guilty of the crimes of which she accused others. Indeed she was deeply suspicious of that middle ground. Moderation, a desire to withdraw from and even deny the extremes of human behaviour, becomes less a symptom of the human sensibility than evidence of failure of will, a withdrawal from a reality which is the more threatening for being ignored. It was an uneasy stance and one which, on a deeper level, she distrusted. The stridency of the wartime plays worked against the understatement and the psychological sophistication which had made *The Children's Hour* such an effective work. But she was nervous of an ambiguity which she too easily mistook for equivocation. Distrustful, politically, of a refusal of definition, of a retreat into ambivalence, she came equally to distrust it as an aesthetic strategy

Apart from three adaptations (*Montserrat*, 1949; *The Lark*, 1955; and *My Mother, My Father and Me*, 1963) and a collaboration (*Candide*, 1966), Lillian Hellman wrote only two further plays. For both of them she returned to the

South. *The Autumn Garden* (1951) is set in the Tuckerman house in a small town on the Gulf of Mexico, a hundred miles from New Orleans, in September 1949. It is autumn not only in terms of the season but more crucially in the lives of many of those gathered in the modest guest-house. They live in a world of illusion, of memories reconstructed to afford a convenient absolution for wasted lives. It is a world drained of truth and hence of a sense of moral responsibility. As one of the characters remarks, in the South 'nothing is ever anybody's fault'.⁴² The theme is a familiar one. Hellman is insisting that people are indeed responsible for their actions, that they are the sum of their choices. The South becomes what it had been in her earlier work, a symbol of a world in which a supposed concern with history is in fact a profound desire to deny its force. The evil of the South, as she had hinted in the early plays, had lain precisely in its denial of the real and hence of the moral responsibility which it spawned. Written in the years of the Sartre–Camus debates, the play is offered as an existential assertion of the need to acknowledge one's responsibility for creating one's own essence. Indeed one character is given a speech which is virtually a précis of Sartre's *Existentialism and Humanism*. It was a speech which summed up not only this work but the position outlined in her wartime plays. Ironically it was also a speech which, in its final form, was written for her by Dashiell Hammett – by her own account the only direct contribution which he made to her work. 'At any given moment,' observes General Griggs,

> you're only the sum of your life up to then. There are no big moments you can reach unless you've a pile of smaller moments to stand on. That big hour of decision, the turning point in your life, the someday you've counted on when you'd suddenly wipe out your past mistakes, do the work you'd never done, think the way you'd never thought, have what you'd never had – it doesn't just come suddenly. You've trained yourself for it while you waited – or you've let it all run past you and frittered yourself away. I've frittered myself away.⁴³

The characters do indeed all seem to have lived provisional lives and, being Hellman's creations, are apt to tell us so ('if you asked me, I just wouldn't know what I thought or believed, or ever had...What have I built my life on?'⁴⁴ 'Most people like us haven't done anything to themselves; they've let it be done to them.'⁴⁵). They are briefly shaken out of their protective illusions by the arrival of Nick, a failed artist who acts as a catalyst. But the play ends with the ripples almost stilled, with an assertion of the need for illusions which must now be ironic: 'Most of us lie to ourselves. Never mind.'⁴⁶

For some critics the play was Chekhovian rather than Ibsenesque, to the degree that it presented the past as less a repository of concealed truths generating present tensions, than a world of lost opportunities and betrayed visions; to the extent that it saw character as less an agent of moral debate than an expression of cultural reality. Certainly the provincial location of the play operates for Hellman rather as it does for Chekhov. It becomes an image of a hermeticism which stifles aspirations, an apt setting for those who have accepted their cultural and historical irrelevance. It is not the source of that surrender of will to imagination but its correlative. But the spiritual and moral limbo which they inhabit is not simply Southern. This form of provincialism now seems a shared fate which equally involves a Europe which in a vague way is invoked on a linguistic and factual basis. This vagueness, however, dissipates the force of a play which is clearly offered as something more than a psychopathology of the South.

Meanwhile the characters are accused of betraying a self which we never glimpse. They are in love with a romanticism which we are supposed to recognise as the underside of decay but, never seeing the truth thereby concealed, are in a poor position to judge. At least in *The Searching Wind* we were granted that privilege. It is, of course, a problem which Chekhov equally set himself in *The Seagull* and *The Cherry Orchard* and solved by establishing a cultural context which itself had the force of character. Here that element is suppressed precisely to the degree that Hellman wishes to transcend the Southern setting. As a consequence her characters' sad reveries have no cultural sanction. For Chekhov his characters' obsession with the past was a consequence of an excitable nature which 'quickly gives way to exhaustion'.[47] That exhaustion is clearly felt by Hellman's characters too, but this is not rooted in a clear sense of cultural identity. Chekhov had said of his characters, particularly in *Ivanov*, that:

> hardly has he reached the age of thirty or thirty-five when he begins to feel weariness and ennui...he says 'Don't get married, old man. You'd better trust my experience.' Or, 'After all, in essence what is liberalism?'...Such is the tone of these prematurely exhausted people. Further, sighing very positively, he advises, 'Don't marry thus and so...but choose something run-of-the-mill, grayish, without bright colors, without extra flourishes...On the whole, try to plan a quiet life for yourself. The grayer, the more monotonous the background, the better....But the life I have been leading, how wearing it has been!
> – how wearing![48]

This is precisely the mood of *The Autumn Garden*. For Chekhov this tone, and a generalised sense of guilt which it spawned, was specifically Russian. For Hellman it is seen at its most acute in the South, a culture whose roots have manifestly shrivelled. Beyond that, she clearly sees it as a destructive contemporary exhaustion, a failure to act which makes the individual an accomplice to cruelty on a private level as, in her earlier plays, she had shown it to be on a public level. But she is less convincing in establishing this dimension of a play which is at its best in creating the moralised landscape of the South. Indeed if Hellman is Chekhovian on the surface, beneath that she sees herself as a moralist, as a voice calling people to the real world of pain, of difficult moral choices, and of action whose consequences must be accepted if the individual is not to follow the South into a dangerous romanticism, a contemplation of the past which effectively destroys the present.

Lillian Hellman has spoken of the guilt which she felt as a result of her success as a writer in the 1930s, a guilt which eventually led her to political commitment. That commitment was never purely ideological. Certainly she never joined the Communist Party, as Dashiell Hammett almost certainly did. But it was sufficient to bring her to the notice of the House Un-American Activities Committee. In 1951 Hammett was sent to prison for refusing to give the names of the contributors to the jail bond fund of the Civil Rights Congress, of which he was a trustee. It was a testing time. Clifford Odets and Elia Kazan both named names. But when Lillian Hellman was called before the Committee she wrote a justifiably famous letter in which she offered to answer any questions about herself but declined to implicate anyone else. It was a dangerous stance, because it potentially deprived her of the right to take the Fifth Amendment (a protection against self-incrimination) while laying her open to contempt proceedings. But it was a direct statement of her liberal principles, a moral statement which is entirely consonant with the values expressed in her plays:

> to hurt innocent people whom I knew many years ago in order to save myself is, to me, inhuman and indecent and dishonorable. I cannot and I will not cut my conscience to fit this year's fashions, even though I long ago came to the conclusion that I was not a political person and could have no comfortable place in any political group.[49]

It was a stand which effectively deprived her of income from the movies and which forced her to sell her farm in order to meet the back taxes which the Internal Revenue Service suddenly decided that she owed. Like Arthur Miller she felt alienated from America, unsure as to whether she had an audience. And it was a decade before she wrote another original play.

Lillian Hellman, whose career began with a good play, ended with a better. She returned to the world of repressed sexuality, locating her play in a South whose own repressions and tensions heightened, and in some senses generated, the action. For the first time the fact of race obtrudes itself as at least a minor element in her work. In Scoundrel Time she admits that she was not insensitive to the fact that her mother's family had owed some of their wealth to 'the borrowings of poor Negroes',[50] a residual guilt which, wedded to an unstated awareness of sexual exploitation, was equally a guilt felt by the society at large. Stained with such guilt, the past could never be viewed unambiguously and is liable, as here, to be the source of a dangerous moral ambivalence, a pressure of meaning nonetheless real for remaining unstated.

These realities charge the atmosphere of *Toys in the Attic* (1960) with a kind of static energy. They are the buried facts which create the context for a play about more subtle forms of exploitation, about the power of sexuality and the desperate cruelties and simultaneous consolations of love. After a sequence of plays in which character· had been forced to serve symbolic purposes, *Toys in the Attic* engaged the individual psychologies of characters whose failure to understand themselves was the origin of much of their pain. It is a play which strays some distance into Tennessee Williams's territory, with its portrait of a woman kept in thrall by her rich gangster/businessman husband, of two sisters who live a life dominated by the past, of a mentally damaged but sexually liberated young girl and of a man whose battle for success is constantly thwarted. It is close in spirit to *Sweet Bird of Youth*. It is a play that expresses a sympathy for its damaged characters which had hardly characterised her previous work.

Carrie and Anna Berniers are middle-aged sisters living in a somewhat dilapidated house in New Orleans. They have, for a number of years, dedicated their lives to their brother Julian, whose attempts to achieve business success have all foundered. A year before, however, he had married Lily, the immature and mentally fragile daughter of the elegant and wealthy Albertine Prine. Now, however, Julian returns, suddenly wealthy. A former lover, desperate to leave her cruel and avaricious husband, has informed Julian of a land deal which enables him to charge her husband $150000 for two acres of swamp land. They are to divide the money equally, the woman escaping from her husband and Julian realising his dreams. But Lily misunderstands the relationship and, encouraged by Carrie, who harbours an incestuous love for Julian and wishes to reduce him to dependency again, betrays him. Julian is beaten and the woman badly injured. It is clear that in due course Carrie will tell Julian of his wife's action and hence drive her out.

Motives are mixed. There is a hint that Julian may have married Lily in return for money from her mother – money used to finance his sister's eye operation – while Albertine may have encouraged her daughter's marriage in order to be left alone with her Negro lover. Most crucial of all is the love which Carrie treasures for her brother but which she can no more face than can Julian the idea of failure. Hellman creates a society of desperate beings, destroyed by the myths and values of their society and by the passions which lead them to betray one another as well as to reach out across the social barriers.

Hellman no longer parades truth with the same assurance. The South is presented as historically wedded to untruth; in Albertine's words the Southern climate 'Puts mildew on the truth'.[51] But she also confesses that 'truth is often ugly. It burns.'[52] It is this fact, carelessly flourished, which leads to her husband's injuries; it is this truth which Anna uses against her sister when she accuses her of incestuous longings. And Carrie wields what is presumably the truth about her sister's eye operation and the conveniently simultaneous gift of money from Albertine as a weapon against Lily and as a means of destroying her brother's independence.

By contrast Anna has formerly kept from her sister the truth about their brother's affairs, so protecting her from a self-knowledge which might have been too hard to bear. And Albertine advises her daughter not to tell the truth of her betrayal: 'Can you have enough pity for him not to kill him with the truth?'[53] But, like O'Neill's *The Iceman Cometh*, the play is finally less concerned with debating the relative value of truth and illusion than with asserting the central need for compassion.

There are the familiar thematic elements. In the background is a corrupt and menacing capitalism, the threat of a violence stemming from greed. There is the same warning against inertia, against a failure to assume responsibility for one's life which was at the heart of *The Autumn Garden* though now a certain irony is apparent as this is pressed close to cliché ('The leaf came in the spring, stayed nice on the branch in the autumn until the winter winds would blow it in the snow. Mamma said that in the little time of holding on, a woman had to make ready for the winter ground where she would lie the rest of her life.'[54]). Hence the only urgency is to show a real concern, to neutralise a loneliness which is partly a birthright and partly a consequence of social imperatives; to place human before material values. And for this reason the relationship between Albertine and her Negro lover becomes paradigmatic.

In *Toys in the Attic* the South becomes less a place than an image. It becomes an apt expression of unrealised hopes and misdirected passions. The social and racial divisions underscore a natural gulf between people who are locked inside their own myths, dreams and memories. The action takes place in a decaying mansion. The characters are trapped by circumstance. Hellman's gothic figures bear the marks of an experience of loss and failure. They cling together united by situation and a need which they dare not articulate. And these alliances generate the potential for pain and consolation alike. The play displays a linguistic and dramatic reticence which she had seldom achieved before, although crucial facts are still flourished and relationships described which might better have been left unexpressed in language.

Lillian Hellman's works are realistic, well-made plays. They take place in private rooms which are meant to contain not merely private dramas but public issues. Her contribution to the American theatre clearly did not lie in her innovatory approach. Carefully structured and elaborately plotted, her plays were fiercely moral dramas. The South, which was the setting for some of her best plays, was not merely a moralised landscape but a set of myths and values which provided a resonance to the private dramas which were the centre of her concern. The neurotic girl, miscegenation, suggestions of incest, the vital but socially incapacitated young man, the fading spinster, the decaying mansion, are all recognisable elements of Southern writing from Poe onwards. That is to say they are familiar components of a myth which was created to convey a sense of a culture under strain, a world which embraced the trope of faded glory and of anarchy concealed beneath surface order, as a means of communicating a fundamental ambivalence. It was a culture which self-consciously looked to the past for its model as the North projected a future defined in terms of discontinuities. The threat of violence was a social fact become aesthetic device. The denial of history finds its parallel in a concern with individuals who never move to full maturity, who are damaged, whose innocence becomes a menacing fact. So it is here. Hellman's response to this myth is itself profoundly ambivalent. On the one hand she resisted its rationalisations, its corruption into simple lie, into cover for a rapacious materialism sheltering behind a false gentility, a style detached from the real. On the other hand she responded to its recognition of a deconstructive drive, its acknowledgement of decay, of loss, of wilful self-deceit, of a seemingly ineluctable tendency to deny responsibility for the past and involvement in the present, as an accurate account of the world which she had experienced.

The events of the 1930s and 40s had shown her the dangerous power of illusion, the desperate desire to cling to innocence in the face of overpowering evidence of a lethal anarchy; those of the 1950s had shown the readiness with which the individual was prepared to deny the past and hence any access to meaning in the present. So, too, the experience of her final years with Dashiell Hammett had taught her the painful truths of pain and suffering but equally the redemptive power of love. The moral neutrality of the Southern myth, its ability to obscure basic failures of perception and humanity, were too close to her experience of a quarter of a century of private and public life for her not to see it as an apt image for such hard-won truths. She had come to feel that self-obsession, of which incest is an appropriate symbol, and of which the Southern myth is an expression, was in many ways the primal sin. And if she was at her least effective as a writer when creating plays like *Watch on the Rhine* and *A Searching Wind* in which that proposition was stated explicitly and unequivocally, it remains the subtext of virtually all her work. She was aware that the love which she advanced as equally the basis of personal and social meaning was not untouched by this egotism, and expressed that ambivalence in her final play. But it was finally this love, imperfect, self-doubting, the source of anguish and doubt as well as of compassion and commitment, which she advanced as the only force with the power to neutralise absurdity, the decay of the human machine, the slow unmaking of meaning. The relationship between Albertine and her Negro lover, calm, understated, mutually supportive, sanctioned only by its own quality of restrained emotion, is surely a portrait of her own relationship with Dashiell Hammett. It was in a sense a valedictory, unsentimental, the more powerful for its discretion and its refusal of false rhetoric, for its confident assertion of mutuality. One year after the production of *Toys in the Attic* Dashiell Hammett died. With the exception of an adaptation, she never wrote another play.

I Harvard 47 plays 1913–17

George Pierce Baker established the first university course in playwriting in the United States at Harvard. This became known by the number of the course in the university curriculum – 47. The course was concerned with teaching the principles of playwriting to students from Harvard and Radcliffe. The Workshop Theatre was established in 1912.

Winter season, 1913

Lina Amuses Herself, W. Fenimore Merrill
Educated, Marian F. Winnek
Molly Make-Believe, Eleanor Halliwell Abbott Coburn

Winter season, 1913–14

Home Sweet Home, Violet Robinson
Maitre Patelin; Romance of the Rose, Sam Hume
The Call of the Mountain, Edwin Carty Ranck
His Women Folk, Abby Merchant
Why the Chimes Rang, Elizabeth McFadden
Ivan the Daring, Anna Sprague McDonald
The Revesby Sword Play

Winter season, 1914–15

The Only Girl in Sight, Caroline H. Budd
In for Himself, Mark W. Reed
Nothing but Money, Margaret Champney
Court Favor, adapted from Oscar Wilde's *The Infanta's Birthday* by Astrid Kimba
The Waves of Torre, Ethel Claire Randall
Between the Lines, Charlotte B. Chorpenning

Winter season, 1915–16

The Purple Dream, Donald L. Breed
The Rebound, Thomas P. Robinson
Plots and Playwrights, Edward Massey
Return of the Prodigal, Lewis Beach
The Other Voice, Sydney Fairbanks
Prudence in Particular, Rachael Barton Butler

Summer season, 1916

The Wonder-Worker, Lucy Wright
The Rescue, Rita C. Smith
The Florist Shop, Winifred Hawkbridge
The Glory of their Years, John Redhead Froome, Jr

Winter season, 1916–17

Will o' the Wisp, Doris F. Halman
The Colonel's Commupence, Katharine Clugston
Eyvind of the Hills, Johann Sigurjonsson
Rusted Stock, Doris F. Halman

2 Washington Square Players: Productions 1915–18

Washington Square plays

Lover's Luck, Georges Porto Riche
Sisters of Suzanna, Philip Moeller
Trifles, Susan Glaspell
Another Way Out, Lawrence Langner
Bushido, Takeda Izumo
Altruism, Karl Ettlinger
The Last Straw, Bosworth Crocker
A Private Account, Georges Courteline and Beatrice de Holthoir
The Hero of Santa Maria, Kenneth Sawyer Goodman and Ben Hecht
The Death of Tintagiles, Maurice Maeterlinck
The Life of Man, Leonid Andreyev
Plots and Playwrights, Edward Massey
Sganarelle, Molière
The Poor Fool, Hermann Bahr
Ghosts, Henrik Ibsen
The Hero of Santa Maria, Kenneth Sawyer Goodman and Ben Hecht
Pariah, August Strindberg
The Family Exit, Lawrence Langner
In the Zone, Eugene O'Neill
The Avenue, W. Fenimore Merrill
His Widow's Husband, Jacinto Benavente
The Critic's Comedy, Samuel Kaplan
Neighbours, Zona Gale
The Girl in the Coffin, Theodore Dreiser

1918

Habit, Frank Dare
Suppressed Desires, George Cram Cook and Susan Glaspell
The Sandbar Queen, George Cronyn
Pokey, Philip Moeller
Youth, Miles Malleson
Mrs Warren's Profession, George Bernard Shaw
The Home of the Free, Elmer Reizenstein (Rice)
Lonesome-Like, Harold Brighouse
Salomé, Oscar Wilde
Close the Book, Susan Glaspell
The Rope, Eugene O'Neill

3 Provincetown plays: 1915–27

Provincetown plays

Appendix 3

An Irish Triangle, Djuna Barnes
Money, Irwin Granich
Vote the New Moon, Alfred Kreymborg
Three Travellers Watch a Sunrise, Wallace Stevens
Pie, Lawrence Langner
Last Masks, Arthur Schnitzler
Kurzy of the Sea, Djuna Barnes
Exorcism, Eugene O'Neill

1920–21

Matinata, Lawrence Langner
The Emperor Jones, Eugene O'Neill
What D'You Want? Lawrence Vail
Different, Eugene O'Neill
The Spring, George Cram Cook
Love, Evelyn Scott
Inheritors, Susan Glaspell
Grotesques, Cloyd Head

1921–22

The Verge, Susan Glaspell
The Hand of the Potter, Theodore Dreiser
A Little Act of Justice, Norman C. Lindau
Footsteps, Donald Corley
The Stick-up, Pierre Loving
The Hairy Ape, Eugene O'Neill
Chains of Dew, Susan Glaspell

1923–24

After an interim of one season, the Provincetown Playhouse reopened under the direction of Kenneth Macgowan, Robert Edmond Jones and Eugene O'Neill.
The Spook Sonata, August Strindberg
Fashion, Anna Cora Mowatt
Georges Dandin, Molière
The Ancient Mariner, arranged by Eugene O'Neill
All God's Chillun Got Wings, Eugene O'Neill

1924–25

Operated jointly with the Greenwich Village Theatre, under the direction of Kenneth Macgowan, Robert Edmond Jones, Eugene O'Neill and James Light, at the Provincetown Playhouse.

Provincetown plays

The Crime in the Whistler Room, Edmund Wilson
Patience, W. S. Gilbert and Arthur Sullivan
Michel Auclair, Charles Vildrac
Beyond, Walter Hasenclever
Ruint, Hatcher Hughes
At the Greenwich Village Theatre
The Saint, by Stark Young
Desire Under the Elms, Eugene O'Neill
Love for Love, William Congreve

1925–26

Under the direction of James Light, M. Eleanor Fitzgerald, Harold McGee, Cleon Throckmorton and Henry G. Alsberg.
Adam Solitaire, Em Jo Basshe
The Man Who Never Died, Charles Webster
The Dream Play, August Strindberg
East Lynne, Mrs Henry Wood
Orpheus, Christoph Gluck

1926–27

Princess Turandot, Gozzi. Adapted by Henry G. Alsberg and Isaac Don Levine
In Abraham's Bosom, Paul Green
La Finta Giardiniera (Intimate Opera Company), W. A. Mozart
Rapid Transit, Lajos N. Egri

4 Theatre Guild productions: 1919–40

This list is based in part on bibliographical material to be found in Walter Pritchard Eaton, *The Theatre Guild: The First Ten Years* (New York, 1929); and Roy S. Waldau, *Vintage Years of the Theatre Guild, 1928–1939* (Cleveland, 1972).

1919

The Bonds of Interest, Jacinto Benavente
John Ferguson, St John Ervine
The Faithful, John Masefield
The Rise of Silas Lapham, Lillian Sabine

1920

Power of Darkness, Leo Tolstoy
Jane Clegg, St John Ervine
The Dance of Death, August Strindberg
The Treasure, David Pinski
Heartbreak House, George Bernard Shaw

1921

John Hawthorne, David Liebovitz
Mr Pim Passes By, A. A. Milne
Liliom, Ferenc Molnar
The Cloister, Emile Verhaeren
Ambush, Arthur Richman
The Wife with a Smile, Denys Amiel and Andre Obey
Bourbouroche, Georges Courteline

1922

He Who Gets Slapped, Leonid Andreyev
Back to Methuselah, George Bernard Shaw
What the Public Wants, Arnold Bennett
From Morn to Midnight, Georg Kaiser
R.U.R., Karel Capek
The Lucky One, A. A. Milne
The Tidings Brought to Mary, Paul Claudel

Theatre Guild plays

1923

Peer Gynt, Henrik Ibsen
The Adding Machine, Elmer Rice
The Devil's Disciple, George Bernard Shaw
Windows, John Galsworthy
The Failures, H. R. Lenormand
The Race with the Shadow, Wilhelm von Scholz
Saint Joan, George Bernard Shaw

1924

Fata Morgana, Ernest Vajda
Man and the Masses, Ernst Toller
The Guardsman, Ferenc Molnar
They Knew What They Wanted, Sidney Howard

1925

Processional, John Howard Lawson
Ariadne, A. A. Milne
Caesar and Cleopatra, George Bernard Shaw
The Garrick Gaieties, Richard Rodgers and Lorenz Hart
Arms and the Man, George Bernard Shaw
The Glass Slipper, Ferenc Molnar
The Man of Destiny, George Bernard Shaw
Androcles and the Lion, George Bernard Shaw
Merchants of Glory, Marcel Pagnol and Paul Nivoix

1926

Goat Song, Franz Werfel
The Chief Thing, Nikolai Evreinov
At Mrs Beam's, C. K. Monro
The Garrick Gaieties, Richard Rodgers and Lorenz Hart
Juarez and Maximilian, Franz Werfel
Pygmalion, George Bernard Shaw
Ned McCobb's Daughter, Sidney Howard
The Silver Cord, Sidney Howard

1927

The Brothers Karamazov, Jacques Copeau, based on Dostoevsky's novel
Right You Are If You Think You Are, Luigi Pirandello
The Second Man, S. N. Behrman

Porgy, Du Bose and Dorothy Heyward
The Doctor's Dilemma, George Bernard Shaw

1928

Marco Millions, Eugene O'Neill
Strange Interlude, Eugene O'Neill
Volpone, Stefan Zweig's version of Ben Jonson's play
Goethe's Faust (Part I), Graham and Tristan Rawson
Major Barbara, George Bernard Shaw
Wings Over Europe, Robert Nichols and Maurice Browne
Caprice, Sil-Vara

1929

Dynamo, Eugene O'Neill
Man's Estate, Beatrice Blackmar and Bruce Gould
The Camel Through the Needle's Eye, Franktisek Langer
Karl and Anna, Leonhard Frank
The Game of Love and Death, Romain Rolland
Red Rust, V. Kirchon and A. Ouspensky
Meteor, S. N. Behrman

1930

The Apple Cart, George Bernard Shaw
A Month in the Country, Ivan Turgenev
Hotel Universe, Philip Barry
The Garrick Gaieties (various authors)
Roar China, S. M. Tretyakov
Elizabeth the Queen, Maxwell Anderson
Midnight, Claire and Paul Sifton

1931

Green Grow the Lilacs, Lynn Riggs
Miracle at Verdun, Hans Chlumberg
Getting Married, George Bernard Shaw
He, Alfred Savoir
The House of Connelly, Paul Green
Mourning Becomes Electra, Eugene O'Neill
Reunion in Vienna, Robert E. Sherwood

Theatre Guild plays

1932

The Moon in the Yellow River, Denis Johnston
Too True to be Good, George Bernard Shaw
The Good Earth, Owen Davis and Donald Davis from the novel by Pearl S. Buck
Biography, S. N. Behrman

1933

American Dream, George O'Neil
Both Your Houses, Maxwell Anderson
The Mask and the Face, W. Somerset Maugham (translated from the Italian of Luigi Chiarelli)
Ah Wilderness!, Eugene O'Neill
The School for Husbands, Arthur Guiterman and Lawrence Langner
Mary of Scotland, Maxwell Anderson
Days Without End, Eugene O'Neill

1934

They Shall Not Die, John Wexley
Races, Ferdinand Bruckner
Jig Saw, Dawn Powell
A Sleeping Clergyman, James Bridie
Valley Forge, Maxwell Anderson
Rain from Heaven, S. N. Behrman

1935

Escape Me Never, Margaret Kennedy
The Simpleton of the Unexpected Isles, George Bernard Shaw
Parade (various authors)
If This Be Treason, the Rev. Dr John Haynes Holmes and Reginald Lawrence
The Taming of the Shrew, William Shakespeare
Porgy and Bess (founded on the play *Porgy* by Du Bose and Dorothy Heyward)

1936

Call it a Day, Dodie Smith
End of Summer, S. N. Behrman
Idiot's Delight, Robert E. Sherwood
And Stars Remain, Julius J. and Philip G. Epstein
Prelude to Exile, William McNally
Jane Eyre, Helen Jerome (a dramatisation of Charlotte Brontë's novel)

1937

But for the Grace of God, Leopold Atlas
The Masque of Kings, Maxwell Anderson
Storm Over Patsy, Bruno Frank
To Quito and Back, Ben Hecht
Amphitryon 38, Jean Giradoux (adapted by S. N. Behrman)
Madame Bovary, Gaston Baty (dramatisation of Flaubert's novel)
The Ghost of Yankee Doodle, Sidney Howard
Wine of Choice, S. N. Behrman

1938

The Seagull, Anton Chekhov (Alfred Lunt and Lynn Fontanne production)
Washington Jitters, John Boruff and Walter Hart
Dame Nature, Andre Birabeau
The Merchant of Yonkers, Thornton Wilder

1939

Jeremiah, Stefan Zweig
Five Kings (Part I), Orson Welles
The Philadelphia Story, Philip Barry
My Heart's in the Highlands, William Saroyan
The Time of your Life, William Saroyan

1940

The Fifth Column, Ernest Hemingway
There Shall Be No Night, Robert E. Sherwood
Love's Old Sweet Song, William Saroyan
Twelfth Night, William Shakespeare
Battle of Angels, Tennessee Williams

5 Group Theatre plays: 1931–40

1931

The House of Connelly, Paul Green
1931, Claire and Paul Sifton

1932

Night Over Taos, Maxwell Anderson
Success Story, John Howard Lawson

1933

Big Night, Dawn Powell
Men in White, Sidney S. Kingsley

1934

Gentlewoman, John Howard Lawson
Gold Eagle Guy, Melvin Levy

1935

Awake and Sing!, Clifford Odets
Waiting for Lefty, Clifford Odets
Till the Day I Die, Clifford Odets
Weep for the Virgins, Nellise Child
Paradise Lost, Clifford Odets

1936

Case of Clyde Griffiths, Erwin Piscator and Lena Goldschmidt
Johnny Johnson, Paul Green

1937

Golden Boy, Clifford Odets

Appendix 5

1938

Casey Jones, Robert Ardrey
Rocket to the Moon, Clifford Odets

1939

The Gentle People, Irwin Shaw
My Heart's in the Highlands, William Saroyan
Thunder Rock, Robert Ardrey

1940

Night Music, Clifford Odets
Retreat to Pleasure, Irwin Shaw

6 Federal Theatre Living Newspapers*

Living Newspaper	Author(s)	Produced/Unproduced
Dirt	Don Farran Ruth Stewart	Unproduced
Ethiopia	Arthur Arent	One performance for press, 1936
Flood Control (scenario)	Richard Oliver	Unproduced
The High Walls	John M. Caldwell	Unproduced
Hookworm (scenario)	Herb Meadow	Unproduced
Injunction Granted	Living Newspaper Staff	Produced, 1936
Just Politics	San Francisco Theatre Union	Unproduced
King Cotton	Betty Smith Robert Finch William Peery Clemon White	Unproduced
Land Grant	T. C. Robinson Kena M. Vale	Unproduced
Liberty Deferred	Abram Hill John Silvera	Unproduced
† *Living Newspaper Follies*	Lawrence Martin Sylvia Martin	Unproduced
Living Newspaper Lives (scenario)		Unproduced
Medicine Show	Living Newspaper staff	Produced after closure of Federal Theatre Project
‡ *Men at Work*	Howard McGrath	Produced, n.d.
Milk (scenario)	Max Gandbard	Unproduced
1935	Arthur Arent	Produced, 1936
One Third of a Nation	Arthur Arent	Produced, 1938
Poor Little Consumer	Robert Russell	Unproduced
Power	Arthur Arent	Produced, 1937
Russia (fragment)	Living Newspaper staff	Unproduced
Scenario/Colossal/Horse Opera	Emmet Lavery John McGee	Unproduced
The South	Living Newspaper staff	Unproduced
Spanish Grant	Eugene Deaderick Max Mansbach Lorin Raker	Unproduced

* Based on a list of scripts held at the Research Center for the Federal Theatre Project, George Mason University. (See their publication, *Federal One*, I, i (November 1975), pp. 3–5.)

† Hallie Flanagan lists two further productions, *Living Newspaper, First Edition* and *Living Newspaper, Second Edition*, 1936, in *Arena: The History of the Federal Theatre*.

‡ Not listed by Flanagan or Jane De Hart Mathews, in *The Federal Theatre, 1935–1939: Plays, Relief and Politics*.

Appendix 6

Spirochete	Arnold Sundgaard	Produced, 1938
Stars and Bars		Unproduced
Straphanger (A British Living Newspaper)	Otis Chatfield-Taylor	Unproduced
Tapestry in Linen	Shotwell Callvert	Unproduced
The Ten Million	William Dorsey Blake	Unproduced
Timber	Myrtle Mary Moss Burke Ormsby	Unproduced
Townsend Goes to Town	George Murray David Peltz	Unproduced
Triple A Plowed Under	Living Newspaper staff	Produced, 1936
War (first draft)	Living Newspaper staff	Unproduced
War and Taxes (first draft)	Living Newspaper staff	Unproduced

NOTES

1 Provincetown: the birth of twentieth-century American drama

1 George Steiner, *The Death of Tragedy* (London, 1961), p. 109.
2 Anthony Caputi, ed., *Modern Drama* (New York, 1966), p. 318.
3 William Coyle and Harvey G. Damaser, eds., *Six Early American Plays* (Columbus, 1968), p. 205.
4 *Ibid.*, p. 270.
5 Quoted in Lise-Lone Marker's *David Belasco: Naturalism in the American Theatre* (Princeton, 1975), p. 9.
6 David Belasco, *The Theatre Through Its Stage Door* (New York, 1919, reprinted 1969), p. 61.
7 *Ibid.*, p. 77.
8 Adolphe Appia, *Music and the Art of the Theatre*, trans. Robert W. Corrigan and Mary Douglas Dirks (Miami, 1962), pp. 7-8.
9 Floyd Dell, *Homecoming: An Autobiography* (New York, 1969), p. 218.
10 *Ibid.*, pp. 216-17.
11 Arthur Waterman, *Susan Glaspell* (New York, 1966), p. 47.
12 *Ibid.*, p. 53.
13 Hutchins Hapgood, *A Victorian in the Modern World* (New York, 1939), p. 379.
14 Susan Glaspell, *The Road to the Temple* (London, 1926), p. 167.
15 *Ibid.*, p. 171.
16 *Ibid.*, p. 189.
17 *Ibid.*, p. 192.
18 *Ibid.*, p. 194.
19 Oliver Sayler, *Our American Theatre* (New York, 1923), p. 91.
20 *Ibid.*, pp. 73-4.
21 Dell, *Homecoming*, pp. 265-6.
22 *Ibid.*, p. 267.
23 Arnold Goldman, 'The culture of the Provincetown Players', *Journal of American Studies*, XII, iii (December, 1978), 304.
24 Appia, *Music and the Art of the Theatre*, pp. 4-5.
25 Glaspell, *Road to the Temple*, p. 222.
26 Robert Edmond Jones, *The Dramatic Imagination* (New York, 1941), p. 77.
27 *Ibid.*, p. 82.
28 Appia, *Music and the Art of the Theatre*, p. 5.
29 *Ibid.*, p. 33.
30 Sayler, *Our American Theatre*, p. 97.
31 Travis Bogard, *Contours of Time* (New York, 1972), pp. 73-4.

32 *Ibid.*, p. 176.
33 Sayler, *Our American Theatre*, p. 78.
34 *Ibid.*, p. 79.
35 *Ibid.*, p. 87.
36 *Ibid.*, p. 84.
37 Susan Glaspell, *Plays* (Boston, 1920), p. 27.
38 *Ibid.*, p. 190.
39 *Ibid.*, p. 188.
40 *Ibid.*, p. 107.
41 Susan Glaspell, *Inheritors* (London, 1924), p. 29.
42 *Ibid.*, p. 101.
43 Waterman, *Susan Glaspell*, p. 79.
44 Susan Glaspell, *The Verge* (Boston, 1922), p. 10.
45 *Ibid.*, p. 20.
46 *Ibid.*
47 *Ibid.*, p. 29.
48 *Ibid.*, p. 53.
49 *Ibid.*, p. 54.
50 *Ibid.*, p. 59.
51 *Ibid.*, p. 62.
52 *Ibid.*, p. 47.
53 Waterman, *Susan Glaspell*, p. 81.
54 Montrose J. Moses and John Mason Brown, *The American Theatre As Seen By Its Critics: 1752–1934* (New York, 1934), pp. 254–5.
55 Thomas Dickinson, *Playwrights of the American Theatre* (St Claire Shores, 1972), p. 211.

2 Eugene O'Neill

1 Arthur and Barbara Gelb, *Eugene O'Neill* (New York, 1973), p. 147.
2 Oscar Cargill et al., *O'Neill and His Plays* (New York, 1961), p. 107.
3 *Ibid.*, p. 104.
4 Arthur Schopenhauer, *Complete Essays*, trans. T. Bailey Saunders (New York, 1942), book 4, p. 56.
5 Arthur Schopenhauer, *The World as Will and Representation*, trans. E. F. J. Payne (New York, 1966), p. 560.
6 Sigmund Freud, *Beyond the Pleasure Principle, The Standard Edition of The Complete Works*, vol. XVIII (London, 1955), p. 38.
7 *Ibid.*, pp. 49–50.
8 Eugene O'Neill, *Strange Interlude* (London, 1928), p. 73.
9 Egil Tornquist, *A Drama of Souls: Studies in O'Neill's Super-Naturalistic Technique* (New Haven, 1968), pp. 13–14.
10 Susan Glaspell, *Inheritors* (London, 1924), p. 29.
11 Letter to Arthur Hobson Quinn.
12 Schopenhauer, *Complete Essays*, p. 75.

13 Friedrich Nietzsche, *Thus Spake Zarathustra*, trans. R. J. Hollingdale (Harmondsworth, 1961), p. 216.

14 *Ibid.*, p. 59.

15 Gelbs, *Eugene O'Neill*, pp. 260–1.

16 Nietzsche, *Zarathustra*, pp. 21–2.

17 *Ibid.*, p. 141.

18 *Ibid.*, p. 143.

19 Cargill, *O'Neill*, p. 129.

20 Gelbs, p. 260.

21 Eugene O'Neill, *The Plays of Eugene O'Neill* (New York, 1955), p. 468.

22 *Ibid.*, p. 471.

23 Nietzsche, *Zarathustra*, p. 26.

24 *Ibid.*, p. 668.

25 *Ibid.*, p. 72.

26 Eugene O'Neill, *'Beyond the Horizon' and 'Marco Millions'* (London, 1960), p. 162.

27 *Ibid.*, pp. 95–6.

28 *Ibid.*, p. 175.

29 Gelbs, p. 5.

30 Friedrich Nietzsche, *The Will to Power*, trans. W. Kaufmann and R. J. Hollingdale

31 Friedrich Nietzsche, *The Gay Science*, trans. W. Kaufmann (New York, 1974), p. 9.

32 Eugene O'Neill, *'The Emperor Jones', 'The Straw' and 'Diffrent'* (London, 1958), p. 195.

33 Karl Gustav Jung, *The Portable Jung* (New York, 1971), p. 60.

34 O'Neill, *The Emperor Jones*, p. 270.

35 Freud, *Standard Edition*, vol. v, trans. James Strachey (London, 1958), p. 613.

36 *Ibid.*, vol. vi, p. 258.

37 *Ibid.*, vol. vi, p. 259.

38 *Ibid.*, vol. vi, p. 260.

39 Robert Edmond Jones, *The Dramatic Imagination* (New York, 1941), p. 26.

40 Eugene O'Neill, *All God's Chillun Got Wings* in E. Martin Browne, ed., *Eugene O'Neill* (Harmondsworth, 1966), pp. 203–4.

41 *Ibid.*, p. 223.

42 *Ibid.*, p. 228.

43 *Ibid.*, p. 234.

44 Freud, *Standard Edition*, vol. xiii, trans. James Strachey (London, 1958), p. 17.

45 O'Neill, *All God's Chillun Got Wings*, p. 217.

46 Freud, *Complete Works*, vol. xiii, p. 17.

47 Gelbs, p. 537.

48 O'Neill, *All God's Chillun Got Wings*, p. 204.

49 O'Neill, *The Hairy Ape* (London, 1923, rpt 1958), pp. 30–1.

50 *Ibid.*, p. 35.

51 *Ibid.*, p. 50.

52 *Ibid.*, pp. 13–15.

53 *Ibid.*, p. 20.

54 *Ibid.*
55 *Ibid.*, pp. 71–2.
56 *Ibid.*, pp. 76–88.
57 *Ibid.*, p. 5.
58 Eugene O'Neill, *Desire Under the Elms* in E. Martin Browne, ed., *Eugene O'Neill*, p. 314.
59 *Ibid.*
60 Edgar F. Racey, Jr., 'Myth as tragic structure in *Desire Under the Elms*', in John Gassner, ed., *O'Neill* (Englewood Cliffs, 1964), p. 59.
61 Isaac Goldberg, *The Theatre of George Jean Nathan* (New York, 1968), p. 135.
62 *Ibid.*, p. 159.
63 O'Neill, *Strange Interlude*, p. 305.
64 Tornquist, *A Drama of Souls*, p. 20.
65 Eugene O'Neill, 'On Masks', Yale Collection.
66 Eugene O'Neill, '*The Great God Brown*' and '*Lazarus Laughed*' (London, 1960), p. 47.
67 *Ibid.*, p. 63.
68 Walter Kaufmann, *Basic Writings of Nietzsche* (New York, 1966), p. 42.
69 Travis Bogard, *Contours of Time* (New York, 1972), p. 280.
70 O'Neill, '*The Great God Brown*' and '*Lazarus Laughed*', p. 60.
71 Nietzsche, *Zarathustra*, p, 304.
72 *Ibid.*, p. 247.
73 O'Neill, *Lazarus Laughed*, p. 121.
74 Arthur Schopenhauer, *Essays and Aphorisms*, trans. R. J. Hollingdale (Harmondsworth, 1970), pp. 72–3.
75 Eugene O'Neill, Letter to Joseph Wood Krutch, 15 July 1927, Yale Collection.
76 *Ibid.*
77 *Ibid.*
78 O'Neill, *Strange Interlude*, p. 11.
79 *Ibid.*, p. 24.
80 *Ibid.*, p. 30.
81 *Ibid.*, p. 71.
82 *Ibid.*, p. 72.
83 *Ibid.*, p. 156.
84 *Ibid.*, p. 73.
85 *Ibid.*, p. 291.
86 Schopenhauer, *Complete Essays*, book 2, p. 139.
87 O'Neill, *Strange Interlude*, p. 11.
88 Schopenhauer, *The World as Will and Representation*, vol. XII, p. 542.
89 *Ibid.*, p. 535.
90 O'Neill, *Strange Interlude*, p. 40.
91 O'Neill, Letter to Joseph Wood Krutch, 11 June 1929, Yale Collection.
92 Bogard, *Contours of Time*, p. 320.
93 *Ibid.*, p. 321.
94 Eugene O'Neill, *Mourning Becomes Electra* (London, 1973), p. 92.

95 *Mourning Becomes Electra* (Working notes and extracts from a fragmentary diary), Yale Collection, p. 2.
96 *Ibid.*, p. 5.
97 *Ibid.*
98 Eugene O'Neill, *Mourning Becomes Electra* (London, 1973), p. 92.
99 *Ibid.*, p. 9.
100 *Ibid.*, p. 92.
101 Bogard, *Contours of Time*, p. 340.
102 O'Neill, *Mourning Becomes Electra*, p. 19.
103 *Ibid.*, p. 222.
104 *Ibid.*, p. 228.
105 *Ibid.*, p. 242.
106 *Ibid.*, p. 252.
107 George Steiner, *The Death of Tragedy* (London, 1961), p. 326.
108 *Ibid.*, p. 327.
109 Cargill, *O'Neill*, p. 111.
110 Ms. of *The Iceman Cometh*, act 4, p. 30. Yale Collection.
111 Eugene O'Neill, *The Iceman Cometh* (London, 1966), p. 16.
112 Ms. of *The Iceman Cometh*, act 3, p. 28.
113 Letter from O'Neill to Lawrence Langner in John Henry Raleigh, ed., *Twentieth-Century Interpretations of 'The Iceman Cometh'* (Englewood Cliffs, 1968), p. 20.
114 O'Neill, *The Iceman Cometh*, p. 114.
115 Ms. of *The Iceman Cometh*, act 1, p. 5.
116 O'Neill, *The Iceman Cometh*, p. 180.
117 Albert Camus, *Carnets 1942–1951*, trans. Philip Thody (London, 1966), p. 103.
118 Eugene O'Neill, *'Ah Wilderness!' and 'Days Without End'* (London, 1958), p. 20.
119 *Ibid.*, pp. 64–5.
120 *Ibid.*, p. 79.
121 John Dewey, *Art as Experience* (New York, 1934), p. 16.
122 *Ibid.*, p. 17.
123 *Ibid.*, p. 18.
124 *Ibid.*, p. 17.
125 Eugene O'Neill, *Long Day's Journey Into Night* (New Haven, 1956), p. 45.
126 Ms scenario for *Long Day's Journey Into Night*. Yale Collection.
127 *Ibid.*
128 O'Neill's *Long Day's Journey Into Night*, p. 176.
129 *Ibid.*, p. 61.
130 *Ibid.*, p. 76.
131 *Ibid.*, p. 85.
132 *Ibid.*, p. 97.
133 *Ibid.*, p. 97.
134 *Ibid.*, p. 131.
135 *Ibid.*, p. 153.
136 *Ibid.*, p. 154.
137 *Ibid.*, p. 153.

138 Eugene O'Neill, *A Touch of the Poet* (New Haven, 1959), p. 145.
139 George Steiner, *After Babel* (London, 1975), p. 218.
140 *Ibid.*, p. 227.
141 *Ibid.*, p. 228.
142 *Ibid.*, pp. 297–8.
143 Eugene O'Neill, *Hughie* (London, 1962), p. 36.
144 Eugene O'Neill, *Moon for the Misbegotten* (London, 1953), p. 121.
145 Eugene O'Neill, *More Stately Mansions* (London, 1965), p. 57.
146 W. David Sievers, *Freud on Broadway: History of Psychoanalysis and the American Drama* (New York, 1955), p. 108.
147 Sigmund Freud, *Totem and Taboo*, trans. A. A. Brill (New York, 1927), p. 158.
148 O'Neill, *More Stately Mansions*, p. 40.
149 *Ibid.*, p. 40.
150 *Ibid.*, p. 48.
151 *Ibid.*, p. 54.
152 *Ibid.*, p. 57.
153 *Ibid.*, p. 175.
154 *Ibid.*, p. 178.
155 *Ibid.*, p. 29.
156 Paul West, *The Wine of Absurdity* (University Park, 1966), pp. xiii–xix.
157 *Ibid.*, p. 58.
158 Frederick J. Hoffman, *Freudianism and the Literary Mind* (Baton Rouge, 1957), p. 301.
159 *Ibid.*, p. 300.
160 Georg Lukács, *Writer and Critic* (London, 1970), p. 51.

3 The Theatre Guild and its playwrights

1 Walter Pritchard Eaton, *The Theatre Guild: The First Ten Years* (New York, 1929), pp. 43–4.
2 *Ibid.*, p. 207.
3 Erich Fromm, *The Fear of Freedom* (London, 1960), p. 29.
4 *Ibid.*, pp. 29–30.
5 *Ibid.*, p. 103.
6 Robert Hogan, *The Independence of Elmer Rice* (Carbondale, 1965), p. 67.
7 *Ibid.*, p. 16.
8 Elmer Rice, *The Living Theatre* (New York, 1959), p. 118.
9 Elmer Rice, *Minority Report: An Autobiography* (London, 1963), pp. 190–1.
10 *Ibid.*, pp. 198–9.
11 *Ibid.*, p. 237.
12 Elmer Rice, *Three Plays* (New York, 1965), p. 122.
13 *Ibid.*, pp. 155–6.
14 Letter from Elmer Rice to Barrett Clark. Yale Collection.
15 Philip Barry, *States of Grace: Eight Plays of Philip Barry* (New York, 1975), p. 276.
16 *Ibid.*, p. 558.

17 William Saroyan, '*The Time of your Life*' *and Two Other Plays* (London, 1942), pp. 6–7.

18 *Ibid.*, pp. 7–8.

19 *Ibid.*, p. 9.

20 *Ibid.*, p. 11.

21 *Ibid.*, p. 12.

22 *Ibid.*, p. 18.

23 *Ibid.*, p. 16.

24 *Ibid.*, p. 15.

25 *Ibid.*, p. 85.

26 *Ibid.*, pp. 104–5.

27 Budd Schulberg, *The Four Seasons of Success* (London, 1974), p. 80.

28 *Ibid.*, p. 58.

29 *Ibid.*, p. 69.

30 *Famous Plays of 1933–4* (London, 1934) p. 252.

31 *Ibid.*, p. 256.

32 *Ibid.*, p. 257.

33 *Ibid.*, p. 258.

34 John Mason Brown, *The Worlds of Robert Sherwood: Mirror to his Time* (New York, 1962), p. 277.

35 Robert Sherwood, *The Petrified Forest* in John Gassner, ed., *American Drama* (New York, 1960), p. 194.

36 *Ibid.*, p. 200.

37 John Mason Brown, *Worlds of Robert Sherwood*, p. 319.

38 *Ibid.*, p. 329.

39 *Ibid.*, pp. 333–4.

40 *Famous American Plays of the 1930s* (New York, 1959), p. 224.

41 *Ibid.*, p. 233.

42 *Ibid.*, p. 237.

43 John Gassner, ed., *Best Plays of the Modern Theatre* (New York, 1947), pp. 772–3.

44 Robert E. Sherwood, *Idiot's Delight* (New York, 1936), pp. 189–90.

45 Robert E. Sherwood, *There Shall Be No Night* (New York, 1940), p. xxix.

46 Walter Meserve, *Robert E. Sherwood* (New York, 1970), p. 144.

47 Maxwell Anderson, *Off-Broadway* (New York, 1947), p. 26.

48 Kathryn Coe and William H. Cordell, *The Pulitzer Prize Plays 1918–1934* (New York, 1935), p. 774.

49 *Ibid.*, p. 793.

50 Mabel Driscoll Bailey, *Maxwell Anderson: The Playwright as Prophet* (New York, 1957), p. 57.

51 Anderson, *Off-Broadway*, p. 50.

52 *Ibid.*, p. 28.

53 *Ibid.*, p. 48.

54 Maxwell Anderson, *Winterset*, in *Eleven Verse Plays* (New York, 1948), p. 7.

55 *Ibid.*, pp. 133–4.

56 *Ibid.*, p. 129.

57 John Mason Brown, *Dramatis Personae: A Retrospective Show* (London, 1963), p. 75.
58 *Ibid.*, p. 76.
59 Maxwell Anderson, *Key Largo* in *Eleven Verse Plays*, p. 21.
60 *Ibid.*, pp. 22–3.
61 *Ibid.*, p. 90.
62 *Ibid.*, pp. 110–11.
63 *Ibid.*, pp. 111–12.
64 Denis Donohue, *The Third Voice* (London, 1959), frontispiece.
65 *Ibid.*, p. 13.

4 The Group Theatre and Clifford Odets

1 Harold Clurman, *The Fervent Years: The Story of the Group Theatre and the Thirties* (London, 1946), p. 48.
2 *Ibid.*, p. 58.
3 *Ibid.*, p. 72.
4 *Ibid.*, p. 79.
5 *Ibid.*, p. 92.
6 *Ibid.*, p. 120.
7 *Ibid.*, p. 130.
8 Suzanne O'Malley, 'America's rival acting schools', *Dialogue*, XIII, i, 72.
9 Clurman, *The Fervent Years*, p. 272.
10 *Famous Plays of 1936* (London, 1936), p. 525.
11 *Ibid.*, p. 545.
12 *Ibid.*, p. 551.
13 *Ibid.*, p. 568.
14 *Ibid.*, p. 559.
15 *Ibid.*, p. 554.
16 Michel Contat and Michel Rybalka, *Sartre on Theatre* (New York, 1976), pp. 4–5.
17 *Famous Plays of 1936*, p. 568.
18 Leon Trotsky, *Literature and Revolution* (Ann Arbor, 1968), pp. 137–8.
19 Clarke A. Chambers, *The New Deal at Home and Abroad, 1929–1945* (New York, 1965), pp. 71–2.
20 Clifford Odets, *Six Plays by Clifford Odets* (New York, 1979, originally published 1939), p. 96.
21 Gerald Weales, *Clifford Odets* (New York, 1971), p. 68.
22 Odets, *Six Plays*, pp. 50–51.
23 *Ibid.*, p. 97.
24 *Ibid.*, p. 47.
25 *Ibid.*, pp. 100–1.
26 Weales, *Clifford Odets*, p. 72.
27 Clurman, *The Fervent Years*, pp. 150–1.
28 Weales, *Clifford Odets*, p. 92.
29 *Ibid.*, p. 166.
30 Odets, *Six Plays*, p. 191.

31 *Ibid.*
32 *Ibid.*, p. 199.
33 *Ibid.*, p. 224.
34 *Ibid.*, p. 229.
35 Clurman, *The Fervent Years*, p. 205.
36 Odets, *Golden Boy* (Harmondsworth, 1963), p. 106.
37 *Ibid.*, p. 52.
38 *Ibid.*
39 *Ibid.*, p. 72.
40 *Ibid.*, pp. 53–4.
41 *Ibid.*, p. 93.
42 *Ibid.*, p. 183.
43 *Ibid.*, p. 95.
44 *Ibid.*, p. 105.
45 *Ibid.*, p. 106.
46 *Ibid.*, p. 108.
47 Odets, *Six Plays*, p. 416.
48 *Ibid.*, p. 418.
49 Clifford Odets, *Night Music* (New York, 1940), p. 235.
50 Clurman, *The Fervent Years*, pp. 266–7.

5 Left-wing theatre

1 Michael Folsom, ed., *Mike Gold: A Literary Anthology* (New York, 1972), p. 62.
2 *Ibid.*, p. 67.
3 *Ibid.*, p. 69.
4 *Ibid.*, p. 70.
5 *Ibid.*, p. 65.
6 *Ibid.*, p. 66.
7 *Ibid.*, p. 67.
8 Jean-Paul Sartre, *What Is Literature?* trans. Bernard Frechtman (New York, 1965), p. 279.
9 Leon Trotsky, *Literature and Revolution* (Ann Arbor, 1968), p. 186.
10 *Ibid.*, p. 164.
11 *Ibid.*, p. 200.
12 *Ibid.*, p. 202.
13 *Ibid.*, p. 205.
14 *Ibid.*
15 *Ibid.*
16 Michel Contat and Michel Rybalka, *Sartre on Theatre* (New York, 1976), p. 41.
17 Trotsky, *Literature and Revolution*, p. 209.
18 George A. Knox and Herbert M. Stahl, *Dos Passos and the Revolting Playwrights* (Lund, 1964), p. 21.
19 *Ibid.*, pp. 8–9.
20 *Ibid.*, p. 9.

21 Jay Williams, *Stage Left* (New York, 1974), p. 14.
22 *Ibid.*, p. 31.
23 *Ibid.*, p. 43.
24 *Ibid.*, p. 46.
25 *Ibid.*, p. 48.
26 Van Wyck Brooks, Lewis Mumford, Alfred Kreymborg, Paul Rosenfeld eds., *The American Caravan* (London, 1927), p. 548.
27 *Ibid.*, p. 549.
28 *Ibid.*, p. 584.
29 *Ibid.*, p. 592.
30 *Ibid.*, p. 595.
31 *Ibid.*, pp. 588–9.
32 *Ibid.*, pp. 603–4.
33 *Ibid.*, p. 626.
34 John Dos Passos, *The Garbage Man* (New York, 1926), p. 53.
35 *Ibid.*, p. 151.
36 *Ibid.*, p. 158.
37 Karen Taylor, *People's Theatre in America* (New York, 1972), p. 9.
38 *Ibid.*, pp. 10-11.
39 *Ibid.*, p. 27.
40 *Ibid.*, p. 29.
41 Malcolm Goldstein, *The Political Stage: The American Drama and Theatre of the Great Depression* (New York, 1974), pp. 31–2.
42 Harold Clurman, *The Fervent Years: The Story of the Group Theatre and the Thirties* (London, 1946), pp. 147–8.
43 Clifford Odets, *Six Plays by Clifford Odets* (New York, 1979), p. 31.
44 Clurman, *The Fervent Years*, pp. 141–2.
45 Sartre, *What Is Literature?*, p. 251.
46 *Famous Plays of 1936* (London, 1936), pp. 350–1.
47 *Ibid.*, pp. 358–9.
48 *Ibid.*, p. 374.
49 *Ibid.*, p. 383.
50 *Ibid.*, p. 385.
51 Morgan Y. Himelstein, *Drama Was a Weapon: The Left-Wing Theatre in New York 1929–1941* (Westport, 1976), p. 551.
52 Goldstein, *The Political Stage*, p. 60.
53 Taylor, *People's Theatre*, p. 68.
54 Michel Beaujour, 'Flight Out Of Time', in Jacques Ehrmann, ed., *Literature and Revolution* (Boston, 1967), p. 33.
55 *Ibid.*, p. 37.
56 In Ehrmann, ed., *Literature and Revolution*, p. 188.
57 *Ibid.*, p. 48.
58 Jean-Paul Sartre, *Situations*, trans. Benita Eisler (London, 1965), p. 95.
59 *Ibid.*, p. 92.
60 *Ibid.*, p. 98.
61 *Ibid.*, p. 104.

6 The Federal Theatre and the Living Newspaper

1 Hallie Flanagan, *Arena: The History of the Federal Theatre* (New York, 1940), p. 13.
2 Jane De Hart Mathews, *The Federal Theatre, 1935–1939: Plays, Relief and Politics* (Princeton, 1967), p. 23.
3 Flanagan, *Arena*, pp. 45–6.
4 *Ibid.*, p. 63.
5 Mae Krulak, 'Why Hallie Flanagan?' *Federal One*, III, ii (September, 1978), 2–4.
6 Marc Slonim, *Russian Theatre: From the Empire to the Soviets* (London, 1963), p. 236.
7 Douglas McDermott, 'The Living Newspaper as Dramatic Form', *Modern Drama*, VIII, i (1965–6), 84.
8 Anon., 'Editing the Living Newspaper', *Federal Theatre Magazine*, I, v, (April, 1936), 16–17.
9 Diane Bowers, '*Ethiopia*: the first Living Newspaper', *Phoebe* (Fairfax, Virginia, 1974), p. 7.
10 Mathews, *The Federal Theatre*, p. 58.
11 *Ibid.*, p. 61.
12 Flanagan, *Arena*, pp. 65–6.
13 Mathews, *The Federal Theatre*, p. 66.
14 Flanagan, *Arena*, p. 70.
15 *Ibid.*, p. 71.
16 Ms of *Triple A Plowed Under*, George Mason University, n.p.
17 *Ibid.*, p. 35.
18 Flanagan, *Arena*, p. 71.
19 Ms of *Triple A Plowed Under*, p. 48.
20 Flanagan, *Arena*, p. 72.
21 *Ibid.*, p. 73.
22 Mathews, *The Federal Theatre*, p. 111.
23 Ms of *Injunction Granted*, George Mason University, 1:3, p. 4.
24 *Ibid.*, 13:2, p. 47.
25 *Ibid.*, 18:2, p. 63.
26 Arthur Arent, 'The technique of the Living Newspaper', *Theatre Arts* (November, 1938), p. 824.
27 Ms of *Russia*, George Mason University, 17:1.
28 *Ibid.*, 17:2.
29 Flanagan, *Arena*, p. 390.
30 Ms of *One Third of a Nation*, George Mason University, 1:4:2.
31 *Ibid.*, 2:1:4.
32 *Ibid.*, 2:3:12.
33 Flanagan, *Arena*, p. 367.
34 Quoted in Krulak, 'Why Hallie Flanagan?' *Federal One*, III, ii, 5.
35 *Ibid.*
36 Flanagan, *Arena*, p. 321.
37 *Ibid.*, p. 322.

38 Maria Ley-Piscator, *The Piscator Experiment: The Political Theatre* (Carbondale, 1967), pp. 10–11.
39 *Ibid.*, p. 26.
40 Erwin Piscator, *The Political Theatre: A History 1914–1929*, trans. Hugh Rorrison (New York, 1978), p. 47.
41 *Ibid.*, pp. 93–4.
42 *Ibid.*, p. 94.
43 *Ibid.*, p. 187.
44 Ley-Piscator, *The Piscator Experiment*, p. 13.

7 Black drama

1   Edith J. R. Isaacs, *The Negro in the American Theatre* (New York, 1947), p. 57.
2   *Ibid.*, p. 59.
3   Doris E. Abramson, *Negro Playwrights in the American Theatre 1925–1959* (New York, 1959), p. 27.
4   Adam David Miller, 'It's a Long Way to St Louis', *Drama Review*, XII (Summer 1968), p. 147.
5   Abramson, *Negro Playwrights*, p. 28.
6   James V. Hatch, ed. *Black Theatre USA: Forty-Five Plays by Black Americans 1847–1974* (New York, 1974), p. 134.
7   Abramson, *Negro Playwrights*, p. 41.
8   Alain Locke, *Plays of Negro Life: A Sourcebook of Native American Drama* (New York, 1927), n.p.
9   Donald C. Dickinson, *A Bio-Bibliography of Langston Hughes, 1902–1967* (Hamden, 1972), p. 66.
10 *Ibid.*, pp. 68–9,
11 Flanagan, *Arena*, p. 74.
12 *Ibid.*, p. 63.
13 *Ibid.*, p. 320.
14 Theodore Ward, *Big White Fog* in Hatch, ed., *Black Theatre USA*, p. 289.
15 *Ibid.*, p. 279.
16 *Ibid.*, pp. 278–9.
17 Abramson, *Negro Playwrights*, p. 25.
18 Hatch, ed., *Black Theatre U.S.A.*, p. 263.
19 *Ibid.*, p. 274.
20 Abramson, *Negro Playwrights*, p. 92.

8 Thornton Wilder

1   Richard Goldstone, *Thornton Wilder: An Intimate Portrait* (New York, 1975), p. 80.
2   *Ibid.*
3   Thornton Wilder, *The Angel that Troubled the Waters and Other Plays* (London, 1928), pp. ix–x.
4   *Ibid.*, p. 3.

5   Theodore Dreiser, *Plays Natural and Supernatural* (London, 1930), p. 165.
6   Wilder, *The Angel*, p. 6.
7   Thornton Wilder, *Three Plays* (London, 1958), p. xi.
8   Letter from Thornton Wilder to Alexander Woollcott, 24 June, 1937, Harvard University.
9   Wilder, *Three Plays*, p. 25.
10 *Ibid.*, p. ix.
11 *Ibid.*, pp. x–xi.
12 Iris Murdoch, *The Sea, The Sea* (London, 1978), p. 33.
13 Letter from Thornton Wilder to Alexander Woollcott, 27 January, 1938. Harvard University.
14 Walter Starkie, *Luigi Pirandello 1867–1936* (Berkeley, 1967), p. 207.
15 *Ibid.*, pp. 206–7.
16 Wilder, *Three Plays*, pp. xii–xiii.
17 Starkie, *Pirandello*, p. 217.
18 *Ibid.*
19 Goldstone, *Thornton Wilder*, p. 127.
20 John Malcolm Brinnin, ed., *Selected Operas and Plays of Gertrude Stein* (Pittsburg, 1970), p. xi.
21 Thornton Wilder, 'Some Thoughts on Playwriting', in Robert W. Corrigan and James L. Rosenberg, eds., *The Context and Craft of Drama* (San Francisco, 1964), pp. 233–4.
22 Brinnin, ed., *Selected Operas*, p. xii.
23 Letter from Thornton Wilder to Alexander Woollcott.
24 Robert Corrigan and James L. Rosenberg, eds., *The Context and Craft of Drama* (San Francisco, 1964), p. 239.
25 Karl Jaspers, 'Basic characteristics of the tragic', in Robert Corrigan, ed., *Tragedy: Vision and Form* (San Francisco, 1965), p. 45.
26 Wilder, *Three Plays*, p. xiii.
27 *Ibid.*, p. xiv.
28 *Ibid.*, p. 155.
29 *Ibid.*, p. 202.
30 *Ibid.*, p. 237.
31 *Ibid.*, pp. 247–8.
32 Samuel A. Weiss, *Drama in the Modern World* (Boston, 1967), p. 244.
33 Goldstone, *Thornton Wilder*, p. 180.
34 Wilder, *Three Plays*, p. xiv.

9 Lillian Hellman

1   Lillian Hellman, *Collected Plays* (Boston, 1972), p. 42.
2   Lillian Hellman, *Four Plays by Lillian Hellman* (New York, 1972), p. viii.
3   *Ibid.*
4   Hellman, *Collected Plays*, p. 67.
5   Lillian Hellman, *Pentimento* (London, 1974), p. 114.

6   Richard Moody, *Lillian Hellman: Playwright* (New York, 1972), p. 56.
7   Hellman, *Pentimento*, p. 102.
8   *Ibid.*, p. 123.
9   *Ibid.*, p. 162.
10 Hellman, *Collected Plays*, p. 99.
11 *Ibid.*, p. 123.
12 Hellman, *Four Plays*, p. ix.
13 Moody, *Lillian Hellman*, p. 68.
14 Hellman, *Collected Plays*, p. 140.
15 *Ibid.*, p. 141.
16 *Ibid.*, p. 182.
17 *Ibid.*, p. 197.
18 Alfred Kazin ed., *Writers at Work: The 'Paris Review' Interviews* (London, 1968), p. 121.
19 *Ibid.*
20 Lillian Hellman, ed., *The Selected Letters of Anton Chekhov* (London, 1955), p. x.
21 *Ibid.*, p. xxii.
22 Anton Chekhov, *Plays*, trans. Elisaveta Fen (Harmondsworth, 1959), p. 384.
23 Robert Brustein, *The Theatre of Revolt* (Boston, 1964), p. 145.
24 Hellman, *Pentimento*, p. 180.
25 Hellman, *Collected Plays*, p. 197.
26 *Ibid.*, p. 379.
27 *Ibid.*, p. 368.
28 Richard Gray, *The Literature of Memory* (London, 1977), p. 38.
29 Moody, *Lillian Hellman*, p. 112.
30 Hellman, *Collected Plays*, pp. 230–1.
31 *Ibid.*, p. 219.
32 *Ibid.*, p. 224.
33 *Ibid.*, p. 239.
34 *Ibid.*, p. 263.
35 *Ibid.*, p. 257.
36 Lillian Hellman, *An Unfinished Woman* (London, 1969), p. 119.
37 *Ibid.*, p. 120.
38 *Ibid.*, p. 121.
39 Hellman, *Collected Plays*, p. 296.
40 *Ibid.*, p. 307.
41 Hellman, *Pentimento*, p. 208.
42 Hellman, *Collected Plays*, p. 477.
43 *Ibid.*, p. 542.
44 *Ibid.*, p. 543.
45 *Ibid.*, p. 542.
46 *Ibid.*, p. 545.
47 Hellman, ed., *The Selected Letters of Anton Chekhov*, p. 70.
48 *Ibid.*, pp. 70–1.
49 Lillian Hellman, *Scoundrel Time* (New York, 1976), p. 93.

50 *Ibid.*, p. 41.
51 Hellman, *Collected Plays*, p. 718.
52 *Ibid.*, p. 719.
53 *Ibid.*, p. 750.
54 *Ibid.*, p. 735.

BIBLIOGRAPHY

Abramson, Doris E. *Negro Playwrights in the American Theatre 1925–1959*. New York, 1959

Anderson, Maxwell. *Eleven Verse Plays*. New York, 1948

Off-Broadway. New York, 1947

Anon. 'Editing the Living Newspaper', *Federal Theatre Magazine*, I, v (April, 1936), 16–17

Appia, Adolphe. *Music and the Art of the Theatre*, trans. Robert W. Corrigan and Mary Douglas Dirks. Miami, 1962

Arent, Arthur. 'The technique of the Living Newspaper', *Theatre Arts* (November, 1938), 820–5

Bailey, Mabel Driscoll. *Maxwell Anderson: The Playwright as Prophet*. New York, 1957

Barry, Philip. *States of Grace: Eight Plays of Philip Barry*. New York, 1975

Basshe, Em Jo. *The Centuries*. New York, 1927

Belasco, David. *The Theatre Through Its Stage Door*. New York, 1919; rep. 1969

Bogard, Travis. *Contours of Time*. New York, 1972

Bowers, Diane. '*Ethiopia*: The first Living Newspaper', *Phoebe* (Fairfax, 1974), 6–15

Brinnin, John Malcolm, ed. *Selected Operas and Plays of Gertrude Stein*. Pittsburg, 1970

Brooks, Van Wyck, Mumford, Lewis, Kreymborg, Alfred, Rosenfeld, Paul, eds. *The American Caravan*, London, 1927

Brown, John Mason. *Dramatis Personae: A Retrospective Show*. London 1963

The Worlds of Robert Sherwood: Mirror to his Time. New York, 1962

Browne, E. Martin, ed. *Eugene O'Neill*. Harmondsworth, 1966

Brustein, Robert. *The Theatre of Revolt*. Boston, 1964

Camus, Albert. *Carnets 1942–1951*, trans. Philip Thody. London, 1966

Caputi, Anthony, ed. *Modern Drama*. New York, 1966

Cargill, Oscar, et al. *O'Neill and His Plays*. New York, 1961

Chambers, Clarke A. *The New Deal at Home and Abroad 1929–1945*. New York, 1965

Chekhov, Anton. *Plays*, trans., Elisaveta Fen. Harmondsworth, 1959

Clurman, Harold. *The Fervent Years: The Story of the Group Theatre and the Thirties*. London, 1946

Coe, Kathryn, and Cordell, William H. *The Pulitzer Prize Plays 1918–1934*. New York, 1935

Contat, Michel, and Rybalka, Michel. *Sartre on Theatre*. New York, 1976

Corrigan, Robert, ed. *Tragedy: Vision and Form*. San Francisco, 1965

Corrigan, Robert W. and Rosenberg, James L., eds. *The Context and Craft of Drama*. San Francisco, 1964

Coyle, William, and Damaser, Harvey G., eds. *Six Early American Plays*. Columbus, 1968

Dell, Floyd. *Homecoming: An Autobiography*. New York, 1969

Dewey, John. *Art as Experience*. New York, 1934

Dickinson, Donald C. *A Bio-Bibliography of Langston Hughes 1902–1967*. Hamden, 1972

Dickinson, Thomas, *Playwrights of the American Theatre*, St Claire Shores, 1972

Donohue, Denis. *The Third Voice*. London, 1959

Dos Passos, John. *The Garbage Man*. New York, 1926

Dreiser, Theodore. *Plays Natural and Supernatural*. London, 1930

Eaton, Walter Pritchard. *The Theatre Guild: The First Ten Years*. New York, 1929

Ehrmann, Jacques, ed. *Literature and Revolution*. Boston, 1967

Famous American Plays of the 1930s. New York, 1959

Famous Plays of 1933–4. London, 1934

Famous Plays of 1936. London, 1936

Flanagan, Hallie. *Arena: The History of the Federal Theatre*. New York, 1940

Folsom, Michael, ed. *Mike Gold: A Literary Anthology*. New York, 1972

Freud, Sigmund. *The Standard Edition of the Complete Works*. London, 1951

    Totem and Taboo, trans. A. A. Brill. New York, 1927

Fromm, Erich. *The Fear of Freedom*. London, 1960

Gassner, John. *O'Neill*. Englewood Cliffs, 1964

Gassner, John, ed. *Best Plays of the Modern Theatre*. New York, 1947

Gelb, Arthur and Barbara. *Eugene O'Neill*. New York, 1973

Glaspell, Susan. *Inheritors*. London, 1924

    Plays. Boston, 1920

    The Road to the Temple. London, 1926

    The Verge. Boston, 1922

Gold, Michael. *Hoboken Blues* in Van Wyck Brooks *et al.*, eds., *The American Caravan*. New York, 1927

Goldberg, Isaac. *The Theatre of George Jean Nathan*. New York, 1968

Goldman, Arnold. 'The culture of the Provincetown Players', *Journal of American Studies*, XII, iii (December, 1978)

Goldstein, Malcolm. *The Political Stage: The American Drama and Theatre of the Great Depression*. New York, 1974

Goldstone, Richard. *Thornton Wilder: An Intimate Portrait*. New York, 1975

Gray, Richard. *The Literature of Memory*. London, 1977

Hapgood, Hutchins. *A Victorian in the Modern World*. New York, 1939

Hatch, James V. ed. *Black Theatre USA: Forty-Five Plays by Black Americans 1847–1974*. New York, 1974

Hellman, Lillian. *Collected Plays*. Boston, 1972

    Four Plays by Lillian Hellman. New York, 1972

    Pentimento. London, 1974

    Scoundrel Time. New York, 1976

    ed. *The Selected Letters of Anton Chekhov*, trans. Sidonie Lederer. London, 1955

    An Unfinished Woman. London, 1969

Himelstein, Morgan Y. *Drama Was a Weapon: The Left-Wing Theatre in New York 1929–1941*. Westport, 1976

Hoffman, Frederick J. *Freudianism and the Literary Mind*. Baton Rouge, 1957

Hogan, Robert. *The Independence of Elmer Rice*. Carbondale, 1965

Bibliography

Isaacs, Edith J. R. *The Negro in the American Theatre.* New York, 1947
Jaspers, Karl. 'Basic Characteristics of the Tragic', in Robert Corrigan, ed., *Tragedy: Vision and Form.* San Francisco, 1965
Jones, Robert Edmond. *The Dramatic Imagination.* New York, 1941
Jung, Karl Gustav. *The Portable Jung.* New York, 1971
Kaufmann, Walter. *Basic Writings of Nietzsche.* New York, 1966
Kazin, Alfred, ed. *Writers at Work: The Paris Review Interviews.* London, 1968
Knox, George A. and Herbert M. Stahl. *Dos Passos and the Revolting Playwrights.* Lund, 1964
Krulak, Mae. 'Why Hallie Flanagan?' *Federal One,* III, ii (September, 1978), 2–4
Lawson, John Howard. *Roger Bloomer.* New York, 1923
   Processional. New York, 1925
Ley-Piscator, Maria. *The Piscator Experiment: The Political Theatre.* Carbondale, 1967
Locke, Alain. *Plays of Negro Life: A Sourcebook of Native American Drama.* New York, 1927
Lukács, Georg. *Writer and Critic.* London, 1970
McDermott, Douglas. 'The Living Newspaper as Dramatic Form', *Modern Drama,* VIII, i (1965–6)
Marker, Lise-Lone. *David Belasco: Naturalism in the American Theatre.* Princeton, 1975
Mathews, Jane De Hart. *The Federal Theatre, 1935–1939: Plays, Relief and Politics.* Princeton, 1967
Meserve, Walter. *Robert E. Sherwood.* New York 1947
Miller, Adam David. 'It's a Long Way to St Louis', *Drama Review,* XII (Summer, 1968)
Moody, Richard. *Lillian Hellman: Playwright.* New York, 1972
Moses, Montrose J., and Brown, John Mason. *The American Theatre As Seen By Its Critics.* New York, 1934
Murdoch, Iris. *The Sea, The Sea.* London, 1978
Nietzsche, Friedrich. *The Gay Science,* trans. W. Kaufmann. New York, 1974
   The Will to Power, trans. W. Kaufmann and R. J. Hollingdale. New York, 1968
   Thus Spake Zarathustra, trans. R. J. Hollingdale. Harmondsworth, 1961
Odets, Clifford. *Golden Boy.* Harmondsworth, 1963
   Night Music. New York, 1940
   Six Plays by Clifford Odets. New York, 1939; rep. 1979
O'Malley, Suzanne. 'America's rival acting schools', *Dialogue,* XIII, i
O'Neill, Eugene. *'Ah Wilderness!' and 'Days Without End'.* London, 1958
   'Beyond the Horizon' and 'Marco millions'. London, 1960
   'The Emperor Jones', 'The Straw' and 'Diffrent'. London, 1958
   'The Great God Brown' and 'Lazarus Laughed'. London, 1960
   Hughie. London, 1962
   The Iceman Cometh. London, 1966
   Long Day's Journey Into Night. New Haven, 1956
   Moon for the Misbegotten. London, 1953
   More Stately Mansions. London, 1965
   Mourning Becomes Electra. London, 1973

The Plays of Eugene O'Neill. New York, 1955
Strange Interlude. London, 1928
A Touch of the Poet. New Haven, 1959
Piscator, Erwin. *The Political Theatre: A History 1914–1929*, trans. Hugh Rorrison. New York, 1978
Raleigh, John Henry, ed. *Twentieth-Century Interpretations of 'The Iceman Cometh'*. Englewood Cliffs, 1968
Rice, Elmer, *The Living Theatre*. New York, 1959
Minority Report: An Autobiography. London, 1963
Three Plays. New York, 1965
Saroyan, William. *'The Time of Your Life' and Two Other Plays*. London, 1942
Sartre, Jean-Paul. *Situations*, trans. Benita Eisler. London, 1965
What is Literature? trans. Bernard Frechtman. New York, 1965
Sayler, Oliver. *Our American Theatre*, New York, 1923
Arthur Schopenhauer. *Complete Essays*, trans. T. Bailey Saunders. New York, 1942
Essays and Aphorisms, trans. R. J. Hollingdale. Harmondsworth, 1970
The World as Will and Representation, trans. E. F. J. Payne. New York, 1966
Schulberg, Budd. *The Four Seasons of Success*. London, 1974
Sherwood, Robert E. *Idiot's Delight*. New York, 1936
The Petrified Forest in John Gassner, ed., *American Drama*, New York, 1960
There Shall Be No Night, New York, 1940
Sievers, W. David. *Freud on Broadway: History of Psychoanalysis and the American Drama*. New York, 1955
Slonim, Marc. *Russian Theatre: From the Empire to the Soviets*, London, 1963
Starkie, Walter. *Luigi Pirandello 1867–1936*. Berkeley, 1967
Steiner, George. *After Babel*. London, 1975
The Death of Tragedy. London, 1961
Taylor, Karen. *People's Theatre in America*. New York, 1972
Tornquist, Egil. *A Drama of Souls: Studies in O'Neill's Super-Naturalistic Technique*. New Haven, 1968
Trotsky, Leon. *Literature and Revolution*. Ann Arbor, 1968
Waldau, Roy S. *Vintage Years of the Theatre Guild, 1928–1939*. Cleveland, 1972
Ward, Theodore. *Big White Fog*, in James V. Hatch, ed., *Black Theatre USA: Forty-Five Plays by Black Americans 1847–1974*. New York, 1974
Waterman, Arthur. *Susan Glaspell*. New York, 1966
Weales, Gerald. *Clifford Odets*. New York, 1971
Weiss, Samuel A. *Drama in the Modern World*. Boston, 1967
West, Paul. *The Wine of Absurdity*. University Park, 1966
Wilder, Thornton. *The Angel that Troubled the Waters and Other Plays*. London, 1928
'Some Thoughts on Playwriting', in Robert W. Corrigan and James L. Rosenberg, eds. *The Context and Craft of Drama*. San Francisco, 1964
Three Plays. London, 1958
Williams, Jay. *Stage Left*. New York, 1974

Bibliography

Manuscripts

Injunction Granted. George Mason University
One Third of a Nation. George Mason University
Triple A Plowed Under. George Mason University
Eugene O'Neill. 'The Iceman Cometh'. Yale Collection
    'Long Day's Journey Into Night'. Yale Collection
    'Letter to Joseph Wood Krutch, July 15, 1927'. Yale Collection
    'Letter to Joseph Wood Krutch, June 11, 1929'. Yale Collection
    'Mourning Becomes Electra: Working Notes and Extracts from a Fragmentary
    Diary'. Yale Collection
Elmer Rice. 'Letter to Barrett Clark'. Yale Collection
Thornton Wilder. 'Letter to Alexander Woollcott, June 24, 1937'. Harvard University
    'Letter to Alexander Woollcott, January 27, 1938'. Harvard University

INDEX

Index

Index

Index

Index

Index

Index

Index

342